CREATING AMERICAN REFORM JUDAISM

THE LITTMAN LIBRARY OF
JEWISH CIVILIZATION

Dedicated to the memory of
LOUIS THOMAS SIDNEY LITTMAN
*who founded the Littman Library for the love of God
and as an act of charity in memory of his father*
JOSEPH AARON LITTMAN
and to the memory of
ROBERT JOSEPH LITTMAN
who continued what his father Louis had begun
יהא זכרם ברוך

'*Get wisdom, get understanding:
Forsake her not and she shall preserve thee*'
PROV. 4: 5

*The Littman Library of Jewish Civilization is a registered UK charity
Registered charity no.* 1000784

Creating American Reform Judaism

◆

The Life and Times of Isaac Mayer Wise

◆

SEFTON D. TEMKIN

London

The Littman Library of Jewish Civilization
in association with Liverpool University Press

The Littman Library of Jewish Civilization
Registered office: 4th floor, 7–10 Chandos Street, London WIG 9DQ

in association with Liverpool University Press
4 Cambridge Street, Liverpool L69 7ZU, UK
www.liverpooluniversitypress.co.uk/littman

Managing Editor: Connie Webber

Distributed in North America by
Oxford University Press Inc., 198 Madison Avenue,
New York, NY 10016, USA

First published in hardback in 1992 by Oxford University Press
on behalf of the Littman Library of Jewish Civilization
as Isaac Mayer Wise: Shaping American Judaism
First issued in paperback with new title 1998

Catalogue records for this book are available from the
British Library and the Library of Congress

ISBN 978-1-874774-45-7

Design: Pete Russell, Faringdon, Oxon.

Printed and bound in Great Britain by
CPI Group (UK) Ltd., Croydon, CR0 4YY

Prefatory Note

THE years that have elapsed since this project was begun have left their deposit in the form of countless debts of gratitude to numerous teachers, co-workers, and friends; and the accumulation is great enough for anything approaching verbal repayment to add a chapter to this book.

I was attracted to Isaac Mayer Wise by the contrast between Wise's personality and the pioneer field in which he worked and the tradition-bound situations which the writer had assumed to be universal, and I recall with gratitude the encouragement given me by the late Samuel Sandmel, provost of Hebrew Union College, to take a fellowship in order to study the subject in detail. At Hebrew Union College I came under the guidance of Jacob Rader Marcus, who, in establishing the American Jewish Archives on the Cincinnati campus of the college, had provided the student of anything bearing on American Jewish history with unrivalled documentary material, but whose kindness to his disciples extends far beyond anything that can be expressed in documents—a spirit which he has transmitted to his staff, particularly Stanley Chyet, Abraham Peck, and Fannie Zelcer. Through my connection with the American Jewish Archives, I have benefited from the generous interest of Wise's granddaughter, the late Mrs Arthur Hays Sulzberger. I record also the help of the Lucius N. Littauer Foundation and the 'Three G's' Family Foundation.

The inclusion of this volume in the Littman Library is due to the kindness of my friend, the late Louis Littman. His untimely passing is mourned not only by a wide circle of friends but by all who are concerned for the development of Jewish scholarship in England. On behalf of the Library, the late Vivian Lipman, CVO, gave considerable time and thought to the shaping of the manuscript; and it has had the benefit of a number of suggestions from Jonathan Sarna, formerly of Hebrew Union College, now at Brandeis University.

The appearance of this volume indicates the view that there was room for another biography of the Isaac Mayer Wise. At the same time I must pay tribute to my predecessors in the field, on whose work I have drawn extensively.

S.D.T.

Albany, New York
July, 1992

Contents

List of Plates

All plates are reproduced with the permission of the American Jewish Archives, Cincinnati Campus of Hebrew Union College–Jewish Institute of Religion.

Abbreviations

AJA
American Jewish Archives, housed on the Cincinnati campus of Hebrew Union College.

May, *Isaac Mayer Wise*
Max B. May, *Isaac Mayer Wise: A Biography* (New York, 1916).

1910 Year Book
Year Book of Beth Emeth Congregation, Albany (New York, 1910).

Reminiscences
Isaac Mayer Wise, *Reminiscences*, trans. and ed. David Philipson (Cincinnati, 1901).

The World of My Books
Isaac Mayer Wise, *The World of My Books*, trans. Albert H. Friedlaender (Cincinnati, 1954).

Note on Transliteration

BECAUSE this work incorporates a large number of quotations from contemporary sources whose authors were not always the most learned, multiple transliterations are sometimes to be found for the same term. An indication of the range will be found in the Glossary; it is assumed that readers will be sufficiently familiar with the problems of transliterating Hebrew and Yiddish to cope with this. (It is to be noted that the Glossary includes only terms that appear repeatedly in the text; other terms are explained *in situ*.)

The text itself follows a simplified version of the system used in the *Encyclopædia Judaica*—simplified in the sense that no diacritics are used. The letters *chet* and *chaf* are both represented simply by 'h', except where 'ch' is the customary rendering. The *tsaddi* is represented by 'ts'. The *taf* is simply rendered 't', except where 'th' is the accepted usage; *tet* is likewise rendered 't'.

For names of communities the text uses the form given in the *Encyclopædia Judaica*.

I

Bohemia (1819–1846)

1. METTERNICH'S EUROPE

In an antiquarian bookstore in the city of Prague I found a collection of English American prints, and in it a set of journals from the years 1780 to 1790. I purchased the whole, and read with the heart more perhaps than with reason. That literature made me a naturalized American in the interior of Bohemia.

(From the sermon preached by Isaac Mayer Wise on the occasion of his jubilee in the rabbinate on 21 October 1893, as reported in the *American Israelite*, 40 (26 Oct. 1893), 4.)[1]

ISAAC MAYER WISE was born in Steingrub, Bohemia, on 20 March 1819 (3 Nisan 5579). The village of Steingrub (now known as Kamenny-Dvur) lies in the north-west corner of Bohemia, then part of the Austrian Empire, close to the German frontier and not far from the point where Bavaria and Saxony meet. It is in the *Bezirk-hauptmannschaft* ('administrative county') of Eger, the nearest town, or, to give it its present name, Cheb (historically famous as head-quarters of the Imperial Army during the Thirty Years War, and the scene of the assassination of its commander, Albrecht Wallenstein, in 1634). Eger was morally the heart of the Sudetenland, the German-speaking area which fringes on the western border of Bohemia. When in the nineteenth century Czech nationalism raised its head, the *Deutschtum* of the Sudetenland became inflamed in response. From the time that the independent Czechoslovak Republic was established,

---

[1] On p. 14 of *Selected Writings of Isaac M. Wise*, ed. David Philipson and Louis Grossman (Cincinnati, 1900), Philipson states that Wise 'had picked up in a book store in Prague several volumes of the Federal Farmer, an American publication'. It has not proved possible to identify a publication answering to that description. May, *Isaac Mayer Wise*, 40, states that he had read 'several volumes of American English reprints, among which were contained letters of Richard Henry Lee under the nom-de-plume "Federal Farmer"'. May's account appears to be sounder. Neither biographer appears to have questioned whether a young Bohemian Talmud student is likely to have read English.

Eger was the centre of the separatist movement which in 1938 was temporarily successful. When they regained their independence in 1945, the Czechs, fearing the presence of an element which might again become the agents of a foreign enemy, expelled the Sudetens into Germany. Today the quarrels of Habsburgs and Wittelsbachs and Wettins, which made the tramp of marching soldiers familiar in Eger, are no more. Until the pull-back of 1989 it abutted the uneasy border between the two republics of Germany and was the westernmost point to which, through her satellites, the power of Russia reached.

The countryside which Wise knew as a boy today gives the impression of solitude, even of desertion. The road ascends as it leaves Eger, leading eventually to a broad plateau of meadowland whose flatness is emphasized by the distant prospect of the Erzgebirge mountains. After traversing this plateau, one repeats the ascent until a few nondescript buildings by the road mark the village of Steingrub. Not many years ago an army barracks, tank barriers in the fields, shrapnel marks, and German Gothic lettering were a reminder that the days of war were not far behind; and perhaps this accounts for the solitariness of the atmosphere.[2]

Of the first twenty-seven years of the man who said that he became a naturalized American amid these surroundings, very little is known. His grandson and biographer, Max B. May, who was very close to him, wrote, 'He could not be induced to talk about his early years, and often said they were too terrible to contemplate.'[3] Sometimes in his voluminous writings he dealt with conditions in the land of his birth, but declared autobiography is incidental.

Wise was born into a fettered society; and its chains were heavier because they had been reimposed after a period of near freedom. The French Revolution and the Napoleonic wars had spread throughout Europe the aspiration for popular sovereignty and the rights of nationalities: the Congress of Vienna gave scant recognition to the new forces and set about restoring the *ancien régime*. The genius of

---

[2] This description is derived from recollections of a visit which the writer made in 1961. Steingrub was too insignificant to appear on atlas maps, but it appeared on an Austro-Hungarian military map in the Vienna Staatsbibliothek (also to be found in the Library of Congress).

[3] May, *Isaac Mayer Wise*, p. viii. After Wise's death information was difficult to obtain. In the *American Israelite*, 62 (1 Feb. 1917), 1, Gotthard Deutsch wrote that he wrote to Ronsperg and Radnitz in 1900, receiving no reply from the former and from the latter merely a statement that old people remembered Rabbi Wise.

those who set themselves to thwart the allied forces of liberalism and nationalism was Clemens von Metternich (1773–1859), Austrian Foreign Minister from 1809 till 1848, and it was in the Austrian Empire that, despite his awareness of the need for reform, Metternich's system operated to worst effect. The government was absolutist in form and tightly controlled from Vienna. Nor was the absence of parliamentary institutions or autonomy for the various nationalities of the Habsburg dominions redeemed by that bureaucratic enlightenment which helped to advance the power of Prussia. There was administrative anarchy; industry and commerce were left to languish, strangled by an antiquated system of internal as well as external tariffs; reform was attempted, but in the interests of the great landholders, who escaped their proper share of the national burdens and retained privileges which belonged to the feudal era; the press was rigidly controlled; there was a close alliance between Throne and Altar, resulting in clerical control over education.[4]

The strangulation of hopes for a more enlightened order was the more oppressive not only because men had seen a new dawn in the French Revolution, but because, even before that upheaval, Austria had felt the winds of change. Joseph II (reigned 1780–92), advancing beyond the example set by his mother, Maria Theresa, had set about reforming the fabric of Austrian society and earned for himself the title of 'Revolutionary Emperor'.

For the Jews of Austria—and, indeed throughout Europe—the post-1815 period was one of intense disappointment. The enlightenment of Joseph II had extended to his Jewish subjects. With good intentions, though, unfortunately, with little tact or discretion, Joseph had set about loosening the hold of the Church and improving the lot of the Jews and other depressed classes. Joseph's reforms did not go the whole way, and after his death the march of tolerance came to a halt. Laws affecting Jews were interpreted restrictively (sometimes, indeed, fresh restrictions were imposed), and the Jew found himself again at the mercy of the petty official. Restrictions on the right of residence, a prohibition against owning land,[5] special taxes, and the *Familiantengesetz*, by which the number of marriages allowed to Jews

---

[4] Wise, writing in *Israelite*, 3 (24 Apr. 1857), 330, expressed himself volubly on the Austrian system as he had known it.

[5] Decrees of 1827 and 1835 rendered it harder for Jews to obtain real property. See A. Stein, *Geschichte der Juden in Boehmen* (1904), 95. Stein, incidentally, served as rabbi in Radnitz, the community in which Wise officiated from 1843 to 1846.

was kept down,[6] were among the humiliations continued after the defeat of the French Revolution. Under such conditions Jews and liberals might sustain themselves by dreams founded on memories, circumventing the law where necessary in trying to bring their dreams nearer reality. The aspirations of the Enlightenment were kept alive, notwithstanding all the efforts of the Austrian censorship to prevent the infiltration of heretical ideas: 'forbidden books were the only ones read and forbidden newspapers the only ones believed'.[7] Across the border, Karl von Rotteck (1775–1840) and Friedrich Schlosser (1776–1861) brought the prestige of their academic standing to the struggle against the *ancien régime*.[8]

Wise was a boy of 11 living with his grandfather near Carlsbad (now Karlovy Vary) when the July Revolution of 1830 demonstrated to the intellectuals of Germany that to overthrow a reactionary government was not an idle dream. The change in Paris was felt almost as keenly in Germany; it struck at the Romantic movement in German literature, whose ideas, transferred to the domain of practical religion and politics, had proved reactionary in their effects: it was the signal for the young German writers of the day to throw themselves into politics.[9]

In 1835 the German Confederation issued a decree suppressing the writing of the literary school known as 'Young Germany'. Five writers were mentioned by name, of whom the most famous was Heinrich Heine (1797–1856). Not mentioned in the decree was Ludwig Boerne (1786–1837), and among its representatives in the domain of scholarship were David Friedrich Strauss (1808–74), whose sensational *Leben Jesu* appeared in 1835, and the philosopher Ludwig Feuerbach (1804–72). The fears of authority show that in intellectual life new forces were taking the lead—the protagonists of a generation which saw no finality in the Holy Alliance and the Carlsbad Decrees and which demanded intellectual and political liberty.[10]

---

[6] The *Familiantengesetz* laid down which marriages might be permitted. Applicants for permission had to submit to an examination by the local rabbi in the presence of a government official. See Wise, Isaac Mayer, *Selected Writings* (1900), 327. The point is also referred to in Daniel Ehrmann's novel *Die Tante*.

[7] *Encyclopedia Britannica* (11th edn., 1910) iii. 13.

[8] *Encyclopedia of the Social Sciences* (1931) xiii. 442.

[9] *Cambridge Modern History* (1st edn., 1910), x. 410.

[10] See generally article 'German Literature' in *Encyclopedia Britannica* (11th edn., 1910), xi. 794–5; also *Cambridge Modern History*, x. 383.

2. JEWISH LIFE IN AN AGE OF REACTION

Isaac Mayer Wise grew up at a distance from the intellectual circles whose aspirations evoked the fears of authority. Whether they came at fourth hand or fifth hand, and however alloyed or reworked in the course of transmission, it would be surprising if the ideas which these men coined and the ideals they held aloft did not colour the ambitions of the Bohemian *yeshivah bocher* (Talmud student) in whom a chance encounter with literature written in the strange but free English language had stirred feelings for something other than the orthodoxies of his day.

In the pamphlet he picked up in Prague we find the following statements:

The happiness of the people at large must be the object with every honest statesman, and he will direct every movement to this point.

The essential parts of a free and good government are a full and equal representation of the people in the legislature, and the jury trial of the vicinage in the administration of justice.

The great object of a free people must be so to form their government and laws, and so to administer them, as to create a confidence in, and respect for the laws; and thereby induce the sensible and virtuous part of the community to declare in favor of the laws, and to support them without an expensive military force.[11]

Discount as we will the rhetorical exaggeration that this literature made him a naturalized American in Bohemia, its effect on a young man brought up in the stuffy atmosphere of Metternich's Austria must have been vivid indeed.

The influence on Wise of the eighteenth-century Enlightenment can be judged from the way it remained with him. Repeatedly he extolled the power of reason and the rule of progress. He was past 50 and had been in America for a quarter of a century when he wrote 'The nineteenth century ... subsists on the wealth of the eighteenth',[12] an exception for 'natural science and mechanical arts' making it clear that he referred to man's political and intellectual heritage.

---

[11] *Observations Leading to a Fair Examination of the System of Government, Proposed by the Late Convention; and to Several Essential and Necessary Alterations in It. In a number of Letters from Federal Farmer to the Republican* (New York, 1787), 11, 15.

[12] 'Reformed Judaism' (1871), in *Selected Writings of Isaac M. Wise*, 298.

Liberty is not an artificial product of some ingenious minds, it is an innate principle of human nature ... despotism is an imposition, an unnatural and violent check upon the natural motions and actions of man; wherefore liberty comes by itself, and takes care of itself, if the natural qualities of man are not corrupted, while despotism must be invented, studied, imposed and guarded.

The passage comes from a lecture given by Wise in New York in 1852, entitled 'The End of Popes, Nobles and Kings',[13] these three classes being the agents of despotism. We hear an echo of Rousseau laying down that 'Man is born free, and everywhere he is in chains', and that nature gave no man rights over his equals. The power of the popes and the nobility had ceased to exist, and the dominion of the kings had been greatly impaired, Wise argued. In North America, liberty found a home for the first time in modern history; in Europe, the French Revolution, inspired by the spirit of American republicanism, had burst upon the trembling tyrants. Wise was writing, it is true, six years after he had landed in America, and after his energetic mind had been given full opportunity to embrace the concepts of freedom embodied in the Constitution of the United States and the Bill of Rights. But those concepts were not unrelated to the European Enlightenment, and the fact that in the lecture in question he quotes from Karl von Rotteck shows that his thinking had not been unaffected by the intellectuals who were active in the Central Europe of his youth.

Steingrub, the little corner of Central Europe in which Wise was born, was stated in 1845 to have eighty-two houses and 755 inhabitants.[14] Seven years later the number of its Jewish families was given as nine.[15] But at that time the town of Eger itself recorded only three Jewish families, and Steingrub's Jewish community was the largest in the *Bezirkhauptmannschaft*. By the year of Wise's death (1900) the number of Jews in Steingrub had declined to two.[16] These population changes reflect a pattern common to nineteenth-century Europe. The records of Jews in Eger go back to the thirteenth century, but the townspeople secured their expulsion in 1430. It often happened that on being expelled from a town, Jews found refuge on

[13] Wise, *The End of Popes, Nobles, and Kings* (New York, 1852), 6.

[14] Franz Raffelsperger, *Allgemeiner geographische-statistisches Lexikon aller Österreichen Staaten* (Vienna, 1846–53), v. 1286.

[15] Albert Kohn (ed.), *Die Notablenversammlung der Israeliten Böhmens* (Vienna, 1852), 407.

[16] This figure is from the Austrian Census of 1900. The article on Bohemia in *Jewish Encyclopedia* (New York, 1902), iii. 209, does not mention Steingrub.

the estates of nobles in the neighbourhood; when in 1849 residence restrictions in Bohemia were removed there was an immediate drift from the villages to the towns.

Though the immediate vicinity of Eger is apparently an exception, most of the Bohemian territory that abuts on Bavaria and Saxony is of poor soil, and before industry developed and the laying of railways made the spas accessible the inhabitants must have led a narrow existence.[17] The political background was not conducive to economic advance. Reference has already been made to the general incompetence of the Austrian government in such matters.[18] Western Bohemia suffered through the additional circumstance that the use of its natural trade outlet, which lay through the valleys of the Eger and the Elbe to Hamburg, was discountenanced: after the War of Austrian Succession relations with Prussia were impaired, and for overseas commerce the Austrian government favoured the use of far distant Trieste.

The Jews of the Bohemian villages shared the poverty of the land by acting as pedlars, usually taking off from Sunday until the onset of the Sabbath.[19] Such small, scattered communities could not sustain an elaborate religious organization. They needed kosher meat, and therefore a *shochet*, a person qualified to slaughter animals according to ritual law, and they needed someone to teach their children; probably both these functions were combined. Jewish custom required no specially consecrated house of worship; the schoolroom, if there was one, or the home of one of the members, sufficed for the purpose of prayer. Naturally a sizeable community, even if only in a village, would have a synagogue building, but the few Jewish families in Steingrub—even assuming that the number in 1819 was double the figure of nine reported in 1852—could hardly have needed anything large.

In two articles written in 1854, Wise alludes to conditions in his native land in terms rather more inviting than those indicated by his grandson.

The family life among the country people is of a patriarchal nature. The husband and father is the independent sheik of the house and wife and mother is second in rank. This dominion is often regulated by the laws of love and

---

[17] See Gotthard Deutsch, 'Wise's Early Career', in *Year Book of Central Conference of American Rabbis*, xxix (1919), 193.

[18] See sect. 1 above.

[19] See Oskar Donath's monograph, *Böhmische Dorfjuden* (Bruenn, 1927), 16, 17, 19.

respect, but sometimes degenerates into a kind of petty tyranny. Unconditional obedience is required of the children, without distinction of sex or
age; no vocation in life can be selected, no marriage can be contracted without
the permission of the parents. Married children are considered independent
of their parents; still it is a matter of good deportment to pay distinguished
respect to parents. There is that mutual attachment in the families which
distinguishes patriarchal family life, and domestic quarrels are rare, and
almost never grow up to violent disaffection.

The days of labor are devoted to business, and none are idle. The father
and the sons who have left school attend to some useful employment, many
working hard. The mother and her daughter care for the domestic comfort.
The Sabbath and holydays are highly valued. On Friday the whole house is
cleaned and set in order, and all the cooking required for the Sabbath is done.
On the Sabbath evening, every one in the house changes their clothing, and
the male portion of the family repair to the synagogue. Meanwhile the lamp
with six to twelve lights is kindled, a white cloth is spread over the table, and
two loaves of bread and a cup of wine are set on it. The mother reads the
prayers, and every thing around it is clean, and assumes as it were, a festive
look. When the father and his sons have returned from Synagogue, every
child salutes his parents, with the solemn 'Good Sabbath', after which the
blessing is received. 'May God let thee be as Sarah, Rebecca, Rachel and
Leah' concluding with the blessing prescribed to the priests 'may God bless
thee and guard thee' etc. Then the whole family sing the hymn 'Shalom
Alechem', every one washes his hands, and takes a seat at the table; the father
arises and recites the benediction over the wine and bread, after which the
cup is given to the mother and then to every child according to age; the father
then breaks the Sabbath bread and gives a piece to every one in the above
order. This is followed by the Sabbath supper, which is generally of an
excellent kind. Meat is never missed, and if possible, fish must grace the
table. After the meal, several hymns are sung (Semiroth) after which the
father loudly speaks the grace. So, every Friday evening is a family feast to
the poor, as well as to the rich, the exceptions are very rare. If there is a
domestic quarrel in a house, the Sabbath eve brings peace. This is regarded
so highly, that the poor are sent flour, oil, money, and meat on Thursday, to
have it for the Sabbath.[20]

Besides the Jewish holidays, the 'extra festivities of such a place are,
the circumcision of a boy, the marriage of a couple, and also the
Sabbath after such a marriage'. Marriage celebrations he describes in

---

[20] *Asmonean*, 9 (24 Mar. 1854), 175. This article concluded with the indication that
it would be followed by recollections of Prague, but in fact the series was broken off.
In *American Israelite*, 63 (1 Feb. 1917), 1, Gotthard Deutsch calls attention to
inaccuracies in these articles.

some detail, mentioning the former custom, which he said had fallen into disuse, of the bridegroom delivering a 'learned talmudical discourse during the nuptial dinner'. Other festive occasions were the anniversary of the congregational benevolent society, the dedication of a new synagogue or the acquisition of a new *sefer torah*.

The falling away in the custom of having bridegrooms give a talmudic discourse at their wedding feasts was one example of the neglect of talmudic learning which had set in.

There every thing is revolutionalized; there are but a few traces left of the old Bohemian Jews; every one is modernized or at least assumes the appearance of being so. Language, customs, habits, schools, Synagogues, and views underwent a mighty change. In Prague, Toeplitz, Brandeis, Leipsic and other places, Synagogues with choirs, organs, and good preachers occupy the places of the old 'Shuhl' and good schools, under examined and experienced teachers have almost extinguished the old 'Hedar'. Talmudical celebrities have become very rare, and are only sought for, if they are in possession of a good university education. The sacredness of the ceremonial laws is almost lost, and many a merchant violates the Sabbath.

The young rabbins of larger cities consider the Talmud a secondary affair, and spend their time in the acquirement of modern sciences, although there are but a few of them who have not a considerable knowledge of our national literature.[21]

It was not in the towns alone, but in the villages also that the study of the Talmud had declined; and the decay set in, according to Wise's estimation, even before the 1848 Revolution freed the Jews from many of the restrictions on residence and occupation under which they had laboured previously.

The Yeshiboth and the Talmud study in general have given way during the past fifteen years to a modern education. When we left Bohemia there was almost no trace any more in the villages and smaller towns of Talmud instruction. Those unhappy old men who know nothing besides the rabbinical literature held very poor places in small congregations and not a few subsisted on public charity. The rabbi must have gone through a course of studies in a university, and the Hazan [cantor] must be either a musician or an examined teacher, and at length it became difficult for a teacher to find a place who could not show certificates either from the State normal School or from the Hebrew normal school at Prague. The schools were improved by this change. Able boys now study Latin, Geography, History, etc. instead of Talmud. After they are thus prepared they go to an academy, to the polytechnical

[21] *Asmonean*, 9 (24 Mar. 1854), 181.

institute or to a commercial institute (Real Schule). Others who intend to devote themselves to a learned profession, go to a Gymnasium where they are prepared for the university, and then to the university. Talmud and other Hebrew branches are studied by those only who intend to become rabbins, and they must do so in private schools and after the college hours. An attempt had been made some years ago to establish a rabbinical college, but it had proved a failure.[22]

The educational system which Wise describes as having obtained in the villages reflects, one assumes, what he knew in his own childhood (twenty-five to thirty years before he wrote, and as a tutor and student at a later period).

Children may visit the village schools, and do so in many places, then they visit the Hebrew schools besides; but more generally the Jews have extra schools. Instruction begins at 8 a.m. and is continued until noon, generally in Hebrew branches; it is resumed at 1 p.m. in winter and continues until dark, and evening again, till 8 or 9 p.m. is used to the instruction of the higher Hebrew classes. A child learns there in his early youth three different languages, the Sclavonic spoken in the greatest part of the country, the German spoken by all Jews there and taught in all schools, and the Hebrew as the language of the Bible which is understood, by the majority of Bohemian Jews. Reading and writing in these languages, grammar, Rashi (a rabbi-commentary to the Bible) arithmetic, and some Geography make the course of elementary education. Besides these congregational schools rich families and those who live too far distant from the larger places, have private teachers, and they are treated in those houses with especial distinction. It is often the case that a man spends his whole property on the education of his sons who support him and their sisters after they have entered upon public functions. In former times Talmud was one of the principal studies of every school, on which were spent three to four hours daily. When a child was six to eight years old and could read Hebrew it was set in a Talmud class. When a boy had learned something, so that he was deemed capable of a higher education, he was sent to such places where a Talmud teacher of some distinction resided. Wealthy parents paid for their children's board and tuition; but the poor did not suffer, he had tuition gratis, most always also lodging, and good people gave him what they call their 'board days', viz. one day's board weekly gratis; even such good men supported a poor student. We lived to see, that one man had twenty five such young fellows in board, one day three and the other day four, who were treated as kindly as the man's own children. Having made considerable progress in the Talmud the young students went to *Yeshiboth* where the higher Talmud studies were pursued under a distinguished master, and the young men were educated to be rabbins and

[22] *Asmonean*, 9 (24 Mar. 1854), 175.

teachers. The poor were supported in those places in the same manner, some got Sabbath-board free, and others earned a living by instruction of either younger students who could pay or other children. After some time was thus spent the young man returned to the business of his father, or he finished his education for the rabbinical office.[23]

After noting, in a passage already quoted, that Talmud study had since become a matter for those interested in the rabbinate professionally, Wise concludes the article:

Poor students are supported in the way, as we have mentioned before; it is therefore not surprising if we say, that two thirds of the young Jews in Bohemia who visit the institutes of learning are the sons of poor parents, and it is a fact deserving notice, we know one man who almost subsisted on charity, now living with his sons, two of whom are distinguished rabbins, one is a celebrated physician, and the fourth a promising young lawyer; and another man who worked a day for so much money as 12 cents, has three sons all of whom are physicians, and the oldest one is medical officer in the Austrian army. Hundreds of such facts may be mentioned.

One of the greatest deficiencies among Bohemian country Jews, is that their girls do not receive more than a common education; it is a rare exception that one is sent to a city for the purpose of receiving a better education. But this is a common fault of Europe, and it is not quite rectified in this country.

The country Jews in Bohemia are very religious, sometimes superstitious, have good morals, are industrious and enterprising.[24]

The picture was a happy one. When he drew it Wise was grappling with the uncharted seas of American life, and he may have had momentary pangs of yearning for the more stable order of the Jewish community which he had left. Economic analysis was no part of his purpose, and there is no reason to disturb the representation of village poverty given by other writers.

The position of the Jewish religious functionary in a small Bohemian community is worth examining a little more closely because, as far as can be made out, it was into such a household that Wise was born and it was that office which he filled before he left Europe.

Some information comes from an article in the *Univers Israelite* reproduced by Wise in 1857.[25] Bohemia knew three grades of Jewish religious functionaries: district rabbis, local rabbis, and *Religionsweiser*. The qualifications required of the first two were set by the government and included 'having gone through a gymnasium and a regular course of philosophical studies'. Appointments needed

[23] Ibid.   [24] Ibid.   [25] Ibid.

government confirmation and carried security against dismissal by
the congregation. The position of officials in the third grade was
different:

> Those congregations that cannot or will not keep a local rabbi, are compelled
> to keep a 'Religions-weiser' who in that case acts as rabbi. This arrangement
> has contributed greatly to lower the estimation in which the rabbis are held.
> They need not be men of either extensive rabbinical knowledge or learning
> of any kind, and require for their appointment merely a certificate from the
> district rabbi, as to their knowledge of the rule of slaughtering, and a
> qualification for teaching children.[26]

The article goes on to describe the supervisory functions assigned by
the government to the district rabbis, which brings out the dependent
status of the *Religionsweiser*.

Of the three classes of functionaries the lowest must have been the
most numerous. There were 347 congregations (only 9 had more than
a hundred families and 22 more than fifty); the number of district
rabbis was twelve and the number of local rabbis forty. Assuming
that the government did compel every other congregation to maintain
a *Religionsweiser*, the number in that category—292—would have
been far greater than that of the superior grades.

From a slightly later source we obtain a picture of the atmosphere
in which the *Religionsweiser* worked. Gotthard Deutsch draws attention to *Die Tante*, a novel by Daniel Ehrmann, in which, he says, the
life of the minister in a small community 'is vividly described, though
somewhat idealized'.[27] The author of *Die Tante* had himself served
as a rabbi in Bohemia; the novel was published in 1881, and the scene
is the small community of Weilenheim first at the turn of the century
and then after the end of the Napoleonic Wars. Ehrmann, evidently
conscious of the change which the rabbinate had undergone in the
German-speaking world, described the position of the rabbi at Weilenheim in these terms:

> The congregation had a rabbi in the person of Herr Frohmann. However,
> this title is not to be taken in the modern meaning of the word. In our time
> the Jewish clergyman has to deliver sermons once or twice a month, decide
> ritual questions, which occur ever more rarely, and incidentally give religious
> instruction to the young for a few hours a week. That is about the measure

[26] *Asmonean*, 3 (15 May 1857), 357.
[27] *Hebrew Union College Monthly*, 5 (Cincinnati, 1919), 140. From 1891 till his death
in 1921 Deutsch taught Jewish history at Hebrew Union College.

of the rabbi's professional calling in the larger congregations.... Frohmann circumcised the eight-day old boys and slaughtered beasts and birds; he instructed the little girls in spelling and forming syllables and the boys in Torah and Talmud; he prayed for the sick and chanted for the healthy; he admonished and instructed the living, buried and blessed the dead. In short, scarcely anything whatsoever was related to the religious life of the Jews, but that it went through his hands or through his mouth.[28]

Die Tante also tells how functionaries of this class were selected. Quarterly fairs were held at Pilsen, and thither came not only merchants but minor communal officials in search of employment. The cheese market was the site favoured by this class and hence they received the nickname *Käserabbiner*.[29]

The world in which the struggling pedlar dragged his load from village to village and in which the religious functionary plied for hire at a public market was one with very narrow horizons. Railways and telegraphs did not exist, and for those who ventured from home the wagon and the barge were the means of transport—unless they went by foot. The Austrian government did not encourage newspapers, and whether many Jews in the Bohemian villages would have read them is uncertain.[30]

Nevertheless, there were stirrings which within a generation had transformed the life of Bohemian Jewry; and the details, quoted earlier, which Wise set to paper in 1854 indicate that they had begun to take effect before he left the country in 1846. The career of Moses

[28] Ibid.

[29] The use of a similar term—*Käsrebbe*—is testified to by Gotthard Deutsch in *Scrolls*, 2 (1917), 236, where he describes it as a 'term of contempt used in Bohemia for the minister of a small congregation', and refers to Daniel Ehrmann's explanation of the origin of the term. It has been noted above that the majority of the Jewish congregations in Bohemia were served only by a *Religionsweiser*; Deutsch's own unidealized assessment of the position of the functionary of the Jewish village community is as follows: 'He was hazan, shohet, *shammash*, collector, *mohel*, rabbi, and above all the lightning rod whose duty it was to deflect bad humor of the congregational bosses, who were not many, but as many as there were members in the congregation. The term of such a "rebbe" was as short as that of the American minister in small towns' (ibid.). *Ben-Chananja*, a monthly published in Szegedin, in vols. 2 and 3 (1839–60) laments particularly the lot of the rabbi in the small community. Evidently the standing of the rabbinate did not improve. Deutsch (Scrolls, 2 (1917), 280) recalls that his friends in Nikolsburg, where all stores closed on the Sabbath, considered it a craze on his part that he should devote himself to rabbinic studies.

[30] Abraham Geiger (1810–74), who lived in the city of Frankfurt, could not recall having read a newspaper before he was 20. See Max Wiener, *Abraham Geiger and Liberal Judaism* (Philadelphia, 1962), 139.

Mendelssohn (1729–86) both showed the Gentile world that the despised Jew was able to play an honourable role in the cultural life of the world and widened the intellectual horizons of the Jews themselves. Until his time not only had Jews decided that a society which treated them as pariahs could have nothing worth while for them, but they had shown a restricted, albeit intense, interest in their own heritage: philosophy and poetry they generally neglected; the historical sense was still medieval; while the study of the Talmud, on which they concentrated their mental energies with religious ardour, degenerated into casuistical hair-splitting.

Mendelssohn was able to dovetail the life of the devout Jew with acceptance of the outlook of the eighteenth-century Enlightenment. He wrote impeccable German and translated the Pentateuch, with a view to acquainting his fellow Jews with the language, adding a commentary based on rationalist instead of talmudic exegesis; he encouraged the development of secular education among Jews; he advocated the separation of Church and State and a society based on equality between religions; he expounded a philosophy of religion according to which the fundamental truths of Judaism depended not on revelation but on reason and were therefore common to all men.

It was the American Revolution which first gave concrete political embodiment to the ideals of the Enlightenment, and their acceptance has been axiomatic to the development of American Judaism. However, the birth of the far-off American Republic made little immediate difference to the Jews of Europe.

Three years separated Mendelssohn's death from the French Revolution. The prospect of a new world order, which would include equality for Jews, made them more receptive to his teaching, and the tide did not turn when political reaction set in a quarter of a century later. The movement for religious reform was a logical, though unintended, consequence of Mendelssohn's teaching, but the check to the hopes of emancipation gave it an impetus. Some Jews chose the way of apostasy as a means of passing the barriers erected by the State; others took up the struggle for emancipation, and with this struggle the movement for religious reform was intimately connected. To ascribe the Reform movement solely to political motives would be one-sided. The cultural barriers between Jews and the Gentile world fell long before the political barriers. Their removal brought an intellectual renaissance, and under the critical scrutiny which the tools of contemporary scholarship made available, the forms and concepts traditionally laid down by the teachers of Judaism could not hope to survive unscathed.

The earliest efforts for reform touched only the externals of public worship. In Seesen (Westphalia) Israel Jacobson established a temple (1810)[31] whose ritual included German prayers and hymns, and in 1815 organized similar services at a private synagogue in his home in Berlin. It was not long before the Prussian government, as fearful of innovation in the church as it was in the State, put an end to these services.

The movement took root, however, in the more liberal atmosphere of the Free City of Hamburg. A Reform temple opened there in 1818, and it published its own ritual in which the traditional Hebrew liturgy was abbreviated and German hymns and prayers incorporated. The Hamburg rabbinate forbade the faithful to visit the temple or to use the prayer book, and their action was the occasion of a scholastic polemic in which opinions—mainly hostile—were expressed by notable rabbis throughout Europe.

The literary movement known as *Die Wissenschaft des Judentums*— it might be described as the Jewish New Learning of the nineteenth century—arose at the same time as the early exercises in reform. In 1819 a group of young men—the most famous among its members was Heinrich Heine—formed a *Verein für Kultur und Wissenschaft des Judentums*. The member who made the outstanding contribution in the field of Jewish research was Leopold Zunz (1794–1886). His *magnum opus, Die Gottesdienstliche Vorträge der Juden* (1832), was designed to prove that the vernacular sermon—one of the cardinal objects of early Reform—was a legitimate Jewish institution. One of Zunz's great admirers was Abraham Geiger (1810–74), who made changes in the ritual which, though minor in the light of subsequent developments, were enough to brand him as a dangerous innovator. In 1835 he founded the *Wissenschaftliche Zeitschrift für Jüdische Theologie*, in which he sought to combine historical research with practical recommendations for reform. Two years later he summoned a conference, attended by fourteen of his colleagues, to discuss a practical programme of reform; and in 1838 he was called to the

---

[31] At this time, the word 'temple' began to be used as an alternative to 'synagogue' to denominate a Jewish house of worship. This usage was intended to differentiate the reformed institution from the uncouthness of the pre-Emancipation synagogues and to emphasize its equivalence to the Temple in Jerusalem, since reformed Judaism had abandoned the tradition of looking forward to its reconstruction.

rabbinate of Breslau, an appointment which was objected to by the orthodox, and gave rise to a bitterly fought controversy.

During the period in which Wise was growing up, the decay of the old order and the impulse towards religious reform and the scientific investigation of the Jewish past had become marked; and it is no far-fetched conjecture to assume that they were the subject of excited interest wherever Jewish matters were discussed. The Reform movement was strong enough by 1836 to draw a stirring counterblast in the form of Samson Raphael Hirsch's *Nineteen Letters of Ben Uziel*.

How did this questioning affect the society in which Wise was brought up? In the article on the Jews of Bohemia quoted earlier, he alludes in general terms to the decay of the old outlook, according to which knowledge of the Talmud was the supreme goal, everything else being of minor significance in comparison.[32] A novel (*Er kann noch sein Glück machen*) with a setting in Bohemia, which he began in May 1856 and which in more than one place suggests an auto-biographical flavour, opens with the village priest anxious to encourage a 10-year-old Jewish boy, Samuel Klein, to pursue further his secular studies. The boy's widowed mother tells the *rebbe* (Hebrew teacher), who replies:

'Your late husband was very *fromm* [pious] and loved his children dearly. If the youngster studies what will he become, what can he become—a village dentist—a *poshe Yisroel* [lapsed Jew] of a doctor, or perhaps even an apostate lawyer? His father would turn in his grave should the youngster be faithless to his ancestors. Chaneh, don't let your son study. He learns his *Blatt Gemorroh* [page of Talmud] as well as a fellow of fifteen. The youngster can still make his fortune.' The mother shudders at the thought that her son might abandon Judaism.[33]

This kind of struggle against the corruption of secular study has been authenticated in tales of other times and places and is known even today. Wise's sketch is taken from life.

To the more specific question whether this particular episode is taken from his own life he later supplied the answer. Writing in 1880, he recalled that 'Fifty years ago an old and venerable Catholic priest took half a dozen of us boys under his particular care to give us extra lessons. We usually went to his house in the evening an hour or two

[32] See p. 9 above.
[33] See also *Die Deborah*, 1 (16 May 1856), 316.

after dark.' Wise would have been about 10 at the time, the age of the hero in the novel.

The watershed between the old and the new formed part of Wise's childhood experience. But for the combined influences of poverty and an old-fashioned family outlook his own career might have followed a path opened up by the availability of secular education. While his elders' sense of the primacy of talmudic studies apparently influenced his early course, it left with him an abiding sense of the value of education. His agitation for a college in America for Jewish youth was not directed exclusively to the training of rabbis, and his chiding of American Jews for their eagerness to get their sons into business at the earliest possible opportunity reflects upbringing in a society in which no sacrifice was too great for the sake of education.

Though the former isolation of Jewish religious life was breaking down, there was little attempt within the Austrian Empire to effect the thoroughgoing reform of Judaism that was sought in Germany by men such as Abraham Geiger, Samuel Holdheim, and David Einhorn. To sum up religious developments among the Jews of the Habsburg Empire during this period, Dubnow uses the term *Der Widerhall der Reform*—'The echo of reform'. It is typified by the synagogue erected in Vienna in 1826—the old ritual purged of the obvious excrescences, beautified by the music of Solomon Sulzer, dignified by the eloquent preaching of Isaac Noah Mannheimer. This system formed the model for the progressive section of the Jewish community of Prague, where a temple after the Viennese model was opened in 1836.[34] The moderate nature of the Reform movement which he encountered in his early life may suggest the background for attitudes which Wise showed in his American career: desire for adaptation coupled with distaste for radicalism, acceptance of the structure of the traditional liturgy, rapturous enthusiasm for the music of Solomon Sulzer.

The spirit of adaptation was represented by another figure to whom Wise referred with great respect in later life—S. J. Rappaport (1790–1867), the famous scholar who officiated as chief rabbi in Prague from 1840. In some communities the compatibility of secular learning with the rabbinate (or even with Judaism) was the shibboleth, and in this sense Rappaport showed himself a reformer. The question of establishing a Jewish theological seminary in Prague had been under

[34] *Jewish Encyclopedia*, ii. 333, gives 1837 as the year of the consecration of the 'Tempel für Geregelten Gottesdienst' in Prague.

discussion since 1837. Though the plan came to naught, the Bohemian *yeshivot* did not show the rigid narrowness which excluded from the students' private reading all secular literature and even the works of such Jewish masters as Ibn Ezra and Maimonides.[35] 'Outside of the schoolroom', wrote Wise,

was perfect liberty. There was not in the Bohemian Yeshiboth that bigotry as in Hungary and elsewhere that the students were prohibited from reading belletristical works, or that it was considered a crime to know Ibn Ezra's commentary to the Bible or Maimonides' *Moreh Nebuchim* [Guide for the Perplexed]. On the contrary it was considered an accomplishment to have read Schiller's, Goethe's, Lessing's or Wieland's works, and the young men spent a considerable time on philosophic theological books, such as the Kusari, Moreh, Chaboth &c.[36]

One can be sure that during the years of his study in Prague Wise heard the pros and cons both of Reform in general and of a modern institution for the training of rabbis canvassed with ardour.

3. EARLY YEARS

Leo Weis, the father of Isaac Mayer, was the teacher and general religious functionary of the small Jewish community of Steingrub. The family had lived in that part of Bohemia for three generations at least. Both Leo Weis's father, Isaiah, and his grandfather, also Leo, were physicians who had studied in Padua and lived at Durmaul, near Carlsbad. Isaiah Weis is stated to have been a learned talmudist[37] and also to have dabbled secretly in *kabbalah*.[38] Brought up in such a home and in a Jewish milieu in which graduation from the Pentateuch to the Gemarah was part of the cycle of the years, Leo Weis would have grown up equipped to be a village rabbi on the lines indicated

---

[35] *Asmonean*, 9 (17 Mar. 1854), 175. See also Deutsch, *Hebrew Union College Monthly*, v. 141–2. Eleven years after his arrival in America Wise gave expression to his disdain for the continued attachment to the old ways in what in Prague passed for reform. In *Israelite*, 3 (24 Apr. 1857), 330, Wise reports that Dr Kaempf, preacher of the Prague temple, had given the anniversary oration at the strictly orthodox Prague *chevra kadisha*. 'The preacher on his part attempted to suit the fancy of the society, and delivered instead of a regular oration an old fashioned *Pilpul-Derasha*. Just think of a professor of a university and preacher in the temple delivering a Derasha.'

[36] The works cited are Judah Halevi's *Kuzari*, Maimonides's *Guide*, and Bahya ibn Pakuda's *Duties of the Heart*.

[37] May, *Isaac Mayer Wise*, 23.

[38] Ibid. 25.

in *Die Tante*. He married twice, his second wife being Regina Weis, a distant relative. To this union thirteen children were born, seven dying in infancy. Isaac Mayer Wise was the oldest surviving son. Leo Weis died shortly after the birth of his youngest child.

When Isaac Mayer Wise was 6 he went to live at Durmaul with his grandfather. At Durmaul there was a Jewish 'trivial school' which he attended, and in the evening he received personal instruction from his grandfather. One reason assigned for Wise's being sent to his grandfather was that he showed such precocity that his father was unable to give him individual attention. In all probability, part at least of the truth is that his parents were unable to support him: when his grandfather died he did not return to Steingrub for that reason.

Isaac Mayer Wise was 12 when his grandfather died, and from that time onwards he made his way alone.[39] It is difficult to establish even a chronology from 1831 to 1843. The account which follows is based on that given in the *Biography* by his grandson, Max B. May, though it raises questions for which the answers are not forthcoming.

In Prague there lived the widow of Rabbi Bezalel Ronsperg (1760–1820), an uncle of Wise's mother, who had been *dayyan* (ecclesiastical judge) and head of the *yeshivah* in Prague.[40] The prospect of her assistance and the fact that the family had standing within the rabbinic circle no doubt helped to determine the course of the poor boy for whom his parents' home offered no prospects. With a small bundle of clothes and twenty-seven kreuzers in his pocket Wise started on foot for Prague. When he reached the Bohemian capital he began to attend the *beth hamedrash* attached to the Altneuschul, receiving *kest*, i.e. meals and lodging at the homes of well-disposed Jews, which was the customary means of supporting indigent Talmud students at this period.

As for the impression which the ancient city of Prague made on the poor country boy, we may refer again to Wise's novel *Er kann noch sein Glück machen*. Samuel Klein, the little Jewish boy whom the village priest desired to see educated, has disregarded the *rebbe*'s warnings and—how similar to Wise's case—has made his way to Prague soon after his 13th birthday.

---

[39] Wise's case was not unique: 'It was usual at that time for poor Jewish families to send their sons out into the world when they turned thirteen' (Ruth Kestenberg-Gladstein, 'The Jews between Czechs and Germans in the Historic Lands, 1848–1918' in *The Jews of Czechoslovakia* (Philadelphia, Jewish Publication Society,1968), 35.)

[40] See *Jewish Encyclopedia*, x. 468.

Samuel crossed the bridge and through the broad arch of the Strahofer Gate.
With each step he grew amazed at the great houses, the lofty towers, and the
crowds of well dressed people ... He wandered about the town for two full
hours, and he lacked the courage to ask any of the well dressed men or
women, whom he took for princes, or at least for counts, for information.

While attending the *beth hamedrash* Wise received private instruction in arithmetic, algebra, and geometry. Later he began to attend
the Prague *yeshivah*, and studied under Samuel Freund (1794–1881),
who had come to Prague as *dayyan* in 1832. Living in retirement in
Prague at this time was Herz Homberg (1748–1841), who had been
tutor to the children of Moses Mendelssohn and had helped him to
compile his commentary to the Pentateuch. Homberg was ardent to
the point of fanaticism in his support for Joseph II's policy of ensuring
that Jews received a secular education, and had served the government
as general superintendent of Jewish schools in Galicia. His work there
met with little success, fanning the flames of hostility on the part of
the rabbis to any form of modernization. Wise, who accompanied the
old man on his walks, was later to recall his influence on the *bachurim*
of Prague:

Young students cluster about him twice a week to listen to his story, which
reaches back as far as the year 1760, embracing the political commotion,
changes of empires, wars, revolutions, progress and retrogression, all stored
up in his tenacious memory. We had forgiven him the wrong he committed
on the boys of his days who were obliged to study the Hebrew text of his
catechism, 'Imre Shepher', a dry book of interminable prose. We looked up
to him as to an authority of ancient days. He loved to be compared to Socrates,
though he bore not the least resemblance to him. One of the lads pleased the
old man by writing a Hebrew dialogue, 'Socrates and His Disciples', with
marked reference to him and to his band of young disciples. The writer of
the 'Dialogue' was called Herz Plato for years after, and, if we are not
mistaken, he is still called so by some of his earliest friends ...

In Prague his influence on the rising generation was quite helpful. He was
a man of enlightened principles and of energy. A splendid Hebraist, versatile
in Scriptures and its commentaries, well acquainted with the Hebrew philosophical literature, and possessing enough knowledge of the Talmud to know
its weak points, he was an apostle of reform to the narrow circle of his friends
and disciples, many of whom he enlisted under the banner of progress.[41]

The familiarity with rabbinic texts running in harness with for-

[41] 'Reformed Judaism', in *Selected Writings of Isaac M. Wise*, ed. Philipson and
Grossman, 326–8.

mulations of Judaism based on reason points to the combined influence in his youth of the orthodox system of talmudic education and the teachings of the eighteenth-century Enlightenment. When, having settled in America, Wise began to publish his ideas on Judaism, his dependence on Mendelssohnian thought was obvious. We see the channel in his association with Herz Homberg; the aversion to *kabbalah* and 'mysticism' which Wise exhibited may also have derived from Homberg's experiences in Galicia.

From Prague, Wise went to Goltsch-Jenikau, the seat of a famous *yeshivah*.[42] Its head encouraged his students to acquire secular education, and Wise studied German literature privately. After about two years Wise returned to Prague to work for the secular educational qualifications which a government decree had made a prerequisite for the rabbinate.[43] To support himself he became a tutor in the home of Herman Bloch, a merchant in the village of Grafenried, not far from Eger. 'Within a year' Wise returned to Prague.[44] About five years later Wise married Herman Bloch's daughter, Therese. Considering that the Blochs were the only Jewish family in Grafenried, it is not surprising that a Jewish young man four years her senior won her heart. One may speculate, however, whether the young man's fondness for the daughter had something to do with his departure from the Bloch household. *Er kann noch sein Glück machen* may again have a touch of autobiography. In Prague Samuel Klein led a model life; he was almost ready to enter university when he received word that his mother had died and that his brothers and sisters were destitute. He realized that it was his duty to provide for them, and that his entrance to the university might wait a couple of years. So he took himself to an employment agent, with the result that Samuel Kaufmann, a wealthy man from the country, engaged him as tutor and bookkeeper. The situation which ensued Wise described in these words:

Samuel Klein was now in his twentieth year. His slender figure made an agreeable impression, and his male countenance with melancholy features and his abstracted manner made him interesting. Though the most ardent

[42] May, *Isaac Mayer Wise*, 26, 28; Gotthard Deutsch in *Hebrew Union College Journal*, v. 142. See also *Encyclopædia Judaica*, x. 335.

[43] David Philipson, 'Biography', in *Selected Writings of Isaac M. Wise*, 7. See *Jewish Encyclopedia*, ii. 332. In *American Israelite*, 63 (1 Feb. 1917), 1, Gotthard Deutsch points out that the decree of 1837 merely extended to Galicia that of 1797.

[44] May, *Isaac Mayer Wise*, 30.

emotion, which was restrained only with difficulty, spoke out of his dark eyes, he was by no means put in splint, like a person who was paralysed. His tranquil manner and his native sagacity, well practised in the study of the Talmud, made him an agreeable companion ... No wonder, therefore, if Samuel made a most favorable impression in the youthful heart of his pretty schoolgirl companion, Klara.

Wise's writings about himself in later life show him conscious of the impression he makes on the ladies. The reader is not surprised to learn that the tutor and the daughter of the house fall in love. There is a terrible scene, however, when Kaufmann discovers the pair embracing, and Samuel Klein is immediately thrown out of the house.[45] He makes his way back to Prague and thence (after suffering shipwreck) to New York. Eventually the Kaufmanns also settle in America (as did the Blochs), and the couple marry and prosper.

On returning to Prague from Grafenried, Wise attended the gymnasium for six months and then passed the examination of the fourth and fifth classes. He then took up the position of teacher in the Jewish community of Ronsperg, fifty miles south of Eger. Six months at Pressburg (Hungary) enabled him to take the final gymnasium examination, and he returned to Prague 'at the age of twenty-one',[46] which brings us to 1841. Then Wise attended the University of Prague for two years,[47] followed by one year at the University of Vienna[48]—two years according to another source.[49] It is stated that when he was 23 Wise received the rabbinical diploma in Prague. In 1843 he took a position at Radnitz, near Pilsen.

There is evidence which shows that Wise was never registered as a student at the University of Vienna,[50] and this reinforces the doubts raised by chronological difficulties and confusions between the sources. Probably he did sojourn in Vienna and could easily have attended lectures without being qualified to study for a degree. The

[45] *Die Deborah*, 1 (16 May 1856), 316. The novel appeared in instalments in this weekly.
[46] Philipson, 'Biography', 9.   [47] Ibid. 31.   [48] Ibid.   [49] Ibid. 10.
[50] This is made clear in a letter (dated 2 Jan. 1901) from the archivist of the University of Vienna to Gotthard Deutsch in the AJA. Professor Guido Kisch informed the writer that the archivist was known to him as an extremely careful historian. Philipson's *Life* had been published in 1900, and it is evident that Deutsch, whose own background and education made him personally familiar with conditions in the Austro-Hungarian empire, doubted the account of Wise's education. In *My Life as an American Jew*, which appeared forty years later, Philipson makes clear his resentment at Deutsch's questioning of the accuracy of his statements (p. 152).

dice were loaded against the poor Jewish boy's attempts to scale the barriers, and there is no disgrace in his having failed to do so.

Difficulties in establishing a chronology of Wise's career before he settled in Radnitz and discrepancies between the versions given by biographers who knew Wise personally set a question mark against these statements. Wise's later career suggests impetuosity and a desire to move quickly, rather than the patience to dig deeply, and perhaps at the earlier stages he lacked the self-discipline which would have paved the way to academic status. Obviously the 'D.D.' which Wise sometimes appended to his name was never conferred by a university. A more serious question is: did he ever receive the rabbinical diploma? Explicit statements have appeared in print, based, it is claimed, on information given by Wise, that he passed his rabbinical examination before the Prague *beth din* composed of Rabbis Rappaport, Freund, and Teweles.[51] When, in America, Wise was asked about his diploma, he side-stepped, which was the practice he often followed when he found himself in a difficult position.[52] When Rappaport celebrated his 70th birthday, Wise wrote a long review of his career, obviously based on personal knowledge,[53] and likewise when he died.[54] Both were highly laudatory, but neither mentioned that Rappaport was the source of the writer's rabbinical authority, as might have been expected had it been the case. The question may be regarded as open; I am inclined to answer in the negative. On the other hand, Wise's enemies in America (and they were unmerciful) did not make anything of the issue. But in that era the waters of the Atlantic washed away many a defect, and perhaps, to vary the metaphor, people who lived in glass houses learned to be cautious in throwing stones.

That Wise received some sort of document from the Prague *beth din* there is little reason to doubt. The position he took at Radnitz in 1843 was that of *Religionsweiser*: the community was reported as

[51] Philipson, 'Biography', 10; May, *Isaac Mayer Wise*, 31; *The World of My Books*, 40 n. 8. In his early days in America Wise harked back to the Vienna temple, especially to the music of Sulzer, and the statement that he ate at the homes of Mannheimer and Sulzer accords with the established practice of supporting *yeshivah* students.

[52] See *Israelite*, 8 (4 Apr. 1862), 316. Isaac Leeser had raised the question of Wise's diploma. Wise replied that there would be no point in sending the diploma since Leeser could not read it and no point in publishing it since the oriental style would not be to the public taste.

[53] See ibid., 7 (24 Dec. 1860), 60.   [54] Ibid. 14 (22 Nov. 1867), 4.

having sixty-nine souls in 1838[55] and fifty-seven in 1850.[56] Though in later life Wise was concerned to emphasize his status as a rabbi, he did not so describe himself when he embarked for the United States: the passenger list of the *Marie* in which he arrived in New York gives his occupation as 'instructor', which suggests an attempt to find the English equivalent of *Religionsweiser*. Wise's duties at Radnitz are likely to have included those of *shochet* (ritual slaughterer), and the customary certificate of competence from a rabbinic authority would have been requisite. To this the Prague *beth din* would doubtless have added testimony of the candidate's fitness for his other duties.

What legacy did Wise take from these *Wanderjahre*? They left him with a familiarity with rabbinic literature and a fervent belief in the ideals of the Enlightenment. Of the diplomas which would be so advantageous for a career in Central Europe, or of the aloofness that often went with the possession of such diplomas, there is no sign. His student years seem to have kindled within him an appetite for knowledge and a readiness to impart whatever he had picked up, unrestrained, however, by the mental discipline which habituates a man to the thorough assimilation of what has entered his mind.

Wise preached his inaugural sermon at Radnitz in the autumn of 1843: he left in the spring of 1846, after a stay of two and a half years. On the fiftieth anniversary of his inaugural sermon he claimed to have been paid well and treated well at Radnitz but to have been 'morbidly dissatisfied with everything: the country, the city, Judaism and Christianity'.[57] Admirers have found a causal relationship between Wise's departure from the Habsburg dominions and incidents during his ministry—the expression of radical sentiments from the pulpit, the celebration of marriages contrary to the *Familiantengesetz*, friction with the *Kreisrabbiner* (district rabbi)—and even the gestation of plans for the future of the Jew.[58] Corroboration is lacking, and its absence is the more conspicuous for the lack of anything giving substance to these claims in his fiftieth anniversary sermon.

Wise's career in America showed from the start that self-assertiveness was a significant element in his make-up, and one can imagine him chafing under the restrictions of life in Bohemia. Moreover, there

[55] J. G. Sommer, *Das Königreich Böhmen Statistisch-topographisch Dargestellt*, vol. vi (Prague, 1838), 52.

[56] *Die Notablenversammlung der Israeliten Böhmens*, p. 407.

[57] *American Israelite* (26 Oct. 1893), 4; May, *Isaac Mayer Wise*, 33, 408.

[58] May, *Isaac Mayer Wise*, 36–7.

was nothing in his prospects as a *Religionsweiser* to pierce the clouds: he had shown no signs of becoming an outstanding talmudist, and the community was turning away from that variety of spiritual leadership; neither had he acquired a university degree, which was the passport to rabbinic advancement under the new order.

When Wise resolved to leave Bohemia, the fall of the Metternich regime was only two years ahead (and when he heard of it his first impulse was to return to Europe), but while Metternich was in the saddle the darkness must have seemed impenetrable and interminable. Though the emigration of Jews from Bohemia was not as heavy as that from neighbouring Bavaria, emigration from Bohemia there was.[59] Wise joined the minority that resolved to make a new life elsewhere.

Wise held office at Radnitz in a period when religious reform shared with civil emancipation the attention of European Jewry. The publication of a second edition of the prayer-book of the Hamburg temple in 1842, and the establishment of the Frankfurt Society of Friends of Reform in the same year, provoked arguments far and wide. Out of the polemics a reform alignment appeared, and it was crystallized in three German rabbinical conferences—Brunswick (1844), Frankfurt (1845), and Breslau (1846). In the free atmosphere of America, Wise's reform inclinations developed tentatively; except for preaching in German, there was nothing in his European career to characterize him as a reformer. He was not a member of any of the rabbinical conferences, but we are told that he was a spectator at the second, while visiting Frankfurt in 1845.[60]

4. DEPARTURE

Wise left Bohemia without a passport.[61] From this it is not to be assumed that anything had occurred to necessitate a furtive departure. It has been stated that 'when he had made all his preparations to leave, he applied for a passport to Count Furstemberg which this official refused with a remark, "Do you think we opened schools for you to take your learning to America?"' Such a reply would have been in keeping with the arrogance of a bureaucracy accustomed to

[59] Guido Kisch, *In Search of Freedom* (London, 1949), 23; Hyman B. Grinstein, *The Rise of the Jewish Community of New York* (Philadelphia, 1945), 473.

[60] David Philipson, *The Reform Movement in Judaism* (New York, 1907), 23 ff.

[61] May, *Isaac Mayer Wise*, 41; Philipson, *Life and Selected Writings*, 15.

dealing with subjects rather than citizens. Into the question of obtaining a passport there may have entered the payment of a composition for the special taxes to which Jews in Bohemia were still subject at that time.[62]

Wise made his way to Bremen. He did not go directly, but spent several weeks travelling in Germany, visiting Leipzig, Magdeburg, Breslau, Frankfurt, and Berlin—towns in which some of the leading German rabbis resided. Was he seeking a position in Germany which would satisfy his aspirations before deciding finally to break with the Old World?

Wise begins his *Reminiscences* with 23 July 1846, the day the barque *Marie* arrived in New York: it is as if he felt that his life really began when he set foot on the New World. He does give a few details as to the voyage: it took 'sixty-three tiresome days'[63] and was marred by a smallpox epidemic; he waited on his seasick wife, carried his little child about, and ate onions and herring—presumably he did not think of departing from the Jewish dietary laws, and of the limited fare then available to travellers by sea he had to deny himself an important part. By the time of Wise's voyage steamships were crossing the Atlantic in two weeks, but they were not for poor emigrants. As poor emigrants were sometimes compelled to rely on the power of their own legs to bring them to the seaport,[64] he probably took philosophically the delays which arose thereafter through reliance on the caprice of the winds; or at least he would readily have suffered the delays of the voyage had conditions been tolerable in other respects. The living quarters between decks in an emigrant ship of that period were dark, crowded, and squalid. Rats, lice, and fleas were the passengers' constant companions, and in bad weather the hatches were battened down, so that cooking, which was done on deck, became impossible. Water descended in large quantities and sluiced about the deck in the darkness. Sanitation was neither valued nor understood, and, even if it had been, the facilities on board were so primitive that no proper standard could be maintained.[65] Death from epidemic was a recognized hazard of the crossing, the normal mortality being about 10 per cent.[66]

[62] Kisch, *In Search of Freedom*, 255.

[63] *Reminiscences*, 13.

[64] Oscar Handlin, *The Uprooted* (London, 1953), 39.

[65] E. H. H. Archibald, *Travellers by Sea* (London, 1962), 15.

[66] Handlin, *The Uprooted*, 51.

Though the inherent unpleasantness of the journey was com-
pounded by its length, Wise has nothing worse to say about the
voyage than that 'I railed at the stupidity of my surroundings.'[67] The
Atlantic may have favoured him, though we may note that throughout
his life he travelled great distances with little complaint. The hardships
Wise does not mention. A new life had begun for the writer of the
Reminiscences and what had happened before did not concern him
over-much; what he gives prominence to is a dream which he says
came to him three days before he landed.

On the twentieth of July the captain informed me that we were about fifty
miles out at sea opposite Boston, and that, if the wind continued favorable,
we would be in New York ere long. It was late at night when he told me this.
I was sitting solitary and alone, and surrendered myself entirely to my
emotions. How foolish and daring it is, thought I, to have left home, friends,
position, and future prospects in order to emigrate to a strange land without
means or expectations! My imagination now played upon the dark and spectral
possibilities hidden in the lap of veiled future. I grew more and more
despondent and confused. Finally I dropped off to sleep, and dreamed the
following unforgettable dream:

I dreamed that a great storm which drove the ship towards the land had
arisen. Every one swayed, trembled, feared, prayed; the inky waves rose
mountain high, and broke into seething masses, only to give way to other
watery heights. Convulsively I embraced wife and child, and spoke words of
calm and comfort. It then appeared to me as though a high steep, rocky
mountain was hurrying towards us and threatened to crush us. 'Here we
must land, or we sink' cried the captain, with quaking voice. Scarcely had
these words been uttered ere the ribs of the ship, which had been hurled on
the rock, cracked. I took a daring leap, and stood on the rock with wife and
child. The ocean still roared, a wave seized the ship, and cast it far out into
the seething waters; in a few moments it was swallowed up in the night, and
disappeared from my gaze. So, then, here we were on a rugged rock; at our
feet the waters, agitated by the wild storm, raged; above us and about us
were forbidding rocks, while the darkness added its terrors. Finally, after a
long interval, morning dawned, and revealed the dangerous situation.
'However steep this mountain appears, we must ascend it,' said I to my wife.
I took my child on one arm; tremblingly my wife clung to the other, and
then forward, in God's name! It seemed to me as though an inner voice
called, 'Up above there is help.' With difficulty we clambered from rock to
rock, higher and higher, constantly, untiringly. Then, as though the measure
of woes was not yet full, hollow-eyed, ghostly, grinning dwarfs, lascivious,
ragged goblins, and tiny poodles, with large, hollow, puffed-out head, came

[67] *Reminiscences*, 14.

towards us on the narrow path, opposed our further progress, and mocked me mercilessly. I brushed them aside; but for every ten that I pushed away a hundred arose from out the bare rock. They came in the shape of night-owls, and deafened me with their cries; they sizzed about me like angry wasps, and stung me; they placed themselves, like stupid blocks, in my path; in short, they did everything to harass me and prevent my further progress. My wife at my side wept bitterly, the child in my arms cried for fright, but my courage, strength and confidence grew. I begged, implored, avoided, circumvented them, all to no avail. Then I marched straight through the crowd of dwarfs, paid no attention to their ravings, dashed them aside to the right and the left, until finally, weary and perspiring, we reached the summit of the mountain. Arriving there, I saw the most beautiful and glorious landscape, the richest, most fertile meadows, but I sank fainting; thereupon I awoke, and found that it was all a dream; but I have often thought of that dream.[68]

This was written nearly thirty years after the event. That alone makes it a matter of wonder and suspicion that he should be able to fill out the details. By 1874 Wise was within sight of the green pastures of his dream. He had battled with hostile elements ('ghostly grinning dwarfs, lascivious ragged goblins and tiny poodles ... night-owls ... angry wasps ...') but he had persisted, and the year before he began his *Reminiscences* the object of his strivings had come an important stage nearer realization: the Union of American Hebrew Congregations had been established, with the support of a theological seminary as its primary object. The resemblance between the incidents in the dream and Wise's experiences in America is striking: 'I have often thought of that dream', Wise concludes, hinting broadly that just before he set foot in the Promised Land he was visited with a premonition of the dangers, the struggles, and the victory that were to be his, which he called to mind while they were being experienced.

Wise may have been making casual use of an accepted literary device. Apart from this, the story bears a strong suggestion of fantasy. Clearly it is the leitmotiv for his experiences; clearly, too, there is a strong similarity in both tone and language to the way Wise wrote about himself when he encountered opposition. Early in 1860, for example, during a controversy with a group of New York Jews, he wrote an editorial in a characteristic vein, concluding:

This pen will not stop to cry out, Onward to truth, forward to enlightenment, onward and forward to liberty, right and love. Over extremes and passions

[68] *Reminiscences*, 14–16.

our way leads; we must pass by errors, fictions, prejudices, superstitions and absurdities; over the precipices of malice, excited passions, slander and abuse we must stride as over thorns and thistles; suspicion, lies and calumnies lay in wait like ferocious beasts; still onward and forward to the sublime summit of light and truth.[69]

The story of the dream could have been an amplification of this passage. However, it was not only when Wise was engaged in active hostilities that he had the vision of himself as the lonely champion of truth, striding forward undaunted despite the attacks of the denizens of the underworld—beings who, though they made noises that would frighten others, were really only dwarfs. When he launched the *Israelite* in July 1854, it was with the same vision that he presented himself to its readers.

When we took up our pen after a short interval, to reappear before the people, our past career rose spectre-like before our imagination. What a dreadful vision! Here the blindfolded ghost of superstition threatened with its thunder-bolts of condemnation. There the masked moloch of hypocrisy and bigotry stretched forth its fiery arms to destroy those who refused to sacrifice their children to the fierce god. On this side the rude, envious and shameless dwarf, ignorance, arrayed for battle its lame champions, to shoot the venomous arrows of calumny and misrepresentation, at every one who could drive them from the couch of indolence, and on that side many an idle bystander gazed at the amusing picture, and leaning upon a heap of cherished usages and misusages blamed the intruder who roused those spectres from their state of lethargy—from a long and dreary dream. The pen trembled between the fingers, and many a melancholy thought stole over the heart.[70]

Strain and excitement made him relive the struggles he had encountered earlier. A dream or fear of shipwreck Wise may well have had as the *Marie* neared land—he was undergoing his first frightening experience of the ocean—and thirty years later he embroidered on to that dream a fantasy generated by his years of struggle for leadership among the rabbis of America.

The story reveals Wise as a man possessed by an inner drive and an intense belief in himself: a great storm arises—'Everyone swayed, trembled, feared, prayed'—but he (apparently no one else) 'spoke words of calm and comfort'. An instant and frightful choice has to be taken; he (again, apparently no one else) takes 'a daring leap' into the

---

[69] *Israelite*, 4 (23 Mar. 1860), 300.
[70] Ibid., 1 (15 July 1854), 4.

unknown, and saves those for whom he is responsible as well as himself. Though immediate disaster has been averted, they are still in danger, to avoid which a steep upward climb is needed; so with his child on one arm and his trembling wife clinging to the other he pushes 'forward, in God's name'. They climb 'from rock to rock, higher and higher, constantly, untiringly'. Their further progress is obstructed by the enemies already mentioned. His wife weeps bitterly, his child cries for fright, but his 'courage, strength, and confidence grew'. But his enemies are only dwarfs; he marches straight through them and reaches his goal. Wise sees himself as the lone hero, the instrument of salvation, and the idea of presenting himself to the world in that light does not abash him.

2

New Beginning (1846–1854)

I. YOUNG AMERICA

In 1846, New York was a large village. On Broadway as far up as Canal Street, and in the business section east of Broadway, the beginnings of the metropolis were perceptible, but elsewhere it was like a village. Small, insignificant-looking people went in and out of small houses, small shops, small institutions. The first impression that the city made upon me was exceedingly unfavorable. The whole city appeared to me like a large shop where every one buys or sells, cheats or is cheated. I had never before seen a city so bare of all art and of every trace of good taste.

(*Reminiscences*, p. 17)

There has arrived from Germany a young schoolmaster who also preaches, and is said to possess some Hebrew learning.

(Attributed by Wise to Isaac Leeser)

These quotations express first the impression which in later years Wise says New York made on him when he landed; and secondly the impression left by Wise's arrival. We now leave the shadows and enter a period in which there is always some documentation. When he established himself in Cincinnati in 1854, Wise began to publish two weeklies, for both of which he wrote profusely. For the 1846–54 period the chronicle is less ample, but he did figure in such other Jewish periodicals as appeared at that time, and in other records, for example of synagogues. After his death no diary or other memoranda were found, and few letters had been preserved.[1] In 1874–5 Wise wrote *Reminiscences*,[2] which begin with his arrival in New York and break off abruptly with the publication of his prayer-book *Minhag America* in 1857. Naturally, they form the principal guiding lines for

[1] May, *Isaac Mayer Wise*, p. iv.
[2] Isaac Mayer Wise, *Reminiscences*, trans. and ed. by David Philipson (Cincinnati, 1901), 17–18. They originally appeared in Wise's weekly, *Die Deborah*.

a sketch of his career during these eleven years. However, they cannot be accepted without qualification: Wise, like most authors, is the hero of his own memoirs; and to boot, he was prone to write hastily and inaccurately as to detail. The *Reminiscences* were written at a time when feeling between him and the rabbis of the Eastern seaboard was particularly bitter and the laity of Temple Emanu-El of New York had offered him a personal rebuff. Probably the resentment coloured his recollection of first impressions made.

The *Reminiscences* are the story of Wise the public figure; Wise's private life hardly emerges. They give a picture of Wise travelling, preaching, writing, fighting; his wife, afflicted with illness at the time the *Reminiscences* were written, is a shadowy figure, and of himself as husband and father he has little to say. Recollections of Wise in his old age speak of him as an affable and even an indulgent parent, and it is no far-fetched conjecture to imagine that in the days of his prime the fighter, withdrawn into his own den, relaxed into the same attitudes. But that was not the part of his life which he set out to describe, and one has the impression that his wife played no direct part in his public career.

When Wise and his wife and baby daughter arrived, they were at first cared for by *landsleit* (people from the same region), like so many homeless immigrants. Edward Bloch, Mrs Wise's brother, was clerk for a certain John Lindheim, and to Lindheim's home in Staten Island she went with her child. Wise himself stayed with a Mr Joseph Cohn, whose marriage he had solemnized at Radnitz six months earlier. Soon the Wise family took lodgings at a house in Broome Street. The story is one which must have been repeated in the lives of countless immigrants.

In 1874 New York had shown itself hostile to Wise, and in that year he noted that it had made a decidedly unfavourable impression on him in 1846. The city is hardly likely to have left that impression on Wise merely because of the size. The population of New York in 1846 was 371,000, about the same as that of Vienna, but doubtless the absence of any great buildings made itself felt. For all its numbers, the city would have had nothing to compare with the Hradcany of Prague, crowning the hill that rises by the Vltava, or the palaces of the Bohemian nobles, still less with the Hofburg or St Stephen's Cathedral in Vienna.

Whatever justification for Wise's impressions of New York, he quickly sensed that he was 'no longer an Imperial Royal Bohemian *shutz-jude* but ... breathing a free atmosphere'.[3] The contrast between what he had left and what he found must have been sharp in the extreme. From a society dominated by a ruling order which sought above all things to preserve the acquisitions of the past, and in which, for the individual, inherited status was all-important, Wise came to one in which there was no ruling order, in which the rules limiting the freedom of the individual—whether laid down by law or prescribed by convention—were minimal, in which the original territory of the Republic, considerable in area as it was, even when measured against the amplitude of the Habsburg realm, was a mere springboard to the acquisition of yet greater dominions. The depression of 1837 had passed, and the United States was taking 'a great leap forward'.

Terms such as 'manifest destiny' and 'Young America' do much to express the feeling that was abroad. In the year before Wise's arrival, John L. Sullivan, writing in the *Democratic Review* for July–August 1845, had referred to 'our manifest destiny to overspread the continent allotted by Providence for the free development of our multiplying millions', and for many a year the phrase he coined, 'manifest destiny', reverberating in American minds, was to sum up the urge to conquer and fill the land. 'Young America' captured the youthful spirit of energy and enterprise characteristic of the time.

'Multiplying millions' was no empty phrase. In 1840 the population was some 17.1 million; in 1850 it was almost 23.2 million—an increase of more than one-third in ten years. The rate of expansion appears more vividly by contrasting the mid-century position with that of 1800, when the population was only 5.3 million. Between 1840 and 1850, 1.4 million immigrants arrived, a figure which was doubled in the following decade, but which nevertheless represented a substantial part of the increase in population. Texas had been admitted to the Union at the end of 1845; a month before Wise's arrival in New York the future of Oregon had been agreed upon, and a few days earlier the Stars and Stripes had been unfurled at San Francisco, shortly to become a source of unbounded wealth; seven months later the conquest of California was completed.

'Society is full of excitement,' wrote Daniel Webster, 'and intelligence and industry ask only for fair play and an open field.'[4] The political and intellectual climate matched this feeling. Jacksonian

[3] *Reminiscences*, 17.
[4] Quoted in R. B. Nye and J. Morpurgo, *The Growth of the United States* (Harmondsworth, 1955), 371.

democracy, symbolized by the crowd of rough, rowdy, back-country people who thronged Washington and ruined the carpets of the White House when the violent-tempered Andrew Jackson took over the presidency from the austere John Quincy Adams in 1829, was in vogue. The eighteenth-century doctrines of natural goodness and human perfectibility, already expressed in the Declaration of Independence and the Bill of Rights, were geared to the expansionism and dynamism of the 1840s. Faith in the people was no longer the substance of things hoped for, but an expression of pride in things achieved; equality among men did not need to be tempered by the leadership of a natural aristocracy of education, talent, and worth, but implied an unequivocal confidence in the common man's innate natural wisdom and his ability to cope with almost any problem. The decorous, orderly, and dignified democracy of Jefferson had been left behind and replaced by something that was rude, vociferous, powerful, and aggressive.

If the newcomer had been blind enough not to realize for himself that the term 'New World' was something more than a geographical expression, it would have been dinned into his ears. The progress of the country—its material prosperity was unequalled, and nature, in making it secure from attack, as well as assuring it with boundless resources, provided a basis for stable government—justified the hopes of the founders of the Republic and buttressed the belief of its citizenry in the inherent superiority and eventual triumph of American institutions. That belief was no 'inarticulate major premise' but was spelt out on all levels: in the press, from the pulpit, and even in casual conservation the superiority of Republican institutions was not left to inference, but driven home by black-and-white comparisons with those of the 'effete monarchies of Europe'. This was a spirit which the naturalized American from the interior of Bohemia came conditioned to accept.

The Jacksonian confidence in the worth of the common man had its counterpart in the realm of thought. 'A man contains all that is needful to his government within his soul', wrote Ralph Waldo Emerson (1803–82), and 'The highest revelation is that God is in every man'. This was the kernel of the thinking of a man who was recognized as emancipating American thought from its European leading strings.

The thinking of Emerson and his Transcendentalist followers had no direct influence on the voters who supported the ideas of Andrew

Jackson: one was, as suggested earlier, the counterpart of the other. But the principles evolved by philosophers are capable of influencing popular thought, or at least of generating phrases, long after the political turbulences which surrounded their birth have been forgotten; and it was so with the philosophically stated notion of the sufficiency of the individual put forward by Emerson.

Since Emerson found even the Unitarian church too narrow for his individuality, it might seem strange to detect the fruits of his philosophy in the life of the churches. Yet it is there, in the establishment of new sects, or in the disruption of old ones which we find at this time. There had been a religious revival: the deism and rationalism common at the time of the Declaration of Independence had ebbed before a reawakening of Christian belief, a fact which must be borne in mind when considering the reaction to the ideas propounded by Wise shortly after his arrival. Thus, the Jewish community of America was expanding under conditions which favoured the establishment of religious institutions: 'the Awakening meant that the United States, despite the shocks of eighteenth century rationalism and "infidelity," remained predominantly a religious-minded nation, with an emotional, pietistic, moralistic spirit that would color its social, political, and economic thinking for generations to come'.[5]

The religious revival took place in a country in which the state was precluded from supporting any church; it was achieved through the agency of voluntary associations, and it helped to create a society which, unlike those of any part of the Old World, became accustomed to the idea of voluntary association for public purposes. The obverse side of the medal was a tendency to schism. The history of the country from 1830 to the beginning of the Civil War has been termed the period of sectionalism, dominated by the struggle over slavery but also 'characterized by quarrels and contentions and slanders among the churches'.[6]

After a short time in New York City, Wise settled in Albany, where he remained till 1854. Thus the first eight years of his career in America were spent in the State of New York. The general progress of the country was being refracted on New York in an intense degree. In 1825 the Erie Canal had been opened. This made accessible to the coast the prairies of the West and enhanced the commercial position

[5] R. B. Nye, *The Cultural Life of the New Nation* (New York, 1960), 219.
[6] W. W. Sweet, *The Story of Religion in America* (New York, 1930), 373–4.

of the state, so that all the advances in agriculture, commerce, and industry which followed in the country as a whole solidified its leadership. The confluence of these forces was New York City itself, whose population grew from 60,000 in 1800 to 202,000 in 1830 and 312,000 in 1840. This rise of fifty per cent in a decade was almost matched—and in absolute terms greatly exceeded—by the increase from 312,000 to 515,000 in the decade (1840–50) during which Wise arrived.

Advances were being made which placed New York in the first rank as regards painting, music, architecture, journalism, and the theatre; the level of popular education was low, but progress towards a public school system was being made. In the field of higher education the most noteworthy development was the founding of several important colleges under denominational inspiration.[7]

2. JEWISH LIFE

The general trend was matched within the Jewish community. Twenty-three refugees from Brazil, unwillingly received by the governor of Nieuw Amsterdam in 1654, made the beginning. When the Republic was founded there were, it has been estimated, 2,500 Jews in the United States; in 1840 the number was 15,000, but by 1850 it had risen to 50,000. When the ending of the Napoleonic wars reopened the channels of emigration, the deferring of the hope of Jewish emancipation and the upsurge of anti-Jewish feeling in Germany stimulated the desire to leave, and the coming of the steamship made the journey less of an obstacle. ('By steamship these days it is a pleasure trip of eleven days', wrote Joseph Goldmark to a friend in Switzerland in 1850.)

A high proportion of the newcomers came from southern Germany; some were craftsmen, many were pedlars. They swelled the Jewish population of New York City, and they founded new Jewish communities elsewhere.[8] Thus the predominance of New York was established among the Jewish communities of the country. The estimated number of Jews in the city rose from 500 in 1825 (when a second

[7] David M. Ellis *et al.*, *A Short History of New York State* (New York, 1957), 317, 318, 322. See also *Dictionary of American History* (2nd edn., New York, 1949), iv. 117.

[8] Rudolf Glanz, 'The Immigration of German Jews up to 1880', *YIVO Annual of Jewish Social Science*, 2–3 (1947–8), 81 ff.

congregation was formed) to 7,000 in 1840 and 12,000 in 1846.[9] More
striking was the establishment of new Jewish communities in the
hinterland. Forty-five congregations were established between 1776
and 1849.[10]

However, every solution creates a problem. There were problems
of adjustment and acculturation facing the individual, and they form
part of the problems besetting the organized Jewish community. In
both aspects their essence is described by Leo Baeck (1870–1953),
the prominent German-Jewish thinker, in a passage which, while
dealing with the later migration of East European Jews, applies
substantially to this earlier period also. 'The many who ... year after
year, sought their place in the new world had left an area into which
the revolution for human rights had not yet penetrated. They were
now received into a land which had begun its history with a revolution
in the name of human rights.'[11]

No struggle for emancipation conditioned the religious thinking of
the American Jew; he was called upon, however, to confront the fact
of emancipation from the moment he set foot on American soil.
Language and culture were different; he left a world which was all
tradition and found himself in a world which had no traditions. In
Baeck's words:

they came out of a world of traditional and community piety in which the
old way of their religion blew into every door and window and enfolded
everyone in every street. Now they were to live in a land of individual piety,
in which every one selected the manner of his religion, in which religiosity
was not present from the beginning, waiting for him and then surrounding
him, but in which each had to prepare a place of his own.[12]

In the first congregations, strung along the Eastern seaboard, the
Sephardi element had predominated. Fewness of numbers and an
inherited sense of insecurity had encouraged self-discipline; the thin
stream of newcomers fed existing congregations without overflowing
into new groupings. After 1820 the increase in numbers, the casting
together of groups of individuals hailing from diverse areas, and
the formation of new congregations far distant from the established
communities led to fissiparousness. American was a land of pioneers;

[9] Hyman B. Grinstein, *The Rise of the Jewish Community of New York* (Philadelphia, 1945), 64.
[10] B. W. Korn, *Eventful Years and Experiences* (Philadelphia, 1954), 28.
[11] Leo Baeck, *This People Israel* (Philadelphia, 1965), 381.
[12] Ibid.

the pioneer is notoriously an individualist; there was schism in the
church, and the Jew, it has been said, 'is like the people among whom
he lives, only a little more so'. Neither a hierarchical structure nor
a synodal system limited congregational independence, and the in-
formality with which Jewish law allows congregations to be organized
and worship to be conducted facilitated disunion. It might have been
different had the immigrants to America included a leavening of rabbis
and communal leaders. They did not. If by chance the immigrant came
well versed in talmudic law, the difficulties of his new environment
gave him little encouragement to apply or develop his knowledge. 'In
America a man must be either all head or all back. Those who are all
head remain in Europe; those who are in this country must be all
back, and forego all intellectual pursuits.'[13] This was the black-and-
white picture given to Wise when he arrived. The immigrants were
poor, and, though the land was rich in natural resources, they could
establish themselves only by unremitting toil. One of the privileges
of the ill-informed is to make great issues out of trivial points of
difference, and the stability of congregational life often hung on minor
customs peculiar to the part of Europe from which a group of members
had come.

Twenty-seven years after his arrival, Wise described the position
in 1846 in these terms:

The prospects for improvement and progress were very slim, because most
were poor, none considerably rich, and intelligence was not very abundant.
Most of the so-called 'better class' despaired of the future, and many kept aloof
from Hebrew society. This was the condition of the Hebrew congregations in
this country in 1846, not quite twenty-seven years ago. The worst of all,
however, was the low standard of the ministry. Anybody, almost, who
could chant well, and was a *Shochet*, was good enough to be minister. The
congregations did not know any better. They asked no more.

The great misfortune then was that united action among those congregations was impossible. In the first place, the Portuguese, English,
German, and Polish were four hostile elements, with strong prejudices toward
one another. In the second place, there was so much petty jealousy among
the various congregations in the same places that cooperation was altogether
out of question. In the third place, there was not intelligence enough to feel
and see the necessity of cooperation and mutual support. But by far the worst
of all the disunited elements was the reform question.[14]

---

[13] *Reminiscences*, 28.
[14] *Israelite*, 10 (20 June 1873), 4.

These words form part of an editorial in the *Israelite*, and it might be thought that Wise thickened his sombre colours in order to bring out the progress of the three decades. It is true that in an article addressed to the German Jewish public twelve months after he reached America Wise expressed himself buoyantly,[15] but not long afterwards he was writing that the majority of the congregations were 'generally composed of the most negative elements from all the different parts of Europe' and were 'governed for the greater part by men of no considerable knowledge of our religion'.[16] In fact, the whole record, including Wise's own struggles, goes a long way to establishing the correctness of his later assessment. Noting changes which the passage of time had made evident, Wise referred with satisfaction to Judaism as having been 'naturalized', or 'Americanized'. The implication is that when he landed it remained something alien, despite the equal status accorded by the American system. Just as Gentile prejudices were not always obliterated by the Constitution and the Bill of Rights, the prolonged Jewish experience of being treated as an outcast left its residue of fear and suspicion; the siege mentality did not disappear overnight; the opportunities for integration did not in all spheres overcome the barriers set up by the instinct for survival.

No ecclesiastical sanction was needed for a person to officiate as a minister; the small congregations which were coming into existence could not afford to be choosy, and there was no reservoir of trained men on which they could draw. Facilities for training rabbis in America did not exist, and to the sedentary disposition of the European rabbi the strange pioneer life of the New World held out little attraction: it was something to be resorted to *in extremis*. In 1846 there were two ordained rabbis in New York—Leo Merzbacher (1810–56) and Max Lilienthal (1815–82). The latter was more influential, but he seems to have been a man of moods and to have been content both in New York and Cincinnati, to work on the local scene.[17]

The 'free-lance' system produced one man of vision in Isaac Leeser (1806–68). Like Wise, he was largely an autodidact, though he had the advantage of a more sustained gymnasium education

---

[15] *Allgemeine Zeitung des Judenthums*, 51 (13 Dec. 1847), 741.

[16] See Wise's 'Call', sect. 4 below.

[17] For Lilienthal's activities in Russia from 1839 to 1844, including his service as adviser to the Russian government on Jewish affairs, see Michael Stanislawski, *Tsar Nicholas I and the Jews* (Philadelphia, 1983).

(in Germany) than is claimed for Wise. He came to America in 1824, and at first followed a commercial career. In 1829 he became *hazan* (minister) of the Mikveh Israel Congregation in Philadelphia.

Leeser's work for Judaism in America extended far beyond his congregation. In 1843 he founded the *Occident*, 'a monthly periodical devoted to the diffusion of knowledge on Jewish literature and religion', to quote from the description on its title-page; he translated both the Sephardi and the Ashkenazi prayer books into English; single-handed he produced a translation of the Bible; he travelled constantly, preaching throughout the land. This largely forgotten figure was responsible for many of the 'firsts' of American Jewish history and was a pioneer advocate of many of the causes which Wise brought to fruition. At the time Wise arrived in the country the *Occident* was the one national platform available to the Jews of the United States, and Leeser had already made two attempts, neither of them successful, to form a union of congregations.

Until the year of Leeser's death the careers of the two men frequently intersected, sometimes in harmony, more often in conflict. Leeser was willing to make changes in the external procedures of the synagogue, where no conflict with the Law was involved, but in doctrine and in practice he would admit of no deviation from the rules of Orthodoxy. Moreover, despite his energy and self-sacrifice, he appears to have suffered from an inferiority complex: he was over-diffident as to his intellectual attainments, over-sensitive as to his personal disadvantages, and awkward in manner.[18] Wise was inhibited by no such drawback.

The openness of society in America, the absence of any legal or conventional restraints on innovation or difference in religious affairs, the inevitability of change as part of the process of the acculturation of immigrants, made America fertile soil for reform. Little had appeared by 1846, though in Europe the movement had made progress. The French Revolution brought in its wake a movement for the emancipation of the Jews, and the emancipation of the Jews, whether realized or only desired, brought in its wake a movement for change in Judaism. The seed-bed of reform was in Germany, where struggle for emancipation was the most difficult. The opening of the Hamburg temple in 1819, the Geiger–Tiktin conflict at Breslau (1838–

[18] For the fullest account of the career of Isaac Leeser, see *Year Book of the Central Conference of American Rabbis*, xxviii (Philadelphia, 1918), 213 ff. For some sidelights, see David Philipson, *Letters of Rebecca Gratz* (Philadelphia, 1929), 108, 193, 246.

42), and the rabbinical conferences of 1844–6 kept before the Jewish world the problem of reform as to the contents of the synagogue service, the obligatory character of traditional observances, and theological principles basic to both. One does not get the impression that these learned controversies had touched the lives of the humble Central European Jews who made their way to America, though some reverberations must have entered their consciousness. In the circles in which Wise moved in Europe the issues must have been argued out passionately, though there is no sign that he had taken a stand before he settled down in Albany in 1846.[19]

A whiff of Reform had crossed to America by that year. In 1824 a reformed congregation had been founded in Charleston, South Carolina, apparently influenced by the example of the Hamburg temple. The milieu was, however, unlikely to affect the immigrants from Germany. In 1845 a group of German Jews in New York founded Temple Emanu-El, from its inception an avowedly Reform institution. But the reforms it made in the ritual were very modest, and no Reform doctrine was articulated. At that period Max Lilienthal's religious position was analogous to Isaac Leeser's; in the synagogues under his jurisdiction in New York he sought to curtail the abuses that had crept into the synagogue service, being careful to justify his changes in terms of traditional ritual law.[20]

This, in bare outline, was the position of American Jewry when Wise arrived, with a few letters of introduction but penniless and without position. There is no evidence which suggests that he had a settled intention to follow any particular calling; there is evidence which suggests that he had not come to America with the settled intention of continuing as a rabbi.[21] His first attempt at earning a

[19] For the development of the reform movement, see David Philipson, *Reform Movement in Judaism* (1st edn., New York, 1968); W. G. Plaut, *Rise of Reform Judaism* (New York, 1963); and id., *Growth of Reform Judaism* (New York, 1965); Jakob J. Petuchowski, *Prayerbook Reform in Europe* (New York, 1968).

[20] Lilienthal described his activities in a letter to the *Allgemeine Zeitung des Judentums*. I have published a translation in B. W. Korn (ed.), *A Bicentennial Festschrift for Jacob Rader Marcus* (Waltham and New York, 1976), 589.

[21] In the *Reminiscences* Wise says little that is positive about his intentions on arriving in the United States, but pp. 18 ff. suggest that he may have wavered for a time between one idea and another. May (*Isaac Mayer Wise*, 43) declares: 'He came to America with definite plans and purposes, chief among these was to liberate the Jew from his bigoted environment, to secure for him the enjoyment of equal political and religious rights, and to make political and religious rights, and to make him an independent and respected citizen of the community in which he lived.' No authority

living was by teaching English, but this only lasted a week or two; certain physicians to whom he brought letters of introduction advised him to peddle or to learn a trade.[22] This may suggest an impression of Wise's attainments. On the other hand, he says that he had 'a good prospect of receiving a professorship at a prominent college'.[23] It was Lilienthal, one gathers, who either by advice or by example, encouraged Wise to serve as a rabbi.[24]

By 1 August,[25] when he met Merzbacher, Wise had decided to continue in his former career. Later in the month Lilienthal sent him to consecrate a new synagogue at New Haven. This is the first public act which Wise performed in the United States, and the commendatory note in the New Haven *Palladium* declared that Wise's lecture 'is spoken of by those who understand the language as a most excellent discussion and the speaker, certainly in his manner, gave evidence of a most perfect style of oratory'.[26]

Wise himself was impressed by the honorarium of $60 which he received for his services.[27] Early in September he again went to dedicate a synagogue as substitute for Lilienthal, this time at Syracuse, which gave him his first occasion to visit Albany. Shortly afterwards he Anglicized his name, changing it from Weis to Wise. A New York

is cited for these 'definite plans and purposes'. The passage quoted follows a reference to Wise's desire to go to Europe during the 1848 Revolution and may be no more than a rhetorical flourish on the part of the author. However, if Wise did have such 'definite plans' and intentions—and as to these his grandson may have had direct information—it should be noted that they point as clearly in the direction of a political career as in any other. He tells us (*Reminiscences*, 16) that he arrived in New York with 'much luggage'—sufficient for a German with a horse and cart to ask six dollars for transporting it to Essex Street. Elsewhere he says 'I left my library in the old country' (*The World of my Books*, 11). The terms 'much luggage' and 'library' are not exact measurements; but, while Wise's position in Bohemia would not have afforded the means to acquire a large collection of books, the basic rabbinic texts would be likely to have been in his possession; they were scarce in America, and his arrival in New York with 'much luggage' but without the tools of hs trade gives further point to the question whether a change of occupation was intended.

[22] *Reminiscences*, 19.
[23] Ibid. 24.   [24] Ibid. 20.
[25] Ibid. 23. *Reminiscences* says 'July 1', but this is clearly an error. The same is true of the reference to 'the third of July' on p. 25.
[26] 29 Aug. 1846. The quotation is given as reproduced by Isidor Lewi in *Isaac Mayer Wise and Emanu-el* (New York, 1930), 3. In *Reminiscences*, 28, Wise refers in a feeling manner to the president of the congregation, Leopold Wasserman (later Waterman). See also Guido Kisch, 'Two American Jewish Pioneers of New Haven', *Historia Judaica*, 4 (Apr. 1942), 16.   [27] *Reminiscences*, 28.

friend gave him an introduction to his brother-in-law, who was at that time president of the Albany congregation (Beth El), and *en route* to Syracuse Wise spent a weekend at Albany, preaching in the synagogue on 29 August. He later recorded that the reaction to his sermon there was none too favourable and, though it produced an invitation to return for the ensuing high holidays, 'aggravated and humiliated' him. Wise was delayed in Syracuse because the dedication of the synagogue had been postponed and did not take place till 'the Friday and Saturday preceding the Jewish New Year in 1846', i.e. 18 and 19 September. The first day of the New Year was Monday 21 September. Wise had to be in Albany by the afternoon of the 20th to take advantage of the invitation extended to him for the festival, and this made him abandon a plan to visit Cincinnati.[28]

In Syracuse Wise seems to have obtained a more optimistic outlook on the prospects of American Judaism. His New Year appearance in Albany he recalled as one unrelieved triumph.

At the close of the service the people crowded about me, overwhelmed me with congratulations and compliments, accompanied me as procession from the synagogue to Stern's hostelry, and well-nigh crushed me beneath the weight of South German Jewish phrases, until Moses Schloss (president of the Congregation) finally took pity on me and carried me home to dinner.[29]

His success at Beth El spread his fame beyond its walls. The officers of the second congregation, Beth El Jacob, waited on him, and, with the permission of his hosts, he preached for them on the second day of the festival. At Beth El Jacob 'policemen had to be placed before the doors of the synagogue for fear lest the great mass of people would break down the old house, the synagogue being on the second floor of a building that was not very strong. My fortune was made as far as Albany was concerned.'[30] *Veni, vidi, vici*: but the story rings true. Wise's forceful personality would have made an impression, sermons in German elevated the status of the service, and his background gave his message the authenticity of the Old World Judaism from which they had sprung. Beth El speedily made Wise its rabbi, and that fact provides the backing for his recollections of triumph.

Emissaries of the congregation, he says, began their negotiations as early as the afternoon of the first day of Rosh Hashanah,[31] and a

[28] Ibid. 40. [29] Ibid. 44–8.
[30] Ibid. 46–7. [31] Ibid. 44.

formal request came on the second day.[32] 'Write a petition to the congregation,' he was told, 'setting forth that you wish to remain here, preach and open a school. This evening we have a general meeting, and you will be elected unanimously.' Wise makes clear that salary did not bother him but status did. To be a religious functionary of indeterminate status, be it *hazan*, minister, or *Religionsweiser*, did not satisfy him; he insisted that he was to be called to the office of rabbi: 'If you wish to elect me, you must elect me as a rabbi. That is my province. I will preach and open a school. I leave to you the determination of the amount of salary because I do not know how much is needed here. I will write no petition. I have never sought a position and will never do so.'[33] Beth El accepted his terms. By the time Wise reached New York on the day after Rosh Hashanah, a telegram announcing his unanimous election as rabbi of Albany was awaiting him. He returned to Albany for Yom Kippur and with his family settled into their new home, 77 Ferry Street, during the festival of Succoth.

3. RABBI IN ALBANY

The Albany Jewish community was of recent origin.[34] It was one of those which had come into being as part of the expansion of American Jewry in the post-1815 period, and more particularly after the opening of the Erie Canal in 1825.

The records show that one Assur Levy settled in Albany as early as 1661. The origins of an organized congregation can be traced back to 1838, the petition for the incorporation of the 'Trustees of the Bethel Jewish Synagogue in the City of Albany', presented on 3 August 1838, showing that the congregation had met on 25 March of that year. On 16 December it decided to purchase a house at 116 Bassett Street as a place of worship, and, as the sum required ($1,500) was beyond its means, an appeal for $500 was made to the other Jewish congregations in America. Rules adopted in 1840 fixed the annual dues as $6 and prescribed that the annual meeting be held during Passover—when the pedlars who formed a substantial proportion of the membership would be at home. The congregation grew, so that by 1841 the Bassett Street Synagogue was no longer suitable. A second congregation, under the name of Beth El Jacob, was organ-

---

[32] *Reminiscences*, 46.   [33] Ibid.
[34] Congregation Beth El had been formed in 1838.

ized in that year, but it appears to have remained much smaller than Beth El.[35] The senior congregation purchased for $2,500 a church building in 76 Herkimer Street, which was dedicated on 2 September 1841.[36]

'Not brilliant financially' is how Wise began a description of his position in Albany.

My salary was two hundred and fifty dollars a year, and nine dollars for each pupil in my school. Albany was poor. There were four firms; viz., Schloss, Blattner, Cohen and Sporberg; two grocers, Schmidt and Schwartz and several mechanics. All the other members of the congregation were peddlars. The yearly congregational dues amounted to six dollars, besides *shnoder* money [offerings]. There were but few families in Albany that had parlors furnished with carpets, cane-seated chairs, etc. The majority lived in two or three rooms. A silk dress was a rarity among the women. The men smoked three-cent cigars, and drank beer at three cents a glass. They played dominoes for an hour in order to decide who was to pay the six, nine or twelve cents. Yet, despite this, the congregation furnished my house, plainly it is true, but to their satisfaction, and this sufficed for my wife and myself. I rented a house for two hundred dollars per annum, sub-rented the top story, occupied the second, and utilized the first for school rooms.[37]

Comparisons bear out Wise's reflections that his 'position in Albany was not brilliant financially'. Lilienthal's salary in New York was $1,000, and in 1839 the *hazan* of Shearith Israel was receiving $1,500. But Merzbacher at the infant Temple Emanu-El was at that time receiving only $200.[38] The Albany congregation had 130 members at the time of Wise's arrival, which suggests, on the footing of Wise's statement as to dues, a regular income of less than $800. Wise, about whom there has been no suggestion that money was a primary consideration, was well satisfied to have firm ground under his feet, not least the status of rabbi about which he was so insistent.

The relationship between Wise and Congregation Beth El began with acclamation and ended with violence. The tale has been told and retold, but it was Wise who was the literate figure among the combatants, and his version forms the basis of most of what has been

[35] There is no suggestion that any question of religious reform was involved in the formation of a second congregation.
[36] See Louis Silver, 'The Jews in Albany, N.Y. (1655–1915)', in *YIVO Annual of Jewish Social Science*, 9 (1954), 222–5. A description of the building appears in *Occident*, 7 (Nov. 1849), 416.
[37] *Reminiscences*, 46, 47.
[38] Grinstein, *The Rise of the Jewish Community of New York*, 90–1.

written. At this stage we cannot determine whether Wise's zeal for ritual reform and the congregation's narrowness was the cause of the breakup (as is usually assumed), or whether Wise's self-assertiveness and the congregation's insistence on maintaining its control was the basic reason. Rabbi–congregation relations still retain a considerable grey area in which the authority of one party as against the other is unsettled. How much more unsettled must the position have been when communal organization was in its infancy and had to grapple with the problems and reckon with the temperaments of members of an uprooted society.

The deterioration in relations did not come overnight, and inferences as to how feeling had developed can be made from the contract entered into two and a half years after the original appointment and a year and a half before the breach. If the parties felt any need to spell out in detail their reciprocal rights and duties at the time of the original appointment in September 1846, the terms have not been found; probably in the enthusiasm of the moment such questions did not arise. As events developed, the congregation felt the need to lay down its rabbi's obligations in a specific and formal manner by means of a detailed contract, dated 14 April 1849;[39] the form of the document suggests that it had been drafted by a lawyer, and some of the points may reflect matters which had been at issue between rabbi and congregation once their honeymoon period had ended.

The first clause declares that 'Congregation Beth El has engaged the services of Rabbi Wise for two years, to wit: from April 14th 1849 to April 15th 1851 at the annual salary of $550 ...'. Wise gives the term of the contract as three years and the salary as $800.[40]

Clause 2 indicates the nature of the rabbi's duties:

In return for said payment of $550 Dr. Wise obligates himself to perform all such duties as belong to the office of preacher, as: to preach on Sabbath and festivals, to decide gratuitously questions of Jewish law for members of the congregation, and officiate at weddings.

There follows a provision specifically forbidding him from making changes in the ritual without the consent of the congregation; and

[39] Material dealing with Wise's relations with Beth El is to be found in Naphtali J. Rubinger's article, 'Dismissal in Albany', *American Jewish Archives*, 24 (Nov. 1972), 160. Some material is contained in a chapter in the *1910 Year Book*, entitled 'A History of the Jewish Community of Albany, 1836–1910', by the Revd Dr M. Schlesinger and Simon W. Rosendale.

[40] *Reminiscences*, 95.

one infers that the laity were determined to stop a practice in which he had indulged. Whether anything is to be inferred from the fact that the generality of his functions is subsumed under the title 'preacher', not the title 'rabbi' on which he was so keen,[41] is less certain: the intent may have been the same.

Several clauses relate to the conduct of the school and indicate a desire on the part of the trustees to obtain closer control. Non-observance by Wise of certain specified clauses relating to the school were, if repeated, to be brought before the congregation, which might declare the contract void.

3. Dr. Wise shall open a school for children or continue that which is now in existence when such English instruction shall be given as is given in the public schools; also arithmetic, penmanship, geography and history, hebrew [*sic*] and translation shall be taught. This educational institution shall be under the superintendence of a school committee, elected by the Trustees, the advice of which must be obtained (by the Rabbi); also the engagement of assistant teachers and school rooms shall be made only with the consent of the Trustees and the School committee.

4. For every child frequenting this school Rabbi Wise shall be entitled to a tuition fee of $9 per annum and every term (school course) shall consist of 6 months at $4.50 which Dr. Wise may collect from the parents of the children monthly or quarterly. Every 3 months the sexton of the congregation shall gratuitously collect for Dr. Wise the tuition fees that are in arrears.

5. Dr. Wise shall furnish suitable school rooms and have them sufficiently heated. Only tables and benches shall be furnished by the congregation—maps and other school apparatus, as well as stoves which are the property of the school can be used, but in future shall neither be furnished nor repaired by the congregation. Suitable school rooms we declare to be only such as are located in the first or second story of a house.

6. Dr. Wise himself is required to teach during school hours with the assistance of an English Lady or Gentleman teacher, or such English, German or Jewish assistant as shall be approved by the Committee or Trustees.

7. The school hours shall be daily from 9–12 A.M. and from 1–4 P.M. so that the children receive 6 hours daily instruction, except Friday 5 hours and Sunday 3 hours instruction shall be given.

8. Besides the Jewish holidays Dr. Wise shall have only ten days vacation.

13. Non observance of articles 5, 6, 7 ... if repeated by Dr. Wise after the School Committee has called his attention to it, shall be laid before the meeting, at the regular congregational meeting when, at the pleasure of the congregation this contract may be declared null and void. In such a case

---

[41] Ibid. 46.

however Dr. Wise shall be heard in his self defense and self justification before a vote is taken.

These details suggest an intention to curb Wise's freedom of action.

By 1849 the congregation felt the need to keep a closer rein on its rabbi. Wise's own account of how he came to tear up the contract and throw it in their faces shows that the negotiations led the parties to the verge of a complete rupture. The change in feeling Wise saw against the background of his own idealism, though he also presents himself as a man of moods.

An idealist, dreamer, and enthusiast I had shaped all things as they ought to have been. The world appeared to me most excellent, just as I wished it to be. The reforming spirit was innate in me; it was my foremost characteristic. In addition to this, I was an enthusiast on the subjects of America and freedom, and was convinced that every one thought and felt just as I did. Consequently I could begin at once to reform and to improve the world. I vented my views awkwardly and unreservedly. After I had spoken in public a number of times, and the auditors did not praise me nor sing hallelujah, I began to despair, and to entertain seriously the thought of retiring from the pulpit. Whereas, I was too dreamy and too impractical to understand, and to take the world as it was. I imagined that the people did not comprehend the nobler things. I began to grow disheartened after I had delivered a few sermons.[42]

In 1849 he actually began to prepare himself for a legal career, and this determination persisted into December of that year. In 1848, when the outbreak of revolution seemed to promise a liberal Austria, he had been ready to return to Europe; he actually resigned his position, though without giving the reason. Owing to his wife's refusal, however, he abandoned the idea of returning to Europe. Next he planned to go to Louisville to speak at the dedication of the new synagogue there in anticipation of being elected rabbi, but gave up owing to the difficulties of the journey.[43]

At this point the 1849 contract appears to have been drawn up. Albany, alarmed at the prospect of his departure, elected him for a further period (three years according to the *Reminiscences*, two years according to the contract) at an enhanced salary. This is the salary provided for by the document of 14 April, and one infers that, despite the comic opera episode which followed, this term remained valid.

[42] *Reminiscences*, 49, 50.
[43] Ibid. 82, 87, 120.

Agreement was not reached without difficulty. Wise had opponents, and at a stormy meeting held during the intermediate days of Passover they were active; evidently the rejection of the contract was a possibility. Wise, about to take the steamer to New York, marched into the meeting, tore up his contract, and went immediately to the steamer. He says that he had 'intended to take a trip to New York'. It is, of course possible that he had planned to take a holiday during the intermediate days of the Festival, especially as in 1849 the major days fell on Saturday and Sunday. One suspects that, as mercurial as his flock, Wise despaired of Albany and that the purpose of this visit was to obtain a position in New York—possibly with the union of congregations which he was then active in furthering. In a letter to the *Occident* dated 14 February, Wise had declared: 'I will never accept any salaried office from this convention.'[44] In New York he found his project for a union of congregations—to be discussed later— in low water. Telegrams and letters were sent to him in New York bidding him continue his ministry, and when he returned to Albany, he preached to a crowded synagogue on the last days of the festival. Immediately after the conclusion of the festival the adjourned meeting of the congregation took place, and at eight o'clock in the evening 'a committee composed of my most violent opponents' informed him that he had been elected unanimously for three years at a salary of $800. This figure from the *Reminiscences*[45] is an exaggeration on Wise's part.

Thus, by the spring of 1849, Wise's position with Congregation Beth El was extremely unstable, and it is not surprising that the conclusion of the new agreement proved to be a temporary truce rather than a lasting peace. What was the cause of the strife? 'Notwithstanding the new agreement,' wrote Max B. May, 'the dissensions in the congregation continued. The ultra-orthodox element was dissatisfied with even the moderate reforms introduced, and whenever a new reform was advocated the storm broke out anew.'[46] It is necessary to leave Wise's own account, and likewise the accounts which were based on Wise's story, and trace the course of events in Congregation Beth El as far as this can be done from contemporary records.

Beth El had conducted its affairs on Orthodox lines, no different from those of other congregations of similar origin, and there is no

[44] *Occident*, 6 (Mar. 1849), 616.
[45] *Reminiscences*, 95.
[46] May, *Isaac Mayer Wise*, 84.

suggestion that Wise had embraced the ideas of Reform Judaism. Early in his ministry, however, he took measures to improve the service. 'Through the exertions of Dr. Wise,' writes a correspondent ('Leopold') in the *Occident*,[47] 'a better mode of public worship is about to be introduced. The Rev. Mr. Traub is about to form a choir for the proper participation in the same, as has been already done in several European congregations.' It was not plain sailing. To Wise's opponents the choir 'was a thorn in their side. They bewailed the disappearance of the old sing-song and there were constant bicker-ings.'[48] A school of thought persists which finds religious objection to choirs, even if confined to males. It is not difficult to visualize the existence of a faction who would cry to heaven that the substitution of Sulzer's new-fangled 'fancy' music for old-fashioned *hazzanuth* (cantorial chants) was a first step to turning the synagogue into a church. And to make matters worse, the rabbi had introduced female singers, in defiance of talmudic precept. 'In 1847,' Wise wrote twenty-four years later, 'the editor of the *Israelite* was condemned by the rabbis of London and some Americans because he admitted girls to the choir.'[49]

The choir became an added source of irritation when, in order to accommodate it, extra seats were built in front of the ladies' gallery, which had the effect of demoting those ladies who had been front-seat occupants. So great was the resentment that the new portion had to be removed. 'The gallery was removed,' Wise observes, 'but not the bitterness against me.'[50]

Wise next sought the elimination of the *piyyutim*. These are additional poems inserted within the regular liturgy on special occasions. For the most part they are complicated in form and obscure in content, and their recitation is more a matter of local custom than of religious law. The optional character of these insertions has often been a moot point since while they add to the length of the service, there is usually a party which regards as inviolable anything that has ever been printed in the prayer-book. Now the serious question arose as to what was to be done with all the prayers, since the music and the sermon took up so much of the time.

We held a *post mortem* examination on the *piyyutim* [liturgical poems], *qinnoth* [lamentations] and *s'lichoth* [supplications]. My answer to the question put

---

[47] *Occident*, 4 (Mar. 1847), 599.   [48] *Reminiscences*, 112.
[49] Ibid.   [50] Ibid.

me by the directory on this subject was: Since the authors of those different liturgical pieces were all alike holy and learned, I do not feel justified in discriminating among them. I therefore recommend that all these liturgical selections be dispensed with. This recommendation was concurred in at the next congregational meeting in reference to all the services, excepting those of *Rosh Hashanah* and *Yom Kippur*.[51]

Again it is not difficult to visualize the existence of a faction which would have been outraged at their rabbi's elimination of a treasured if little-understood part of the ritual.

The milieu in which Wise worked was neither urbane nor sophisticated. His flock had inherited a Judaism that had become a matter of rote. They would work through the synagogue service much as a railway engine travelled along the rails: the mechanical processes, and the noises they gave off, would be the same whether passing through hill or dale, town or country. A break in the routine, however, would immediately arrest attention. Heresy in fine points of theology would not by itself have brought about much excitement in Albany, but the omission of a *piyyut* (liturgical poem) or a chant that had been remembered from childhood was something on which the least educated worshipper could fasten, and to stand for Orthodoxy by fighting for its retention cost very little.

4. ORGANIZING AMERICAN JEWRY

While difficulties persisted in Albany, Wise developed broader concerns. (Was the rabbi's attention to outside concerns part of the reason for tighter definition of his duties to the congregation laid down in the contract of April 1849?) This began within a few weeks of his becoming rabbi of Beth El. A *beth din* is the traditional Jewish authority in ritual matters, and after Max Lilienthal became chief rabbi of the United German Congregations of New York he took up the establishment of such a court. Lilienthal was able to announce the establishment of his *beth din* in the course of a sermon on *Shabbat Bereshit*—17 October 1846.[52] Wise was one of the four members, the others, apart from Lilienthal himself, being Herman Felsenheld and Herman Kohlmayer. The *beth din* held a preliminary meeting on the

[51] Ibid. 53–4.
[52] Ibid. 50. See also *Occident*, 3 (Feb. 1846), 575, 578; ibid. 5 (May 1847), 109, 111; and my 'A Beth Din for America', in Arthur A. Chiel (ed.), *Perspectives on Jews and Judaism* (New York, 1978), 409.

following day. Its tasks were to be wider than answering such questions on ritual as might arise in the three constituent congregations—'their services were ready to be given', Lilienthal declared, 'to every Jewish congregation in America, without claiming any clerical rights or dues.' A comprehensive range of activities was to be initiated—Lilienthal was to prepare a history, Felsenheld a catechism, and Kohlmayer a Hebrew grammar. To Wise was assigned the task of preparing a *Minhag America*—a prayer-book offering a ritual which would be available for all the Jewish congregations in America to adopt.

These plans came to naught. Wise says that he worked diligently on his allotted task during that first winter in Albany, and as his energy was always unflagging we may readily believe him when he remarks that he had his manuscript in his case when he went to New York for the second meeting of the *beth din* on 18 April 1847. The report in the *Occident*, as far as the ritual is concerned, indicates that a common ritual for American Jews was needed because experience taught that in most places different congregations were set up, and the strength of the Israelites was divided, 'because every immigrant brings his own *Minhag* from his home, and the German will not give way to the Polish, nor he to the English, nor the latter to the Portuguese Jew. Such a cause for dissension would be obviated by a Minhag-America which would promote the harmonious development of the young congregations.' Whether these words actually originated with Wise we do not know, but they are consistent with the line of thinking he advocated for the rest of his career.

Details of his plan have not come to light, but again the report in the *Occident* conforms to this phraseology. 'The project of the Minhag as introduced by Dr. Wise, treats of the Tephillah [prayer] according to the *Din* [religious law], upon scientific principles and the demands of the times, and shows plainly, that the new Minhag must be based on those three pillars, to be entirely satisfactory.'[53] Acceptance of *din* as the basis is clear, and, while there would be a party which would regard the least change as unorthodox, it is clear that Wise was not offering a Reform concept.

To give the members time for deliberation consideration was deferred, but no further meeting took place; Lilienthal's *beth din* simply expired. Wise's liturgical proposals were reported in the *Occi-*

[53] *Occident*, 5 (May 1847), 110.

dent for May 1847.[54] There are passages which indicate that an attitude which was to form a central thread in Wise's subsequent activity had already crystallized.

What stands out is not so much reform as union. 'To bring unity among the members of every congregation as well as among all the American synagogues' is the first of the two aims stated to be directing the project; and the exposition of Wise's principles concludes with the hope that 'according to them all the congregations of Israel may be led to adore our God, and that the consequence may be to unite all the congregations in America into one great and harmonious body, with revelation as their stronghold, and with peace presiding over their assemblies'.[55]

At the rabbinical conference in Cleveland (1856), Wise agreed to a platform which lost him the confidence of the ideologists of Reform in order to achieve union. In the debates which preceded American Jewry's 'civil war' he put the maintenance of the union first. A union of American Israel was a cause he never lost sight of. It seems as if, coming from a part of the world where the independence of a large number of petty principalities went hand in hand with social and political stagnation, Wise was impressed with the strength and the progress which the voluntary association of the independent units— whether states or congregations—brought about. Though failing in 1847 in the attempt to use the *beth din* as the means to promote a book of common prayer, he soon returned to the charge in a more direct way.

A great part of the *Occident* for December 1848 is taken up with 'A Call to Israelites'.[56] Conciseness was not the rule in those days, and we must digest ten pages of editorial *Vorspeise* before arriving at the main item, which is a call 'To the Ministers and other Israelites' over the name of 'Isaac Wise, D.D., Rabbi of Albany' dated 'the Ninth Day of Marchesvan, 5609, A.M.' This five-page statement is a call for union. In the opening paragraph he sounds the trumpet:

To my brother Israelites in North America, I call in the name of my God

'Be firm, and let us strengthen each other in behalf of our people.' The Rev. Editor of this periodical has granted me the favour to give publicity to my views about the association of Israelitish congregations in North America, to produce one grand and sublime end—to defend and maintain our sacred faith, to the glory of God and for the benefit of Israel and all mankind.

[54] Ibid. [55] Ibid. 106, 163. [56] Ibid. 6 (Dec. 1848), 421 ff.

Then he gives expression to a sense of his own unworthiness, coupling it (as is not unusual in such cases) with a reference to the higher power of which he is the vehicle.

Brethren! though I am a stranger among you, unknown and unimportant,— though I am aware that there are men among you much better than myself, 'Whose little finger is thicker than my loins',—though my years are but few in number, and among you are men gray-haired and high experienced,— notwithstanding all this, I make use of the Rev. Editor's permission to express publicly my views on this important subject, because I think with Elihu, son of Borachel, the Buzite of old, 'Verily it is the will in man' (that renders him able to speak and act), 'it is the spirit of the Almighty that gives understanding to them' (who have a good will devoted to God and virtue,)—or if I shall express the same idea in a Talmudic form of speech, I may say I trust 'in the help of heaven'.

Wise dwells upon the mission of Israel and urges that in order to fulfil this mission Israel needs to be 'united as one man'. He called for something more than union; and, with a messianic zeal recalling the purpose with which Joseph Caro compiled the *Shulhan aruch*, he laid down that Jews should be 'linked together by the ties of equal views concerning religious questions, by uniformity in our sacred customs, in our form of worship, and religious education. We ought to have a uniform system for our religious institutions.' Wise calls attention to the defects of the existing situation. First, the laity leaves much to be desired:

The majority of our congregations in this country have been established but a few years back; they are generally composed of the most negative elements from all the different parts of Europe and elsewhere; they have been founded and are now governed for the greater part by men of no considerable knowledge of our religion, and generally of no particular zeal for our common cause.

Then congregations are law unto themselves:

Each congregation pursues its own way, has its own customs and mode of worship, its own way of thinking about religious questions, from which cause it then results that one Jew is a stranger in the Synagogue of the other Jew.

Ministers and teachers are unqualified:

Any man who is so happy as to have a license to kill from some unknown person, can become the minister of a congregation, and the teacher of the youth.

Without union there would be disaster:

It is lamentable, but true, that if we do not unite ourselves betimes to devise a practicable system for the ministry and religious education at large,—if we do not take care that better educated men fill the pulpit and the schoolmaster's chair,—if we do not stimulate all the congregations to establish good schools, and to institute a reform in their Synagogues on modern Jewish principles,— the house of the Lord will be desolate, or nearly so, in less than ten years, and the zeal of the different Christian missionaries will be sufficient to make among us a large number of unprincipled infidels.

'Something must be done', he proclaimed, 'to defend and maintain our sacred faith', and he called upon ministers and laymen to 'be assembled in order to become united … Let the place of assembly be Philadelphia … and let the time of meeting be the second day of Rosh Hodesh Iyar, 5609' (23 April 1849).

Wise's proclamation—it is entitled to a description no less portentous—strikes one immediately for its oracular tone. It breathes self-confidence, an impression which the show of humility in the second paragraph only heightens. Could this be the work of a young man, who, the humble *Religionsweiser* of an obscure Bohemian township, had arrived in the United States two and a half years earlier? Wise's whole career, particularly the list of his writings, is a story of self-confidence. American life was shot through with self-confidence, and it had not taken Wise long to exhale the air he breathed.

The idea of a union of congregations was not new. Leeser had put it forward in 1841, but his plea went unheeded. Now Leeser and Wise were collaborating in an attempt to put it into effect. Exhortations in favour of the Philadelphia meeting rang through many issues of the *Occident*, but the project came to nothing. The venue was changed to New York and the date postponed to 11 June. The plan assumed a more ambitious form, developing into a proposal for a convention of the Jews in the United States. Wise and Leeser agreed to a division of labour in making propaganda, and Wise spoke twice in New York in support of his plan. It is evident that he needed to overcome suspicion of himself on two counts: first, that he sought office for himself, and second, that he was a reformer. Further, his description (general, it is true, and not relating especially to New York) of the congregations as 'composed of the most negative elements from all the different parts of Europe' and 'governed for the greater part by men of no considerable knowledge of our religion' was less than tactful. It was at this stage that Wise felt the need to state his attitude to reform. 'You aver that I am a reformer', he wrote in the *Occident* for March 1849,

to prejudice the people against this sound plan; to be sure, I am a reformer, as much so as our age requires; because I am convinced that none can stop the stream of time, none can check the swift wheels of the age; but I have always the *Halachah* [traditional Jewish law] for my basis. I am a reformer, if the people long for it, but then I seek to direct the public mind on the path of the *Din*; but I never urge my principles upon another, nor do I commence to start a reform in a Synagogue.[57]

Unfortunately, while Wise parried the suggestion that he was an advocate of reform, it became apparent that he had close relations with a group known as the *Lichtfreunde* and may even have inspired its foundation. His manœuvres concerning this association, which harboured tendencies of a radical character, are extremely obscure, and while they were proceeding the movement for a convention fizzled out. The minimum of twenty congregations was not forthcoming: only eight (including Leeser's in Philadelphia and Wise's in Albany) gave their approval. The one New York congregation to do so was the recently established Shaarey Tefillah. One suspects that the union movement was in low waters when Wise dashed to New York during April 1849. Whether, had he not needed to mend his fences in Albany, Wise would have been able to pull it round is a matter of speculation. In the course of a letter addressed to Leeser on 16 September 1849, Wise remarked 'As to our convention, I'd rather write nothing about it. My heart bleeds!!!'[58]

An analysis of the suspicions and the intrigues which accompanied the failure of this plan would help us to assess the characters of the participants. For the failure itself a deeper reason must be assigned. Wise and Leeser were ahead of their time; both men of vision, they were thinking of the needs of the American Jewish community at a range far more extended than that of the isolated and recently established congregations. They had to overcome apathy and indifference. The small leavening of well-established Jews might have been more inclined to take up the cause had they not looked down upon the

[57] *Occident*, 6 (Mar. 1849), 616.
[58] Original letter in Leeser papers, Dropsie University.

newcomers. For the newcomers, life was a struggle—first to earn a living, then to adjust themselves to the language and culture of a strange society. If resources of time and money were left over, the imperative claims of their local organizations would swallow them up.[59]

Moreover, neither of the protagonists of the union carried sufficient weight. Leeser, for all his tireless devotion to the public good, was not a forceful personality ('laboured impotence' was the characteristic once unkindly ascribed to him by Richard Lyon, the editor of the *Asmonean*, the New York-based Jewish weekly), and Wise was new to the scene. The status of the rabbi had yet to be established. After three years in the country, attached to a non-metropolitan congregation and without the means of making his voice heard far and wide, Wise did not have the commanding position to get his idea across. Yet he had already taken hold of certain ideas—union of congregations and a ritual for American Jews to use in common—which he was to fight for throughout his prime.

5. EARLY WRITINGS

After the failure of the union effort, Wise seems to have remained in the background for a while. He was not idle. His school took six hours of the day, besides which he spent two or three hours weekly with the synagogue choir and gave time to preparing his sermons. The appetite for knowledge was strong, and he used to frequent the New York State Library. There he not only added to his reading but rubbed shoulders with the literati of the neighbourhood. These contacts gave him a sense of the unfavourable impression of Judaism left by Christian preachers, and the lack of Jewish literature in reply, and the determination to provide the reply was not long in following.[60] While there is no evidence to suggest that contemporary American theology shaped Wise's thinking, it may be that in the realm of practice those with whom he mingled provided the role model for the rabbi.

During the summer of 1849 he suffered a severe personal blow: cholera raged in Albany, and it carried off his 2-year-old daughter,

[59] It may be of interest to examine the reasons for this failure given by B. W. Korn in *Eventful Years and Experiences*, 38–9.

[60] See an editorial written for *Israelite* in 1868, quoted in Dena Wilansky, *Sinai to Cincinnati* (New York, 1937), 142.

Laura. The loss affected him severely: 'I had frequent attacks of hypochondria, and became entirely unfitted for society', he writes in his *Reminiscences*.[61] The genuineness of his grief is not to be doubted, but one wonders whether his mood at this time did not also flow from defeat over the union scheme. Early in 1850, when he was still confined to his limited sphere in Albany, he 'coughed terribly', and his physician ordered him south. But on the steamer to Charleston, probably comforted by the belief that his election to the pulpit there was likely, he discovered that his illness was imaginary.[62]

As a result of the epidemic, Wise writes, 'An armistice was declared' in the running fight between a section of his congregation and himself.[63] Instead of the upsurge of sympathy which his loss would naturally evoke, lengthening the armistice into a durable peace, it soured quickly. 'At the funeral of my Laura,' *Reminiscences* tells us,

the 'pious' members of the congregation wanted to cut the *K'riah* [ritual rending of garment for mourning] for me. I repelled them and forbade the women to even suggest this observance to my wife. People visited me after the funeral, but they did not find me sitting on the floor; further, my feet were shod in boots; in short, I observed none of the traditional mourning customs.[64]

He offers no reason for his rejection of personal observances connected with death. It may have been a manifestation of the 'Protestantization' of his Judaism; or the mainspring may have lain deeper.

Wise comments: 'This fanned the slumbering embers of the old quarrel into flame.' One is not surprised. Despite the minor liturgical changes introduced by Wise, and whatever the personal habits of its individual members, the Albany congregation could only be classed as Orthodox. In such congregations the members looked to the rabbi to set an example in personal observance, even where they did not observe; how much more in regard to practices (such as those of mourning) to which the non-observant usually continued to adhere. Many members of the congregation must genuinely have felt shocked when their rabbi peremptorily cast aside the traditional mourning rites. They followed them themselves and regarded them as the inevitable Jewish manifestation of grief and reverence. 'During the fall holidays I was the subject of the most violent and bitter discussions

----

[61] *Reminiscences*, 125.   [62] Ibid. 127–8.
[63] Ibid. 124.   [64] Ibid. 125.

on the street, in the saloons, at the gaming table.'[65] This is not difficult to believe of a rabbi who did not keep *shivah* (the week of confined mourning). And the vigour of these discussions would have been heightened by the fact that Wise did not hesitate to upbraid his flock about not observing the Sabbath. One can almost hear the bewilderment (and the resentment too) of the untutored pedlar and storekeeper, a little guilty at following his calling on the seventh day, harangued by the rabbi for not keeping *mitsvot* whose observance involved personal sacrifice, finding that his pastor had *motu proprio* discarded another *mitsvah* whose observance would have involved him in no sacrifice.

Amid these troubles Wise seems to have kept steadily at work. His regular duties as rabbi and teacher were substantial; he wanted to turn his back on the rabbinate and continue his study of the law: 'I wanted to become a lawyer as quickly as possible in order to protect my family against future eventualities.'[66] Wise also set to work on his first book, on the Jewish religion. On 1 December 1849 we find him writing to Isaac Leeser ('Regarding you, as I do my best friend in this world of flattery and falsehood, since you never hesitate to tell me truly what you think about'), enclosing the first three chapters and asking for an opinion.[67] Though he was feeling peeved with Wise on account of the version of the union project which he had given to the press, Leeser obliged by publishing in the *Occident* for January 1850[68] a summary of the three chapters together with some flattering personal references. The book failed to see the light of day. In February 1851 Wise wrote: 'the want of pecuniary means and the efforts of my opponents to decry me as a base denier of our faith have prevented me from publishing it'.[69]

However, before 1849 drew to a close, there had opened up a new opportunity for Wise to make himself known beyond the confines of Albany. In October, Robert Lyon, of New York, began the publication of his weekly *Asmonean*. Immediately Wise addressed himself to the editor, and this personal manifesto appeared on the front page of the third issue.

The first number of the *Asmonean*, he begins, 'reached me in my solitary closet, behind the dusty barricades of the large books of

---

[65] Ibid.   [66] Ibid. 126.
[67] Original in New York Public Library.
[68] *Occident*, 7 (Jan. 1850), 436.
[69] Ibid., 8 (Dec. 1850), 443–4.

antiquity'.[70] The American Jew had the twofold mission of promoting truth and liberty. The promotion of liberty they furthered through their citizenship of the United States.

In respect of promoting truth, I thought it proper and advantageous, that Israel form a religious unity of his little republics (congregations), that this centre may animate light, where darkness yet prevails, that instruction may be brought to every heart, at home and abroad. Therefore I left last year my solitary closet for a short moment to call on my brethren earnestly and solemnly, to unite for the accomplishment of our holy mission to be strictly combined in our sacred cause.

But, sir, ashamed and disappointed, I had to retire from the stage of public activity! My call died away, my design was misinterpreted, the cause which I warmly advocated was misrepresented, and all the pious efforts of my orthodox friends proved a total failure. Therefore do I sit again in my solitary closet behind the barricades of vast tomes of antiquity, and study restless dead letters to forget the living presence, to forget the shame and disappointment which I experienced.

There follows a paragraph in which Wise heaps blame on himself for the failure:

I am candid enough, sir, to know, and sufficiently meek to confess publicly, that I myself am the real cause of the disappointment; a stranger, unknown and unnamed as I am, scarcely able to read and write the language of the country, having no popularity, no especial renown either for piety or learning, could not possess the confidence of the people, the most energetic words and efforts rather tended to arouse the suspicion of the true hearted, it was feared that I probably had a design of my own to be affected by such a convention, or that I probably a heretic, or at least a wild reformer, intended to overthrow the rock of venerated Judaism, and making machines of my own of the majority of the delegates, I might accomplish what I like and orthodoxy disliked, but I was innocent of any such chimerical notions, and so I retired, disappointed, yet with the pure self-satisfaction of having done what I could, I am to blame for not having studied circumstances enough.

'Take that grand standard'—the cause of unity—'out of my feeble hand and represent it to the people. . . . You have revived my hopes to see speedily realised what I was too weak to accomplish', the last paragraph continues. But the first to do battle, wounded though he is, waits ready to do battle again.

[70] *Asmonean*, 1 (9 Nov. 1849), 17.

If you think it advantageous to the sacred cause that I leave again my solitary closet, then call on me, and though opposed by the prejudices of a world, I will render my assistance; it is true I lost the battle, my hosts lay slain on the battle field, but I have saved the mighty banner, under which yet new forces may assemble; but if you think my cooperation (as I do) injurious to the sacred cause, then say it frankly and openly, and henceforward I will be dumb, I will continue to forget myself, to subdue and to bury my wishes, but with the glorious triumph of union I will triumph too, when this grand statue shall be erected amidst the American Israelites, I will rejoice, likewise. God grant you this divine favor.

It shows some hardihood and an intense belief in himself for a man of thirty, occupying an unimportant position, the centre of strife in his congregation, and lacking any record of achievement, to advertise his meekness and assume the character of a wounded sage, the long-suffering servant of the people who has withdrawn far from the 'madding crowd's ignoble strife' and broods over higher things in solitude. But Wise had shown himself susceptible to the milieu in which he lived: he had grasped that in the democracy of Andrew Jackson it was not the meek who inherited the earth. Above all, he was waiting ready to thrown himself into the fray once more. The appearance of a Jewish weekly in New York opened up straight away the possibility of a worthwhile platform, and through the verbal device of stating that he will be dumb if his co-operation be thought injurious to the cause, he asks for an invitation to a place on it.

Wise's collaborator in the earlier effort 'to form a religious unity' was put out of countenance at Wise's usurping of the stage for a public soliloquy. 'Surely', Leeser asked, 'Dr. Wise does not mean to say that the plan of union was entirely his own—that the thing was not heard of till he left his study last spring to propound the subject to the German congregations of New York?'[71] This comes in the course of a reasoned article in which the ever-serious Leeser takes to pieces Wise's *Asmonean* letter. 'It is possible, indeed,' Leeser observes, 'that neither Dr. Wise nor ourself is the fit man to unite the people. Well, what of this? It is no matter, so the union takes place; and we agree with him, that we shall feel a triumph in the result, though its ultimate accomplishment succeeds in other hands.' Leeser did not understand his man. Whatever words Wise used, the veil of self-abnegation in which Leeser assumed Wise to be ready to join in covering himself was a garment to be donned and shed at will.

[71] *Occident*, 7 (Dec. 1849), 436.

Wise was to do battle again, but for the time being no one showed such interest in the cause as to require him to emerge from his solitary closet. Apart from Leeser's reply, there was no follow-on of any kind to Wise's manifesto in the *Asmonean*, and Wise himself had to give attention to other concerns.

Not long after the *Asmonean* piece first appeared, the *Occident* contained an advertisement indicating that the position of rabbi of the Congregation Beth Elohim, Charleston, South Carolina, was vacant and it was this that drew his attention. In every respect it was a better position than that which he occupied in Albany and Wise resolved to apply for it. The congregation was of a definitely Reform complexion, and Wise now showed himself ready to come down on that side of the fence.

6. SORTIE IN CHARLESTON: BACKLASH IN ALBANY

Early in 1850 Wise made the journey south—no everyday occurrence in days of indifferent transport—and eventually he reached Charleston. This was in a period which has been described as the golden age of Charleston Jewry. No longer the largest Jewish community in the country, as it had been in the post-Revolutionary period, in wealth and culture it still ranked high. There had been Jews in Charleston since the seventeenth century, and Congregation Beth Elohim, founded in 1749, could boast a hundred years of history, as compared with the mere decade of the one which Wise was then serving. Moreover, the congregation had taken a stand on the issue of reform, and its position was confirmed by the secession in 1841 of the Ortho- dox members.

In his *Reminiscences*, Wise attributes his journey south to the state of his health following the death of his daughter in the previous summer. He went to New York and then to Philadelphia.[72] In Phil- adelphia, Leeser told him that the Revd M. J. Raphall was to go to Charleston 'to lecture and to champion the cause of the orthodox congregation,[73] whereupon 'I informed him that I intended to spend ten or twelve days in Washington, and that I might then go to Charleston if a favorable opportunity presented itself. Leeser fur- nished me at once with the address of the prominent members of the reform congregation of Charleston.'

[72] *Reminiscences*, 126.   [73] Ibid. 131.

The next chapter deals with the visit to Charleston: 'I had not been in Washington many days before I received an official invitation from the reformed congregation in Charleston, in which my attention was particularly called to Dr Raphall's attack on the Reform movement.'[74] (The reader might gather, though this is not clear, that he was being invited to address them in reply to Raphall's anticipated attacks.) It was only after he had addressed Congregation Beth Elohim that the Charleston minister, Gustavus Poznanski, told him that he intended to resign.[75] A few days after he returned home he received a telegram that he had been elected rabbi at $1,000 per annum plus a house.[76]

Although it turned out to be an incident on his journey to Charleston, Wise's sojourn in Washington had an important effect on him. He was counting no Charleston chickens before they were hatched, and if the law proved to be the only alternative to an uncongenial rabbinate in Albany, he would find himself in front of the traditional doorway into a political career. The Senate impressed him deeply, and he listened to its debates for lessons in English oratory. William Henry Seward introduced him to President Zachary Taylor, to whom he bore himself with suave politeness, and Henry Schoolcraft, who represented the Albany district in Congress, introduced him to Daniel Webster. Seward also introduced him to the Austrian ambassador, and the cordiality with which the ambassador received him—'a fugitive countryman'—struck Wise with the difference between the free and easy equality of America and the status-ridden rigidity of his native country.

My sojourn in Washington exerted an Americanizing influence upon me on this very account. I felt that I was one of the American people, although I had not yet been naturalized, and from that time I said 'we,' 'us,' and 'our' quite unconsciously whenever I spoke of American affairs. I felt greatly uplifted and aroused by this intercourse with the great spirits of the country and the kindly reception wherewith I met.[77]

Wise's description of his experiences in Washington helps to invest the visit to Charleston with a casualness designed to avoid any suggestion that he went as an applicant for rabbinic office. In fact the congregation had been seeking a minister for two years when Wise arrived on the scene. The first attempts had come to nothing and

[74] Ibid. 141.   [75] Ibid. 147.
[76] Ibid. 150.   [77] Ibid. 139.

were renewed by the announcement of the vacancy in the *Occident*.[78]
Wise wrote to the congregation applying for the position on 24 January
1850 and offering to visit the congregation to put himself on trial; and
on 3 February the congregation resolved to invite him to Charleston.[79]
It was plainly contrary to the truth for Wise to suggest to his readers
that it was only during his conversation with Poznanski that he learned
that the Charleston pulpit was vacant and that he was to be asked to
occupy it.

Wise leaves his readers to infer that his presence in Charleston
arose only through the intelligence imparted to him by Leeser that
Raphall would be in the town to speak for the Orthodox congregation,
and that the Reform congregation, learning of his availability, invited
him to champion its cause. Though the facts are otherwise, we can
believe that once in Charleston Wise was not backward in taking up
the cause of Beth Elohim. 'One or other of us', he wrote, referring to
the presence of Raphall, 'spoke in public nearly every day, in order
to weaken the arguments of his opponents, and we each had large
audiences.'[80]

He became friendly with Raphall, who tried to turn him from the
path of reform, but Wise replied that he could see no future for
American Orthodoxy. The two controversialists continued their
verbal shooting match, and, naturally, Wise ran up the more impressive score: 'A Christian lawyer who had followed the controversy
closely, gave the following opinion: "Raphall expresses himself beauti-
fully; Wise has the power of conviction." This was the general verdict.'
However, it was Wise's intervention in a debate between Raphall and
Poznanski which had more direct consequences for his career.

But the controversy was to have a lamentable ending. Raphall and Poznanski
had determined to hold a public debate, in which the one was to try to
convince the other. This was decided upon before my arrival in Charleston.
This was a foolish and purposeless procedure; but it had been resolved upon,
time and place had been fixed, the public was on the *qui vive*, and the comedy
had to be enacted. The doughty champions appeared on the appointed day.

---

[78] *Occident*, 7 (Dec. 1849), 477. This reference is to the literary section. The
advertising pages containing the announcement itself have not been bound with the
volume to which I had access.

[79] Records of Congregation Beth Elohim, Charleston, SC, in AJA. Material relating
to this period was lost during the Civil War. Charles Reznikoff and Uriah Engelman
in *The Jews of Charleston* (Philadelphia, 1950) hardly go beyond the version given by
Wise in his *Reminiscences*.

[80] *Reminiscences*, 146.

A long table stood in the upper part of the hall. On it lay the folios to be used in the fray. Dr. Raphall, a rotund little man with a black velvet skullcap on his head, sat at the head of the table, and next to him Mr. Poznanski in full dress, stiff, cold and self-satisfied. The *chazan* and the officers of the orthodox congregation sat at Raphall's side, while the officers of the reform congregation, with myself at the head, sat at Poznanski's side. The house was crowded with the adherents of both parties. I had gone thither with the firm resolution not to laugh, happen what would, although the whole affair seemed to me most laughable and ridiculous. During the course of the debate I wrote a German poem, which I refrained from publishing because I did not wish to encroach on Heine's preserves. Poznanski had read the proceedings of the rabbinical conferences, and the writings of Jost, Geiger, Zunz, Holdheim, Solomon, Kley, and Mannheimer; besides, he still retained some Talmudical reminiscences from his early youth. Raphall ignored the German literature, and referred exclusively to the rabbinical codex of Maimonides. Poznanski cited Albo. But beyond this there was no reference to literature. When I noticed that Raphall had dog's-eared his *Rambam* in order to find his citations readily, I opined that he was not particularly *au fait* with the contents, and when he began to murder Talmudical passages, I began to grow angry; but I held my peace. Two persons who knew the rabbinical literature only from secondary sources were debating dogmatic questions. No principle of procedure was established; no judges had been appointed. The debate was a kind of *pilpul* in a new form, but without basis. No especial acumen was displayed. Raphall was being worsted, for Poznanski was a skilled dialectician, and remained calm; while Raphall grew excited, and declaimed violently. Finally Raphall grew angry, and glowed with holy zeal. Instead of arguing, he began to catechize. He asked the public, and finally myself personally: 'Do you believe in the personal Messiah?' 'Do you believe in bodily resurrection?' I have never refused to answer a direct question; therefore I answered Raphall's question with a loud and decisive No! This ended the drama. Raphall seized his books, rushed angrily out of the hall, followed by his whole party. He had apparently given up the fight. The reform party was satisfied with the result; the whole affair appeared ridiculous to me. I preached on the following Sabbath, and left in the evening for New York by steamer, for I wished to take an ocean trip.[81]

On 10 March, the Charleston congregation considered the question of 'an immediate election for a minister' but adjourned for two days. On 12 March it resolved to elect Wise for a probationary term of two years.[82]

When he received the telegram announcing his appointment to

[81] Ibid. 147.
[82] Congregation Beth Elohim Minutes, Charleston, SC.

Charleston, Wise made arrangement to leave immediately. He gave notice to his Albany congregation;[83] he also gave notice to the world through an announcement in the *Asmonean* for 27 March.

Notice—The Rev. Dr. Wise, of Albany, N.Y. notifies his friends and correspondents, that having received a call, which he has accepted, from the Congregation of Beth Elohim, of Charleston, S.C., he has resigned his office in the Ministry of Albany, and will D.V. leave the latter city for the South in the 15th of April.

Albany, N.Y., March 22, 5610.[84]

And in the same issue the Albany congregation advertised for a successor.

The *Asmonean* for 5 April contains a report, undated, of a testimonial to Wise for Congregation Beth Elohim. It is signed by 'T. Schulz, President; Isaac Cohen, Ex-President, four trustees, two ex-trustees... and many others'. It was accompanied by a monetary gift.[85] Then there was a change of mind. By 10 April he had resolved to stay in Albany, and on 15 April had signed a fresh contract with Beth El.[86] According to Wise his decision to leave Albany stimulated resolutions and deputations urging him to remain. 'If you leave Albany,' one member declared, 'Judaism and reform will receive a death-blow, for your friends will take no more interest in the congregation nor in Judaism.'[87] Finally, reports of the prevalence of yellow fever in Charleston upset his wife, and he eventually allowed himself to be persuaded to remain in Albany, being re-elected for three years. 'The joy was great; feasts of reconciliation were celebrated; I was overwhelmed with costly gifts; the heavens were without a cloud.'[88] Knowing that he was acting 'foolishly and wrongly', he wrote his letter of withdrawal to Charleston. 'This was received in ill part there.'

---

[83] *Reminiscences*, 151.

[84] *Asmonean*, I (27 Mar. 1850), 180.

[85] Ibid. 189.

[86] This contract is similar in general purport to the one described above. The salary remains at $550 per annum, but the period is for three years. In clause 2 the term 'rabbi' replaces the term 'preacher': 'Dr. Wise engages himself to execute all such duties incidental to the office of Rabbi, likewise to preach on Sabbaths & Holy-days & to decide Jewish laws & to execute marriage ceremonies without pay.' Again there is specific provision on a matter which was liable to cause friction: '3. Dr. Rabbi Wise shall not change the prevailing Rituals without consent of the trustees.'

[87] *Reminiscences*, 152.

[88] Ibid.

Wise's dealings with Charleston, though far from being the origin or the sole cause of the dissensions surrounding his position in Albany, added to the poison in the atmosphere. In Charleston he unfurled his colours as a reformer without any equivocation, which was grist to the mill of enemies who professed concern for Orthodoxy. By accepting election to the Charleston rabbinate he broke his contract with Albany, which had two years to run (in Wise's own version three years to run) from April 1849. By accepting re-election at Albany he broke faith with Charleston, which made its feelings known in Albany.

On 5 May the Charleston congregation recorded its receipt of Wise's letter withdrawing from his agreement, adding starchily that 'subsequent reflections upon the nature of its tenor has entirely dissipated the feelings of mortification and disappointment which for the moment were engendered'.[89] The real sting came in the expression of surprise that Dr Wise had not returned the $149 expended on his account. A copy of this letter was sent to the Albany congregation, doubtless a hint that Albany was responsible for effecting payment. Since the congregation had originally given Wise leave of absence to go south to recoup his health, the suggestion that they now meet the expenses incurred by another congregation would not have put him in good light; and it is probable that the sum of $200 paid to Wise from non-congregational sources when he decided to remain with Beth El[90] was raised in order to meet this liability.

Wise felt the need to justify himself before the public. The *Asmonean* for 19 April 1850 prints a letter from Dr Wise 'Albany, April 15, 5610', enclosing both the German text and an English translation of a letter, not published elsewhere, signed 'One for Many' and dated 10 April 1850.[91] The anonymous writer first refers to Wise as 'a man of great knowledge and powerful elocution' and 'among the men who advocate a decided reform in the Jewish religion'. He then says that the reformers 'greeted with joy the tidings that you were

---

[89] The *1910 Year Book* of the Albany congregation quotes a letter from the secretary of the Charleston congregation in which they 'demand that they return to him one hundred and forty dollars which they expended on his account'. Writing from Charleston in *Sinai*, 1 (Sept. 1856), 242, Maurice Mayer, who had taken the position of rabbi of Beth El, records Wise's acceptance of and withdrawal from the office and adds that 'a correspondence that was not very comforting to him ensued'. See also Records, Congregation Beth Elohim.

[90] *Occident*, 8 (Aug. 1850), 308. Rubinger, 'Dismissal in Albany', 117–18, throws additional light on this subject.

[91] p. 219.

elected preacher of Charleston, where we hoped that an extensive field was opened for your acting and longing in a liberal sense'. Why, then, had he decided to stay in Albany? As 'a flash of lightning from the slanderer's sting', the intelligence came that he had been given an increase in salary. Having quoted and translated this anonymous letter for the readers of the *Asmonean*, Wise proceeds to give them his answer. He acknowledges that he has wronged Congregation Beth Elohim, whose members are 'gentlemen of noble heart, of pious sentiments, and of truly Jewish feeling', but the 'bitter tears', 'the feelings of love and attachment', the prophecy that a 'much loved edifice would become a howling ruin' had kept him in Albany. As to the cause of Reform, it was for him to remain in Albany rather than to go to Beth Elohim where 'every member was "a true hearted reformer," a heroic defender of the sacred cause of progress'. Lastly, Wise emphasizes his Reform convictions and suggests that by re-electing him, Albany had indicated its acceptance of his position:

A congregation that re-elects a man to the ministry, who was called to the ministerial duties to the congregation Beth-Elohim in Charleston must know, that the man is a reformer in the strictest sense of the word; and they must, therefore, be willing to give ear to such principles and doctrines which constitute a sound reform, since nobody likes to make a hypocrite of a minister. Was I not Rabbi of Albany when I publicly stated in New York, before an innumerable audience, that the duration and the prosperity of Judaism is bound on the condition of a temporal reform—Did I ever hesitate to pronounce my inmost conviction? or did my congregation ever oppose my views? They did not; and they gave me the best proof of their agreement with my views by the re-election of my humble self.

Thus Wise is using his turn-round between Charleston and Albany to assert a mandate to proceed with a reform programme. This, it appears from the petition (mentioned below), was the position he took up in the pulpit immediately after his re-election. One would be surprised to learn that the congregation had expressed any such attitude; one would not be surprised to learn that the Orthodox party argued that by accepting re-election Wise had accepted the status quo in Albany.

Wise's communications to the *Asmonean* smack of an attempt to parry criticism that he had abandoned the cause of Reform; to the Orthodox, whose suspicions he had probably been trying to assuage with assurances that his reforms were all within the framework of

Jewish law, this, following his courtship of an 'advanced congregation', would have been further evidence of duplicity. The straw was dry, waiting for a spark that would set it ablaze.

Incident followed incident; each fed upon the other; with the atmosphere growing more and more charged with hostility the light of rationality would become more and more feeble. On 13 May the president of the congregation remonstrated with Wise over doctrines he had expressed in a confirmation sermon:[92] Wise responded with what he called 'indifference' (it is difficult to believe that this meant complete silence). Wise then remonstrated with a member of the board who kept his store open on the Sabbath, and when the reprobate failed to mend his ways indicated that he might allude to the matter from the pulpit: the president, fearing a public scene, ordered Wise not to preach on 1 June.[93] Wise paid no attention to the behest, even when repeated, and preached despite the president's threatening attitude. Some members considered this sermon heretical and on the next day addressed to the president a petition requesting that a copy of the sermon be obtained: to the president's request for a copy Wise replied that he did not keep copies of his sermons.

At about this period a quarrel erupted between Wise and Veist Traub, the *hazan–shochet*. He dismissed Traub from the office of *shochet* and apparently of his own accord appointed a replacement. What was the genesis of this quarrel? Wise alludes to Traub's visiting of saloons, drinking, and playing cards as the cause of his action. What one knows of Wise's 'hail fellow' demeanour makes it strange that he should take an austere line with a subordinate religious official. Traub did bring an action for libel against Wise on account of words uttered by him in the course of a sermon. Whether the libel action brought about the suspension or was its consequence is difficult to say. The terms of the settlement between Wise and Traub lead to the inference that it was Traub who had reported the language of Wise's sermon of 1 June to the president and had thereby brought down on his head a denunciation by Wise which he regarded as defamatory. In the meantime, having dismissed Traub, Wise urged his flock not to purchase meat killed by him, which drew a complaint to the president from two butchers who continued to use Traub (26 June).

[92] *Reminiscences*, 156. By this time F. Schulz, who had been president when Wise decided to remain in office, had withdrawn. Louis Spanier, who replaced him, had supported Wise's re-election.
[93] Ibid. 158.

The waves set up by the rabbi's intervention in the Raphall–Poznanski debate continued to break on the Albany shore, for nine members sent a letter to the president on 23 June bringing charges against Wise in respect of the heresies uttered by him at Charleston and requesting that he 'be suspended from his duties until this matter has been resolved'.[94] The trustees met on 1 July; the charges against Wise were embodied in six counts and forwarded to Wise with an order to send his defence in writing not later than 14 July at 10 a.m.[95] On that day the same nine members sent a further letter to the president containing eleven paragraphs and sub-paragraphs of charges against Wise.[96]

Wise had already replied (3 July) to the earlier bill of complaints. His manner combined truculence with a side-stepping of the issues—a characteristic of his method in controversy which we shall encounter again.[97] The president, Louis Spanier, regarded this answer as personally abusive. Before it was received, however, and possibly before the meeting on 1 July, he evidently took care to have the charges against Wise authenticated, because he requested and received from three leaders of the Charleston Orthodox congregation an affidavit confirming that they had heard Wise deny belief in the coming of the Messiah and the resurrection of the dead.[98] With the help of a friendly post office official, Wise was informed of the source of Spanier's correspondence, and evidently the latter was in communication with rabbinic authorities in Europe.[99]

Wise states that when his answer came before the board he was sustained by three votes to two.[100] What this signified is uncertain, since the next board meeting (24 July) of which record exists voted three to two to withhold Wise's salary until the whole matter had been brought before the general body of members.[101] It was a mercurial situation, and sentiment could change from day to day.

[94] Archives, Congregation Beth Emeth, Albany, NY.
[95] Ibid.
[96] Ibid.
[97] Ibid. In *Reminiscences* (p. 63) Wise reproduces two of the six counts set out in this letter and one ('That I had preached a God of reason') which is not there; four of them he does not mention.
[98] *Asmonean*, 2 (27 Sept. 1850), 180; ibid. (19 July 1850), 116.
[99] *Reminiscences*, 160.
[100] Ibid. 158. Rubinger, who examined the congregational records, points out that apart from Wise's statement, no record exists of any such meeting ('Dismissal in Albany', 135).
[101] Archives, Congregation Beth Emeth, Albany.

On 24 July the affidavit from Charleston would have been before the board. What is more, Spanier had acted to bring the Albany quarrel before the world through a letter to the *Asmonean*, published on 19 July.[102] He enclosed the affidavit from Charleston and enquired 'whether a man who denies two fundamental Articles of the Jewish faith is a fit and proper person to hold the office of Rabbi and preacher in a Jewish congregation'. Presumably this is what Wise had in mind when he stated that 'the next thing that occurred was that a new bull of excommunication'—his customary description of any statement unfavourable to his opinions—appeared in the *Asmonean* on the following Friday.[103]

If the temperature in Albany that July had been high, Spanier's action in writing to the *Asmonean* must have raised it several degrees further. The editor observed in the next issue that Spanier

appears to have operated as a firebrand amidst the worthy gentlemen comprising the congregation, Beth El, of Albany. Jealous of the character and standing of their Rabbi, the zeal of many of the parties outruns their discretion, and in the outpourings of their indignation they convene meetings and pass resolutions which eclipse anything we ever read as the conclusion of a deliberate meeting.[104]

The *Asmonean* alluded to but did not publish the resolutions of this group of Wise's friends. The paper was plainly hostile to their tone and standpoint, and asked them to concentrate on the question whether the statement 'that two of the cardinal points of belief in Judaism had been rejected by an officer of the synagogue' was true or untrue. From Wise's side came insinuations that the *Asmonean*'s attitude was due to 'want of impartiality' and 'accessibility to bribery', but he gave no direct answer to the statements against him.

Wise remained at his post without receiving his salary until the congregational meeting took a decision. The meeting was held on 5 September 1850, two days before Rosh Hashanah. Wise says that the dice were loaded against him in several ways; the pedlars would be home, which meant a stormy meeting; the meeting was usually held after, not before Rosh Hashanah; there was a fair in the city that week, which made members reluctant to leave their businesses; the meeting was held in the daytime instead of at night; and the special

---

[102] *Asmonean*, 2 (19 July 1850), 100.
[103] *Reminiscences*, 162.
[104] *Asmonean*, 2 (27 July 1850), 108.

business that was to be brought before the meeting was not indicated in the notice.[105] In the event, the charges against Wise were debated from three o'clock to eleven o'clock. At that point the meeting resolved to depose Wise, and he was given written notice on the following day. The excitement and the confusion are not difficult to imagine. In Wise's version the motion for dismissal was put after the adjournment had been carried and his supporters had left the meeting; in Spanier's version the motion for the adjournment had been rejected.[106]

Wise did not take things lying down. He regarded the motion deposing him as not having been validly passed—and this view was eventually sustained in a court of law[107]—and he at once gave notice to the president that 'according to the law and at the request of the majority of the Trustees he shall remain in office and perform all the duties pertaining thereto'.[108]

This was the day before Rosh Hashanah. Within a few hours the Beth El Synagogue would be crowded for one of the major services of the year. This time, the congregation would be divided into hostile factions, one accepting and the other rejecting Wise as its rabbi. Both parties came prepared to do battle. It was the practice for the *mitsvot* (at least for Rosh Hashanah) to be sold before the festival. So that he should not have to ascend the pulpit only in order to preach, or otherwise perform the duties of the office that was in dispute, when he might have met with obstruction, Wise's friends bought for him the *mitsvah* of opening the Ark for the Reading of the Law. Spanier, scenting the possibility of trouble, deemed it prudent to apply to the sheriff for aid in maintaining the peace of the service, and on the morning of the New Year, learning of the purchase of a *mitsvah* for Wise, cancelled all sales of *mitsvot*.[109] The vice-president occupied the rabbi's seat. At the time for taking out the Torah scrolls Wise went to the Ark but was assaulted by Spanier and pushed down. 'This was the signal', recalled Wise, 'for an uproar the like of which I have never experienced.'[110] That day's Albany paper reported what must have been a near riot in these terms:

---

[105] *Reminiscences*, 163.
[106] Ibid. 163, 164; see also Rubinger, 'Dismissal in Albany', 179.
[107] The terms of the judgment in Wise's favour given on 17 May 1851 are set out in *Occident*, 9 (June 1851), 166.
[108] Rubinger, 'Dismissal in Albany', 182.
[109] *Asmonean*, 2 (11 Oct. 1850), 197.
[110] *Reminiscences*, 165.

During the last two or three days the members of the Hebrew Congregation worshipping in Fulton Street, have been in great excitement. It seems that they are not at all united in love for the Rev. Mr. Wise, their spiritual adviser, and one portion have labored with great zeal to remove him from his pastoral station; while the other portion have been equally zealous in maintaining him in his position.

On Thursday, it seems, an election was held to test the question, when, we understand, there were other feelings than those of brotherly love strongly manifested. This morning, being the Jewish Sabbath, the congregation assembled very early, when a strife arose between the two sections as to whether the Rev. Mr. Wise should, or should not officiate. It seems that as soon as the attempt was made by Mr. Wise to conduct the ceremonies, a general melee commenced. Argument, persuasion and conciliation were dispensed with, and angry words, threatenings and even blows were resorted to, and several severe assaults were committed.

The peace of that portion of the city finally became so alarmingly disturbed, that it became necessary, for the safety of the public, and for the belligerents themselves, to call in the interposition of the police authorities. Sheriff Beardsley repaired promptly to the spot, accompanied by a strong force, and soon cleared the synagogue of both parties, locked the doors and took the keys in his possession. This had the desired effect, and the riot and disturbance then terminated.

Several of those who were in the melee soon afterwards applied to the police for warrants, charging each other with assault and battery. They will have a hearing probably on Monday, if they do not, previous to that time, reconcile matters among themselves, which we hope they may do.[111]

Wise says that on his return home he was arrested and marched through the streets of Albany to the police station, but that instead of being arraigned in court he was heard by the police judge in private and allowed to go home.[112] The arrest of a rabbi after a synagogue riot on a holy day would have been a scandal of such dimensions as hardly to escape contemporary reference in the press. The absence of such reference makes one wonder whether Wise's memory was at fault.

On the second day of Rosh Hashanah Wise conducted services in his own house, with the choir in the front hall and the congregation in the two parlours. On Monday, 9 September, he said farewell to his

[111] *Albany Evening Atlas*, 7 Sept. 1850. Two days later the paper published a correction of the address of the synagogue. The Albany newspapers disclose no reports of court proceedings, which suggest that the parties did to some extent 'reconcile matters among themselves' over the weekend.

[112] *Reminiscences*, 166.

school and made arrangements with his friend Amos Wood to be admitted to the bar on the following day, rounding off the morning with a convivial lunch. But it was not to be. In the evening he attended a meeting of his supporters. They decided to form a new congregation, naming it Anshe Emeth ('Men of truth'), with Wise as their rabbi.

Here was a great turning-point in Wise's career. For a few hours it seemed that he might desert the ministry for the law. Instead he remained wedded to the rabbinate, but his was a fighting rabbinate. In his native Bohemia, indeed in most parts of Europe, some officer of government would have issued a decree regulating the affairs of the congregation, and a rabbi who proved recalcitrant would probably have found himself debarred from exercising rabbinical functions anywhere in the country. In Breslau, Geiger's right to officiate, despite being a reformer, was settled by the Royal Prussian government; in Budapest Einhorn's Reform temple was closed by state authority. Most of those officiating in American congregations had grown up in that atmosphere and would have submitted, either by following the line indicated by the laity or by withdrawing from office.[113] Wise did neither: he fought.

The story is not the black and white one depicted by Wise and repeated by his admirers. In his own portrayal he stands a picture of thrusting bumptiousness, abusive when criticized, blustering and evasive when he sensed that he might be cornered. He clearly commanded a following in Albany, and this was due primarily to the force of his personality, though intellectually too he stood out in his environment. Above all, he acknowledged no superior, and was ready to fight for his position; and in young America the fighter was respected—when he won.

This quarrel has become something of a *cause célèbre* in American Jewish history. For one thing it was recorded, whereas in the pietistic style of writing communal history such incidents are rarely disinterred. The strands in Wise's case were of mixed texture: the rabbi's personal relations were interwoven with his championing of a theological position, and with the advance of the Reform movement this event has grown in significance. A rabbi had insisted that he was an independent figure, something other than an employee beholden to the laymen who appointed him; and he had asserted his independence in the cause of reform. Thus the strife in Albany marks a turning-

[113] Comparison may be made with the withdrawal from office of Isaac Leeser (Philadelphia) and Max Lilienthal (New York) at this period.

point not only in Wise's life but in the life of the American rabbinate. Wise seems to have taken a lesson from his Beth El experience. He worked in the American rabbinate for another half-century, and, though he was ever ready to take up arms, in a most important respect his career was remarkable for its stability. For another four years he remained in Albany, and then he accepted a call to Congregation B'nai Jeshurun, Cincinnati, where he remained for the rest of his life. These years are remarkable for the absence of strain between him and the laymen of his congregation. There are no grounds for believing that in the second half of the century a sudden stability overtook Jewish congregational life. Was the situation made more difficult by the combined inexperience of both parties? The inexperience of rabbi and congregation was concurrent. Wise was holding office as an independent rabbi for the first time, and Congregation Beth El had enlisted the services of a rabbi for the first time. Was Wise unfortunate in the coincidence of personalities and events in his early Albany experience, circumstances rendering a clash of personalities inevitable? Did that experience teach him to curb his temper and exercise more restraint when criticized? Did the fight he made in Albany cause him to be treated with unusual deference? Did the wider ambitions which he formed in Albany and to which he devoted himself in Cincinnati provide all the outlets which his combativeness needed and make him cherish quiet on the home front?

7. ANSHE EMETH

Fifty-six members of Beth El followed Wise into the new congregation, and they were joined at the outset by twenty-six people who had not previously been connected with either of the synagogues. Joseph Sporberg, who had been vice-president of Beth El, was the lay leader. The congregation was incorporated on 11 October 1850, and Wise became its rabbi.

Yom Kippur was approaching when the decision to establish Anshe Emeth was taken. The new congregation rented a loft at the corner of Lydius and South Pearl streets in the business district (it had lately been used as a razor-strop factory) and hastily procured benches, chairs, and two *sifrei torah*. A little table, donated by the wife of one of the members, served as the reading desk. In these improvised surroundings Wise conducted Yom Kippur services. Soon the congregation moved to other rented rooms at 77 South Ferry Street.

The explosion seems to have cleared the air, for arrangements were arrived at early in October which enabled the two groups each to go its own way. Legal actions were withdrawn, except Wise's suit against Spanier, already referred to; those members of Beth El who seceded gave up their rights, save that of burial for the next two years; Wise's contract was annulled, but he received $800 as compensation.[114]

Early in October Wise went to New York, Philadelphia, and Baltimore with a commission to raise funds for the new congregation.[115] 'I was coldly received everywhere in New York, except at Lilienthal's house,' he recalls. 'After spending one day in New York I understood perfectly well that I was discredited.'[116]

Wise then went to Philadelphia. Though they differed on religious principles, Leeser, through the pages of the *Occident*, had been friendly, and he published a generous account of the two sermons and lecture which Wise gave in Philadelphia on 12 and 26 October.[117] Between these dates he visited Baltimore and Washington. Again he made the acquaintance of leading politicians. His *Reminiscences* recall a meeting with Judah P. Benjamin, later secretary of state in the confederacy, during this visit to Washington,[118] but, despite the detail that Wise gives, doubt has been cast on the accuracy of his recollection.[119]

The account of this visit to Washington brings the first mention in Wise's *Reminiscences* of a 'Mrs. F.'[120] Returning one afternoon to his hotel, he was told by the clerk that a lady had been waiting for him for several hours. 'Mrs. F.' had followed him from Philadelphia to Baltimore to hear him speak, and then from Baltimore to Washington with the same object, and then back to Philadelphia. On the journey

---

[114] Details of the settlement effected between Congregation Beth-El and the supporters of Wise are given in Nathan Rubinger's doctoral dissertation 'Albany Jewry of the Nineteenth Century', 145–63. Presumably the passions did not cool overnight, but a letter in *Asmonean*, 7 (12 Nov. 1852), 42, states 'the re-echoes of the late troubles are heard only among the extreme partisans on both sides, and on the whole, peace and good understanding are restored'.

[115] *Reminiscences*, 176.

[116] Ibid. 197.

[117] *Occident*, 8 (Dec. 1850), 473.

[118] *Reminiscences*, 184.

[119] See B. W. Korn, 'Judah P. Benjamin as a Jew', in *Eventful Years and Experiences* (Philadelphia, 1954), 83 ff.

[120] It is believed that 'Mrs. F.' was a Mrs Florance—Hannah Levy, daughter of Hart Levy, who married Jacob Levy Florance. Mrs Levy died in Philadelphia in 1870.

she hands him a poem about a young orator who is 'the morning star of American Judaism', and when he preaches in Philadelphia she does not take her eyes from him. 'Mrs. F.' reappears in the *Reminiscences* at various points, counselling and warning Wise, visiting Albany for the consecration of his synagogue, encouraging his literary work. One is tempted to assume that some sort of liaison may have come into being, but the very candour with which Wise describes their association makes it unlikely that it assumed an illicit character. In recounting his visit to Charleston he wished the world to know what an impression he had made on the ladies, and the same conceit is at work here; as usual Wise presents himself as the hero.

Wise makes for this journey the modest claim that he 'had brought back for the congregation some money and much encouragement'.[121] The delay in entering into possession of the South Pearl Street Baptist Church, which Anshe Emeth had contracted to acquire, combines with this cautious statement to suggest that the financial results were meagre. Nevertheless, the fact that Wise was ready to make the effort exhibits him as a fighter, just as much as his stand in Congregation Beth El. This was the first, but not the last time that Wise was to show a willingness to go about the country to solicit funds for a cause in which he was interested, and this tireless energy and lack of inhibition was in due time to establish his position as a leader of American Israel.

The synagogue was consecrated on 3 October 1851, by Wise's friend Lilienthal.[122] The day was Shabbath Shuvah (the Sabbath between New Year and the Day of Atonement), and one wonders whether it was with the idea of providing a *locus poenitentiae* that Anshe Emeth invited the members of Beth El to participate. It might have been expected that the establishment of their own congregation by the pro-Wise, pro-Reform group would lead to a pronounced move in the direction of Reform: it did not, which confirms that Wise was not pressing in the direction of radicalism. Congregation Anshe Emeth made arrangements for *shechitah* (ritual slaughter) early in its history, and not long afterwards gave orders for the construction of a *mikveh* (ritual bath). The most remarkable innovation came when the new synagogue was opened and an organ and family pews (instead of the traditional segregation of men and women) were introduced and

---

[121] *Reminiscences*, 198.
[122] The address which Wise gave on this occasion he later published in *Israelite*, 5 (10 Dec. 1858), 180.

accepted. (Whether this innovation sprang from any decided conviction or was merely an accommodation to the building taken over
is uncertain.)[123]

A third innovation related to the music of the service. Apparently
it was not chanted by the officiant. 'All the singing was done by the
choir and I myself read the prayers.'[124] Wise felt very strongly that a
rabbi should not be called upon to chant prayers: 'singing ministers'
was one of the epithets he flung about, directed no doubt, at ecclesi-
astics in the position of Isaac Leeser. Wise looked upon the abolition
of chanting as an important reform.[125] When asked shortly before he
left for Albany for his view, Wise responded that it would not be
against Jewish law to reduce to three the number called to the Reading
of the Law.[126]

Although in breach with the senior congregation, Wise was the
only rabbi in the town, Beth El being confined to the services of its
hazan, Veist Traub. Contemporary reports suggest that it was Anshe
Emeth, under Wise, which made the running.[127] His services attracted
visitors (Gentiles included), and during the week ending 17 January
1852 he officiated as chaplain of the Legislature of the State of New
York. Wise himself states that he had to secure this position over the
protests of the Christian clergy, who did not wish a rabbi to fulfil the
duty.[128]

From the time of his arrival in New York, Wise saw the need to
train Jewish ministers in America. The crowning achievement of his
life was to become president of a theological seminary, but the task
attracted him long before he had firm ground under his feet. The
following advertisement appeared in the *Asmonean* on 5 March, and
was repeated in the three succeeding weeks:

THEOLOGY—A young man desirous of accomplishing his education for the
Jewish Ministry, either in one or all the branches of learning necessary to
hold such an office, can avail himself of a good opportunity in the house of

---

[123] *1910 Year Book*, 51, 52; *Asmonean*, 5 (21 Nov. 1852), 53.

[124] *Reminiscences*, 224.

[125] See *Israelite*, 11 (5 Aug. 1861), 43. This point arose in the 'kite' which Wise flew
in *Asmonean* while he was negotiating for his position in Cincinnati. See ch. 2 sect.
11 below.

[126] *1910 Year Book*, 52; *Asmonean*, 7 (15 Apr. 1852), 372.

[127] As to the strength of the three congregations, see n. 174 below. Rubinger, 'Albany
Jewry of the Nineteenth Century', ch. 4, adduces evidence as to the development of
Congregation Anshe Emeth.

[128] *Asmonean*, 5 (31 Jan. 1852), 113; *Reminiscences*, 218, 219.

the undersigned, provided the applicant be willing to teach the undersigned's pupils the elementary branches of the Hebrew and German or Hebrew and English languages. A knowledge of music will be essential.

Isaac M. Wise, D.D., Albany, New York[129]

The offer indicates Wise's belief in his own capabilities. It was bold, but Wise was a pioneer in a pioneer world, and among the American Jews of 1853 he was establishing himself as the regular popular exponent of theological and philosophical questions to the Jews of America.

In October 1849, the New York Presbyterian Synod issued an address to 'the Israelites within their District', inviting them to join their church. This naturally roused the editor of the *Occident*.[130] Wise was not the first to intervene, but between August 1850 and March 1851 he contributed three articles to the *Occident* replying to the pro-Christian contribution of M. R. Miller, for which Leeser—rather strangely—found space.[131]

8. FORMULATING HIS BELIEFS

While this series was running, Wise became involved in another battle. In September 1850, Leeser began to publish a series of articles on 'Judaism and its Principles'.[132] The series was intended to illustrate the idea of the Messiah and the resurrection of the dead as based upon scriptural grounds,[133] and was called forth (as Leeser later admitted) by Wise's negation of these doctrines. Leeser gave him space in the *Occident* for a series of letters in reply.

In these three letters Wise makes his first attempt at anything like a systematic exposition of the basic ideas of Judaism. The sequence suggests that he did not think out the three articles as a whole, and the context is overlaid with sermonic matter. In the first place he expounds a Maimonidean viewpoint as regards the Bible: 'the Bible is a divine truth as a whole and in all its particulars ... all laws of nature and all experience of history' are as true as the deductions of mathematics. If the one is proved to contradict the other then

[129] *Asmonean*, 5 (5 Mar. 1853), 193, 211.
[130] *Occident*, 6 (Dec. 1849), 487.
[131] His *Reminiscences*, 121 leave the impression that until Leeser called on him there was no one to take up the pen in defence of Judaism.
[132] *Occident*, 8 (Sept. 1850), 265; (Oct. 1850), 325; (Nov. 1850), 373; (Dec. 1850), 433; (Jan. 1851), 481: (Feb. 1851), 529; (Mar. 1851), 581.
[133] Ibid. (Sept. 1850), 265.

the expounder made a wilful or accidental mistake.... Wherefore we must come to the conclusion, that as dogmas have been taught, and even proved by biblical texts, which are contradicted by the laws of nature, or by the facts of history, whoever has so expounded them, must have taken an erroneous view of his subject, or has misinterpreted the word of God.[134]

In the second letter Wise expounds the basic doctrines of Judaism. 'Judaism', he declares, 'is based upon four leading ideas and has, therefore, four principles.' Doctrines and observances which did not correspond to these ideas had to be rejected as 'anti-Jewish and foreign to our system'. The four principles were:

1. There is but one God, who is the Creator, Preserver, and Ruler of the Universe; an absolute, pure, and eternal Spirit; the primitive life, Power, Intellect and Love; who has revealed himself in the Bible, in all nature, and in all history.
2. Man is the image of God, and is therefore not only endowed with all the superior capacities which are the necessary qualifications of an image of the most High, and bound in duty to develop them to the utmost extent; but he is also immortal in this respect, in quality of his being made in the image of his Creator.
3. Man is accountable to God for all his deeds, for which he is rewarded or punished here and hereafter.
4. God has chosen the people of Israel to promulgate through them these divine and sublime truths to mankind at large.[135]

Except for the fourth, these principles repeat the religious ideas of the French Enlightenment; and the fourth is a Mendelssohnian addendum to that viewpoint. The four truths, Wise says, 'are plainly announced in the Pentateuch, reechoed by the Psalmist, and by all and each of the Prophets; nature and history do not merely not contradict them, but they are the living witnesses, they bear the strongest evidence, to the verity of all these four dogmas'.[136] This doctrine Wise continued to put forth in later years, and it led him to question the authority of the Talmud. Conflict between the Bible and the law of nature could only be apparent, the fault of the expounder; conflict between the Talmud and the law of nature meant that the talmudic doctrine must be wrong since it conflicted with part of God's revelation.

By contrast with the Bible, the Talmud and the Midrashim were

---

[134] *Occident* (Jan. 1851), 494.
[135] Ibid. (Feb. 1851), 541.   [136] Ibid. 542.

'of a human origin, liable to mistakes, fallible in many respects, and therefore subject to a sound and scientific criticism'.[137] He venerated these incomparable treasures for their great value as a whole, 'but— where the Talmud comes in conflict with the facts of natural philosophy, and their logical consequences, or with the events, as experienced in history, and their natural results, I am fearless on the side of truth'. That, however, was not enough. He had to clinch his statement of principle with an attack on the influence of talmudic Judaism.

Where the Talmud imposes upon us doctrines or the observances of ceremonies, which are foreign to the Bible, and which infested us for many centuries with the spirit of intolerance, and of separation; which degraded religion into a compendium of blind and insignificant rites; which depressed the youthful spirit of Judaism, and drove thousands from our community; or where the Talmud comes in conflict with the demands of our age, which if listened to, will bring destruction and ruin in its train; there I am fearless on the side of reform; and if thousands of learned or not learned doctors say, 'The Talmud is divine', I must a thousand times pity them, for that they lack the moral courage to speak the truth.[138]

It was a strong line, and one which must have angered the Orthodox; but he did not stick to it. If an honoured place for the Talmud would bring the Orthodox under his umbrella, he was prepared to give it. We can imagine with what joy Leeser discovered at Cleveland in 1855 that the man who had written these words now advanced the principle that biblical laws must be expounded and practised according to the comments of the Talmud, and with what anger the reformers must have viewed Wise's Cleveland declaration as a recantation of his former position. Was Wise reacting to events? He attacked the influence of the Talmud on the morrow of the breach with Beth El, and he was bitter with those who made of Judaism 'a compendium of blind and insignificant rites'.

Wise's concern in the course of these letters with the resurrection of the dead must also be ascribed to controversies in which he had been engaged immediately before. The immortality of the soul, he says, is biblical doctrine, because in the Bible 'man is called an image of God'.[139] On the other hand, the 'dogma of an immortal body' is not of biblical origin, and because it is not biblical its exposition in

[137] Ibid. (Jan. 1851), 493–4.   [138] Ibid. 495.   [139] Ibid. 9 (Apr. 1851), 15.

the Talmud needs to pass the test of reason before it can be accepted. This it fails to do because 112,200,000,000 individuals must have lived on earth in the 5,611 years that had elapsed since Creation, and it would be irrational to expect that so many people could live on earth at the same time. The talmudic view that, when the resurrection of the body takes place, the revived will live in an unnatural, supernatural, or preternatural state, was like demonstrating from the Bible that 3 × 3 makes 8, which was contrary to his postulate as to the harmony of the Bible with Reason. He rejects it: 'erroneous, contrary to and impairing the truth and divinity of the Bible, which allows no contradiction to nature, the handiwork of the same Maker'.[140]

Leeser printed this letter with a closely reasoned rejoinder.

No man can have the power to revive the dead.... Life is not within man's gift, he only can work with and move within the spheres of forces which outward nature yields to his manipulation.... If, however, we assume that there is a Being not bound by nor circumscribed within the powers of outward nature, what is there absurd in the proposition that He should be able to revive the dead?

Leeser buttressed his argument with ample citation. Of greater interest, in view of the reaction they provoked in Wise, are some observations of a more personal character which he added:

We know not indeed that in our whole editorial career we have given publicity to an article with more pain and unwillingness than in laying the above letter 'on the resurrection' before our readers.[141]

To the flames that he had kindled by his attack on Wise's reasoning, he added fuel by a reply to Wise's attack on talmudic Judaism.

It is indeed strange that professed successors of the Rabbis, those who exercise functions which ought not to exist if the Talmud were a tissue of errors, should be found among the followers of Eisenmenger and McCaul, and libel by their satire or invective those who have transmitted to us with so much care the undefiled Bible, the pure word of God, without admixture and addition. If they had meant to propagate error, they would have been cautious how they preserved the scriptures, contradict as these would do their assumption on every page. We had hoped that our ministers and preachers would have hesitated long before they cast reflections so unjust upon our

---

[140] *Occident*, 9 (Apr. 1851), 16–18.   [141] Ibid. 19.

glorious predecessors. But it is useless to deny the fact that our destroyers
are members of our own household.[142]

Leeser's reply goaded Wise. Being classed with Eisenmenger and
McCaul might well have drawn fire from a man with less of a
disposition to irascibility, and yet was it not the quality of Leeser's
measured tones which was as galling to Wise as anything else?[143] His
reply is dated 9 July, which indicates that he must have written
immediately he had seen the *Occident* for that month. It is a good
sample of Wise's early polemical style.

Whenever I sit down to write something for the people, I always do it with
a cheerful mind, because I am convinced the people read my humble essays;
and, since I always commit to writing the most sacred truths, according to
the best of my conviction, I am confident of God's assistance. But this time
it is with indignation that I take up my pen. I detest to speak or to write in
my own behalf. You will admit that I have written more during the last five
years than any one of my colleagues; but I never wrote one letter in my own
behalf. You turned a philosophical dispute into personal invectives of the
most abusive kind; and, though I am aware that you will either not publish
this communication, or affix again to it a host of notes full of ironic compliments and new invectives, still I cannot resist the desire to answer you.[144]

However, he is an astute enough controversialist to disclaim any
intention of answering Leeser's argument as to the substance of their
differences. As on other occasions, his reply to a direct probing of his
defences is to make a violent attack from another flank; he, Wise, is
the victim of an attack. The weapons of Scripture and tradition, which
others can handle just as well, are laid aside. Instead he fires off the
batteries of vigorous, dogmatic assertions.

To answer your notes to my letter on resurrection would be a folly, which to
commit I shall deliberately beware; for neither you nor your allies, whom
you summoned to partake in the crusade, have done the least injury to my
fortifications; and if you cannot bring forward better evidences in your favour,
and better contraevidences to my statements, you will hardly succeed to
discomfit the fatal 'No' which I hazarded to pronounce in the presence of
the uppermost exponent of your so-called orthodoxy. You came again and

[142] Ibid.

[143] Johann Andreas Eisenmenger (1654–1704) was a German anti-Jewish author
who collected from rabbinical literature all that was calculated to bring it into
disrepute. Alexander McCaul (1799–1863) was a leading English conversionist who
wrote on matters pertaining to Judaism.

[144] *Occident*, 9 (Sept. 1851), 288–9.

over again with the worn out arms of mysticism, and so do your friendly
allies; but I am no Don Quixotte, that I shall fight the air. Friend Leeser, it
becomes you to know that the philosophical investigations of our age have
shaken the foundations of mysticism; its pillars, its strongholds are dashed
in pieces, and everything based upon it exists but in a dream of bygone ages.
Whatever is irreconcilable with the plain facts which nature represents to us,
can be vindicated no longer, because it is a useless waste of time.[145]

To Leeser's suggestion of heresy he replied with a full-blooded
attack.

You state (p. 196), 'We have no rule to declare any one a heretic; but this
much is certain, that we cannot trust any one as a teacher of religion, who
denies what this religion teaches.' ... But, my dear sir, I advise you not
to trouble yourself; not to disturb the sweet repose of your friends, to
excommunicate an humble and decried individual—a harmless, not cared
and not called for man as Isaac M. Wise, of Albany. Such a great trouble
was in its right place when Rabbi Jehudah Hallevi, Maimonides, Aben Ezra,
Spinoza, Mendelssohn, and Solomon Maimon were excommunicated as
heretics ... Christian doctors persecute me on account of my criticism on the
New Testament; so neither Abraham nor Paul (?) would open me the gates
of heaven. But who shall excommunicate me? You? Oh, you wage no personal
warfare with me, you are so much inferior to my humble self in erudition,
in Jewish learning. Did you not say so? I will take the fruits of your lofty
imagination for truth. Shall your erudite and sagacious friends do it? Tell
them I am not afraid to discuss with them any one theological question,
provided they abstain from personal warfare. Shall the people do it? You may
rest assured, that your views are not those of the majority of Israelites in
America. That class of people who think, think with me; and those who think
not, do not think with you either. 'You have no confidence in me as a religious
teacher.' That is a real pity; but I am accustomed to be perfectly satisfied if
I can have confidence in myself—if my conscience whispers that I have
spoken truth on behalf of my sacred cause of Israel, though it undermines
my reputation, my very existence; though I am opposed by dozens of fanatics,
who spare no trouble to ruin me. I am content if my conscience whispers
that I have done my duty, have not harmed my fellowman, have not advanced
doctrines which I myself do not believe in, have not become arrogant and
overbearing. And, my dear sir, I have this satisfaction, and also this one, that
hundreds whom I taught the pure word of God, whom I withdrew from
immorality, from superstition, and prejudices, from sin and indifferentism,
whom I connected closer with God and Judaism, have full confidence in me
as a religious teacher. And I am satisfied; when we once will meet as

[145] *Occident*, 9 (Sept. 1851), 288–9.

disembodied spirits before the throne of mercy, you will perceive that I am satisfied.[146]

Such an outpouring, standing fast in print, reminds us that the pastor with whom the laity of Congregation Beth El had to deal was no modest and unpretending shepherd. Wise's invective is remarkable both for its sensitivity to criticism and the belief in self which it breathes. The protagonist of reason is in no humour for reasoned argument; disagreement with his views is an attempt to do him injury; the suggestion that he might be wrong is a decree of excommunication. He is ready to discuss theological questions with anyone, though he refrains from taking up the arguments to which he is supposed to be replying; all thinking people are on his side; he has spoken the truth though there is a conspiracy against him. Wise draws his tirade to a close with the first person still to the fore:

And so I abandon the dispute, and I hope my name will be mentioned no more in American Jewish Journals; nor will I reply to any charge brought against me. I shall henceforth pursue my way without journals. In twenty years hence, the reader will be astonished that I could waste so much time in the discussion of questions decided long ago; that men disputed matters which were as clear as the sun at noon. They will pity me, that I lived in this critical and unsettled age, when the war of opinions is waged all over the civilized world, and also between the opinion of the people and the editors. They will be the evidences for my doctrines.

I can easily forgive you the injuries done to me; for I pity you, and I hope that the day is not far when the *Occident* will advocate the doctrines of reform.

I will remain an honest friend of Isaac Leeser, but with the Editor of the *Occident* I am done; wherefore I bid a hearty farewell to its readers.

Fraternally yours,

Albany, July 9th, 5611   ISAAC M. WISE D.D.[147]

Thus there came about a breach between Wise and Leeser, and for some time Wise's name was little mentioned in the *Occident*. But the wild waves could abate if the deeper current underlying them moved on to different channels. The following year Wise was ready to return to the pages of the *Occident*, but Leeser was stand-offish. Wise found another and more effective platform.

---

[146] Ibid. 301–3.   [147] Ibid. 305.

9. THE *ASMONEAN*

The *Asmonean* began publication on 26 October 1849. Its attitude to
Wise during the strife at Beth El had been reserved—its quest for
straightforward answers to plain questions Wise was ready to attribute
to a conspiracy against him. Wise was not one to allow rancour over
the past to get the better of him if he could come to an agreement as
regards the present; and the *Asmonean*, for its part, was more concerned to cater for all tastes than to make a stand on issues of policy.
At the instance of 'Mrs. F.', Wise tells us, Robert Lyon wrote to offer
Wise the 'editorship'.[148] This was not control of the contents as a
whole, but direction of the 'theological and philosophical department'.
Emphasizing that *'the principles of the paper will be unaltered'*, the
Asmonean announced the appointment on 10 September 1852. 'A cry
of dismay escaped the abused and betrayed orthodox party,' Wise
says. 'Robert Lyon was bombarded with threats and letters; but all
to no avail.'[149]

In the same issue as that in which his appointment was announced
Wise gave out his platform:

It will be my first endeavour to promulgate correct information on Jewish
learning. ... prejudice is ... the second foe against which I shall direct my
arrows. ... I hate long articles on little subjects ... Wherefore I shall be
concise and cogent. ... I intend to aim at instructing the people at large,
wherefore I shall make choice of the most popular and simple style. I ...
acknowledge every man's right to his own opinion, and am not vexed if my
views are gainsaid by others; wherefore I shall utter truth boldly, and only
notice arguments of opponents for refutation or acknowledgment when they
are founded upon truth, sound in their logic or free from personal feelings.[150]

Having set forth his aims in these high-flown terms, Wise proceeded
to the struggle against ignorance and prejudice, Judaism's two adversaries, by imparting New Year greetings in a style which showed none
of the hatred of 'long articles on little subjects' to which he had
confessed earlier.

Week by week the articles poured from Wise's pen. The field they
covered was wide.

I wrote three lengthy essays, 'The Bath Qol,' included later in part of my
'Origin of Christianity;' a biography of the first Hillel, as the precursor of

---

[148] *Reminiscences*, 200–1.
[149] Ibid. 202. See also *Asmonean*, 10 (28 Apr. 1854), 13.
[150] *Asmonean*, 6 (10 Sept. 1852), 199.

Jesus; and 'The Jewish Constitution, based on the Code of Maimonides.' Nothing was known in this country of the German Jewish literature. Hence I was compelled to translate in order to bring the names of our German litterateurs to public notice. I translated successively the chapter on the Book of Chronicles in Zunz's *Gottesdienstliche Vortraege der Juden*, Geiger's *Divan des Jehuda Halevi*, Frankel's *Der Gerichtliche Beweis*, etc., and various writings of Rapaport, Reggio, Luzzato, Krochmann, Munk, Carmoly, Holdheim, Jost, and Graetz (from his magazine). In addition, I published weekly a rabbinical legend from Talmud or Midrash. This had to be rendered from the original sources.[151]

Wise's *Asmonean* articles display all the rough energy of Young America. It was harnessed first to the author's voracious appetite for reading, and then to the need, no less compelling, to feed the press week by week. Equally apparent is that the material was not properly digested nor subject to the scrutiny of a tutored mind.

As contributions to literature or scholarship, therefore, these articles would not rate high, but in their time the wide familiarity with great thought which they display must have created an impression. By all appearances the *Asmonean* was a successful weekly, with a popular touch that was lacking in the *Occident*. Its contents were selected to give it an appeal to a wide variety of readers, and it must have had no small effect on Wise's standing in the American Jewish community that his name was before it week after week and that he became an interpreter of Jewish literature to its reading public. The *Israelite*, which Wise founded after leaving Albany, and the capacity for prolific writing which he displayed as the editor, reflect the lessons he had learned during his apprenticeship in popular journalism with the *Asmonean*. Finally, being chained to his books and pen must have helped the mental equilibrium of a man of huge energy who would otherwise have been confined to a small congregation.

Wise's articles were programmatic as well as literary.[152] The necessity for a college was raised more than once, but in discussing another favourite concern, 'A Conference of the Israelitish Clergy', Wise was inclined this time to pour cold water on the idea, possibly because of memories of the earlier failure, possibly because Isaac Leeser had raised it earlier in the same month.[153] Among the reasons for his scepticism was that it might have the effect of instituting an ecclesi-

---

[151] *Reminiscences*, 206–7.
[152] See e.g. *Asmonean*, 7 (28 Jan. 1853), 73; 8 (19 Aug. 1853), 144.
[153] Ibid. 7 (14 Jan. 1853), 18.

astical authority, which was just his reason for advocating it on other occasions but which he 'hated to hear or see proposed under present circumstances'.

The reason is not theological but practical, the want in America of ministers of 'eminent learning', 'consistency in the principles which they professed to be theirs', and 'honesty of purpose and activity to achieve them'. Wise's view was that in America, where the majority rules, such an institution would merely lead to the virtuous minority being subject to the decisions of their less worthy brethren. It was the settled principle in America that the majority ruled. But could 'the few literary men, who have sacrificed their health and the joys of youth to obtain the knowledge and learning necessary to their position, and who now resign everything for which others long, and spend days and nights in literary pursuits, ... go to a conference to be instructed in their duties by others, who never thought it necessary to have a scientific education?' This is interesting as self-portrayal; interesting also because in later years, when he was in conflict with the university-trained German rabbis, we find Wise on the opposite side.

There were occasions when Wise soared aloft on a homiletical wing. 'Love is the beginning, the center and the end of the Judaic system', he states in the opening paragraph of an article entitled 'The First Principle of Judaism'.[154] 'Judaism is not a sectarian religion; it is destined to become the religion of mankind,' he declares, 'and therefore love is its beginning, its center and its end—universal love is another name for Judaism.' Christianity had departed from this principle, and 'many of our Israelites also fell into inconsistencies'. He specified some of the beliefs and practices which represented a departure from the first principles of Judaism:

The doctrine of eternal punishment, which some of the last talmudists and their followers teach: the existence of a Satan with his host of evil spirits ... the ascetic practices of which the bible teaches nothing, of fasting so many days in a year, not shaving and eating no meat, and drinking no wine, for so many days annually, the rising after midnight to say prayers, the custom of ... of fasting Mondays, Thursdays and the day before New Moons-day; the custom of sitting on the floor on the ninth day of Ab...are strange inconsistencies.[155]

Those who invented these doctrines never understood the spirit of

[154] *Asmonean*, 7 (14 Jan. 1853), 41.
[155] Ibid. 8 (19 Aug. 1853), 41.

Judaism. Weeping might be inevitable in the European night, but joy alone was compatible with the American dawn. The ascetic had no place in a society devoted to the pursuit of happiness.

The word 'reform' does not occur in this article, but it indicates how Wise was prepared to sift what had come down from the past. For all his talk of the supremacy of reason, his sifting was highly personal. Barnacles, false to its essence, had attached themselves to the original, pure Judaism; and it will be noted that these excrescences are all observances demanding seriousness or deprivation. Wise had indeed been taken hold of by a society devoted to the pursuit of happiness.

The need for reform he touched upon early in February in an article entitled 'Life and Religion'.[156] The theme is that, when the Jews led an 'active life', Moses and the rabbis reconciled life and religion and that contemporary conditions made it necessary for this principle to operate again. 'If we carefully investigate ancient history,' he wrote, 'and then study the Pentateuch, we shall find that Moses opposed the notions of ancient religion, according to which man was conceived to be a non-entity; a part of the divine essence, which ... became absorbed in the great whole which was the reigning Deity.' The Israelites had absorbed this idea and

were unfit to be a political community as long as they despised the idea and this life. Therefore we see Moses recalling the people to life by giving them laws and directions how to live.... He showed to them, that God finds pleasure in noble and righteous actions; that he rewards such actions as well as he punishes wicked actions.... An age came when the Mosaic institutions were no longer efficient to reconcile life and religion ... then came our fore-fathers, the ancient Rabbis and they altered, amended and abolished according to the best of their judgment; and so they reconciled life and religion.[157]

This process became dormant, Wise continues, 'only when the Israelite had been driven away from the stage of active life', by which, presumably Wise means the centuries of dispersion: 'the Israelite was limited to religious pursuits; in all other respects he did not live'.

The approach is nearer that of the *maggid* (preacher) than of the scholar of the new age in which Wise expressed fervent belief. The corpus of rabbinic literature showed that the need to reconcile religion

[156] Ibid. 7 (4 Feb. 1853), 187 ff.   [157] Ibid.

with life did not perish with the 'ancient Rabbins', and that their successors continued their activity. Wise, however, was content to draw the picture of the centuries of dispersion as if the whole was represented by the milieu in which he grew up. The contrast between the restricted life of the Jew in Bohemia and the free life of the Jew in America was starkly before him, and it pointed to the need to reform the institutions of Judaism.

The Israelite has reentered on the stage of active life; the political, scientific, commercial, social and active life has re-opened its gates to receive the sons of Israel; and they have flocked in by millions. There is again a conflict between life and religion: the world has powerfully progressed, but the customs of the Israelites are unaltered for many centuries. Does not the reflecting Israelite daily perceive the conflict between the necessities of life and the institutes with which his religion is surrounded? Are we not aware that the people reconcile this disparity as well as they can? That they do it without a firm and leading principle, and so they invade, they must invade the province of religion itself; forgetful that Judaism requires sacrifices, and will not give way to the demands of life. Judaism is a living active system of immutable principles; it has changed its exterior forms with varying ages without the least disadvantage; it can, it will undergo such other adaptations to times and circumstances without being in the least impaired.[158]

Here we have familiar arguments in favour of reform.

10. A BIBLE HISTORY

Extensive as were Wise's weekly writings, they did not exhaust either his appetite or his ambitions. By the end of 1852 he had resolved to write a history of the Jews; being unable to find a publisher, he assumed that responsibility also.[159] The intention was to complete the work in four volumes; in fact, only the first, carrying the story from Abraham to the destruction of the First Temple, saw the light of day. [160]

'Having discarded all prejudices, national and religious,' he explained in his Preface, 'we are able to lay before our readers a complete and pragmatical history of the Israelitish nation, derived

---

[158] *Asmonean*, 7 (4 Feb. 1853), 187 ff.

[159] *Reminiscences*, 204, 215; *Asmonean*, 7 (7 Jan. 1853), 139.

[160] *History of the Israelitish Nation from Abraham to the Present Time*, vol. i (Albany, 1854). A continuation, entitled *History of the Hebrews' Second Commonwealth*, was published in 1880. At one stage Wise had in mind a translation of Jost's history which had lately appeared in Germany.

from the original sources, written in a spirit of philosophical criticism, independence and impartiality.'[161] This involved the exclusion of the miraculous from the domain of history, a deviation from Orthodoxy which was striking to a generation brought up to believe that, if recorded in Scripture, an event must have taken place as recorded. With every sign of pain, Leeser observed that 'Dr. Wise has spoken out so plainly against the truth of inspiration of the Bible and the truth of the miracles, or even the facts as there plainly recorded, that no one who believes in the ancient method can be deceived.'[162]

Wise expounded his views as to the distinction between history and religion in his Introduction. One key passage may be quoted. 'Miracles do not belong to the province of history. Miracles can be wrought by God only, and history records what men have done. The historian may believe the miracles, but he has no right to incorporate them in history.'[163]

The man who was unorthodox in regard to miracles believed firmly in revelation and believed revelation to be enshrined in the Bible; but he equated revelation with reason. Hence in his view no miracles were necessary to support the religious and moral truths of the Bible. Miracles could be expounded in any way or shape; they did not affect the truth of the Bible; Judaism based no doctrines on them; and they were not rational.[164] However, Wise's attachment to the Bible prevented him from discarding the stories involving the miraculous as completely as his principles suggest: 'the action itself may be historical, and can be adopted in history if it can be ascribed to common and natural causes'.[165] This desire to find naturalistic explanations of events described in the Bible led Wise to read into the narrative explanations for which any rational basis was as tenuous as the traditional explanations which he was concerned to discard.

Some examples of Wise's interpretations (he makes it clear that where the authorities differ he exercises his own judgement) will indicate his approach. Gen. 21: 1 states that the sons of Laban were jealous of Jacob's prosperity, and verse 3 that 'the Lord said ... Return unto the land of thy fathers.' Wise says that Jacob 'perceived a divine call—probably his mother had sent the promised mes-

[161] *History of the Israelitish Nation*, p. xii.
[162] *Occident*, 12 (Jan. 1854), 150.
[163] *History*, i. xv.
[164] Andrew F. Key, *The Theology of Isaac Mayer Wise* (Cincinnati, 1962), 18.
[165] *History*, i. xvi.

senger—to return into the land of his fathers'.[166] The man with whom
Jacob wrestles (Gen. 32: 24) was 'probably a freebooter' who attacked
him.[167]

The *History* begins with Abraham and therefore does not deal with
the story of Creation, but Wise appears to characterize the early
part of Genesis as a reconciliation by Moses of various streams of
folklore.

In Egypt he heard of Hermes, Thaut and Manes; but in Arabia he heard of
Abraham, Isaac and Jacob. He had heard the history of the creation of the
first human parents, of the primitive ages, of the flood, from the Egyptians
and the Hebrews, now he heard it from the Arabs—each nation on the globe
has the same stories covered under other fictions—he compared the myths
and with the help of God, he produced the first eleven chapters of Genesis,
in which the Egyptian and Arabic accounts, as well as the master pen of
Moses, are plainly visible. He then compared the traditions of the Hebrews
regarding Abraham, Isaac and Jacob, with those of the Arabs, on the same
subject; he also most likely visited all the spots which tradition had pointed
out to him—his exact knowledge of the geography of Palestine is a plain
demonstration that he must have been in that country—he probably saw the
altars built by the patriarchs, found inscriptions, marks, and, most likely, also
documents; he compared again, exercised his own judgment; and, with the
help of God, he compiled the rest of the book of Genesis.[168]

The events which lead up to the crossing of the Red Sea Wise
explains thus:

It is not unlikely, that Moses co-operated with the kings of Thebes, who
were led by Amosis, the founder of the eighteenth dynasty, to which the
terms of the Bible, 'And they (the Israelites) saved Egypt,' is no mean support;
therefore, Moses manœuvred about in the desert, either to hold Pharoah in
a state of excitement, and so to withdraw his attention from the commotions
in the south of Memphis; or to attract him with his army into the desert,
where he might find the end of his power by the waves of the Red Sea; or,
if this was not effected, Amosis could find time to occupy Memphis. Therefore
they directed their steps towards the Red Sea.

Next we come to the miracle by which Moses drew water from the
rock:

Moses, probably either knowing that there was a well of water in a rock, or
digging one with the aid of his friends, and covering it with a large stone

[166] *History*, i. 21.   [167] Ibid. 23.   [168] Ibid. 60, 68, 69.

which was thin enough to be split by a forcible blow with a stick, produced by the command of God plenty of water from a rock, as our sources inform us.

Wise associates the Elders with the promulgation of the legislation referred to in Exod. 19:

He then constituted a legislative body, consisting of seventy of the elders of Israel, in whose company, together with Aaron and his two sons, Nadab and Abihu, he retired to the mountains in order to have a solitary place for calm and considerate deliberation; while the nation celebrated the feast of the covenant, and prepared themselves to receive the fundamental laws, being, as it were, the compact between God and Israel, between the king and his people. Meanwhile, Moses and his legislative body deliberated on the mountain, and prepared the first constitution ever given to a nation; an instrument which has outlasted thirty-three centuries; which has become the original compact of civilized society; every word of which still testifies its divine origin.[169]

The dietary laws are naturally interpreted as having a sanitary purpose:

He did not prohibit the use of animal food; but he prescribed laws as regards the health of the animal, the like of which existed also in Egypt, where special officers watched over those laws ... It appears, therefore, that Moses did but renew an ancient and established custom of the nation. It must be considered, that we stand too far from that age, in order to ascertain all the climatical influences, the predominant diseases and other circumstances which influenced the legislator in the adoption of this law. Some sanitary causes must have been at the bottom; as this was the case with the swine, which was greatly abhorred in Egypt, because the enjoyment of that meat produced cutaneous diseases; and the fish kinds, which Moses prohibited, which produced cholera morbus, and still do so in warm climates.[170]

The Day of Atonement, as described in Lev. 16: 29–34, appears to have been intended in political affairs as a day of general amnesty.[171]

These explanations fluttered no intellectual dovecotes when they were published and today are of antiquarian interest only. The Preface is a review of Jewish history and is noteworthy for the pride in the Jewish past which breathes through its pages. We find a passage which scholarship may dismiss as unsubstantiated by the biblical text (let alone the fruits of archaeological and anthropological research)

[169] Ibid. 78–9.   [170] Ibid. 140.   [171] Ibid. 157.

but which is an expression of Wise's Enlightenment faith and one of the leitmotifs of his strivings.

Extolling Moses as 'the grandest character of antiquity', he declares that he 'promulgated the unsophisticated principles of democratic liberty and stern justice in an age of general despotism and arbitrary rule'. He went on to find fulfilment of the teachings of Moses in the American system: 'Moses formed one pole and the American the other, of an axis around which revolved the political history of thirty-three centuries'. The principles of government embodied in the Constitution of the United States were linked directly to the truths revealed on Sinai. This was a standpoint to which Wise adhered throughout his life. Half a century later he could write: 'the government of the United States in principle and form is identical with the Mosaic State as laid down in the Pentateuch'.[172]

The book was a failure—it 'lay in the bookstores unsold, and I was in dire straits. I had debts like an Austrian staff officer, and no prospect of paying them. What distressed me most was that I could not pay my friends the money they had advanced.' A gift from Mrs F. helped to recoup the financial loss, but despite some words of praise from Theodore Parker (who nevertheless found the work too Orthodox) the sting of the reception given his work remained with Wise. As late as 1896 he wrote, 'I was reviled, cursed, called a heretic, in the same measure by Jews and Christians, or rather in the same measureless fashion.' Nothing wrong could be found with the book, he asserts, with his unshakeable self-confidence.

This may be passed over as one more example of Wise's extraordinary sensitivity (or at least of his automatic resort to hyperbole) when reacting to criticism. One would have wished for a more complete statement of the Unitarian minister's opinion of the rabbi's approach to biblical history. Early in his ministerial career, Theodore Parker (1810–60) had espoused a point of view too radical even for the Unitarian clergy of Boston. He had denied the necessity of believing in biblical inspiration and in miracles (1841); he had shown himself an adherent to German Bible criticism, as exemplified by de Wette (1780–1849), who had asserted that Deuteronomy had been composed not by Moses but centuries later, during the reign of King Josiah. The inspiration of the Bible was the cornerstone of Wise's system, and, though he spoke of religion without mysteries or miracles,

---

[172] *American Israelite*, 45 (29 Dec. 1898), 4.

the revelation on Sinai formed its core. Even when garnished with a rationalist Midrash, this was an orthodoxy which Parker had left behind. Wise remained a child of the Enlightenment when his contemporaries among the liberal Christians of America were reacting against it, finding guidance in Coleridge and German philosophical mysticism. Hence there was little scope for any relationship at an intellectual level.[173]

More immediately, there was no market for Wise's book. If orthodox Christians would not look to a rabbi for the exposition of sacred history, and he had no message for the liberals, his prospects among the Jews were no brighter. There were perhaps fifty thousand Jews in the country, most of them recent immigrants, German-speaking, and confined to the immediate demands of earning a living. A 600-page Bible history was not among their necessities. To compound these factors, Wise lacked the machinery for distribution. Not for the last time Wise had bitten off more than he could chew, but persistence was not least among his qualities, and before his busy life was over he had managed to attach a long list of books to his name.

11. HEADING WEST

By the time Wise's *History* appeared, he had other concerns. A vacancy occurred in the ministry of Congregation B'nai Jeshurun, Cincinnati, Ohio. Cincinnati was then truly the 'Queen City of the West'; it was growing rapidly, so that by 1860 it was third city in the nation. Albany, after the advance given it by the opening of the Erie Canal, had reached a plateau from which no further ascent seemed imminent. Congregation Anshe Emeth had been successfully launched, but there is no suggestion of any great accession of strength, such as would justify its large synagogue.[174] This lack of elasticity must have affected Wise's personal position, particularly in relation

---

[173] The absence of any relationship between Wise's thinking and that of contemporary American theologians extends later than his biblical history. He had a brief flirtation with the Free Religious Association founded by O. B. Frothingham in 1867 but probably found its basic attitudes unpalatable.

[174] In 1852 Anshe Emeth, with 95 dues-paying members, was the largest of the three Albany congregations; Beth El had 63 and Beth-El Jacob 41. Anshe Emeth also had the largest debts ($4,000), as against $3,000 for Beth-El Jacob and $1,900 for Beth El. Revenues showed a similar order. A count of worshippers on Kol Nidre night showed 850–900 at Anshe Emeth, 175–190 at Beth El, and 160–70 at Beth-El Jacob (*Asmonean*, 7 (12 Nov. 1852), 42).

to his school; of this period he himself writes: 'because of my debts, I could not hope for money'.[175] Cincinnati was in a key position for contact with the leading towns in the country. Albany was accessible enough to New York and Boston, but not so to the then important centres of the South. In New York and Philadelphia Wise had established no following, but 'There in the West', he wrote, 'is a new world that comes into but little contact with the East.'[176] Congregation B'nai Jeshurun was well established; it obviously offered possibilities that Wise could not expect in Albany.

The generally accepted version of Wise's appointment to Cincinnati is that in August 1853 Jacob Goodheart, then treasurer of the congregation, wrote to Wise out of the blue asking whether he would accept the position of rabbi; that Wise stipulated election for life, no trial sermon, and not taking up his duties before a lapse of six months, and a salary that would make him independent of gifts; and that five days after communicating the requirements he 'received a telegram to the effect that he had been unanimously elected rabbi of the congregation on his own terms'.[177]

This story can be traced back to Wise's *Reminiscences*, where he says he received Goodheart's letter while he was in a mood of defeat and self-pity following the failure of his *History*. But the *History* bears the imprint '1854', the preface being dated 'December 1, 1853'. Goodheart's letter he says came in August 1853. By the time the *History* appeared, Wise had received the Cincinnati appointment. Wise was in communication with Congregation B'nai Jeshurun by July 1853. *Pourparlers* appear to have been opened by a letter from Wise read to the Board of Trustees on 10 July.[178] On 18 September the Board of Trustees resolved to invite him to visit the congregation, but apparently there was no trial sermon because on 27 October the congregation resolved to 'elect the Revd. D. I. M. Wise [presumably 'D.' here stands for 'Dr'] during good behavior as our Minister, Reader and superintendent of the Talmud Yelodim School at a salary of $1500 per annum'.[179] It is a measure of the impression which Wise had created that even from a distance he was able to secure an appointment on these advantageous terms.

---

[175] *The World of My Books*, 175.

[176] *Reminiscences*, 234.

[177] David Philipson and Louis Grossman, *Selected Writings of Isaac M. Wise* (Cincinnati, 1900); *Reminiscences*, 233–5.

[178] B'nai Jeshurun Minutes, in AJA.   [179] Ibid.

The minutes of the congregation indicate the outcome of the manœuvrings rather than the tactics employed. It is obvious that Wise used the space in the *Asmonean* at his disposal to fly kites which would catch the eyes of the people in Cincinnati. The first, which purported to be an enquiry from a correspondent whose identity could not be revealed, suggests duties customarily undertaken by ministers which Wise regarded as beneath his dignity.

A party, whose name we are not permitted to mention, wrote a letter to another person who has expressly prohibited us from giving his name to the public, requesting information as to whether the latter would not accept a call as minister of a certain congregation of which the writer is a member, promising him a pleasant and influential position, connected with a liberal salary, &c. &c., to which the response was as follows:

I have been very much pleased to learn from you that the——congregation considers me able to be their minister, although I have to boast neither upon extensive learning nor especial popularity, still I most respectfully decline to accept the position if offered to me. I hate to commit suicide of my principles. I am told that it is not seldom in American congregations that a minister is required to be a singing master; nay, that even the accidental execution of a Lechah Dodi or Anim Semiroth [hymns of the Sabbath liturgy] is a matter which decides frequently the future of the minister. I never sing any kind of song in the house of the Lord. I have assigned that performance to a choir of young people; the house of the Lord is much too sacred to me for that I could sing in it. A sacred earnestness fills every recess of my heart whenever I enter the consecrated spot, and in such a humor one may pray, he may praise the Lord, he may teach, he may expound the word of the Lord, but he cannot sing; nor have I ever read that Moses or the prophets sung when in the house of God.

I am told that it is not seldom in American congregations, that if the minister when reading the Law, chants a Sakef for an Esnachta, he is stopped by one or more of the hearers, or that he is declared to be unfit for his office. To me the word of God is much too sacred that I should permit one reading it in my presence, or when reading it myself, to disfigure or rather dishonor it by an antiquated chanting, which causes the audience to bestow attention upon the chanting and not upon the words, and deprives them of their effect, beauty and influence. I want to hear the Law read in an impressive manner to the benefit of the community. I am told that many American congregations are thus attached to outward forms; that if the minister should recite a verse twice which is recited generally three times, or if he should say Adon Olam, when it is customary to say Yigdal, or if he should omit one iota of the Piutim, Selichoth or Kinoth, even of those which have no connection with our age, as, for instance, the Yekum Purkon, in which they pray for the Resh Golutha and the schools in Babylonia, which have expired a good many centuries ago—he would be stopped and corrected, or he would be reprimanded afterwards by the Parnosim. While I cannot see the benefit of prayers which none understand: in which so many talmudical allegories are contained, which breathe the spirit of the middle ages, and neither in style nor in contents befit our age. Therefore I recite but the simple prayers of our forefathers, as Rapaport and Zunz have recommended, to which I add compositions which befit our age, and which are calculated to satisfy the religious desires of the heart.

I am told that it is not infrequently in America, that those who visit the Synagogue but two or three times a year, who keep very few of the Mosaic precepts, violate the Sabbath, and seldom, if ever, read a chapter in the Bible, are the loudest and most inflexible opponents of progress and improvement, while 'tis my belief—and I always act accordingly—that such men must not speak, and if they do they should not be heard regarding the Synagogue, for they cannot possibly speak bona fide; hypocrisy and superstition are the most dangerous foes of Judaism. I am told that public favor in America depends not so much on scientific accomplishments, activity on behalf of society and honesty of purpose, that it depends on the conformity of the recipient to the notions and views which are afloat, therefore, I am told, that it occurs not seldom that men who lack both education and activity, stand much higher in public favor than others, and that men who have the power of both knowledge and education and who unite with a restless activity an honesty of design, are therefore feared by the community, because many are afraid they might convince others that they are right. My principle, however, is, that truth is the only desireable object for man, inaction and death are synonymes, or rather two different names of the same thing.

I am told, that it is not uncommon in America, that the ignorant considers himself better informed on religious questions, and more pious than the learned and upright; therefore they have no confidence in their ministers, and rather oblige the ministers to act on their views and dictates. My principle, however, is, let him speak who knows what to say, and let him be silent whose tongue utters what his great-grandfather thought, and which he, nine times out of ten, does not understand. I am told that in America, he who does the most, must not reckon upon the largest share of public confidence, but he who does the least, and whatever he does is done under the mast of doing a great deal to the public benefit. My principle, is, 'He tries hearts and reins, the God of the righteous.'

I am told, that in America many ministers are business men, i.e., they are led away by the raging disease of materialism, and they try every way to make money, excusing themselves with the spirit of the age. He whose mind is engulphed in business affairs, cannot do justice to his office as a spiritual leader of a congregation; he cannot point his flock towards heaven, when he himself is fastened to earth with iron chains. I am also told that many American congregations think so little of a preacher, that if they cannot hear sermons for nothing, or for a trifle a year, they would not hear a sermon at all. I think, and Dr. Zunz has proved it, that the reading of the Law and the expounding of it are the main objects of the Synagogue, and it was so ever since the Bamoth have been changed for the Synagogue, by the labors of the Prophets, and as early as the days of king Jehoshaphat, men were sent to the congregations to teach them the Laws. (II Chron.) I am also told, that it is by no means required of a preacher that he be honest in what he says, or that he understand Judaism by scientific investigations into its enormous literature, if he only has read the poets and knows how to speak agreeably; if he only succeeds in making a few weep, and accommodates his sermons to the whims and notions of his audience; but woe unto him if he ventures to express his own sentiments, and three times woe, if he understands the spirit of Judaism and is bold enough to preach it.

The rest of the letter is void of public interest, therefore we stop here. We lay this letter before the public to let them judge whether the author of it is correctly informed on American affairs, we are too much confined to our study to have a correct judgment on public affairs. If things really stand so as this man says, it is almost best that an honest man be anything but a minister; but we hope it is not so, at least we do not find it so in our community.

W.[180]

The second piece appeared in the *Asmonean* for 10 September. Negotiations with B'nai Jeshurun were in progress, and Wise was concerned to parry an attack that was being made on his Orthodoxy.

A man, pretending to be a Jewish Minister, without having ever visited a Hebrew institute—pretending to be a Rabbi, without having the Marenuar Hatorah of any one authority in the world, travels in the United States as it appears, for the purpose of publishing slander against me, in the following words:— 'If you believe in the Yareh Deah you are not yotse to let that man preach in your Shul; for he does not believe in Tehiyath Hamethim and the Meshiach.' After the numerous explanations which I have given on this subject in the Asmonean, I am entitled to declare that man to be a malignant and wilful slanderer, who, too ignorant to build up a reputation for himself, endeavors to become popular by slandering me and misrepresenting my words. I challenge that man to come forward as a man of honor, and avow himself, and discuss the matter in a public paper, when he shall always find me ready to defend my principles; but as long as he creeps in the dark like

[180] *Asmonean*, 8 (20 Aug. 1853), 92.

the venomous serpent, I despise him as a malignant slanderer, and the principle cause of the trouble in Albany, some years ago.

ISAAC M. WISE

Here is one polemic among many, but its style and content deserve attention. Wise wants to be considered as working within the parameters of rabbinic tradition, and he appeals to an audience with whom a familiarity with the diction of the traditional synagogue can be taken for granted: 'Marenua Hatorah'—a corrupted transliteration of the Hebrew term signifying rabbinic ordination, 'Yareh Deah' (*Yoreh de'ah*), one of the four sections of the *Shulhan aruch* (authoritative code of Jewish law); 'yotse' (*yotseh*), a technical term signifying fulfilment of the requirements of rabbinic law; *shul*, the familiar term for a synagogue; *tehiyath hamethim*, the resurrection of the dead (echoes of Charleston); and the 'Meshiach' (*Mashiah*), or Messiah.

Wise is astute enough not to identify his assailant, and that gave the assailant every encouragement not to reply. On 14 September M. J. Raphall—the adversary in the Charleston encounter—had visited Cincinnati to consecrate the new synagogue of Congregation Bene Israel, and with the news abroad of Wise's candidacy at the sister congregation what is more likely than that hostile comments would have fallen from his lips? Wise makes the nature of his beliefs as little clear as he does the identity of the person to whom he is replying: but he builds up the position that there is nothing about them of which a congregation which hitherto had not diverted from Orthodoxy need be fearful.

Wise's unwillingness to indicate a theological position stands out more forcefully from the letter which he wrote to B'nai Jeshurun (31 October) on being informed of his election.

Being in possession of your favor of the 28th I repeat what I have informed you by telegraph, That I accept the Office. I shall be in Cincinnati in December as I promised and will enter upon my duties the first of May next. I promise nothing but that I shall honestly attempt to give satisfaction to the K. K. Bnai Jeshurun, and to deserve that unconditional confidence which that Honorable Body has been pleased to put in me. The intelligence and pious will for which your congregation is reputed promise that we soon succeed to elevate it to a model congregation for the whole West and South, to maintain and defend the honor of our sacred faith opposite to all religious sects. I am a friend of bold plans, and grand schemes, therefore I entertain the hope that the Talmud Yeladin will in a few years realize my fervent wishes of a Hebrew College in which our national literature will flourish on the side of a classical and commercial education, as I have frequently uttered the idea in the Asmonean. Please sir to assure your congregation of my highest esteem.

Albany, October 31, 5614   Isaac M. Wise.[181]

He is looking beyond the established parameters of congregational life and entertains 'bold plans and grand schemes', but as to Reform he is silent.

The election completed, Wise made his way to Cincinnati in December, there to acquaint himself with his new parishioners. Prickly points of doctrine were not the staple which he offered them. According to his *Reminiscences*:

I scattered so many blossoms and flowers upon the congregation from the pulpit, used so many flowers of speech and so much poetical imagery that there were enough bouquets to go around and every one went home bedecked. I had not said one word about principles; but my reputation as a speaker was established at once, my fortune was made; even the semi-orthodox were won over. I was satisfied with my success, and the congregation was overjoyed in not having been deceived in its choice. They deserved to have a speaker who could speak well in both English and German and they believed that they had found such a one.[182]

Wise returned to Albany to wind up his affairs. His last contribution to the *Asmonean* appeared on 5 April, and a week later, announcing that in consequence of his removal to Cincinnati he could not continue his weekly articles, the editor placed on record that 'our connection with Dr. Wise ends as it began, reciprocally with the highest respect and friendship'.[183] On 15 April he conducted his last confirmation service. On 23 April the Congregation Anshe Emeth passed a resolution acknowledging his eminent services to it and the irreparable loss it would sustain by his departure; and as a memento it presented him with a silver salver.[184] On 25 April he left Albany; his feelings at the change—pugnacious as well as sentimental—were expressed in a letter to the *Asmonean*.

Dear Sir,—Having missed the western train, am obliged to stop here for a few hours, and so I have a chance to send you a friendly salutation from this beautiful town of Western New York.

[181] Minutes, Congregation B'nai Jeshurun.
[182] *Reminiscences*, 242.
[183] *Asmonean*, 9 (5 Apr. 1854), 204.   [184] Ibid.

The last sounds of my friends in Albany still re-echo in my heart, and if I was able to give utterance to my sentiments, I could write you a beautiful and touching letter, but I apprehend being yet too much moved to be capable of giving a distinct picture of the most sincere and profound sentiments of gratitude, love, and the painful emotions connecting with the moment of departing from friends, who supported me patiently and untired, when I was deserted and condemned by thousands to whom, I, unfortunately, was misrepresented. Allow me, dear sir, a small space of the Asmonean to assure my friends in Albany, in the presence of a world, that if my services were and will be of any value to the house of Israel, the thanks for it are due to my Albanians; for without their faithful attachment and support, I would have been obliged three years ago to have quitted my position and enter upon the legal profession. That 'country congregation,' as Isaac Leeser styled them, consists of men who adhere to principles which I advocated; they adhered consistently to those principles and under all circumstances, and this is certainly more than Isaac Leeser can say of his supporters. That 'country congregation' of one hundred and twenty contributing members, are the readers of the Occident, because they adhere to principles; hence Isaac Leeser must at least try to injure its reputation. That 'country congregation' could not be persuaded to be satisfied with a singing minister, or with a preacher who is unable to read a passage in the Talmud, such as we have plenty. They will have again a learned Rabbi, as Isaac Leeser will say. The Rev. E. Cohn, at present Rabbi of Brandenburg, in Prussia, will be the next Rabbi of Albany, and the opponent of ignorance, impertinence, and hypocrisy, which are always linked together. It was a 'country congregation,' Isaac Leeser says, which I accepted seven years ago; but this same 'country congregation' is now in every respect far ahead of the city congregations. Let Isaac Leeser try to do the same.[185]

Why did the man who could be so circumspect when it came to revealing his religious outlook to his new flock feel the necessity of taking a swipe at Isaac Leeser? At that point of time Leeser was without position: Wise was marching to fresh triumphs. Leeser's reference to the humbler position which Wise had occupied on his arrival in the United States may have been gauche, but it could be read as a tribute to Wise's achievements, and in the American view humble beginnings were nothing to be ashamed of. Do we have an instance of Wise's extraordinary sensitivity where anything that might hinder his ascent was concerned; and, however ineffective Leeser

[185] *Asmonean*, 10 (28 Apr. 1854), 13. Elkan Cohn was Wise's successor at Anshe Emeth, Albany, where he remained until 1860. As he had not taken up his duties at the time Wise wrote to the *Asmonean* it was premature to describe him as the rabbi of Albany, and in any case he was rabbi of one congregation only.

might appear at this distance in time, did the only other cleric with
extra-parochial concerns seem a threat to his 'bold plans and grand
schemes'?

Earthly strivings were not the sole concerns which filled Wise's
mind as he made his way to Cincinnati. Waiting at Columbus, Ohio,
for the last stage of his journey, he noted in his diary: 'I am troubled
with anxious forebodings, now that I reach my new home, which I
will reach in a few hours. I cannot pierce the veil of the future. God
wills that I should not. Wherefore this fear? Is it the echo of the past,
or a magical voice from the future? O Lord God, thou alone knowest.'
This was the reverie which he recorded in his *Reminiscences*.[186]

[186] *Reminiscences*, 252.

3

Cincinnati (1854–1900)

I. M. Wise, the great Cincinnati agitator, comes along offering
as a panacea for all evils, as a universal remedy against all
complaints, the establishment of a union of all Jewish congregations... Twenty-five years ago Dr Wise was already
engaged in forming a union, though not for the purpose of
forming a college, but a Jewish Sanhedrim of which he was to
be the head ... Had he then been successful, reformed Judaism
would have been smothered in its very cradle. What did Dr Wise
care for the reform principles he had in some way or another
preached before? In order to become the leader of American
Judaism, he shook hands with the representatives of orthodoxy,
sure to atone for his once confessed liberalism by the completed
union... Judaism knows of no organized union. It kept its fresh-
ness while and because its strength did not consist of one man's
power or in a few men's authority, but in the intelligence and free
conviction of its individuals ... Certainly, a union of American
Jewish congregations formed twenty-five years ago would have
left Judaism to ignorance, while our best men would have become
estranged from their inheritance. And in what respect can a
union benefit us today?

(From a lecture by Kaufmann Kohler, delivered on 23 May
1875, reported in the *Jewish Times* (New York), 28 May 1875)

1. QUEEN CITY OF THE WEST

'I was fortunate in finding a splendid element in the congregation—
men who, without any great exertion on my part, desired, favored,
and actively supported every forward and progressive movement. I
met with no obstacles in the congregation itself; everything was
peaceful and harmonious.'[1] On several occasions the accuracy of
Wise's *Reminiscences* has been questioned, but there are no grounds

---

[1] *Reminiscences*, 258.

for doing so when he writes of the good relations cemented immediately upon his arrival at Congregation B'nai Jeshurun. In Cincinnati he remained for the rest of his days. From the start he seems to have impressed himself on the congregation. They accepted his ideas for reforms within the synagogue; they stood by him in the difficulties which his larger schemes involved; in forty-six years there were few disagreements, and only one serious incident—his candidature for the Ohio Senate during the Civil War—marred their relationship, and the speed with which it was passed over confirms that basically there was a happy association which neither party wished to endanger.

In 1854 Cincinnati was in truth 'the Queen City of the West'. Between 1840 and 1850 the population all but trebled, rising from 46,000 to 115,000. By 1860 the figure was 161,000, and in 1900, the year of Wise's death, it was 325,000. Cincinnati was first settled at the end of 1788. It was incorporated as a village in 1802 and was chartered as a city in 1819. Its emergence as 'the Queen City of the West' was an outcome of the age of water transportation. The frontier was being pushed westwards, but when the nineteenth century had reached half-way point the movement had placed Cincinnati in approximately the middle of the country. It was half-way along the Ohio between Pittsburgh and the Mississippi, and the completion of the Miami Canal in 1830 joined the Ohio river system to the Great Lakes. Agricultural produce and manufactured goods could be moved easily between Cincinnati and all the then settled parts of the United States, and in the wake of the entrepôt trade came industry. The destructive effect of the Civil War on the economy of the South, the receding of the frontier farther west, the building of transcontinental railways which converged on Chicago to the north, caused other cities to deprive Cincinnati of the lead which it had early established. That, however, was yet to come. Between 1830 and 1860 there had been extensive immigration from Germany, and the presence of these industrious (and in some cases cultivated) people helped to solidify the gains brought by a favourable geographical position.

In view of Cincinnati's expansive prosperity, in view of its business relations with all parts of the United States, in view of its position as a meeting-place of merchants, it would be only natural for Wise to encounter a broader outlook than would exist in most congregations; for a man who harboured 'bold plans', plans which extended far beyond the confines of a single town, his position was ideal.

Within a short time, Wise had begun to put into operation many of these 'bold plans': a weekly newspaper, which would carry his voice through the land; a synod which would provide a religious authority and a common liturgy; a college which would train rabbis—all with Wise in charge. Success did not come immediately, and it was his persistence that won him the war where his impetuosity lost him many battles. He had come to Albany unknown; he arrived in Cincinnati with a reputation. He also came to Cincinnati with greater experience, and one thing which he showed he had learnt was that he could not hope to conquer outlying territory if his home base was insecure.

I was very moderate, considerate, and argumentative (as far as externalities were concerned) in the pulpit [he wrote] ... I had to address every Saturday a very mixed audience. My hearers comprised, not only the members of the three other congregations of Cincinnati, but also the inhabitants of near and distant towns, because business brought many merchants of the West and South to Cincinnati at that time. I was therefore compelled to speak carefully and tactfully if I wished to succeed, and I was determined to succeed.[2]

The violence which Wise had shown in Albany did not desert him after 1854, and his energy in writing, travelling, and lecturing increased. He uses the strongest expressions against rabbis and laymen who acted contrary to his views, against organizations which he did not control, against Christians who insulted Jews, or denied them their rights; he had local quarrels, but with members of other congregations.[3] With Congregation B'nai Jeshurun he remained on good terms, and, though this must be due in large measure to the strength of his personality, for it cannot be that the lion was reborn as a lamb each moment it entered the portals of the synagogue, it also appears to be the case that he had learned not to push his flock too hard or to run too far ahead of them. Indeed, it seems to have been of the essence of Wise's capacity as a leader that, while he stood above and ahead of his followers, it was never at such a distance that they could not see him. He was ahead of them not only in his theological equipment, but also in his capacity to use English; but that did not lead him off the road along which they were travelling, though it did enable him to articulate their needs and soothe their fears, to assert

---

[2] *Reminiscences*, 257.
[3] There was a confrontation between rabbi and congregation in 1863 over Wise's decision to seek election to the Ohio Senate: see ch. 3 sect. 22 below. There were occasional disagreements during the same decade over times of services, but they did not amount to anything substantial.

their equality, to defend their rights, and to promulgate a religious system which would be as American as any that flourished in the New World.

The Jewish community of Cincinnati was about a third of a century old when Wise made his home in the town. In 1820 there were enough Jews in the town to celebrate the festivals; in 1824 they formed themselves into a congregation—Kehillah Kedoshah Bene Israel.[4] The founders of the congregation came principally from Great Britain, and their *minhag* followed that customary in England.

The considerable German immigration (between 1830 and 1860) brought with it a number of German Jews. These at first joined the existing congregation, but differences—personal, linguistic, and liturgical—were a barrier to full harmony. The first meetings of a second congregation took place in 1840, and in 1842 it was incorporated under the name of B'nai Jeshurun. In 1848 B'nai Jeshurun erected its first synagogue building, in Lodge Street, where it remained till 1866, when it moved to the present structure in Plum Street. It began with 50 members; by 1854 there were 169 and by 1859 the number had jumped to 220.[5] Thereafter the congregation seems to have grown but little, at least till the Plum Street temple opened; and the compactness of its membership together with the circumscribed range of activities then conceived possible, allowed a rabbi of Wise's energies the time for the extra-congregational activities on which his fame rests.[6]

The congregation took the initiative in 1849 in establishing the Talmud Yelodim Institute, which served first as a parochial and later as a Sabbath school and which, though under a separate constitution, was an adjunct of B'nai Jeshurun. The rabbi was also superintendent of the Talmud Yelodim Institute.[7]

Unless some half-hearted attempts to organize a choir can be viewed in that light, there was nothing in the record of B'nai Jeshurun to suggest a tendency to Reform. Indeed, Wise's immediate predecessor,

---

[4] Literally, the Holy Congregation of the Children of Israel. The first settler in Cincinnati was Joseph Jonas, whose recollections, reprinted in Jacob R. Marcus (ed.), *Early American Jewry* (Philadelphia, 1951), i. 203 ff., form the best account of the early days of the community.

[5] James G. Heller, *As Yesterday When It Is Past* (Cincinnati, 1942), 229.

[6] Wise's extra-congregational activities appear in no instance to have been directed to personal gain.

[7] The minutes of the Talmud Yelodim Institute do not suggest that Wise played an active part in its affairs.

the Revd A. L. Rosenfeld, had come under fire because of alleged deviations from the stricter requirements of Orthodoxy.[8] How was it, then, that Wise, apparently without opposition, was able to introduce reforms—gradual, it is true, but still no different from those which at Albany had brought down fire on his head? The answer may be that the passage of a short period of time, or the somewhat wider outlook of the leaders of his Cincinnati congregation, had lessened the hold of the minutiae of Orthodoxy; but it must also be in the good relations, springing partly from his reputation as a writer and partly from his added experience, which Wise established in Cincinnati from the start.

2. CONGREGATION B'NAI JESHURUN

Changes in the B'nai Jeshurun service did not lag far behind Wise's arrival. First he set about introducing a choir, which had been attempted before but without lasting success. Overcoming the doubts of the president, Wise persisted, and when the trustees met on 8 August 1854, a letter from Wise was read announcing that the choir, twenty-five in number, would be ready to take part in the service on the ensuing Friday evening. The repertoire was taken from Sulzer and Naumbourg.[9]

He went on to suggest a number of liturgical modifications. With one exception (the omission of the talmudic passage *Bameh madlikin*, dealing with the laws of the Sabbath lamp), these affected style rather than content.[10] Wise's letter, the record states, was 'on Motion ordered to be spread on the Minutes'.[11] For these changes it could be argued that they were merely modifications in the performance of the ritual, designed to incorporate a more musical rendering and not involving any religious principle; and Wise went no further than 'suggest for your consideration'.

Six days later the trustees held a special meeting, at which the sales of *mitsvot* were abolished and the *misheberachs* (sponsored prayers for the well-being of individuals) severely curtailed. On 25 November

[8] See *Occident*, 10 (Nov. 1852, Jan. 1853), 408, 487; Heller, *As Yesterday When It Is Past*, 70–2.

[9] The training of the choir must have involved considerable work. An advertisement in *Israelite*, 1 (21 July 1854), 16, shows that rehearsals were being held on five evenings during the ensuing week.

[10] Congregation B'nai Jeshurun, Trustees' minutes.

[11] Ibid., meeting of 14 Aug. 1854.

the trustees resolved, on the recommendation of the Committee on Religious Rules and Regulations, to adopt the modifications in the ritual communicated to the Board by Dr Wise:

Approved of, and adopted:
  1. The Shir Hayichud, Anim Semiroth, the Mismor, the Kadish Derabbonon, and all other Kadeshim, with the exception of Kadish Yosem after Olenu shall henceforth be said before Boruch Shehomar.
  2. Yekum Purkan, Pittum Haktoresh and all Yozeresh or Piuttim with the exception of Rosh Hashanah and Yom Kipur shall be discontinued.
  3. The Choir shall co-operate always in divine service during the evening and morning of every Sabbath and Holiday.
  4. This shall take effect the next Schabes Channukah 5615. No other business the meeting closed.

Such is the record in the minute-book of the congregation. Wise's own version is that on the second Sabbath of his incumbency, the president, of his own authority, announced that the *piyyutim* were abolished and they were never discussed thereafter.[12]

'I recognized that all things would turn out right if I would be content to make haste slowly,' Wise observed; and a little later, 'Although the external reforms were introduced slowly, I was much less timorous in regard to enlightenment in the school and in the pulpit.'[13] In the course of time, further liturgical reforms proved acceptable. Three years after his arrival in Cincinnati, Wise brought out his own prayer-book, *Minhag America*, and when it was ready he communicated the fact to the trustees. A committee of three was set up to examine the book, and as a result of their report a general meeting on 24 September 1857 adopted *Minhag America* as their prayer-book. The ritual again came before the trustees in July 1860. A special committee recommended further changes, including the triennial cycle of the reading of the Torah and the abolition of the wearing of the *tallith* save for officiants and persons called to read from the Torah. At a meeting of the trustees held on 1 September 1860 Wise declared the proposed changes legal, and at a meeting of the congregation held on the 23rd they were substantially accepted— the voting on the triennial cycle being seventy to thirty-three. The concentration on the Sabbath morning service implies that it was still the congregation's principal service.

[12] *Reminiscences*, 258.   [13] Ibid. 260.

A further reform which Wise proposed and which the congregation accepted on 2 October 1859 was to abolish the second days of the festivals, except Rosh Hashanah. The second day of Rosh Hashanah went in 1873, and in the same year the obligation to worship with covered head was abolished. Throughout Wise's ministry the congregation held daily services but Wise was dispensed from attending them because he had objections to laying *tefillin*: 'there was a "live and let live" atmosphere'.[14]

Seen from the distance these reforms suggest a negative character; no grand principle stands out. Did Wise and his followers regard the observances they dispensed with as barnacles encrusted on the hull of the ship whose removal would facilitate its progress? Did they take it for granted that the motive power on which that progress depended would remain effective without great effort?

The most eloquent tribute to the impact made by Wise's ministry is that, on 5 November 1854, a little more than six months after he assumed office, the Congregation Bene Israel, between which and B'nai Jeshurun there had been at times a little friction, invited him to be their rabbi too. A member of Bene Israel, Orthodox in sentiment, who held Wise in no great admiration, said that Wise's eloquence as a preacher had advanced the position of B'nai Jeshurun while the senior congregation 'was fast sinking'.[15]

In his *Reminiscences* Wise states that the resolutions appointing him to Bene Israel were passed by ninety-three votes to twelve.[16] 'It was a fairly won battle,' he adds, 'a victory for the cause of progress in Judaism, for the B'nai Israel congregation was looked upon as the mother congregation of western Jewry and as the camp of simon-pure orthodoxy.'

We had warm and, we believe, honest and pious opponents in this congregation when six months ago we came to this city. It cannot be denied that

---

[14] The text reflects the general impression left by a perusal of the congregational minutes and *As Yesterday When It Is Past*. In his Introduction to the *Controversial Letters and the Casuistic Decisions of the Late Rabbi Bernard Illowy, Ph.D.* (Berlin, 1914), Dr Henry Illoway, who would have had personal knowledge of conditions in Cincinnati, writes (p. 2): 'It was not until the congregation removed to its new temple ... (1866) that the more radical measures were carried into effect.' Illoway is making the point that his father, an Orthodox rabbi, also of Bohemian origin, did not regard Wise as so far removed from the right path for it to be out of place to argue with him.

[15] *Occident*, 13 (Dec. 1855), 459.

[16] *Reminiscences*, 277.

we had for years ago warm and true-hearted friends in this community, but our opponents formed a vast majority. We may confess without fear of contradiction, that we in the discharge of our duties used no policy whatever, for furtherance of our personal position. Boldly and without the least caution we expounded the Word of God according to our limited intellect, not only because we were backed by a congregation of zealous and approving friends, but because we are accustomed always to act so and not otherwise. Isaac M. Wise had not changed his principles and views, nor has he hidden them under the veil of ambiguous language.

On the other side it must be confessed, K. K. [*kehilah kedosha*—holy congregation] Benai Israel has not changed; its members still hold different opinions on the questions of progress and of stability. But also this is true, that men of all shades of opinion have cast their votes in our favor.[17]

Wise went on to describe at length the 'cause of this revolution', and as regards Congregation B'nai Jeshurun added 'that we are entitled to expect, that things will be adjusted, as they should be'.

B'nai Jeshurun was not prepared to comply. On 25 November they approved a letter to Wise which in language that was polite but firm made it clear that they were unwilling to share his services with the sister congregation.

Wise was not the kind of man to hold back while others debated the propriety of his action. Between the making of the appointment by Bene Israel and the communication to him of his own congregation's refusal of consent Wise had assumed the second office, preaching at Bene Israel on Saturday afternoons and opening a school called Noyoth.[18]

Four years later, Wise wished to accept an invitation to preach once a month in Louisville; on 21 November 1858 a general meeting of B'nai Jeshurun rejected the proposal. By this time some of the flock must have thought that the shepherd was roaming too far from the fold; the attempt was made at this meeting to curtail Wise's travels through a resolution that in future only the board of trustees, and not the president alone, should have power to permit him to leave Cincinnati; but the minutes record that this was lost 'by a very large majority'.[19]

[17] *Israelite*, 1 (7 Nov. 1854), 147–8.
[18] *Reminiscences*, 278. For another view of this episode, see *Occident*, 13 (Dec. 1855), 458 (written in Oct. 1855).
[19] The trustees had declined the Louisville request on 7 Nov., and the general meeting which sustained them was convened by petition. Immediately thereafter the trustees acted favourably on a request by Wise that his salary be increased.

Bene Israel renewed the search for a rabbi, and their choice fell on one with whom Wise had formed a friendship from the time of his arrival in America—Max Lilienthal, who was then running a 'Hebrew and Classical Boarding School' in New York.[20] In the tenth number of the *Israelite* (15 September 1854) Lilienthal's name had appeared immediately under Wise's as 'corresponding editor' for the first time. It may be that Wise's influence played a part in securing Lilienthal's election. The two remained closely associated until Lilienthal's death in 1882.

3. THE *ISRAELITE*

By the time he took over (albeit temporarily) the second pulpit, Wise had added the responsibilities of a newspaper editor to those of a preacher. The first number of the *Israelite*, flying at its masthead the flag 'Let there be Light', bears the date 'July 15, 5614, AM, 1854 AC'.[21]

It would be hard to overemphasize the role played by the *Israelite* in establishing Wise as a leader of American Jewry. It carried his voice throughout the land, and made some people fear his censure and others curry his favour. It brought him callers and information from all parts, and, as in those days many railways provided free passes for newspaper editors, it gave him the means of undertaking the many journeys to distant congregations which did so much to enhance his influence among the communities of the South and the West.[22]

As Wise had settled in his new position only as recently as April, and had been involved in all the distractions incidental to removing himself and his family and to taking over his pastorate, the appearance of the *Israelite* in June testified to his determination and energy. Wise relates that he planned the *Israelite* before he left Albany, and that in New York he 'received very encouraging promises, many of which

[20] For Lilienthal's activities in Russia from 1841 to 1844 and his attempts to introduce a government school system for the Jews, see Michael Stanislawski, *Tsar Nicholas and the Jews* (Philadelphia, 1983).

[21] The date is that of a Saturday, and one of Isaac Leeser's correspondents wrote to him in scandalized tones of the rabbi's weekly being hawked about the streets on the day of rest. The date of the second issue was that of a Friday. See I. Mayer (Cincinnati) to Isaac Leeser (Philadelphia), 14 July 1854, copy in AJA.

[22] The writer is indebted to the Association of American Railroads for information concerning this practice.

were even kept, but money simply was not available at that time, at least not for me'.[23]

If he was to have a paper, it had to be published somehow. No one among the Jews had the necessary experience, and Christian publishers 'declared bluntly that a few Jews could not insure the success of any paper'. Finally he engaged Dr Schmidt, owner of a German evening paper, to publish the *Israelite*, guaranteeing him against losses for the first year.[24]

The pages of the *Israelite* bear out Wise's claim that he 'possessed rare facility in the use of the English language' and that 'writing itself was a mere play after I had thought out a theme'.[25] This 'rare facility' must be appreciated in relation to Wise's circumstances: he was self-taught, and he did not live in a literary environment. His 'facility' was a matter of energy rather than grace. In later life, when he could look at these early efforts in the mellow light of success, he lifted the curtain on struggles which, though not world-shattering in their dimensions or effects, must have been difficult enough to the early participants. The first issue of the *Israelite* mentions that its appearance had been delayed in consequence of the severe sickness of Charles Schmidt, the publisher, so one can understand that the labour pains, inevitable when any new weekly is born, were acute. Everything, Wise says, had to be written or edited by him. With the readiness to try his hand at something new so characteristic of the American pioneer, Wise wrote novels himself when the translations of French and German stories promised by friends failed to materialize. The first instalment of his novel *The Convert* is in fact the *Israelite*'s opening piece, and, even had not Wise subsequently admitted authorship, the first scene ('At the eastern end of the Eger Valley in Bohemia'), being that of Wise's birthplace, would have revealed the author. The same applies to his novel *The Catastrophe at Eger*, the first instalment of which appeared on 29 September and which opens 'In the North-western part of Bohemia . . .'.[26] Wise is candid as to his literary technique:

How did I write novels? I wrote the required chapter every week, but no sooner than I had to. The first pages were set up while the last were being written. On one occasion I was in a sorry plight. I had made two maidens fall in love with one and the same character, and I had to get rid of one of them. I was in sore straits. How was I to get rid of a lovelorn female? I had

[23] *The World of My Books*, 18. [24] *Reminiscences*, 265–6.
[25] Ibid. [26] Ibid. 270.

no experience in such things, and yet I wanted to dispose of her decently, romantically, and effectively. I therefore had the poor thing become insane; and the unhappy creature had to jump from a window during the conflagration of the ghetto of Frankfurt and thus meet her death. The poor creature was greatly mourned and wept for the following Saturday, and all the tears fell upon my burdened conscience. The most serious feature of the whole matter was that my wife made sport of me every Thursday evening, and declared stoutly that I had forgotten entirely how to enact a lover's part.[27]

Elsewhere, Wise adds: 'usually the manuscript went red hot from my pen to the printing press, often without being checked, and generally without even having been outlined in advance'.[28]

The impromptu manner in which Wise carried on the *Israelite* was not concealed from its readers, as the following announcement shows:

The Editor having gone east, the continuation of the Novel, which usually occupies our first page, will be omitted until his return; and perhaps, some other unfinished articles, will be left in the same situation.[29]

Ten years later we find him bringing to an end with these words an article giving his impressions of New York Judaism: 'There, the bell rings, visitors are on hand, I must close. I will continue at my next leisure hour.' This is no journalistic device to round off an article. In fact many an editor would have cut off these sentences since they flow over into a fresh column. Moreover the article had begun in the same conversational style which makes much of what Wise contributed to the *Israelite* a substitute for a recording of his voice.

I am in New York, the city with ten thousand mercantile palaces and public mansions, with a population as large as the kingdom of Saxony, and money enough (beside the sum in my pocketbook) to purchase Palestine, to rebuild the Temple of Mount Moriah. I am always astonished, why our old fashion friends weep over the destruction of Jerusalem and the Temple, and pray for the restoration of Israel and the holy city. Let them pay for it and they shall have it. The Sultan needs money, no wonder a man does, who has so many wives to go out shopping—well then, the Sultan needs money, and our friends are 'as rich as a Jew'; let them make a fair offer to the Sultan and, I am positively informed, he will not refuse it. Let them go back then to Palestine, and rebuild the Temple, if they can find none to be King, high priest, and

---

[27] *Reminiscences*, 270–1.   [28] *The World of My Books*, 21.
[29] *Israelite*, 4 (28 Aug. 1857), 58.

to have the balance of the public offices, let them appeal to American generosity, we can furnish them with plenty of magnanimous men who never refuse an office.[30]

One can picture Wise in an affable mood, enjoying a tankard of ale, perhaps digging one of his Orthodox friends in the ribs and laughing hugely at the joke about the sultan's expenses.

When, during the Civil War, Cincinnati came under martial law, an issue of the *Israelite*, in common with other newspapers, failed to appear. That was a case of *force majeure*, and causes no surprise, but there were occasions when pressure of other work was given as the reason. Wise had been busy that summer with the establishment of the Union of American Hebrew Congregations; between 3 and 18 September he had been on a visit to the East; the New Year had fallen on 22 September. Still, one would have thought the *Israelite* firmly enough established by 1873 to be independent of the engagements of its editor.

The agonies that go on behind the firm mask of print could hardly have spared the *Israelite*. At one time (apparently in the early days) there was a typesetter by the name of Hainebach, who took it upon himself not only to correct the spelling and grammar of the copy handed to him, but also to alter statements with which he did not agree, from which treatment not even the contributions of the editor-proprietor were exempt.[31] There is no means of knowing where the opinions which we ascribe to Wise should be credited to the over-zealous typesetter.

The *Israelite* did not match the unrelieved solemnity of the *Occident*. Unpolished as they were, the editorial articles of the *Israelite* (and they were numerous) breathed fire and energy. Besides such articles, and novels and news from home and abroad, there were also snippets of all kinds. While the rabbis were debating a synod in Cleveland in 1855 there appeared the following:

Miss Rachel[32] causes in the East such a dramatic furor [*sic*], that even the Episcopalian and other clergymen cannot help attending her masterly representations.—In due course we shall appoint her Chief of a Jewish missionary establishment.[33]

[30] *Israelite*, 19 (9 Aug. 1867), 4.
[31] *American Israelite*, 71/2 (Seventieth Anniversary supplement) (24 July 1924), 29.
[32] Rachel (d. 1888) was a celebrated, perhaps notorious, actress in her day; for further details, see *Oxford Companion to English Literature*.
[33] *Israelite*, 2 (17 Nov. 1855), 149.

Two years later we find Ada Isaacs Menken, another somewhat scandalous actress of the period, making her appearance.[34]

In layout the *Israelite* was modelled on the *Asmonean*. The resemblance goes to appearance only. Robert Lyon was making a living by purveying news; Isaac Mayer Wise's publication subserved the ideas which he wanted to advance in the American Jewish community. Robert Lyon was not an anonymous editor, but he did not obtrude his personality on the *Asmonean*; the readers of the *Israelite* shared the agonies and the ecstasies of its editor.

Wise's methods of working and the fact that he had little assistance meant that the *Israelite* reflected his personality with little distortion. There was no editorial blue pencil to consign Wise's writings to oblivion or even to curb his verbosity; there were no trained sub-editors to correct his English. We hear a rough, uncultivated voice; sometimes it snorts or bellows, sometimes it caresses, but within the whole range of human experience there is no question to which it does not have a confident answer. It knows science as well as religion, it delves into history and pronounces on the future, it expresses the random thoughts of the traveller and orders the affairs of the American Jewish community, it hectors the sluggards and rises to a crescendo of abuse at the opponents.

While the *Israelite* was much more the auditorium for one man's voice than a forum for the exchange of opinions, his control of the paper would have fostered his contacts with Jewish communities far and near. He would have been the first to receive news for publication; visitors to the city—and it was a great mercantile centre for the South and Midwest—would have made themselves known to him; and, in particular, congregations seeking rabbis and rabbis seeking positions would have sought his advice and even his favour. Thus, well before the presidency of Hebrew Union College and the Central Conference of American Rabbis gave the seal of office to his status, his influence would have been accepted on a personal basis. Isaac Leeser gave testimony—regretfully—to the power Wise had obtained in parts of the country, and the visit paid to him by another critic, rabbi and writer Henry Illowizi was the result of assurances that Wise 'had lots of positions to give away'.[35]

The columns of the *Israelite* which Wise filled betray all that

[34] *American Israelite* (24 July 1924), 31. See also Bernard Falk, *The Naked Lady* (London, 1952), 25, 33.
[35] See pp. 194–5 below.

insistent versatility which is needed to impress and to master a community of pioneers, themselves self-assertive and without the discrimination that is given by the presence of scholars or men of leisure. We smile at the poor style of his articles (and often their poor taste too) and laugh at their naïvety, but the strength of the man's voice still comes through; and sometimes we get the impression of the recording of a man's voice—an impression which is no doubt heightened by the contrast with the desiccated style which a century later characterizes writing and speaking on public Jewish affairs.

Neither calmness nor consistency informed Wise's writings. The extracts which follow are taken from the same page of the *Israelite* (the issue of 4 November 1859)—and they are a fair example of how Wise reacted to what he heard or read—and show that his zeal was not always, in the words of his spiritual descendants, 'tempered by wisdom and guided by regard for other men's faith'.

In the *Boston Evening Journal* for 22 October there had appeared a dispatch from its New York correspondent which, after commenting on the moving of a synagogue uptown, because its present location had become unsuited for a 'fashionable congregation', continued: 'The better class of Jews are wealthy and numerous. Much of the importing is in their hands. Wines and liquors, laces, German goods and toys are mostly in their hands ... surely they are commanding and controlling much of the solid and profitable foreign business of New York.' Aloof and patronizing, we might think, but, as with Leeser's reference to his being rabbi of a 'country congregation', it was enough to set a fuse to this tirade:

We will say nothing of the narrow-minded Knownothingarian spirit that speaks through every line of this paragraph, as we are used to see the foreigners insulted by Boston journals, legislators, preachers, orators, and other public mediums who in their unholy zeal, place the foreigner far below the native negro, and treat them with their thousands of men who [are] much higher in science and art than the scribblers and talkers of Boston, its pariahs, low plebians, a rabble of dirty and ignorant fellows. But when the man with the narrow sons speaks of a FASHIONABLE Jewish congregation abandoning their location, because the vicinity is 'filled with foreigners', we can only pity his ignorance; as that very fashionable congregation consists one-half at least of foreigners, and their minister too is a foreigner. A fashionable congregation is so outlandish a thing in our estimation that we can say nothing to characterize it. It must be a congregation that worships God in a fashionable style with black suits and diamond breast-pins; gold watches and chains and diamond rings; the ladies all dressed in silk, velvet, gold and jewels, and the minister wearing white kid gloves. This appears to us a fashionable congregation composed of the upper tendom. We do not know how much God and the angels are pleased with such a fashionable congregation, how much dearer beloved its fashionable members are to God, than the ordinary mortals—we can not tell which prophet or saint gave a description of such a fashionable congregation, or where the tailors, dress-makers, hatters, milliners, shoemakers, &c., live who make such fashionable congregations:— Thus much we know that the Jews are free of that plague or rather that ridiculous, narrow idea, which the New York correspondent of the Boston Journal calls a fashionable congregation. We maintain all men (also the foreigner in Massachusetts) are equal and fashionable before God. As much as we know, the congregation in question built a new house of worship because their members reside farther uptown, and the present location is too far from their residences.

Codfish aristocracy and ignorance are natural concomitants. This is also the case with the New York correspondent of the Boston Journal. He says of the Jewish importers: 'Wines and liquors, laces, German goods and toys are mostly in their hands'. How dim the eyes of that poor man must be, if he could not see that besides the Opera house and other musical celebrities of N. Y., a good many other things are in the hands of the Jews.

Wise then went on to enumerate some of the other trades in which New York Jews were prominent and finally wound up:

But it must not be forgotten, that many of those merchants are foreigners and no Negroes, hence that aristocratic correspondent can not descend so far as to know that they do exist, and if he should do so he would be suspected of vulgar and illoyal conceptions in the American Athens of isms and eccentricities. We can only advise the Boston Journal to have a correspondent in New York who is better posted in local matters.[36]

Here we see an example of Wise's extreme sensitivity where anything was concerned which might affect his personal authority extended also to statements which might carry the implication of an attack on the Jews or a derogation from their status as American citizens. We see also the recent immigrant's and democratic Westerner's resentment at the superior airs and superior culture of the Bostonian (a homeliness which also made the swagger of New York distasteful to him) and, finally, his suspicion of the solicitude for the Negro slave which was then widespread in New England and casting the shadow of disruption over the Union he loved so dearly.

[36] *Israelite*, 6 (4 Nov. 1859), 140.

The second occasion for Wise's vexation that week had a more solid basis, though the manner of his reply showed more insensitivity to the feelings of others than that of which he was given to complain. His torrent of words made boasts which, in their way, were as derogatory of Jews as the simile of which he complained.

The Rev. Dr. Comfort in a communication to the Christian Advocate and Journal of New York says of them [the Jesuits]: 'They shall be worse than Jews, having no resting place on earth; and then shall a Jew have more favor than a Jesuit.' To which Jews does the Rev. Doctor refer, to Jesus of Nazareth or Paul of Tarsith? to the father, grandfathers, mother, grandmothers or brothers of his God?

After expounding the contribution of the Jews to religion, Wise declared that 'as the simile stands now, not a rational man unless insane with fanaticism or purblind with ignorance can tell what the learned reverend doctor intended to say'. And after demonstrating how Jews had real homes in many countries of the world, he wound up an article whose length exceeded a column thus:

What kind of a God Dr. Comfort imagines we can not tell; but thus much we know, this is the real characteristic of black fanaticism; it is not satisfied to stigmatize and poison the object of its hatred in this world, in this life; it raises its serpentile head to the heaven and also there spits its venom on those who unfortunately differ with it in religious views.

Finally, on the very same page he has this to say about an article by Henry Ward Beecher affirming, without any reference to Jews, his belief in the Virgin Birth:

If the doctrine of Mary's virginity ever was ridiculed, if ever words were used to make sarcasm sarcastic, the following passage of a sermon by Henry Ward Beecher, published in the Independent, is a master work; if he, however, is in earnest about the matter, we can not comprehend how a man can use such lubric language in the Lord's house, or how he can expect for a moment to convince any body of the peculiar christian, unnatural and immoral doctrine of the immaculate conception, which is for the ear of any moral or intelligent man.

His vocabulary would have been strained indeed had a Christian paper written about one of the doctrines of Judaism in such terms.

The same man who could wax indignant when the Russian Jews who journeyed to Palestine were referred to as filthy describes the San Francisco *Catholic Guardian* as 'written by barefaced demagogues for the lowest class of Irishmen';[37] and when the Cincinnati *Catholic Telegraph* commented adversely on one of his lectures on Christianity, he retorted that 'vulgar Irishmen', especially when they were subject to fits of religious hatred, called the Jew 'Christ-Killer'.[38]

Between Wise and the *Israelite* the relationship was intensely personal. Year by year, as each volume closed and its successor opened, Wise opened his heart to his readers on the progress which the paper had made, on the difficulties which it encountered, on the destiny which it served. At the end of the first year, when, according to his later reminiscences, he must have been at his wits' end to carry on, he beats the big drum with defiant bluster.

The progress of the *Israelite* during the first year of its existence has no precedent in the history of journalism. The causes of the brilliant success are manifold. There is the known zeal and unabated enthusiasm of its editor on behalf of Judaism and the nation professing it, which finds a re-echo in every noble heart, and the opponents of the editor are obliged to confess, that the *Israelite* is borne on by a thoroughly Jewish spirit, that it breathes in every line enthusiasm and devotion for the cause which it pleads and is fully and truly what it professes to be. The liberal and scientific spirit, in which it is conducted, is the true spirit of our age. The boldness of its language in self-defence equals fully the insolence and arrogance of its assailants.[39]

Here Wise goes on to refer to 1,600–1,700 subscribers in four hundred different places:

Nothing can make us timid or hesitating in the defence or exposition of principles which according to the best of our knowledge are true, sacred and eternal. None shall succeed, by arguments or invectives, direct or indirect attacks, haughtily or rather cowardly ignoring the existence of The Israelite; none, we are sure will ever succeed in silencing our voice, frightening us away from the field of sacred action changing our garment before the eyes of the community, or sharing our confidence in the good sense of our people, the uprightness and fidelity of our friends and the sacredness and godliness of our cause.[40]

A proclamation of similar intent, though varying in form with the mood of the day, is to be found in succeeding years. They show that, although Wise may not always have advocated the same course, he

---

[37] *Israelite*, 19 (7 Mar. 1873), 4.   [38] Ibid. 15 (29 Jan. 1869), 4.
[39] Ibid. 2 (13 July 1855), 4.   [40] Ibid.

was consistent in presenting himself as the man beholden to a higher
mandate. Only one further example can be quoted here. In the first
issue of volume 4 he wound up the customary introduction with this
peroration:

We send out again the *Israelite*, and pray to God, that it weekly may be the
harbinger of divine instruction, the messenger of cheerful tidings to humanity,
the instrument, in the hands of Providence, to promulgate divine truth among
our fellow-citizens, that Israel may flourish, that truth and humanity may be
triumphant, and the will of God be done for ever and ever.[41]

This was no tailpiece added for the sake of a little uplift. ‘"Here I
am",’ the article had begun, ‘unimpaired and unterrified, as willing
and vigorous as ever, to serve in the sacred cause of God and Israel.’
The opening paragraph goes on to remind readers that ‘Here I am’
was the response of Abraham and Isaiah when they heard the Divine
Call. Those words were his own response too.

‘Here I am,’ is also the sincere and hearty response of the humble writer of
these lines, from the innermost and fervent desire of his mind, to benefit the
cause of Judaism and humanity. ‘Here I am,’ he exclaims with a glowing
devotion to the cause for which he pleads, with a heart grateful to the
Almighty, who affords him the eminent opportunity to work prominently in
the vineyard of the Lord, and with a filial attachment to God and Israel—
my God and my people.[42]

If such was the response, the reader of the *Israelite* might ask, was
there not a divine call to Isaac Mayer Wise? If Wise responded as did
the heroes of Scripture, had he received a call as the prophets of old
had done? Wise was not so incautious as to make an affirmative
statement to this effect, but the language in which he continued did
nothing to suggest the negative. He declared his rejection of the
caution that would bring material benefit to his paper:

Conviction, the inmost conviction of the soul, breaks through this spider net
of dishonest sophistry, and cries with the irresistible voice of thunder. ‘The
course pursued hitherto is right!’ and its editor responds ‘Here I am,’ and
here I remain, careless of consequences, opinions, approbation or blame,
without fear or hope. ‘Here I am,’ and no earthly power can drive me one
inch from the position which I have occupied hitherto in behalf of God and

_____
[41] Ibid. 4 (10 July 1857), 4.   [42] Ibid.

Israel, reform and progress, Jews and Judaism, instruction and enlightenment; for no man can successfully resist his own conviction.[43]

This was no isolated flash. Wise began the seventh volume (when indeed the Civil War, in addition to its general troubles, made the going difficult for the *Israelite*) with these words:

'The voice of the Lord is with power'; therefore we come before our readers with this seventh volume of the *Israelite*. Our loins are girded. 'I am yet today as strong as on the day when Moses sent me; my energy then—as my energy now to war, to go out, and to come in.' ... Let others write and publish papers to have an organ, make money and hold a position in society; we handle our pen in a sacred cause, for the future of Israel and mankind; we shall not yield ....

Therefore, we again appear before our readers, reluctantly, we can not deny it, but we appear; for 'the voice of the Lord is with power,' and nothing that man can do, death excepted, shall prevent us from serving our sacred cause.[44]

The *Israelite* was the platform of the man of destiny, and as we read these editorials we are reminded of the character of the dream which Wise said visited him as his ship neared America.

In the unrestrained hands of a man who was animated by this feeling and who could write in this vein, a newspaper could be a dangerous instrument, for a sense of destiny heightens a man's contempt for those who stand in his way and allows him to use any weapon he chooses to beat them down. Nothing was too imposing to be spared Wise's invective. Of the assaults which he delivered at those who in his view disparaged or disregarded the equal rights of Jews, examples have been given and we shall see more later.

Frequent occasions for Wise's polemic were provided by language which suggested that the United States was somehow a 'Christian country'—Thanksgiving proclamations often had this statement, while proposals for a 'Christian clause' in the Constitution or for religious instruction in the public schools were more obvious in their significance. With the *Israelite* so much its editor's mouthpiece, the impression it left on its readers is not easy to gauge. Did they look upon Wise as one might look upon a volcano—to be admired from a distance but dangerous if one drew too close? The ferocity of Wise's eruptions was without precedent: and one can imagine his contemporaries agreeing on the one hand with the principles he asserted but not themselves wishing to tangle with the Gentile majority. Wise

[43] *Israelite*, 4 (10 July 1857), 4.   [44] Ibid. 1 (27 Apr. 1855), 355.

proved correct in his assessment of the American system, and it is fair to conclude that his assertiveness enhanced his status in the eyes of the Jewish community. Enemies within he attacked without inhibitions, and sometimes there were personal scores to pay off.

Violent language could be repaid with violent language, and in one case it became evident that Wise was using his editorial liberties to pay off personal scores. A piece lampooning one Joseph Abraham, a Cincinnati lawyer, and which, when cornered, Wise described as a 'piece of fun', appeared in the *Israelite* for 23 October 1857. When Wise failed to print Abraham's rejoinder, the latter had it inserted in the *Occident* as an advertisement.[45] It covered three pages and contained damaging insinuations against Wise, which Wise met by an evasive reply.[46]

Twelve months later, Wise's quarrel with Joseph Abraham took another turn, resulting in a journalistic foray on Wise's part whose details seem to have been deliberately obliterated. In October 1858 a bitter election campaign was being fought. The Cincinnati newspapers were using strong language, which was being matched by even stronger action in the streets. Wise issued three numbers of a special supplement to the *Israelite* (the last two called *Isaac M. Wise's Weekly Observer*) with a political character.

The appearance of this supplement caused a strong reaction within the Jewish community. When a protest in the name of a group of Jews in the city appeared,[47] Wise seems to have taken it for granted that his old enemy was responsible, and in the second issue of his supplement directed his fire principally at Abraham,[48] to which Abraham replied with nearly a full column of the Cincinnati *Daily Commercial* for 9 October 1858, attacking Wise in the same style as that he had employed in the *Occident*.

The quarrel did not end there, though later details are hidden in obscurity. The matter went to arbitration, and the award, published in the *Israelite* for 5 November, while not exonerating Abraham, apportions the greater part of the blame to Wise.[49]

---

[45] See *Occident*, 15 (Dec. 1857), 450.   [46] Ibid. (Jan. 1858), 498.

[47] *Israelite*, 12 Oct. 1858.

[48] In fact the reply was the work of one Frederick Lewis, Abraham merely having been one of the signatories: see letter from Lewis, *Cincinnati Daily Commerical*, 9 Oct. 1858.

[49] *Israelite*, 5 (5 Nov. 1858), 143. The quarrel subsided. In the *Israelite* 18 (1 Aug. 1871), 9, we find a commendation of the candidature of Mr Joseph Abraham for the office of judge of the Common Pleas Court.

Wise's publishing enterprises appear to have cost him dearly in money. When he arrived in Cincinnati he was in debt.[50] These debts were cleared within a year,[51] but no sooner had the ship been pumped dry of the waters of the first storm than it was again steered into uncharted seas. Wise says that he lost $600 on the *Israelite* during its first year,[52] though shortly before he says that the losses had been guaranteed.[53] Schmidt had lost enough on the *Israelite* during the first year not to wish to continue with it, so Wise and his brother-in-law, Edward Bloch, set up as printers and publishers (July 1855). They bought machinery on six months' credit and started business with debts of $3,000. A German supplement to the *Israelite* had been promised as soon as the circulation reached a thousand, but it was still, one surmises, far short of that figure, and losing money, when *Die Deborah* was launched.[54]

This journal, which Wise also edited, made its first appearance on 24 August 1855, and thereafter Wise often wrote in counterpoint. Its subtitle described it as 'A Supplement to the *Israelite*, Devoted to the Daughters of Israel'. *Die Deborah*, however, was more than a women's sheet. Wise still wanted to laugh and cry in the language in which he had first learned to do so, and the question must always be asked whether it was not in *Die Deborah* that the feelings closest to his heart were aired.

The business depression which began in 1857 coincided with the check to Wise's schemes for the establishment of a college and the union of American Israel.[55] Contemporary references in the *Israelite* make it clear that money was urgently needed to keep it going, and that here also a reverse might have been very close at hand.[56] Besides having to keep his two weeklies afloat, Wise had somehow to pay for *Minhag America*, the prayer-book which he had launched in 1857 at his own expense. He could not have been long out of these difficulties when the crisis of the Civil War supervened. In July 1866 Wise heaved a public sigh of relief that the *Israelite* was at last on a firm foundation;[57] more than ten years of uncertainty as to where the ship

[50] See ch. 2 sect. 10 above.
[51] *Reminiscences*, 292.
[52] *The World of My Books*, 22.   [53] Ibid. 19.
[54] *Reminiscences*, 293.
[55] See ch. 3 sects. 22, 23 below.
[56] *Israelite*, 4 (20 Nov. 1857), 158, 162; ibid. (14 May 1858), 359; ibid. (2 July 1853), 412.
[57] *Israelite*, 13/1 (6 July 1866), 4.

would next spring a leak were now behind him. The losses on these publications must have been a trial even to Wise's buoyant spirit; the fact that he let nothing stand in the way of these plans is evidence of his grit.

4. ZION COLLEGE

However, if Wise had financial headaches he also had something he valued more—a platform from which to propound his 'bold schemes'. Long before the *Israelite* was on its feet—in fact in its twelfth number—Wise began to project another venture that was close to his heart. On 29 September 1854,[58] the paper contained an announcement calling the Jews of Cincinnati to a general meeting with a view to establishing 'a college on the pattern of German universities, connected with a theological seminary, and a seminary for teachers, in order to promulgate science and the interests of Judaism among our fellow-citizens'.

Wise's optimism was undiluted—'We', i.e. the Jews of Cincinnati, he wrote a week later, 'have the financial and the literary powers, plenty of money and men, why should we not be able to achieve a brilliant victory.'[59]

The meeting was duly held. It resolved to establish the Zion Collegiate Association, elected officers, and fixed a fee of $1 for admission to membership and $2 as the annual subscription. The object of the association was 'the establishment of a university in Cincinnati, the theological faculty of which shall be Judaism'.[60]

Two German papers voiced opposition to the scheme, and Wise answered them with his accustomed vigour.[61] On 27 November regular officers were elected, Wise becoming 'Recording and Corresponding Secretary'. By 1 December, Wise was able to announce that two hundred members had enrolled in the Zion Collegiate Association and that 'the nucleus is formed to produce the fruit of the tree of knowledge for American Jews'.[62]

An institution of the dimensions contemplated needed more than local support, and Wise immediately took the lead in organizing such support outside Cincinnati. He spoke in Louisville on 7 March

---

[58] Ibid. 1 (28 Sept. 1854), 94.   [59] Ibid. (6 Oct. 1854), 100.
[60] Ibid. (13 Oct. 1854), 100.   [61] Ibid. (24 Nov. 1854), 156.
[62] Ibid. 164.

1855, with the result that a local 'Zion Collegiate Association' was established,[63] and two months later he embarked on a major tour of the East—the first of many such tours which he was to make and the forerunner of the 'national campaign' which was to become an important feature of American Jewish life. His time was packed with travel and meetings. First there were forty-four hours by river boat to Wheeling, where he induced sixteen of the twenty-seven members of the congregation to subscribe to the *Israelite* and *Die Deborah*.[64] Thence he moved to Baltimore (9 May), Philadelphia (17 May), and New York (22 May), addressing literary associations, preaching in synagogues, leading meetings in support of Zion College. A Zion Collegiate Association was formed in Baltimore and in Philadelphia; in New York two such associations, one at a meeting in Temple Emanu-El, a second at a meeting of the B'nai B'rith lodge. On the return journey he spoke first at Albany and then at Syracuse. He had been away for five weeks and therefore 'hastened home', regretting that he had been unable to visit a number of important communities.[65] The fatigue of this lengthy speaking tour did not worry him; in fact the experience seems to have lifted him to a peak.

This 'tour to the East' gives fresh evidence of Wise's wide-ranging interests and self-confident versatility. He had written on theological matters; he had written history; he had written novels. Now he turned his hand to descriptive writing. The Baltimore and Ohio Railroad had not long been opened, and the engineering feat represented by the construction of this difficult line across the Alleghanies excited him, as did 'the iron horse in which fire and water struggle for dominion'. Theology was never far from his mind, and the Baltimore and Ohio Railroad had implications for theology as well as for commerce and industry; it was evidence of the powers of man and exposed the weakness of Christian doctrine which demonstrated that 'man was nothing but a weak, sinful and wretched being, if not redeemed by' Christian belief. More, it showed that progress was the keynote of the age, nowhere better exemplified than in youthful America, and

[63] *Israelite*, 1 (16 Mar. 1855), 283.

[64] Ibid. (25 May 1855), 364.

[65] Ibid. (29 June 1855), 401–2. Wise's journeyings were accompanied in *Israelite*, 1 (8 June 1855), 381, by descriptions in overflowing terms from himself and others. A more sceptical approach to Wise's efforts is expressed in *Asmonean*, 14 (11 July 1856), 103.

advance in technology would go hand in hand with elevation on the moral plane.[66] The advances in communication that have become familiar a generation later have been accompanied by new fears, and it is difficult for us to savour the exhilaration which the steam engine brought to Wise.

The mood of optimism remained after Wise had returned to his workaday tasks. On 6 July, with no hint of the financial troubles which, according to his *Reminiscences*, were encompassing him, he brought the first volume of the *Israelite* to a close on a note of exultation.[67] His journey had convinced him that (*a*) the people were 'susceptible of intelligent instruction', (*b*) 'the cause of reform had been misrepresented', (*c*) 'a national university will be established', and (*d*) 'the Israelite is a popular and much read journal, not one line of it escapes the notice of our readers, the hearts of our people are with us, as our sentiments and energies are devoted to them and their sacred cause'. So he was able to 'close the first volume of the Israelite, satisfied with the blessings of God, and the good sense of our people'.

Just as Wise had not been satisfied to wait until his first weekly rested on a firm foundation before launching a second, so, in his attempts to solve the problems of American Israel at once and under his own leadership, he was taking up another project before the university had left the drawing-board stage. In the same month Wise was reviving his old plan for a rabbinical conference, which actually met in Cleveland before the year was out.

So important an event deserved to be celebrated, and in the style of the times a banquet was held on 1 November, when the company of 150 gentlemen included Salmon P. Chase, governor-elect of Ohio, the president of the City Council, and two local judges. Wise himself both presided and responded to the toast to 'The Zion College— the first cornerstone of the intellectual superstructure of American Judaism'.[68] The report in the *Israelite* of the florid oratory which graced this occasion—there were twelve toasts in all—is one of a number designed to build up the impression that the Zion College idea had taken root.

'The company retired at a late hour of the evening well pleased, we suppose,' Wise concluded his report of the Zion College banquet

---

[66] *Israelite*, 1 (25 May 1854), 364.
[67] Ibid. (6 July 1855), 412.
[68] Ibid. (16 Nov. 1855), 156.

in Cincinnati. But if joy endured for the night, heaviness came in the morning. On 2 November, the morning after the banquet, the *Asmonean* appeared in New York with a lengthy statement by the Zion Collegiate Association of that city declaring the steps taken in Cincinnati whereby Zion College 'was created by a single association' to have been 'a breach of the covenant whereon all other associations were founded'. 'We are excluded from acting', the statement continued, 'and we do not consider consistent with our dignity and position to continue our labours under the auspices under which we have been appointed.'[69] The New York Association had considered this statement at a meeting on 28 October and had resolved unanimously to dissolve its connection with the Cincinnati body.

Wise's reaction to the New York statement did not show him at his best. He tried bluff and bluster, evading the substance of the complaint against him. The *Israelite* published a lengthy article headed 'Reply to the Anonymous Calling Himself the Committee of N. Y. Zion Collegiate Association No. 2'. Throughout the article, Wise persists in insinuating that the protest published in the *Asmonean* in the name of the New York Association was the work of an individual animated by impure motives.

There are a number of human beings in this sublunar world who are composed of heterogenous materials, and enlivened by the spirit of negation; hence they feed upon quarrel and opposition and subsist on schisms. They are best known as the opponents of somebody, scheme or system, and if they even happen to give birth to an original idea, they soon make opposition against themselves. This class of human beings are very noisy, talkative and officious; they speak first and last, again and anon, of themselves and their gigantic schemes for the salvation of mankind. If it was not for them (so they say) the system of the universe would be reduced to atoms, and if it was not for their philosophy, learning and incessant labor the structure of the moral world would have been long ago shaken to its center. A natural history of this class of human beings must be very interesting, indeed. We are sorry, however, that our limited knowledge would not permit us to do justice to this species. . . .

But in taking up the last week's issue of the Asmonean, we found an article which we give below, putting to shame all our philosophy on the human mind. The report of a committee without names attached to it! the resolutions of a society published again without official authority, nay, without the

[69] *Asmonean*, 13 (2 Nov. 1855), 20.

support of a name! a scribbler feeds on the most sacred interests of man, education, tramples upon the most precious cause of Judaism, union, throws his slurs into the face of a respectable and outraged community, and forgets to write his name under the ignoble produce of his pen. Why do you feel ashamed to give your name to the world?[70]

In the same spirit Wise gave voice to his feelings a week later, in an article entitled 'The little big-men of New York'.[71] This made no reference to the Zion College controversy; it merely vituperated against New York and everything connected with it. Whether Wise might have retrieved the situation had he replied with elementary civility to the New York protest (there was nothing offensive in the language used by New York) is an open question. An additional reason for his need to tread carefully was the suspicion of his ambitions which the Cleveland conference had just engendered. If there had been any chance of bringing Cincinnati and New York together, Wise's intemperate abuse destroyed it.[72]

Support for the college melted away. The affront felt in New York must have been a solvent of the enthusiasm that other communities had expressed. There were, one suspects, other factors. American Jewry was as volatile as it was disorganized. Under the spell of Wise's personality, members of an audience would come forward and pledge support; when he had departed and the effervescence subsided, other problems would come into view and the promises would be forgotten. The stage had not been reached when a national body—such as the union of congregations which Wise had advocated and which was eventually established—could solicit support as a continuing operation.

Try as Wise did to carry on, and he was persistent in showing an optimistic face to the world, when 1856 opened the college was near collapse. To a meeting in Cincinnati in January he propounded far-reaching plans,[73] denouncing New York and Baltimore for attempting to upset the boat;[74] early in April he received the endorsement of a

[70] *Israelite*, 2 (16 Nov. 1855), 156.
[71] Ibid. (23 Nov. 1855), 164.
[72] To Wise, of course, the only cause for complaint lay against the attacks made on him. 'Most bitter and venomous attacks emanated one after the other from the East. If we had been horse thieves, gamblers, sharks and tramps, we could not have been more shamefully treated.' (*Reminiscences*, 325.)
[73] *Die Deborah*, 1 (11 Jan. 1856), 161.
[74] *Israelite*, 2 (11 Jan. 1856), 220.

meeting in Louisville for a new plan to finance the venture,[75] but the endorsement was not followed by material support.

That summer he embarked on a second speaking tour. This time he went not to the East, where, one suspects, he was in bad odour, not only because of the *fait accompli* with regard to Zion College but also because of the controversies following the Cleveland conference,[76] but to the West. He left Cincinnati for Indianapolis on 9 July, reaching Chicago on the 24th and returning early in August. His accounts of the journey are full of the wonders of the West and the friendliness of the people;[77] but however idyllic the scenery and however rapturous the enthusiasm which his presence aroused, that degree of financial support which would have enabled Zion College to survive was not forthcoming.[78]

On 1 August 1856 there appeared in the *Israelite* the first of a number of notices stating that Zion College would reopen on 25 August. Then there was complete silence until 24 April 1857 when a general meeting of the association for the purpose of winding up was notified.[79]

Defeat did not mean oblivion. Other projects and controversies occupied his attention, and the financial panic of 1857 discouraged action. In 1859 he turned to the B'nai B'rith, being a leading figure in the affairs of his district, but his attempt to interest them came to naught.[80] In November 1860 he published the full curriculum of a college which he said would open in the following September.[81] Of this too nothing more was heard.

[75] *Israelite*, 2 (4 Apr. 1856), 314. See also ibid. 383. A report on an examination at Zion College, in which it was stated that a vacation had been declared till 25 Aug., appeared in the *Israelite*, 2 (4 July 1856), 420.

[76] See ch. 3 sect. 7 below.

[77] *Israelite*, 3 (18 July 1856), 14; (25 July 1856), 22; (1 Aug. 1856), 29; (8 Aug. 1856), 36; (15 Aug. 1856), 46; (22 Aug. 1856), 52. In the *Israelite* he never states the purpose of his journey, though this is made clear in *Die Deborah*, 1 (18 July 1856), 391.

[78] Wise may have collected something on this tour. Joseph Abraham, the lawyer whose attack on Wise is mentioned above, insinuated that some of the monies collected by Wise for Zion College may not have reached their destination.

[79] *Israelite*, 3 (1 Aug. 1856), 334.

[80] *Menorah*, 5 (July 1888), 27. Evidently there was recurrent ill-feeling between Wise and B'nai B'rith. See *Reminiscences*, 198, 263–5.

[81] *Israelite*, 7 (2 Nov. 1860), 140. Two weeks after the original announcement (ibid. (16 Nov. 1860), 156), Wise gave a hint as to how his plan was being received: 'Nineteen letters full of wise plans, prudent caution, good advice, peculiar themes have reached us from different quarters of the country. Some joke, some doubt, while others let us feel the cup of bitter irony. We have in the first place to say to all friends or opponents:

5. CONFERENCE—UNION—SYNOD

As a counterpoint to the establishment of a university, 1855 was to see the setting up of a synod. Early in the year Wise had begun to renew his agitation for a conference. 'Let us Have a Conference' was the title of an article in the *Israelite* for 26 January. Wise wanted a general 'get-together' without regard to theology. He enumerates some of the questions which lay before American Jewry: Zion College, which had been started in Cincinnati; the orphan asylum which had been started in New Orleans; whether or not to have Jewish parochial schools; 'our standing complaint about the serious want of textbooks for Hebrew schools'. 'The grand problem—to be solved at present is this,' said Wise, 'how to unite all these endeavours into one focus.' Here, indeed, we see a mind working on a grand design for American Jewry. It is a conference on practical issues, not on ideologies, that Wise is advocating. The note is definitely union, not reform.

> We propose a conference, a personal interview of all men who take an interest in the progress of Judaism and its institutions. Let Rabbis, Hazanim and Laymen, if a layity we have—meet, to come to a definite conclusion, what measures should be adopted, recommended to our friends, and advocated by each and all of us. A colloquial and friendly interview can exercise only a benevolent influence on our affairs, and must necessarily tend towards prompt and united action.[82]

In time Wise moved away from this idea to a conference which, though not exclusively rabbinic, had a more ideological flavour; but his premiss, sometimes articulate, sometimes not, was that practical activity came before theological uniformity.

Wise worked on the conference idea with his accustomed force. The theme of union permeates his propaganda, and with this occupying his mind it is not a hierarchy but individualism that is the danger. Thus he criticizes on the one hand the Orthodox for demanding compliance with rabbinical law and on the other the reformers for failing to see

---

we want nothing of any body; not a penny. The College is all finished in all respects—rooms, apparatus, library, museum, professors, proper plans of instruction, government and discipline; all ready and finished to be set in operation by the first day of September next.'

[82] *Israelite*, 1 (26 Jan. 1855), 229.

that 'if we throw off the rabbinical and cabalistical literature, we either cease altogether to be a community . . . or we represent mummies remaining from the Mosaic age, as the Caraites do'.[83] Israel as a nation, he argued, had a sacred mission to perform to humanity, and in order to discharge that mission needed to remain united: 'Grant to every preacher the right to promulgate his own views in the Synagogue and in a few years we present the miserable prospect of a thousand Jewish sects'. He drew attention to the importance of the rabbinical standard of exegesis when it came to the practical applica-tion of the Law, a point of view which contained the seeds of what was to emerge at Cleveland later in the year. The remedy was 'a regular triennial synod'. The staunchest Orthodox Jew must admit that 'the principle of progress lays at the basis of the Mosaic dis-pensation'—otherwise the whole rabbinical development of the Law would be illegal. The principle of progress had been set aside in the Middle Ages. Moses Mendelssohn and his followers had revived the Jewish spirit, and the American and French revolu-tions had transformed the position of the Jew. Some had bridged the gap between religion and life by abandoning Judaism. The efforts of those who had 'reformed Judaism and the institutions, to agree with the demands of the age', he observed, had been harmed by 'modern materialism, infidelity and atheism'.[84] To heal the breach between religion and life and to protect Judaism against the noisy voice of materialism, infidelity, and atheism was needed 'a perpetual synod whose decisions and resolutions are binding upon all Jewish communities'. Such a synod derived its power from the Talmud.[85]

It is not easy to determine what the word 'reform' conjured up when he wrote this article. What does emerge is the view that change must be sought on the basis of the past, and that the proper authority was collective, not individual action.

Five weeks after Wise began, we find him drumming the same theme—'We must have peace and union, at any hazard or sacrifice, principles excepted', is how he begins an article entitled 'The Synod'.[86] Naturally, the application of the term 'principles' leaves open the possibility of endless controversy, but the dominant note is the importance of unity. As a platform on which 'the contending

[83] Ibid. (2 Mar. 1855), 268.   [84] Ibid.
[85] Ibid.   [86] Ibid. (9 Mar. 1855), 276.

parties' could meet, he wanted a regular synod as the highest religious authority in the country, subject to the Bible and the Talmud (a stipulation which was to involve Wise in controversy and set-back) with a standing committee 'to carry out the resolutions of the synod, watch over communal institutions, examine the paid officers of the congregations and schools, and decide on questions laid before them'. 'We expect', commented Wise, 'that these articles of peace must satisfy even the ultra-orthodox, and we were going to say, everyone who reasons on the subject of Judaism.' He then proceeds to an investigation 'whether this platform is legal' and supports his contention that it is with reference to a great number of authorities, for example, Deut. 16: 18 and 17: 8–14, the *Yad* and the *Tur*, and the practice of the Va'ad Arbah Aratsot in Poland.[87] The expression of the hope that the Orthodox should be satisfied obviously proceeds from one who knew that he was suspect within that group, but it shows that he was striving to satisfy them, to work within the framework of tradition, not to break with it.

Presumably there were preliminary negotiations, but they have not emerged (the other participants did not assume a central role); and by 13 April Wise's advocacy bore fruit, and the following 'call' appeared in the *Israelite* for 10 August 1855—the same issue as that which contained Wise's elaborate scheme for Zion College.[88]

THE FIRST CONFERENCE

IN THE NAME OF ISRAEL'S GOD AND ISRAEL'S RELIGION, the ministers and delegates of the Israelitish congregations are respectfully requested to assemble in a conference, to take place the 17th day of October 5616 A.M. in the city of Cleveland, Ohio, to deliberate on the following points:

1. The articles of Union of American Israel in theory and practice.

2ly. A plan to organize a regular synod, consisting of delegates chosen by the congregations and societies, whose powers, privileges and duties shall be defined, to be sent to the several congregations for their approbation.

3ly. To discuss and refer to a committee a plan for a Minhag America, to be reported to the synod at its first session.

4ly. A plan for scholastic education in the lower and higher branches of learning.

---

[87] The *Yad* by Moses Maimonides and the *Tur* by Jacob ben Asher are important medieval codes of Jewish law. The Va'ad Arbah Aratsot was a judicial and rule-making authority of the Jews in Poland.

[88] See ch. 3 sect. 4 above.

5ly. Other propositions either sent in by congregations, or made by the ministers or delegates at the conference.

By order of the American rabbis,

Rev. Doctors COHN of Albany

GUENZBURG of Baltimore
HOCHHEIMER   do.
ILLOWY of St. Louis
KALISH of Cleveland
LILIENTHAL of Cincinnati
MERZBACHER of New York
ROTHENHEIM of Cincinnati
WISE of Cincinnati
ISAAC M. WISE, Corresp. Sec'y.[89]

By August 1855, therefore, Wise seemed set fair to realizing two of his cherished projects, a college and a union, an anticipation which had not faded as 17 October approached. The *Israelite* for 12 October—the last issue to appear before the conference opened—shows in what spirit he set off for Cleveland.

Two of our most favorite schemes, and for which we have incessantly worked these seven or eight years—appear now to be realized at once, and under the most promising auspices. The sentiments as far as we could ascertain them are everywhere in favor of union and progress which should be and we hope will be the motto of the conference, and the leading stars of that venerable body. The eyes of all our brethren are inquisitively directed to Cleveland and the conference, and therefore we hope, that all congregations will be represented, and that the actions of the conference will be guided by a consciousness of the responsibility, lasting [sic] upon that body, and the expectations of the people from their representatives.

But the reader has a right to ask why we put together in one article two different subjects, the Zion College and the Conference? Here is the reply at once; because we hope, nay we expect, that the Conference will adopt some laudable plan to forward the cause of learning, hence also to support the Zion College, and the scheme for establishing a university, this being one of its most sacred duties.[90]

A synod was to be established, and the college was to receive organized backing. The discussion of ideas presupposes no precedence among men, but when the ideas are clothed in institutional form, leaders—or perhaps a leader—must be acknowledged. Wise was 36, the rabbi of a leading congregation, and, one is justified in adding, through his

<hr>

[89] *Israelite*, 2 (10 Aug. 1855), 39.   [90] Ibid. (12 Oct. 1855), 115.

writing, the best-known rabbi in the country. He had achieved much in the short time since he had settled in Cincinnati. If there spun in his mind the thought that Cleveland would set the seal on his pre-eminence, we could not be surprised.

6. DAVID EINHORN

On 27 September 1855 Rabbi David Einhorn arrived in the United States, and on 4 October he preached his inaugural sermon at the temple of the Har-Sinai Verein in Baltimore.[91] He was invited to attend the conference at Cleveland but replied that 'being but lately arrived in this country and still too much engaged with his private affairs' he was prevented from so doing.[92]

Einhorn was ten years older than Wise. He received his talmudic education at the *yeshivah* of Fürth, in his native Bavaria, and at the universities of Munich and Würzburg. Participation in the German rabbinic conferences of 1844–6 marked him out as a reformer and made life in German congregations uncomfortable for him. When a Reform temple was opened in Budapest, Einhorn was appointed its preacher. He gave his inaugural sermon in 1852, but the government, prodded by the Orthodox, and fearful of change anywhere, closed the temple after a bare two months. Without prospects in Europe, Einhorn moved to Baltimore in 1855. In 1861 he had to flee Baltimore on account of his outspoken opposition to slavery, and until 1866 he served Congregation Keneseth Israel, Philadelphia. From 1866 to 1879 he was rabbi of Congregation Adath Jeshurun, New York (later part of Congregation Beth El).

Endowed with considerable talents—eloquence, scholarship, the power of original thinking—but not with the qualities which endear a man to his fellows, Einhorn worked in America a bitter and frustrated man. Denied opportunities in his native Germany, he was obliged to labour in what he regarded as a spiritual wasteland; having laboured diligently to obtain immaculate title-deeds to academic and theological standing, he found himself in a strange world where the ignorant started equal with the learned, and it was the broad-shouldered man of action who wielded influence. This experience seems to have

[91] Einhorn's arrival in New York in the steamer *Washington* is given in *Israelite*, 2 (5 Oct. 1855), 99. The date of his inaugural sermon (correcting a statement in *Occident*) is given by Einhorn himself in *Asmonean*, 13 (14 Dec. 1855), 68.

[92] *Israelite*, 2 (28 Mar. 1856), 309.

strengthened the hold of Germany on Einhorn and the rabbis who
felt like him. He neither wrote nor preached in English, and his
farewell sermon was a plea for the retention of German in American
Reform congregations. To point to the contrast with opponents such
as Einhorn on the one side and Leeser on the other is helpful to the
understanding of Wise's personality and policies. Wise's constant
hammering at the need for an American rabbinate and the naturalization of the Jew and Judaism in America must be seen in the
light of the Einhorn influence; the significance of his constant travels to
outlying congregations stands in contrast to his opponent's aloofness.
What they shared was a readiness for full-blooded conflict.[93]

7. CLEVELAND PLATFORM: QUICK VICTORY—LENGTHY WAR

'There are happy days in Cleveland.' Thus Wise began his first report
on the conference.[94] The mood of elation which had borne him to
Cleveland remained after the meeting opened. Both as regards locality
and viewpoint, diverse congregations were represented. Shortly after
opening, the conference proceeded to elect officers, and Wise was
chosen president, Elkan Cohn, his successor at Albany, vice-president,
and Max Lilienthal, his associate in Cincinnati, secretary. If any
permanent structure was to ensue, Wise would be in an advantageous
position to take first place; more immediately, the election placed
control in the hands of the Reform element and increased the suspicion
felt by the Orthodox.[95] 'It appeared', wrote Wise, 'that a union of
those men was a matter of impossibility, and one of the most influential
members of the old school prepared already for retiring.'[96] The
reference may be to Isaac Leeser, who, when challenged at this point,
indicated that, though a delegate, he was uncertain whether or not he
would participate in the conference.[97]

After the election it was proposed to appoint a committee to prepare

[93] In a farewell sermon delivered shortly before his death, Einhorn emphasized the
importance of retaining German as the language of American Reform Judaism. See
generally, Kaufmann Kohler (ed.), *David Einhorn Memorial Volume* (New York,
1911), 50, 436. His attitude at an earlier date appears in an article in which he
blamed the English element for putting a brake on Reform efforts, of which 'Recent
occurrences in the Emanu-El Congregation of New York' furnish evidence that speaks
loudly enough'; *Sinai*, 4 (Jul. 1859), 161.
[94] *Israelite*, 2 (26 Oct. 1855), 32.
[95] Ibid. See also *Occident*, 13 (Nov. 1855), 410.
[96] *Israelite*, 2 (26 Oct. 1855), 32.   [97] *Occident*, 13 (Nov. 1855), 410.

an agenda. Before the resolution could be put, Wise intervened and produced a platform which at once became the focus around which the business of the conference revolved. Wise's platform 'commenced with two important articles':

1. That all Israelites agree upon the divinity of the Bible, and
2. That the Talmud is acknowledged by all as the legal and obligatory commentary of the Bible.

With this declaration Wise was able to dissipate Orthodox suspicions and plaster together a union on the spot. The report in the *Israelite* (despite the self-praise, to be regarded as Wise's own) continues:

The reading of this sketch produced an immense effect. The doctor expounded his sketch in an eloquent address, during which the Rev. Isaac Leeser who sat on the other side of the hall, advanced gradually as far as to the chair, and his countenance beamed with delight. The orthodox ministers and delegates were so much surprised, that none of them was able to speak.[98]

The clause relating to the authority of the Bible was adopted without discussion. The second clause attracted closer examination. Various amendments were suggested, but eventually an agreed form of wording was accepted. Leeser proposed that the conference adjourn to August 1856, apparently believing that it had accomplished its work, and that, with the clauses relating to the Bible and the Talmud accepted, the adjourned session would attract a more representative gathering, at which plans for a union could be worked out. He thereupon left for home. Leeser knew that the conference was to meet on the following day, though he may have believed that it was not to take any major decisions.[99]

In fact the conference continued its sessions until 24 October.[100] The 'Articles of Union', as finally adopted, were as follows:

The conference of the rabbis and congregational delegates, assembled in Cleveland, actuated by the earnest desire to preserve the union of Israel and its religion by a mutual understanding and union, and convinced that the organization of a Synod is the most efficient means to attain this sacred aim, and whose legality and utility is taught in the Bible, Talmud and history— consider it their duty:
    To convene a synod, and call upon the American Jewish congregations in an extra circular, to send their ministers and delegates to the said synod.

---

[98] *Israelite*, 2 (26 Oct. 1855), 132.   [99] *Occident*, 413.
[100] *Israelite*, 2 (9 Nov. 1855), 149.

The conference also feels obliged to give utterance to the following points on which they unanimously agree to be the leading principles of the future synods.

(1) The Bible as delivered to us by our fathers and as now in our possession is of immediate divine origin and the standard of our religion.

(2) The Talmud contains the traditional, legal and logical exposition of the biblical laws which must be expounded and practised according to the comments of the Talmud.

(3) The resolutions of a Synod in accordance with the above principles are legally valid.

(4) Statutes and ordinances contrary to the laws of the land are invalid.[101]

This was not all. The conference appointed three different committees: one to settle a constitution for the synod and to frame a common liturgy (*Minhag America*); one (consisting of Rabbis Wise, Lilienthal, and Rothenheim, all of Cincinnati, with whom Merzbacher (of New York) was joined for a time) for ritual questions; and one for schools and textbooks. These committees were to report to the synod, which was to meet in Philadelphia in December 1856. Finally, the conference appointed a standing committee to see that its resolutions were carried out. This committee consisted of Wise and Lilienthal, together with Jacob L. Miller,[102] whom we have met before as president of Wise's congregation. Thus control was left in the hands of a Cincinnati group, which Wise dominated. He could be excused feeling well satisfied with the progress of events as he returned to Cincinnati to preside over the opening of Zion College.

Before the storm burst in the East, Wise seems to have had some inkling that he was being inconsistent in putting forward the Cleveland Platform. Immediately after setting it forth in the *Israelite* he adds 'we must protect ourselves against the accusation of having changed our views', which he sought to do by quoting from an earlier article advocating a synod. Having done this he adds:

What will the progressive men of Israel say to these articles of union? Will they not think their cause betrayed by those who advocated it for so many years? We hope not. We rather expect our friends place as much confidence in the advocates of progress, as not to suspect their sincerity. Progress and reform was, is and will always remain our watchwords as long as there is a misconception of Judaism, an abuse of its laws, or a schism between our life and our religion. But every attempt of improvement or progress must be

[101] *Israelite*, 2 (9 Nov. 1855), 149.
[102] Ibid. See also *Die Deborah*, 1 (2 Nov. 1855), 81.

based upon our laws. Our friends knew this, and our opponents know it now, we never sanctioned, and this is true of the rest of our friends in this country—never will give our sanction to illegal reforms, so we always did, and this we now declare publicly. There is no retracing, onward and forward are still our watchwords.[103]

When the conference was an aspiration, Reform was pushed into the wings and union held the stage; when the conference had become a reality, the Reform part of the scenery could again be brought into view. Wise closes the article on the note that he still proposes reforms, though, now expecting to lead a synod, he is willing to bow to its authority: 'we bow our neck before the highest tribunal, because we want peace and union, and for this we are ready to sacrifice any thing, principles excepted'. *Qui s'excuse s'accuse.* But Wise must have been surprised at the force of the indictment which was levelled against his handiwork. The mêlée which ensued coincided with the collapse of the Zion College, and the two fiascos put an end to his chance of emerging forthwith as the leader of a united American Jewry.

The attack came from Einhorn, who did not wait for the final report of the proceedings at Cleveland to get into the *Israelite* but prepared and launched his thunderbolt on the strength of the report that the authority of the Talmud had been accepted. Einhorn does not seem to have been the kind of man to fire one shot where he could fire two. By an unfortunate coincidence, Wise had given offence simultaneously with the Cleveland Conference by translating and publishing in the *Israelite* without permission Einhorn's inaugural sermon, and the offence was heightened by one of those incidents, known even in journals conducted with greater precision than the *Israelite*, whereby parts of the oration were placed in wrong sequence.[104] Einhorn promptly placed the worst construction on this error and fanned the flame of his own indignation accordingly. The president of the Har-Sinai Verein wrote to the editor of the *Israelite* protesting against the breach of copyright.[105] On the same day—5 November—Einhorn advertised his protest in a German paper published in Baltimore, complaining of the 'mutilation of my introductory sermon, by the Rev. Dr. Wise', and insinuating that the reason was 'that the omitted passages stand in little harmony with that FOUL peace of Cleveland'.[106]

[103] *Israelite*, 2 (9 Nov. 1855), 148.   [104] See *Occident*, 13 (Dec. 1855), 448.
[105] *Israelite*, 2 (16 Nov. 1855), 157; *Sinai*, 1 (Feb. 1856), 1.
[106] *Sinai*, 1 (Feb. 1856), 28; *Israelite*, 2 (16 Nov. 1855), 157.

Having set out this complaint, Wise replied that the 'mutilation' was a printer's error which had already been rectified; and he rebuked Einhorn for accusing him of 'impure motives and a foul treachery of the public confidence', adding 'thank God, we have the stomach of an ostrich, we can swallow the stones thrown at us'. Einhorn's attack on the Cleveland Conference he parried.

We can not take any notice of it, being written in a style becoming neither the station he occupies, nor the personal character of a scholar. As soon as the doctor, in a style becoming the dignity of the subject, will address us his remarks against the Conference, we are willing to enter the lists, and to explain the principles and views leading the same.[107]

The declaration of the Har-Sinai Verein took as its starting-point the second paragraph of the articles agreed upon at Cleveland, and set forth the grounds upon which the signatories offered their 'most decided protest'. Many Jews whose attachment to Judaism could not be questioned did not consider as binding the talmudic exegesis of the Bible and those who failed to carry out the rules of the Talmud could not be denied the name of Israelite. The Cleveland Platform

would condemn Judaism to a perpetual stagnation, consign its countless treasures, available for all times, to the narrow confines of an exclusive Jewish nationality, and expose to derision its entire historical development as well as the incontestible results of a wholesome biblical research. ... The declared legitimacy of talmudic authority cannot heal, but, on the contrary, will render permanent our unhealthy religious condition, which consists not in the present conflict of parties, but must be sought for in the demoralizing effects of an antagonism between prescriptive rules and the unyielding nature of religious and social wants. With the Talmud in hand it is no longer possible to obtain the honorable and efficient means of healing the gaping wound in the heart of Israel, and reforms bearing on public worship and the general conduct in life, can at best be only smuggled in by a disregard of law, and a resort to juridical trick and chicanery.[108]

Einhorn illustrated his point by reference to articles then appearing in the *Israelite* whereby the difficulties attendant on the law of *halitzah* were to be alleviated by a pre-marital agreement.

Instead of unlocking with great pomp every door and closet for the entrance of the Talmud, and at the same time to provide a means of escape from its powerful grasp by some back window, we on our part prefer to deny in the

[107] *Israelite*, 2 (16 Nov. 1855), 157.   [108] Ibid.

most unreserved and emphatic language, the legislative legitimacy as an opinion which has been left far in the rear of an improved religious knowledge.[109]

The difference was between those who believed that they could build on the talmudic system to accommodate it to changes in society and those who believed that the talmudic structure was altogether obsolete. The sting, however, came in the insinuation of personal ambitions.

We also appreciate peace in Israel as a precious boon; but a peace which necessarily degrades Judaism, our greatest boon, appears to us to be too dearly bought, and is in the highest degree of a precarious tenure, when a few men in the name of collective Israel set up articles of faith which deny to dissenters a place in the communion of professing Israelites. May the free American Israel keep a strict watch on hierarchal movements which would again forge its chains, though under the most charming lullabies of peace, now in the guise of dogmas, and ere long by a Minhag America. The plan of a consistory, which was originally intended to be established, is an omen of significant import. The great work of peace-making being once finished, and everything brought under one hood into a bishop's mitre—and nothing more reasonable but that the great united flock must needs have a chief pastor—and all is ready for the advent of Jewish Popes. Let us rather thank God for the blessings of religious liberty we enjoy in this country, equally secured to all denominations; and may we not put a yoke on our own shoulders which would interfere with the full expansion of the old and reformatory Judaism, and eventually reduce both to miserable caricatures.

The declaration as printed in the press[110] bears the names of the rabbi and president of the Har-Sinai Verein and adds 'Here follow all the names of the members of this congregation,' though the names themselves are not set forth in the printed version.

It is not difficult to sum up the difference between Wise and Einhorn. Wise was fighting for union, Einhorn for reform. Wise believed that if the disparate elements in American Jewry could be brought into one organization, an American *minhag* would emerge; Einhorn believed that an association except on the basis of a prior agreement as to principle was a 'foul peace'; and where Einhorn's principles presupposed that the new age demanded a new Judaism, Wise was content that the old should be touched up.

---

[109] *Sinai*, 1 (Feb. 1856), 28, referring to *Israelite*, 2/16 and *Occident*, 13 (Dec. 1855), 448 ff.
[110] The extracts here given are taken from the text printed in *Occident*, 13 (Dec. 1855), 448 ff.

The immediate polemics which arose out of the Cleveland Platform were extended enough; the open breach between the two groups of American reformers, between East and West, lasted for a quarter of a century. Indeed, Einhorn went out of the way to refer to the matter in the farewell address which he delivered on retiring from his pulpit in 1879. It was healed only after the Union of American Hebrew Congregations had come into being.

At the outset of this conflict Wise had not one but two weeklies through which to broadcast his views. This he did freely and at the top of his voice. Cleveland had brought within his grasp the possibility of sitting at the controls of a united American Jewry, and to enhance that possibility he was ready to summon arguments which he would not use in his conflicts with the Orthodox and to resort to almost any tactics in trying to discredit those who stood in his way.

In the polemics which filled the *Israelite* during the last weeks of 1855 and the beginning of 1856 we find Wise employing tactics with which the strife in Albany has made us familiar; he side-steps the points raised by his opponent and makes a counter-attack; he professes to disdain to reply to Einhorn but in the very same issue takes a lunge at him, though without mentioning his name; reversing the stand he had taken in the *Occident* a few years earlier he now sings songs in praise of the Talmud ('no Judaism without progressive reforms ... no reform without Talmud'); he even insinuates that Einhorn and his followers are atheists and hints that they ought to leave the Jewish community.[111]

An expression of satisfaction on the opposite flank provoked Wise as easily as did the direct attacks of his Reform critics. Isaac Leeser must have surprised his orthodox friends by joining forces with the heretic, and in his defence he pointed to the articles in the Cleveland Platform which accepted the authority of the Bible and the Talmud. 'Were these not welcome words?' he asked. 'Were they too little compensation for travelling seven hundred miles while labouring under a severe indisposition, in not the most pleasant season of the year? Indeed they were; and we should have travelled farther yet, and labored much to have been sure that this would have been the result of all the contests in which we have been engaged.'[112] He epitomized his satisfaction by declaring that he left 'having accomplished all we

[111] See *Israelite*, 2 (30 Nov., 14 Dec. 1855), 172, 188.
[112] *Occident*, 13 (Dec. 1855), 429.

looked forward to', adding, 'Yes, our opponents surprised us by their generalship in retreating from a dangerous position.'[113] To be commended by the spokesman of Orthodoxy as the general who led the retreat from Reform was the last thing Wise needed. 'If the Rev. Editor of *The Occident* supposes for one moment', he wrote on 21 December, 'that Isaac M. Wise repents what he ever said or wrote, he must be corrected.'[114]

The retort to Leeser is in the natural order of things, but it appears in the midst of an article headed 'He is a Traitor' in which he presents himself to the world as the one who has suffered and bled in the cause of Judaism, to be rewarded only with vilification. It shows an unshakeable belief in himself; without refinement of style it paints the portrait which Wise wanted the world to accept.

Isaac M. Wise, they say, is a traitor to the cause for which he worked incessantly for the last eight years. He is a traitor to the cause of reform and progress, according to his conceptions of the cause of Judaism. He has changed his opinion, he contradicts himself, and therefore we do not trust him—we have no confidence in his words; therefore we are opposed to the Cleveland Conference.

Shame and disgrace upon a man who dares betray a cause, for which he fought and struggled so many years, struggled so manly and boldly when he had scarcely bread to eat, or the means to support his family; struggled boldly and manly when all, a few friends excepted, opposed him with the enthusiasm of religious fanaticism; but now a traitor? without external cause or inducement on sudden a traitor? Why gentlemen? Is it for the sake of material gain? All the money you have ever made in this country, cannot change one iota of his ideas, he despises wealth, the treasures of California offer no inducement to him. He is this day as poor as he ever was, and considers himself as rich as ever before. Not one cent he has earned by the incessant work, not a penny he has yet made by the sacrifice of all earthly interests and joys, by reflecting and writing day and night for the sacred cause of Israel.

Honor? Ambition? You say, these spectres misled Isaac M. Wise, and he became a traitor to the cause which he, unaided and uncherished, advocated for the last eight years? The man whose name is known to every Jewish child in this country, is looked upon with profound respect even by his opponents; the man upon whom our European brethren look as the standard bearer of Judaism and enlightenment in this country, he who is known as a critical writer to the literati of this country and of Germany; the man who was the Rabbi of K. K. Anshe Emeth of Albany, and is now the cherished Rabbi of K. K. Benai Yeshurun of Cincinnati; he who had given the impulse to

[113] Ibid.   [114] *Israelite*, 2 (21 Dec. 1855), 196.

every little or great thing, that has been done in this country by his brethren during the last eight years; he who has continually been the axis, around which the sole American Jewish literature revolved; verily, he stands not in need of any honor, and has become perfectly indifferent to the voices of praise and blame; he has no ear for the cry of glory nor for the shout of treachery; he is perfectly deaf to the flattering sounds of acknowledgement, as to the outcries of men, who attempt to make themselves popular by attacking him.

What, please tell, what can make a traitor of a man who cares not for money, wealth, reputation or position? What can silence him who fears none, dreads none, and regards but the cause for which he labors? And if you cannot name the subject, please to confess plainly, that you do not understand Isaac M. Wise, or you take particular pain to misunderstand him. Please to confess, that you did not bestow sufficient care upon the literature of Israel to comprehend the words of him who has made this the problem of his life.

When, therefore, the reformers cry treachery, it is but an evidence of their frivolity, with which they look upon the books, and men who expound Judaism. If a man is thus self-deceived, that he considers himself and only himself an authority, a friend of truth and of Judaism, he is pitiably blind, and must be told, that there are some honest men besides him. If the Rev. Editor of the Occident supposes for one moment, that Isaac M. Wise repents what he ever said or wrote, he must be corrected. He must be told, that it requires patient and consistent investigation, profound research, and above all an entire renunciation of all carnal interests and pleasures, to comprehend the essence and system of Judaism. He must be told, that strong hopes are entertained, that as he had come so far as to appreciate the course of the reformers, time will come when he will appreciate the immense amount of good, which Isaac M. Wise has done with his 'History of the Israelitish Nation'. All of them must be told, that Isaac M. Wise can sustain his course of actions before the supreme throne of justice.

But if all this is a falsehood, are the proceedings of the Cleveland Conference impaired? The attempt to unite Israel for all great and noble purposes, is independent of the persons who laid the foundation. Is it right or wrong that Israel should be united in this country to build up institutions for the prosperity of Israel? Please answer. Is it right or wrong, that we should be one body in this country, in order to lay a firm foundation for the prosperity of Judaism on this American soil? Please reply. Is it right or wrong, that we should meet on a platform which every Israelite can acknowledge, and which leaves free scope for further reforms and improvements, according to the demands of all ages? Please, let us hear your objections. Is it right or wrong, that the Cleveland Conference refused to depart from the historical basis of Judaism, pointed out by three thousand years of history?

Please, give us some of your wisdom. Is it right or wrong, we ask in the name of common sense, that men uttered freely and boldly their own sentiments on religion? There was no hypocrite in Cleveland; they are men who understand the demands of the age and the doctrines of Judaism; men, whose learning and sincerity have been tried often enough to be known and appreciated.

The opposition waste in vain their words and their paper. Truth will triumph.[115]

When 1856 opened the first storms seemed to have blown themselves out, and Wise displayed a calmer mood. In February Einhorn began to publish the German monthly *Sinai*, and—naturally—a large part of the first number was devoted to questions arising out of the Cleveland Conference, one of Einhorn's articles on the subject being embellished with devastating comments on Wise's *History of the Israelitish Nation*. There was more than enough to goad Wise, and yet another diatribe against Einhorn filled the columns of the *Israelite*.

The immediate controversy spluttered out. Try as Wise might to keep it alive, Cleveland was killed in the war of words. There is no suggestion that the issue between Wise and Einhorn evoked any concern among the self-sufficient congregations, and no word came from the rabbis who had joined Wise in adopting the Cleveland Platform. Did they suspect, once they were out of Wise's presence, that the programme to which they had assented would make him an American Chief Rabbi? Was Einhorn's intellectual authority such that his word tore down the flimsy structure hastily put together at Cleveland? The laity had not advanced in outlook since Wise had arrived in the country ten years earlier; its concerns were localized, and they had not risen to Wise's vision of the broader needs that a united American Jewish community might satisfy: questions of theology were not among their concerns; questions of ritual each congregation could settle in its own way. Wise was still ahead of his time.

Though the engagement was broken off, for long years the war between Wise and the Reform rabbis of the East smouldered and sometimes flared: 'the spirit of faction outlived the cause of faction, and became in itself the new and prolific source of useless and endless strife'.[116] It must have been a saddened Wise, reflecting on defeat, who

---

[115] *Israelite*, 2 (21 Dec. 1855), 196.
[116] I have unfortunately mislaid the source of this wonderful quotation, though I think it is from James Bryce's *Holy Roman Empire*.

146 Cincinnati (1854–1900)

penned the article entitled 'Unser Nachtrab' ('Our Rearguard') which
appeared in *Die Deborah*:

America is a new world, with different people, different customs and different
phenomena. Climate and the products of nature are different here; the same
with the people. Three wholly distinct phenomena characterise America:
Extremes, quick changes, and Bigness. Everything here is extreme—the
weather, the temperature, the people and their affairs, religion, pleasure and
everything else is extreme and changes quickly so that one extreme follows
another in a quarter of an hour. Our mountains and our plains, our rivers,
our lakes and waterfalls, our woods and our forests, but also our railways
and our canals, our navigation and our commerce, our steamships and our
factories—everything is huge, immense, what is small disappears by the side
of what is big, and what is big in other countries here is scarcely visible.

Thus the people also are extreme, fickle and colossal in intelligence or in
folly. Thus it is with all religions, and thus with Judaism. Here the sensible,
thinking, observant Jew, who is true to the faith of his fathers, submitting to
the rational doctrines of religion without insulting or sacrificing his reason,
stands between two extremes, as huge as our mountains in their folly, by
which he will be opposed and condemned, not in a moderate fashion but
with disposition to extremism.

Nevertheless, things change, often very quickly, and what today is still
crass, thoughtless piety, is often extravagant atheism already by the morning,
and what is now frivolity changes in the morning to scrupulous observance
of the smallest and most trivial ceremonial laws. A man here who had thrown
off Judaism lost a child, and he rent his clothes, sat in the dust and let his
beard grow in the old way—and lay in the arms of the other extreme until
he had recovered from his fright. Sickness breaks out, people die, the poor
dear folk take to flight, into the arms of primeval Orthodoxy, so that Death,
cruel thing, shall not accomplish the dreaded result. This or that person will
be informed that religion here is only for the Plebs, for uneducated families;
again he wants to make a claim to being educated; he may be told that the
educated man must also be frivolous, must laugh and ridicule away that
which is sacred, must reject the higher things with mockery and derision, must
be an intellectual, a wit, a freethinker, a bigger, bigger, bigger intellectual; and
he must find everything unreasonable. He can't help knowing everything,
must always be infallibly right, must always be the most sagacious person—
and there you have a blown up fool—look, laughable as a peacock! He knows
neither God, duty nor Judaism, carries on business, eats, drinks, sleeps,
gambles, and dies. We need no Judaism and no religion, no doctrine and no
teacher 'I am clever and wise; no one cheats me so easily' is his song and his
conceit. But a man must still be buried by his rabbi and be buried according
to Jewish rites—yes, and certainly not in the municipal cemetery; the
children must be burdened with the ceremonial of Judaism, but certainly

not learn about it.... No, it is true that the folly is as big as the mountains.

Here, at present, the thinking, rational Jew stands between these two extremes, and should laugh if he doesn't have to cry.

But the rational outlook excels just here, in that it proceeds quietly and assuredly, unconcerned with all excrescences and wrongs, with all criticisms and all passing of judgment, with all hallucinations of folly and egoism, conscious of its aim towards a goal that is prepared by reason, set in its place by the hand of knowledge. The extremes constitute the rearguard; again they follow, blustering and insulting—they have to follow. They easily quarrel in the rearguard, and make a frightful noise; they easily bring the vanguard to a standstill; but it is no use. That which is wise remains wise forever, and cannot allow itself to be ensnared by any clamour, by any artful manœuvre. 'Don't look backwards. Otherwise you will be a loathsome pillar of salt. Forward! The rearguard must follow.'

But, Oh, supposing Amalek should fall suddenly on the rearguard—and kills the weary and the exhausted 'and does not stand in awe of God' and the dissatisfied become involved in commonplace verbiage and strange sophistry; then the rearguard must remain behind in the desolate waste to become Amalek's spoil. But Israel need not lose a man. 'With our young and our old will we go; for we have a feast of the Lord.' Israel must remain a unique body, and united pass through the desert on the way to the Promised Land; therefore the war against Amalek in the name of the Lord, and therefore listening to none but God and reason, and forward to the assured goal.[117]

There is little difficulty in casting the role of the leader who, unconcerned at the yelping dogs around him, keeps to the path pre-ordained by a Higher Power; it is the same hero who appeared to Wise in the dream which came to him as his ship approached New York. It is strange that a man whose performance in controversy showed unmitigated ferocity should see himself as the incarnation of Wordsworth's 'Happy Warrior',

> Whose high endeavours are an inward light
> Which makes the path before him always bright
>
> .   .   .   .
>
> More skilful in self-knowledge, even more pure,
> As tempted more; more able to endure,
> As more exposed to suffering and distress.

His was not that kind of serenity. Repeatedly and for years he

---

[117] *Die Deborah*, 1 (9 May 1856), 305.

exhibited himself to the American Jewish public as the one who had
been slandered and misrepresented merely because he had advocated
forward-looking measures, the innocent victim of opponents filled
with personal rancour.

In October 1857 he made another journey to Baltimore, in connection this time with relations between the United States and Switzerland. As will be shown later, his conduct on that occasion suggests
that a propensity for taking command may have been stimulated by
a desire to show 'the Easterners' what he could do. As he set out, he
painted for the readers of the *Israelite* a picture contrasting the high
hopes he had entertained on his previous journey with the doleful
sentiments that had come to oppress him on the second. 'We imagined
to [*sic*] Israel's glorious future smile through the rosy curtains which
hides the billows of future days in the rosy curtains of time.' The
vision had vanished. His ideas had been 'dissolved into air and gas'.
And why?

Our motives were questioned; 'it is ambition that prompts him,' was the
outcry of our opponents. Yes, gentlemen, while you had the ambition to do
nothing, it was our ambition to work for the benefit of our people; while you
delighted in overthrowing, we took pride in building up. Now, spirit of
negation, behold thy work and the monument set to thy work. On the other
side, petty leaders and petty scribblers, prompted by envy, and agitated by
malice, insulted, slandered, outraged us in public print, to spit gall in our
cup of life, in order to disgust us with all public affairs ... The orthodox
cried: Heresy! the reformers vociferated: Treason! and the people on whom
we did not call personally, betrayed no token of life, or sympathy for either
side. So we were discouraged, disgusted, and a sentiment of indifference
overcame us, and we relaxed.[118]

This is a sample of what appeared many times and, once again, its
tenor has a similarity to that of the dream. Wise's bent for controversy
had found a broader outlet than disputes within his congregation;
but, as in Albany, he still showed himself hot-headed, and relied on
the blustering force of his personality rather than on the soundly
constructed logic of his position. Where Wise's self-portrayal in *Die
Deborah* should gain wider acceptance is in its suggestion of the
persistence which in the end left the 'rearguard' behind.

Twenty years were to elapse before the 'bold plans' which Wise
brought with him to Cincinnati came to anything like fruition. He

[118] *Israelite*, 4 (23 Oct. 1857), 124. See ch. 3 sect. 11 below.

was resilient in defeat; he continued his agitation; on his own authority he published the books which the organization he had tried to set up should have produced.

8. MINHAG AMERICA

The synod which it was intended should follow the Cleveland Conference did not meet, and there was no body which could authorize action upon the recommendations made by its committees. Nevertheless, Wise pushed ahead with the proposed 'book of common prayer' for the Jews of America. The result was the *Minhag America* prayer-book, used by many congregations in the United States until, nearly forty years after it first appeared, Wise withdrew it in favour of the *Union Prayer Book*.

Minhag America can be described as the most important among Wise's many books. History and theology interested a limited few; the market for Jewish literature was thin; but a prayer-book was a minimum necessity. Aided by Wise's promotion, *Minhag America* attained a certain vogue and therefore came into the hands of a larger number of people. It was a practical embodiment of his quest for unity among the Jews of America. Though described as a collective enterprise ('By the committee of the Cleveland Conference'), it was regarded as Wise's very own child. He advanced its claims without inhibition, and attempts to supersede it aroused his protective instincts.

The promulgation of a liturgy for the Jews of America was something for which Wise had striven almost from the moment he had landed in America: he had brought a plan before the stillborn *beth din* which Lilienthal had established, and had the conference which Leeser and he had called materialized it would have found a place on the agenda.[119] Now that he occupied a more commanding position, it had become not less urgent to act. Not only had several Reform prayer-books appeared in Europe, but American rabbis too were entering the field. In 1854 Leo Merzbacher of New York had produced a ritual for Temple Emanu-El. More provoking, in view of the post-Cleveland disputes, Einhorn announced, in May 1856, that his new prayer-book was ready. To the public, the form of prayers was a touchstone of Reform far beyond any learned disputation. Wise had to have a hand.

---

[119] See ch. 2 sect. 5 above.

'While the polemical storm outside raged furiously, the three of us, Kalisch, Rothenheim and Wise, were at work together almost every evening, engaged on this task.'[120] And earlier Wise had described the basis on which this joint effort proceeded:

We had all agreed on the principles that were to mark the prayer-book. It was out of the question to retain the old prayers unchanged, because the belief in the coming of a personal Messiah descended from the house of David had disappeared from among the people. The return to Palestine, the restoration of the Davidic dynasty, of the sacrificial cult, and the accompanying priestly caste were neither articles of faith nor commandments of Judaism, while the lamentations over oppression and persecution, and the accompanying cry for vengeance were untrue, and immoral as far as American Jews were concerned. The cabalistical portions which had crept into the prayer-book, and the obstinate adherence to the doctrine of the bodily resurrection, were regarded as unjustified. We were also agreed that the Sabbath service, including the sermon, should not last longer than two hours. And this was made quite possible by our adopting the triennial cycle of readings from the Torah. We determined further that as little change as possible should be made in the order of the prayers and in the typical prayers; in fact, no more than the principles we had adopted and the length of time of the public service was necessary. We resolved to publish an English and German, as well as a Hebrew, version of the prayers, and that it should be left to the congregation to decide upon what language it wished to use in the rendition of the service.[121]

'*Minhag America: The Daily Prayers, Part I, Revised and Compiled by the Committee of the Cleveland Conference, Translated by Isaac M. Wise*', appeared in October 1857 and was immediately brought into use by Congregation B'nai Jeshurun. It has two distinct sections which are bound in one—the Hebrew original of the prayers beginning on the right, and the English translation on the left. 'Pray in the language thou understandest best' is the injunction at the head of the English section. There was a companion edition with a German translation.

Compared with some of the Reform prayer books which preceded it (and certainly with the *Union Prayer Book*, which replaced it), *Minhag America* is cast in a conservative mould, and close inspection of the contents is needed to determine how far a Reform alloy has modified a traditional content. (A summary is provided in the Appendix

---

[120] *The World of My Books*, 23.
[121] *Reminiscences*, 343. See also *Israelite*, 3 (20 Feb. 1857), 260.

to this chapter.) *Minhag America* comprises two volumes. The Hebrew portion of volume I runs into 144 pages. The rubric is given in Hebrew, and a few sentences regarding prayer taken from Hebrew literature, the first from the *Shulhan aruch*, precede the *Mah tovu* prayer recited on entering the synagogue.

It then goes on to give the prayers for the three daily services, for Sabbaths and New Moons, for the 'High Feasts' (as the festivals of Pesach, Shavuoth and Succoth were termed), for Purim and Hanukkah and the Ninth of Ab. There is grace before and after meals, night prayers, the burial service, and prayers for mourners. The concluding portion of the Hebrew prayers (*Seder haberachot*) contains the full order of blessings customary in Orthodox prayer books, including blessings for putting on the *tallit* (prayer shawl), laying *tefillin* (phylacteries), various kinds of food, thunder and lightning, and seeing men renowned for their wisdom, religious or secular. This section, possibly through an oversight, does not appear in the English version. Volume II, which appeared ten years after volume I, contained the prayers for Rosh Hashanah and Yom Kippur.

Minhag America was not an Orthodox prayer-book. The traditional liturgy is curtailed; talmudic excerpts are omitted, as were some of the occasions for the recital of the Kaddish; some of the particularistic references are modified, but some prayers for the final ingathering of the Jewish people remain. The Kiddush, customarily a blessing over wine, comprises in both Hebrew and English a blessing over bread.[122] The compilers worked hastily and in isolation, and it is easy to find inconsistencies in their work. The changes they made may betray a theology that was as radical as any, but even more important is the impression of continuity which the editors wished to convey. They were at pains to preserve the contours of the traditional prayer-book. The old needed to be modified—to be purged of accretions which were incomprehensible or repetitive and which therefore lent themselves to indecorum, or which lent themselves to the charge, horrible in Wise's eyes, of being irrational, mystical, or kabbalistical,[123] or which did not reflect the American Jewish status as equal citizen in a free republic. These modifications had to be kept to the minimum, so that the worshipper would continue to see before him something which looked like the *siddur*—the traditional Hebrew prayer book—on which he

---

[122] See *Minhag America*, 49 (Eng.), 58 (Heb.).
[123] See *The World of My Books*, 23.

had been brought up and would be able to have the service performed in the language and on the lines to which he was accustomed. In Wise's words, 'They'—Wise means his colleagues and himself—'adhered anxiously to tradition; they had no desire to found a new religion or to institute a new cult. They wished to recast the old and traditional prayers reverently, so that they might be brought into accord with the religious consciousness of the time and the democratic principles of the new fatherland.'[124]

As with his *History*, so with his prayer-book: Wise believed that with a few quick touches of the pen, differing attitudes could be reconciled. The prayer-book had the more direct object of uniting the different elements in the American Jewish community, and his vision even soared to its finding a lodgement beyond the Jewish world. His aspirations emerge in an article he wrote when the new liturgy was introduced into his own synagogue:

All obnoxious passages and useless repetitions are either omitted, or appropriately changed, the Synagogual laws and customs are faithfully regarded, the old substance is regenerated in a new and beautiful form, ... The orthodox has the substance of the old Hebrew prayers, the reformer is not offended by prayers for the restoration of the sacrifices, and Levitic priesthood, the republican hears not the petitions after a king of Israel, yet the Messiah idea, in its highest signification, speaks from every part of the book, ... established theories of the legal reformers are fully incarnated in this mode of worship which fully deserves its name, *Minhag America*, for it is as thoroughly American, republican and cosmopolitical, as it is thoroughly Jewish, and pacificating the conflicting theories on Jewish worship. Every man of any creed can now pray with us.[125]

Wise attributed the ten-year delay in publishing the second part of *Minhag America* to the attitude taken by his opponents to the first part: 'Like every other thing proceeding from our humble pen, the *Minhag America* was so terribly decried by the orthodox and the radicals, that we could not issue the second part.'[126] The most likely explanation for the delay is that Wise had over-extended himself financially on the production of the first part and that the distractions of the Civil War delayed the appearance of the second.

Wise was stretching things by purporting to act in the name of the Cleveland Conference, but the same effrontery enabled him to ride

---

[124] See Appendix at the end of this chapter.
[125] *Israelite*, 4 (23 Oct. 1857), 24.   [126] Ibid. 12 (24 June 1866), 4.

objections to his conduct. In the *Asmonean* that August the editor
referred to the forthcoming appearance of *Minhag America*.[127] He
quoted from an article which Leeser had published in the *Occident*
protesting against Wise's having assumed the right on behalf of the
Cleveland Conference to revise the prayer-book and against *Minhag
America*'s being offered to the world when the committee had not
reported to any synod or conference, and observed that in this matter
what Leeser said was 'entitled to more than ordinary attention'.[128]

Of course Wise had a reply. It is a typical sample of his dialectic.

The Country is Safe.

The country is safe! for the Asmonean has 'popped the question,' about the
Committee on the Minhag America. Zeus is great, so is the editor of the
Asmonean, and so are the productions of his pen; and he says, Isaac Leeser
is a great man, (there was a time when he maintained the contrary), a
theologian of the first class; we doubt not Mr. L. is now very proud—and he
protests against the committee's right, to have their products printed and
published; hence the editor of the Asmonean, troubled in his conscience, and
tickled by some correspondent, 'pops the question.' Now the country is
safe.

The Asmonean, it appears, needs again [to] be galvanized by some spicy
articles against some popular men or measures, as pale death thrones on its
forehead; the times of peace and good will would not suit it, nor can it, by
fair means or original products, render itself interesting, and the editor pops
the question, commences a quarrel with the committee on Minhag America,
to have some quarrel, controversy, literary rowdyism as last year, that attention be attracted to the Asmonean —

But hold on; since last year we have also become one year older, and know
the imprudence of providing food and nutriment to the starving Asmonean,
in which we have not seen an original article for the last six months, at least.
This, of course, is not the fault of its talented editor, who is unable to write
on any subject except lead mines and iron works. It is solely the fault of the
indifferent, lazy, careless and sleepy public, especially the learned, who would
not do anything for the public weal, through the agency of the Asmonean.
We go with the majority, therefore we shall not provide vitality for the
Asmonean, and shall never answer what the learned editor of that paper shall
say or write.

The Committee on the Minhag America have a right to publish their
labors, even without the permission of the editors of the Asmonean and
Occident, and in the absence of a Synod, against which the correspondents

[127] *Asmonean*, 15 (28 Aug. 1857), 156.   [128] Ibid. 242.

of the Asmonean were so violently opposed; they may report to the congregations on nobody's except their own authority, even without the additional luster of the two editors mentioned above, and the congregations will render a verdict, independent of all the ill-will peeping through the remarks of the two gentlemen.

If the editor of the Occident opposes the labors of the committee on Minhag America with blind and desperate zeal, he is excusable in one respect; he might do it in behalf of his religious views and his party, and every man has a right to his opinion. What excuse is there in store for the Asmonean in opposing the labors of legal reform? This paper has already served all masters, borne all colors, sworn to all flags and courted all parties' favor. It has been hyper orthodox, conservative, reform, radical, a railroad, iron and lead works, book trade and theatrical periodical, and sometimes it had all these colors in one week. Why would this color of the committee not suit it? The editor has not seen the book in question, nor is he able to read it if he should happen to see one. He does not say that this or that part of the book or translation is not according to his learned views; no, he pops the question, in order to throw suspicion on the book. Is not this fair?

We do hereby inform the editor of the Asmonean, that none of the committee does care for his saying, writing, supposing, believing, printing, etc., etc., and that it is ridiculous, for a man like him to assume the right to debate on religious questions, or write on religious subjects in a mining journal. It looks, indeed, very funny, to meet with such 'stuff' in America, and in the year 1857.

When we, 12 years ago, came to this country, the Hazanim system was the ruling principle of the Synagogue. Any man who thought he could read Hebrew, sing a song, or read somebody's prayers or sermons, if he could not earn a living by any other means, thought himself called to be a Jewish minister. These very men gradually considered themselves capable also of ruling the Jewish press, and so they did. Learning and knowledge were obnoxious to them. Liberal exposition of religious questions was considered heresy and infidelity. They had nothing to boast upon, and they rode upon the hobby horse of orthodoxy. So they canonized themselves, wore white handkerchiefs, styled themselves Reverends, wore silk gowns, preached, wrote, cut sacred faces, made a farce of the Synagogue, and represented us as a parcel of fools.

This Hazanim system is routed, ruined, sinks into oblivion, and we wish it a happy journey. Its representatives, the Occident and Asmonean, still sustain a pitiable existence. Mr. Leeser's ignorance in Jewish matters is no secret, he does not deny it.—The editor of the Asmonean can not even read Hebrew. Still they could be the editors of Jewish papers as long as the Hazanim System with its ignorance predominated. But now it is too late. Let Mr. Lyon continue his praiseworthy labors in iron works, railroad and mining affairs, or umbrella making; but let him not meddle in Jewish affairs, he is not fit for it in this day of merciless criticism. Let him attend to his own business, and not render himself ridiculous by meddling with matters and things which belong not to his province, and of which he understands least of all. Our school boys know more about it than he does. But if he meddles let him stand the ridicule with which he will and must meet.

This settles forever the question with the editor of the Asmonean, who would have done better in making umbrellas than meddling in theological questions. The country would have been safe without him popping the question.[129]

Sinai (Einhorn's monthly), it is needless to say, was scornful of Wise's effort. *Minhag America* was duly torn apart in three articles (March–August 1858) written by Dr Elkan Cohn, Wise's successor in Albany.[130] Cohn's distaste for *Minhag America* was not based on theological grounds only. Wise naturally promoted his new prayer-book, and after the congregation in Cincinnati which he was serving, what more obvious place was there in which to do so than the congregation in Albany which he had been instrumental in bringing to birth? But the incumbent rabbi seems to have been embarrassed by the idea that the path mapped out by the founding rabbi was the one which the congregation would follow again. According to a communication which Cohn addressed to *Sinai* in January 1858, Wise used the occasion of a visit to Albany towards the end of 1857 to put pressure on Congregation Anshe Emeth to adopt *Minhag America*, to the embarrassment of Cohn's relations with his congregation.[131]

Wise's keenness for *Minhag America* betrayed the love of an affectionate father, rather than the mercenary keenness of a salesman. When the Cleveland Conference became a matter of history, *Minhag America* remained a source of contention between Wise and the Reform rabbis of the East. After it had been put to sleep by a rabbinical conference in which Wise participated, he reissued it. When the book was discarded by the one New York congregation which used it, he appears

---

[129] *Israelite*, 4 (11 Oct. 1857), 76. *Asmonean* regularly gave space to commercial and financial news; hence Wise's allusions to its editor's expertise in regard to lead mines and iron works.

[130] *Sinai*, 3: 837, 978, 995.

[131] Ibid. 2 (Jan. 1858), 788; (Apr. 1858), 889. *Israelite*, 4 (4 Dec. 1857), 172, had reported the decision. Cohn resisted the introduction of *Minhag America*, and the congregation reversed its decision with the result that the president and two members of the board resigned. See Naphtali Rubinger, 'Albany Jewry of the Nineteenth Century', 218 ff.

to have promoted another (B'nai Maimunim) which would use it, and when in 1873 he suddenly decided to take a New York pulpit, bringing *Minhag America* to New York was one of the reasons he gave. By 1870 the prayer-book was being used by fifty or sixty congregations.[132] When finally Wise withdrew it in favour of the *Union Prayer Book*, there was considered to be some self-abnegation in his action.[133] The springs of this intense love we do not know: perhaps the book symbolized the union—under his leadership—of American Jewry for which he was striving; perhaps the derision of his critics redoubled his love for his child.

9. THE ESSENCE OF JUDAISM

Though the revision of a prayer-book gave expression to a theological point of view, the elaboration of a theology was no part of its object. Rather, it related to Wise's grand aim of building up a visible edifice of American Judaism; but the edifice would need appropriate theological foundations, and Wise wrote explicitly in that field. These writings responded to practical needs also: his two weekly newspapers had appetites which had to be satisfied. Constant reading gave him access to a vast corpus of literature, and he had an energetic mind which could draw on it immediately in reaction to events as they arose. Under such conditions consistency is not to be expected, and it is difficult to isolate a well-rounded statement of beliefs. One consistent thread, his stress on Sinaitic revelation and his belief that Mosaic teaching was being consummated in the American system, has already been mentioned.[134] Here was no isolated off-the-cuff observation but a glimpse of a thread that was expressed throughout his life.[135]

Divine revelation to Moses on Mount Sinai was basic to his system. Not only was it witnessed by the tribes of Israel, but it was accepted by Christianity and Islam and therefore represented universal religion.

---

[132] *Israelite*, 18 (29 July 1879), 8.

[133] See David Philipson, *Centenary Addresses and Other Papers* (Cincinnati, 1919), 26.

[134] See p. 94 above. One area in regard to which consistency is difficult to establish is the authority of the Talmud. His controversies with Leeser and Einhorn at different periods on this subject have been mentioned. In *Judaism: Its Doctrines and Duties* (Cincinnati, 1872) he makes the categorical statement 'American rabbis, the author included, having declared in various conferences the authority of the Talmud abrogated, it could only be consulted as a historical record' (pp. 5–6).

[135] Reference may be made to the quotations collected by Dena Wilanksy in *From Sinai to Cincinnati* (New York, 1937), 115–27.

'We know of God, His divine essence and nature, precisely what Moses told us and no more.'[136] The Declaration of Independence, the American Constitution, and the political system that flourished under their rays represented the ultimate fulfilment of what had been begun under Moses and called for the recasting of the ephemeral elements in the Judaism that had come down from the past.

Practical needs dictated an organized statement of Jewish beliefs. American Judaism needed not only a prayer-book but apologetic literature as well, so Wise set about providing it. The result was *The Essence of Judaism*,[137] first published in 1861. Eleven years later this sixty-five page book was reworked into a catechism entitled *Judaism: Its Doctrines and Duties*.[138] This book was intended as a confirmation textbook (the ritual of confirmation having become an accepted part of the Reform programme) and was stated by its author to contain 'a complete abstract of Judaism and a guide to a better understanding and appreciation of the Bible'.

In his 'Introduction' to the later version, Wise states that he 'reads the Bible from its own standpoint, and proves that it contains the complete and rational system of religion for all generations and countries'. Having a basis so universal, Wise saw in Judaism a future as a 'universal religion': 'Judaism is the religion of the future generation, as it was the teacher of the past ones.'[139]

The statements propounded in *The Essence of Judaism* are supported by references to biblical proof-texts, rather than by the texts themselves. In the Preface Wise says that the pupil 'must find, read and understand' the biblical passages himself and, showing a respect for Hebrew similar to that exhibited in *Minhag America*, he adds:

The Bible is Hebrew and should be read in that language to be properly understood. No translation can fully replace the original text. Those who do not understand the Hebrew will not always succeed in ascertaining the sense which the author discovers in some passages, but they will succeed in most instances. Teachers are expected to have the Hebrew Bible before them, if the pupil reads the passages referred to in English, in order to improve the translation if necessary to approximate the original text.[140]

---

[136] *Israelite*, 7 (14 Dec. 1860), 90. See Andrew F. Key, *The Theology of Isaac Mayer Wise* (Cincinnati, 1962), 13–14, and the sources there cited.

[137] *The Essence of Judaism for Teachers and Pupils and for Self-Instruction* (Cincinnati, 1861).

[138] Published in Cincinnati, 1872.   [139] *Judaism: Its Doctrines and Duties*, 6.

[140] *The Essence of Judaism*, 5.

A passage such as this is a useful proof-text for those who would demolish the contention that reform is necessarily anti-Hebraic; further enquiries, however, to which it gives rise show that the practical implementation of this point of view had little place in Wise's concerns.

In *The Essence of Judaism*, Wise defines religion as 'to worship God by doing His will'. The existence of God is testified by 'nature, history, intellect and the revelation'. Israel's religion is revealed by God to Israel directly, and indirectly through Moses and the Prophets (Deut. 5: 19–30, and 17: 13–22). The revealed matter is preserved intact in the twenty-four books of sacred Scripture. Why revelation? Man, Wise says, was not as wicked as he was foolish, and his motives were better than his judgement.[141] 'Therefore God revealed His will to, and made a covenant with the men of his choice, for the benefit of all mankind, to teach them to distinguish properly between right and wrong, justice and injustice, virtue and vice, to know what is acceptable to God and beneficial to man, and what is abominable before God and injurious to man.' Covenants between God and man are several—with Adam, with Noah, with the patriarchs, and finally with Israel.[142] 'The promises which God made to Israel are ... To be his chosen people with a special mission to perpetuate and promulgate His will, and therefore they should stand under His special protection.' Israel's obligations under the covenant are set out in the precepts of the Bible, which Wise divides into four categories, using the terminology found in the Bible, and presented sequentially in one of the familiar prayers of the daily evening service.[143]

First among the four categories are *toroth* ('Doctrines or the light of truth'), which he compares to 'the universal laws of nature' coming 'direct from God everlasting'. *Toroth* themselves are divided into four 'cardinal doctrines'—(a) God, (b) Man, (c) God's government and (d) the Hope of Mankind.[144] Expounding the fourth, Wise takes an optimistic view of the impending fulfilment of the Messianic dream before the eyes of his readers.

History testifies to the progress of truth, justice and prosperity. Every new

---

[141] *The Essence of Judaism*, 10.   [142] Ibid. 12, 14, 16.

[143] This device had been used by teachers of Judaism for many generations. A notable example, belonging to Wise's own day, is to be found in Samson Raphael Hirsch's *Horeb* (Altona, 1847). See Noah H. Rosenbloom, *Tradition in an Age of Reform* (Philadelphia, 1976), 187 ff.

[144] *The Essence of Judaism*, 18–31.

discovery in science is an onward step to the triumph of truth. Every century of history is a step forward toward the sovereignty of justice. Therefore it must be true that not by miracles but by natural development of the original principle and plan of Providence truth and justice will universally triumph (Isaiah XIV, 18 etc.).[145]

The second in the four categories are the *mitsvoth* ('Commandments or moral laws'), which are the laws of Sacred Scripture having a direct object in view and, like the *toroth*, were revealed directly by God.[146] The third and fourth categories, *hukkim* and *mishpatim*, were not so revealed, but at God's command were taught by Moses to Israel. They have an indirect object in view; they contain a mutable element, which accounts for the changes recorded in the Mishnah and Talmud.[147]

As to the distinction between *hukkim* and *mishpatim*, the former are 'religious observances' for which Wise appears to use 'worship' as an alternative expression. Since they belonged to the category of *hukkim*, the biblical prescriptions concerning worship were not immutable, which was of great importance since in the period in which he was working controversies concerning the sacrificial system were always being raised. Sacrifice was the national mode of worship prescribed by the Law because when the Law was given to Israel it was common to all nations. Sacrifice was not the only mode of worship acknowledged in the Bible; and Wise was able to deduce that 'the sacrifices and other ceremonies were merely symbolic actions' required to convey ideas or sentiments to weak or gross minds. Within the Temple the words and music were the main portions of the service. Outside, their place was an exclusive one: they sufficed to instruct and edify the intelligent. Jews were under a duty to be intelligent, and if the Temple should be rebuilt no sacrifices would be made there.[148]

Finally, the *mishpatim* were 'such Biblical laws whose direct object is the dispensation of justice'. These were (*a*) organic laws, which related to the government, (*b*) sanitary laws, and (*c*) penal laws. A staunch republican such as Wise evidently felt some discomfort at the institution of a monarchy under the Organic Laws of the Bible, and

---

[145] Ibid. 30.
[146] Ibid. 32–57. Wise emphasizes the pre-eminence of the Decalogue, 'which contains, expressed or implied, the whole moral law' (p. 32).
[147] Ibid. 58–80.   [148] Ibid. 75.

he concluded that it is 'much more a republican chief called king'.[149]

Wise later described *The Essence of Judaism* as a 'portrayal of biblical Judaism in its entirety',[150] and made it clear that the omission of talmudic references was deliberate.[151] For all that, his approach was essentially midrashic; Scripture was not critically analysed but had rational doctrines read into it.

The presence of a mutable element in the heritage of biblical religion raises the question as to who had authority to change or discard. Wise favoured a synod, but in the absence of a synod regarded the individual congregation as empowered to act.[152] The latter practice prevailed.

Another field of Wise's literary activity was the criticism of Christian origins, an area of some practical importance in view of the activity of the conversionists. In 1868 he wrote *The Origins of Christianity*. It runs to 535 pages and was described as a critical investigation of the Acts of the Apostles with the aid of rabbinic sources.[153] Here he made the identification of Acher (Elishah ben Abuyah) of the Talmud with the Apostle Paul, a claim which has received no credence at the hands of scholars.[154] In 1874 he wrote *The Martyrdom of Jesus of Nazareth—* 'A historic critical treatise of the last chapters of the Gospel, designed to show that it was actually the Romans who were responsible for the crucifixion'. Between 9 July 1869 and 1 April 1870 he published in the *Israelite* ten chapters of *Jesus Himself*, a work which he did not complete. Four years earlier Wise had been confident that there had never been a Jesus.[155] Later he changed his view and, discarding all the miraculous elements in the Gospel story as devoid of historical worth, asserted that Jesus was a 'Pharisean doctor of the Hillel school'.[156]

Any admission that Jesus had really lived involved no concession as to the truth of the characteristic doctrines of Christianity: obviously the miracles surrounding Christian origins ran directly counter to his identification of religion with reason. He objects that Christianity is 'a warfare with philosophy and science, and sustained by constant

[149] *The Essence of Judaism, 78.*   [150] *The World of My Books, 28.*
[151] Ibid. 31.   [152] See sect. 30 below.   [153] *The World of My Books, 31.*
[154] See *Jewish Encyclopedia*, v. 138.   [155] *Israelite*, 13 (7 July 1865), 4.
[156] See Samuel Sandmel, in *Essays in American Jewish History* (Cincinnati, 1958), 325.

appeals to credulity and ignorance'.[157] 'Whatever parts (of the New Testament) are good and true are not original, they are taken from the Old, and those parts which are original are neither good nor true.'[158] The doctrine of the Trinity involved giving up the position of pure monotheism. Original Sin, Incarnation, and Vicarious Atonement likewise incurred his disdain.[159]

At the level of doctrine, Wise's polemic against Christianity could manifest itself in lengthy argumentation; when he lighted upon manifestations close at hand he expressed himself in a contemptuous snort. In May 1861 Pius IX, at the request of John Lynch, Roman Catholic bishop of Toronto, appointed a place of pilgrimage at a church near Niagara Falls, with indulgences for those of the faithful who should make the pilgrimage. The transplantation of Old World 'obscurity and ignorance' on to the free soil of North America was not to Wise's taste. He reprinted the papal decree embedded in an article which began with the heading 'The Folly of the Century' and closed with the words 'this is one of the several comedies enacted by Rome during the last twenty years to the amusement of the literate and the edification of the illiterate masses. No danger yet.'[160] The erection of a shrine was something that was contrary to the 'rationality of the age', out of place in America, and he wished to believe that such institutions could not grow on American soil.

Wise also emerged as a novelist—in fact as 'The American Jewish Novelist', to use the pseudonym under which his imaginative pieces appeared in serial form in the *Israelite*. In 1859 he published *The Combat of the People; or, Hillel and Herod: A Historical Romance of the Time of Herod I*. A year later *The First of the Maccabees* appeared. (Over thirty years later it was published in Jerusalem in a French translation.) By this time Wise was old enough to take a detached view of his early work: 'God forgive me', he reflected, 'for writing ten short stories and historical novels in English and German, and later, for manufacturing rhymed verses in both languages.'[161]

[157] *Origins of Christianity*, 535.   [158] *Israelite*, 9 (4 July 1862), 5.
[159] Ibid. 3 (13 Feb. 1852), 252; 7 (28 Nov. 1860), 100; (21 Feb. 1862), 268.
[160] Ibid. 7 (24 May 1861), 372. There was much else in the article deriding these expressions of religion.
[161] *The World of My Books*, 50–1.

10. FIGHTING FOR JEWISH RIGHTS

These exertions—reorganizing his synagogue and school, starting a college, planning a union of synagogues, revising the prayer-book, editing two weekly papers, writing novels and poetry—did not exhaust Wise's interests or his capacity for action. His polemics within the Jewish community were matched by his 'unbridled belligerency'[162] against its enemies outside: missionaries, denigrators of Judaism, those who swerved by however so little from the American principle of separation of Church and State, as well as obvious antisemites, drew instant retaliation from his pen.

The occasions on which Wise felt called upon to act thus are too numerous, and the torrent of words too copious, to permit a representative selection of these writings. The instances cited here came early in his career in Cincinnati, when Wise had not been three years in the city and the *Israelite* was scarcely established.

When the *Churchman* for 24 March 1855 protested against a rabbi being asked to reply to the toast of 'the Clergy' at a banquet of the New York Legislature, the *Israelite* devoted almost a page and a half to the matter;[163] and when the Speaker of the California legislature made some antisemitic remarks, Wise gave the matter nearly two pages, addressing the offender as 'Haman II', 'Your Majesty', and 'Your Holiness'.[164]

In the following year, Wise had occasion to direct his fire nearer home. On 28 October 1856 the governor of the State of Ohio, Salmon P. Chase, issued a Thanksgiving Proclamation which referred to Thanksgiving as a custom 'highly becoming a Christian people'. Apart from this, the proclamation contained no word of a Christological character; but the governor invited the people to give thanks not only 'for the products of our Agriculture, and of our Arts, for the intercourse of Commerce; for the preservation of Health; for homes endeared by sweet family affections' and much else of this kind, but also 'for the mercies of Redemption and for the hopes of Immortality'.

In a column and a half of the *Israelite* Wise turned his artillery on the governor, going so far as to complain that the Proclamation read like 'a bull of a Pope of the Middle Ages'.[165]

---

[162] See Jacob R. Marcus, *The Americanization of Isaac Mayer Wise* (Cincinnati, 1969), 19.

[163] *Israelite*, 1 (20 Apr. 1855), 324.   [164] Ibid. (11 May 1855), 345.

[165] Ibid. 3 (14 Nov. 1856), 148.

With the man whom he attacked so vigorously Wise had previously been friendly. In the previous year, Chase had been one of the speakers at the banquet which marked the opening of Zion College, and one can readily imagine that the language of the proclamation, framed in the rhetorical terms that had become *de rigueur* for such occasions, was not meant to carry any theological implications. So Chase protested,[166] but Wise was hard to mollify. 'The insult offered in such a document to any portion of the community cannot be eradicated by a private letter ... We are honestly tired of protesting every year against the illiberal and unconstitutional Proclamations.'[167]

One week after his attack on Governor Chase, Wise had the occasion to say in a different context, 'The doctrine of a Christian state is perfectly dreadful to us.'[168] Wise looked upon separation of church and state as one of the sheet anchors of American liberty. As he reacted to events he could take the doctrine far beyond its legal form and declare: 'The entire and complete separation of Church and State appears so desirable a policy to us, that we abhor the interference of religious ministers in political affairs.'[169] He was commenting on the results of the 1856 presidential campaign, in which Abolitionist feeling had been stimulated by a section of the Protestant clergy, and giving reasons why he had 'studiously abstained' from taking sides despite financial inducements. 'In close connection with the atheists', he wrote, the clergy 'made propaganda in favor of a political party. With the pretensions of Godliness, liberality and justice on their lips, they cast the consuming fire of disunion, civic war, and fanaticism among the community.'[170] And he concludes by castigating 'the undue interference of religious ministers in political affairs'.

'Interference' at an early stage of this article becomes 'undue interference' later on. The language is entirely subjective, and nothing demonstrates Wise's flexibility more clearly than the fact that a few years later he became a candidate for political office—this apart from his uninterrupted flow of comment on public events.

Given his strong feelings about separation of church and state, Wise's attitude to Bible reading in public schools could not be in doubt. To a proposal made in 1855 that the Bible be read in the public schools 'without note or comment', he replied: 'There are plenty of mistakes and errors in the English authorized versions of the Bible ... We agree to having the Bible in the public schools

---

[166] Ibid. (21 Nov. 1856), 154.   [167] Ibid.
[168] Ibid. 156.   [169] Ibid.   [170] Ibid.

whenever the public are able to translate from the Hebrew into the English, and their reading of the New Testament should be in exact ratio with their knowledge of the Greek language.'[171] When the matter became a live issue in Cincinnati fourteen years later, his attitude was one of blunt hostility.[172] Wise's insistence that it was contrary to the spirit of American life to favour the religious institutions of the majority extended to comparatively minor matters. In 1857 we find Wise criticizing the Cincinnati School Board for holding examinations on Saturday. Why not on Sunday, he asked?[173] He also criticized the Republican state convention for meeting on a Sunday, but here we see his political prejudice clearly at work. In 1863 he had no objection to being nominated for the office of state senator by a Democrat convention which met on a Saturday.[174]

To the fighter for Jewish rights the foreign relations of the United States also demanded attention. Since 1851 controversy had simmered over a treaty of commerce with Switzerland, which, on account of the tenor of the Swiss constitution, secured certain privileges to Christians alone. Nevertheless, this treaty was ratified by the Senate in 1855. In 1857 an American citizen received notice to leave the canton of Neuchâtel on account of his being a Jew, and immediately Wise called for action 'so that the wrong inflicted on the Jewish citizens of this country be remedied forthwith'. 'Slaves and cowards only will submit to such an outrage; we are men, and must be treated as such.'[175] There were 'indignation meetings' in several places, including Cincinnati. A committee set up in Baltimore convened a conference of representatives of the different communities for 28 October. Wise represented Cincinnati, and as he took up his journey he exhibited to his readers the resentments that were burning within him at the failure of his previous initiatives and, by inference, his determination to assert himself as the pathfinder and spokesman for the Jews of America. He contrasted the circumstances of his mission with those of the journey which he had made three years before; then he had gone in the spring, now it was the autumn; 'then we were carried upon the wings of two

---

[171] Quoted in Wilansky, *From Sinai to Cincinnati*, 147.

[172] May, *Isaac Mayer Wise*, 147 ff.

[173] Wilansky, *From Sinai to Cincinnati*, 253.   [174] See p. 183 below.

[175] *Israelite*, 2 (17 Aug. 1856). On the Swiss treaty question generally, see Sol M. Stroock, 'Switzerland and the American Jews', *Publications of the American Jewish Historical Society*, 11 (1903), 7–52; and Cyrus Adler and A. M. Margalith, *With Firmness in the Right* (New York, 1946), 299 ff.

great and excellent thoughts, the Synod and the University, the union, progress and elevation of Israel, two thoughts which monopolized our whole soul. But now a wrong calls us.'[176]

There followed a passage expressing the hopes he had entertained for his university and his synod and of how it had proved 'a dream, a fairy angelic dream; still a dream and no more'. And why? Because people had questioned his motives and because 'petty leaders and petty scribblers, prompted by envy, and agitated by malice, insulted, slandered, outraged us in public print, to spit *gall* in our cup of life, in order to disgust us with all public affairs'. Now, therefore, 'Nothing' was the sentiment with which he was going East—'To make the Swiss treaty *nothing*, to do nothing and say nothing'. But Wise was still working for his day of triumph. Of that the concluding words of this manifesto leave the reader in no doubt: 'after the fall comes the spring and the summer with its fruits. ... The time will and must come, when Israel will judge between us and our opponents; then we will act again, again, on the same basis and principles, and with the same means.'

A serious financial panic had shaken the country at the time the Baltimore Conference was convened, and the response was small. Representatives of a few cities arrived but, not having heard of any great response, the Baltimore committee had not made any arrangements for a conference and were disinclined to go further.[177] They had not even taken steps to elect Baltimore delegates.

Whatever he had written in the *Israelite*, Wise had not come all the way from Cincinnati to do nothing, and he had not come to the city whence had been disseminated the attacks on his Cleveland Platform without meaning to assert himself as the most effective rabbi in the country. He reached Baltimore on a Friday. On the following day (24 October) he preached in two synagogues. On Sunday afternoon he expounded before 'a large congregation ... the motives of the committee of the Cleveland conference, and the principles regulating their views, in the preparation and publication of the first part of the *Minhag America*'. In the meantime he had been remonstrating about the inaction of the Baltimore group. On Monday, 26 October, he seems to have met the chairman of the Baltimore committee (Dr A. B. Arnold) and, dissatisfied with what he considered

---

[176] *Israelite*, 4 (18 Sept. 1857), 85; ibid. (23 Oct. 1857), 124.
[177] *Asmonean*, 18 (6 Nov. 1857), 28.

his 'evasion', Wise simply took the matter out of his hands.[178] He pushed the matter forward throughout the week. On Friday the committee which he led asked to see President Buchanan, who received them in the White House on Saturday at 1.00 p.m.

Spring had come very soon after the autumn. Wise's dispatches to the *Israelite* now breathe the elation of success. On the day of the interview he reported that the mission had proved successful—the response of the president was direct and decisive, and the initiatives to redress the grievance were in the hands of the secretary of state.[179] The mood of elation remained when Wise came to write his next dispatch. His faith in America had been redoubled: in Europe it would have been impossible to start an agitation, approach the head of state without ceremony, and discuss a problem frankly. There was something more. He had triumphed in the East, in the very city of Baltimore, where superior men had derided him.

Despite the assurances given by the president and the secretary of state, there was no immediate redress of the grievances felt by Jews, and it was not until 1864 that the Swiss government intimated that it was ready to amend the treaty.[180] In the meantime, being little acquainted with the roundabout ways of diplomacy, Wise could congratulate himself on a good week's work. On 1 November the party returned to Baltimore, where there was joy and feasting in honour of the victory; and on Monday evening Wise started on his way home—not directly, but by way of Philadelphia, New York, and Albany. Anger at Wise for having taken the lead with a small and unrepresentative group must have arisen in Baltimore. Wise pointed to the failure of the Baltimore group to follow through on the initiative it had taken and suggested that 'another affair' must have caused their unhappiness at his successful action.[181] 'Another affair' was doubtless his strife with Einhorn and his followers. (Dr Arnold, chairman of the inert Baltimore committee, was one of them.)[182] To have outmarched them was giving Wise occasion to guffaw.

Wise spent one night in Philadelphia, but it was long enough for

---

[178] *Israelite*, 4 (6 Nov. 1857), 142. In Isaac M. Fein, 'Baltimore Jews During the Civil War', *American Jewish Historical Quarterly*, 51 (Dec. 1961), 67–96, Dr Abraham B. Arnold is referred to as a friend of David Einhorn and as the person who translated Einhorn's inaugural sermon into English.

[179] *Israelite*, 4 (13 Nov. 1857), 145.

[180] See Stroock, 'Switzerland and the American Jews', 48.

[181] *Israelite*, 4 (20 Nov. 1857), 156.   [182] See n. 178 above.

him to take a lunge at Isaac Leeser—'The Israelitish community of this city are anxious to hear the word of God expounded by a capable and well instructed man. They are tired of the shallow Quakerism, in an Israelitish garment, which has swayed its scepter in the Philadelphia Synagogue and produced awkward results.'[183] No name was mentioned, but little imagination is needed to see who was being referred to—though compared with other things Wise had written about Leeser, the tone is almost genial.[184]

In New York he made the acquaintance of Samuel Adler, who had succeeded Merzbacher as rabbi of Congregation Emanu-El. Then he proceeded to Albany where he preached twice to his old congregation. He found kind words to say about his successor, Elkan Cohn,[185] but, if any real cordiality ever existed between them, it was soon ruptured by the controversy over the adoption of *Minhag America*.[186]

A year later Wise made another foray into the field of diplomacy, this time in connection with the case of Edgar Mortara, a Jewish child in Rome who was forcibly abducted and baptized. From September 1858 to late in 1859, articles dealing with the Mortara case filled the columns of the *Israelite*. As can be imagined, Wise was unsparing in his denunciations of the church ('the Pope and his numerous soulless lackeys never cared whether the boy is a Christian or a Jew ... Rome's object is not and cannot be the religion of a boy, nor religion *per se*').[187]

The *Israelite* carried an 'Appeal to the Israelites of the United States' signed by Lilienthal, its foreign editor at that time.[188] This invited the congregations to call meetings and send petitions to the president. Wise and Lilienthal were the first to act, but their unfamiliarity with official attitudes enabled the secretary of state to disclaim the right to interfere before there could be concerted action on the part of the Jews of America.

As with his other causes, so with his activities to defend his people: Wise liked to picture himself as the lonely warrior. The threat of Civil

---

[183] *Israelite*, 4 (20 Nov. 1857), 156.
[184] Not long before he had written that Leeser was 'sometimes completely deranged in his mind' and that 'his fanaticism, envy and avarice deranges his mind'; ibid. (4 Sept. 1857), 69.
[185] *Israelite*, 4 (20 Nov. 1857), 156.
[186] See ch. 3 sect. 8 above.
[187] *Israelite*, 5 (17 Sept. 1858), 85, and subsequent issues. See generally B. W. Korn, *The American Reaction to the Mortara Case* (Cincinnati, 1957).
[188] *Israelite*, 5 (22 Oct. 1856), 126.

War had produced a financial panic, and the enterprises for which he had laboured were placed in jeopardy. In April, in a depressing situation, the *Israelite* published an article of which the title and refrain was 'Served Him Right'. This, he said, had been the answer when he stood up against 'benumbed conservatism' and when he annoyed a certain class of reformers by taking reform to the masses, when, after the Cleveland Conference, both wings turned against him. Now he was being told 'serve him right' when his defence of the Jews caused him to be attacked.

Alone again, all alone we must raise our voice against the vileness of petty politicians who administer a thrust to the Jew, if they wish to excite laughter among a vulgar audience—against the prejudices of an inveterate nature. . . . against these and more inimical elements we stand alone, the rest of our journals on the Atlantic shore are engaged in considering their own interests, the editors do not think proper to do any thing except fabricating week after week orthodox lamentations and crocodile tears at the down-fall of their peculiar sort of un-Jewish Judaism.[189]

Wise did not exaggerate his readiness to defend the Jewish name; of this he gave proof throughout his career. But he preferred to fight alone than to fight as a member of a team of which he was not the captain. When he proclaimed in the *Israelite* that he stood alone in his determination to defend the name of Israel, an organization with that object, the Board of Delegates of American Israelites, had been set up. The Mortara case, coming on the heels of the Swiss treaty question, had driven home the need for a representative body of American Jews, and, on the initiative of some leading New York Jews, a meeting, to which every synagogue in the country was invited to send two representatives, took place in November 1859, when the Board of Delegates was established. It was not completely representative; whether by reason of apathy, distance, or differences based on principles or personalities, important elements stood out.

The Board might have been more representative had Wise not opposed the movement, asserting that it was the beginnings of a Jewish political party and an intended attack on the Reform movement. The principal sponsor, the Revd S. M. Isaacs, minister of one of the New York Orthodox synagogues and editor of the *Jewish Messenger*, endeavoured without success to convince Wise that the movement

[189] *Israelite*, 7 (12 Apr. 1861), 324.

was designed to protect Jewish rights at home and abroad. Isaacs did
not succeed, for Wise decided to boycott the board. He even boasted
that he refused to publish anything concerning it or emanating from
it.[190] The reasons given were various: on previous occasions the
English and Portuguese congregations had declined to meet with the
Germans (Cleveland and Baltimore) and 'The Polish invariably go
where they smell Orthodoxy'; it was a conspiracy against Reform. As
to the idea that 'We might go there and outvote them on any question',
that was impossible because the organizers had taken the precaution
of having the seat of that board in New York 'where twenty or
thirty delegates from ultra-orthodox congregations could always be
collected'—'they would not go to a neutral ground, not to some
central part of the country that could be reached by all our congregations'. The board's undertaking not to interfere in the internal
affairs of the member congregations was a piece of deception inserted
to allay suspicion while it gained strength.

As for the board's avowed objects, Wise was equally derisory. A
publication society? Good books would sell without its aid. Hospitals,
orphanages, and so on? These things had been done already. A college?
What the board would organize would be a 'Tsenah Verenah College',
whose graduates would know as much of Judaism as of Buddhism.[191]
Defending the Jews against attacks from outside? 'That is just the
thing we do not want.'[192] All this from the man who had long been
preaching the union of American Israel. In the comprehensiveness of
the indictment we see the petulant side of the one who will not join
the game unless he can play chief.[193]

When, during the Civil War, the Board of Delegates sent a representative to Washington in order to seek legislative sanction for

[190] *Israelite*, 6 (27 Jan. 1860), 236. Wise's later association with the Board of Delegates
is dealt with below.

[191] The name is a corruption of the title of a 17th-cent. commentary on the
Pentateuch written for women; the implication is that the college would be less than
serious.

[192] *Israelite*, 6 (27 Jan. 1860), 236. Wise returned to the attack four weeks later: ibid.
(24 Feb. 1860), 268.

[193] The form of Wise's attacks is, one surmises, similar to that of the criticisms he
received of his various union schemes, and reading them helps to explain the years
of constant arguing needed to bring them to fruition. The minutes of the second
meeting of the inaugural session of the Board of Delegates held on 29 Nov. 1859,
which rejected a proposal by Leeser for the election of a 'highly qualified Ecclesiastical
Board ... who shall be regarded as the expounders of the law for the Israelites of the
United States', do not suggest any inclination to interfere in religious affairs.

the appointment of Jewish chaplains, Wise was among the six Reform rabbis who gratuitously issued a statement to the press denying the board's representative character;[194] and when, with the encouragement of the board, Maimonides College—the first Jewish theological seminary in America—was established, Wise's attitude was virulently hostile. Yet in 1870 we find Wise joining the Board of Delegates: Leeser had passed away and he hoped to get it to take up his proposal for a seminary—more liable, one would have thought, than the protection of Jewish rights to lead to ideological conflicts.

Before this, while he was making clear his contempt for the Board of Delegates, Wise's running conflict with the Reform rabbis of the East broke into the open again. The occasion was a local 'civil war' which disrupted Baltimore Jewry towards the end of 1859 and in which Cincinnati gave aid and comfort to one of the parties, and was perhaps regarded as the principal belligerent. Congregation Oheb Shalom, established in 1853, used *Minhag America*, which presumably did not endear it to Einhorn. In September 1859 a young Hungarian, Benjamin Szold, took up the office of rabbi, and when he published his inaugural sermon and a memorial sermon Einhorn subjected them to a devastating nineteen-page analysis in *Sinai*.[195] The reply of Szold—or Szold and Wise together—went to the length of a special supplement to the *Israelite* (10 February 1860).

The violence of the language in his supplement seems to have given Wise second thoughts; possibly glimmerings of contrition worked from within, possibly intimations of drastic action from outside gave him pause. Two weeks later the *Israelite* carried a half-apologetic note attempting to shuffle off responsibility for the attack.[196] A committee of Einhorn's friends, meeting under the chairmanship of Dr Samuel Adler, rabbi of Temple Emanu-El, was already at work; they were not appeased and published in the press a statement of protest. They suggested that others besides Szold were involved in the attack, and accused Wise of continually venting a grudge against Einhorn, 'the destroyer of the Cleveland Platform of unholy memory'. One paragraph of the resolution they adopted expressed 'deep anger' at the *Israelite* for 'having no scruples at reviling in a disgraceful fashion the character of a man like Dr. Einhorn'. Alluding to 'this disgraceful

[194] See B. W. Korn, *American Jewry and the Civil War* (Philadelphia, 1951), 72.
[195] *Sinai*, 4 (Mar. 1860), 321.   [196] *Israelite*, 6 (24 Feb. 1860), 267.

condition of the Jewish press', they professed the intention to 'employ all the means at our command to avert this nuisance'.

Whether the New York group really contemplated any action against Wise and the *Israelite* is not known; in any case, no action ensued. Their statement did have the effect of blowing away any traces of contrition for having published the attack.[197] In the *Israelite* for 30 March 1860 Wise turned his guns on Einhorn and his defenders. The style they condemned was not his but Einhorn's, he argued: 'The Israelite has never condescended to retaliate in the same style.' He assumed the mantle of the knight who sallied forth in support of a man who had been unfairly and unjustly persecuted, and when that occurred he could not be expected to be an indifferent spectator. This did not suffice to complete the projection of his own personality that week: in another article in the same issue he referred to the hostility he met from Christians and from Orthodox and radical Reform Jewry and proceeded to insist that he would carry his banner 'until the angel of death wrests it from our hands and unfurls it on our graves'.[198]

11. POLITICAL DIVERSIONS

Wise's complaint that the Board of Delegates was a move in the direction of forming a Jewish political party has an almost comic ring about it in view of the way in which he and the *Israelite* had been mixed up in the 1858 election.[199] His incursion, apparently sudden, into the scrimmage in November 1858 is not the first instance, nor is it the last, of Wise's interest in politics, an interest which raises the question whether at any time he considered making politics his career. He had not been long in the United States before he came to know Horace Greeley, then a prominent journalist and politician. On his journey to Charleston early in 1850 he had stopped in Washington, presumably for the purpose of getting to know the leaders of the Federal government; when he visited the East to raise funds for Congregation Anshe Emeth later in the same year he again visited Washington and consorted with leading politicians;[200] and he took the

---

[197] This statement was published in several newspapers, including the *New York Herald*. It appears also in a Supplement to *Sinai*, 5 (Mar. 1860). This was headed *Abfertigung*, lit. 'act of finishing', but also 'reproof', 'snub', 'dismissal'; it is difficult to find a single word giving all that Einhorn intended.

[198] *Israelite*, 6 (23 March 1860), 300.　　　[199] See ch. 3 sect. 3 above.

[200] See ch. 2 sect. 6 above.

first steps to qualify as a lawyer, which would have facilitated his entry into politics. Wise had settled in Cincinnati at a time of political flux as the bitter controversies which preceded the Civil War mounted in force. Six years before, the Whigs had split on the slavery issue. Salmon P. Chase, whom we have met already, had led a Free Soil movement, and out of this grouping the Ohio Republican Party had been born in July 1855. Chase, according to Wise, suggested on several occasions that Wise should attach himself to the Republican Party, instead of working for a religious idea within a narrow circle. Wise declared that he had 'sat at the round table at which that party was born and baptised', but that 'some wounded apostles of the atheistical stripe' drove him out.[201] At a time of Republican domination (he wrote his *Reminiscences* in 1874–5), Wise may have been harking back to a 'might have been'. His 1858 foray into politics— like his candidature for a state senatorship in 1863—was directed against the Republicans.

It is evident, moreover, that Wise's action in 1858 reached out to something larger than local Cincinnati politics. On 9 November he wrote to Stephen A. Douglas, who had just waged a successful campaign in the State of Illinois, to congratulate him on his 'triumph' and, forwarding a copy of the election sheet he had brought out, he emphasized the senator's claims to the presidency in 1860. Wise offered Douglas the support of his paper and suggested that after a year or so it be transformed into a daily in Douglas's favour.[202]

Douglas did not answer this letter. Wise wrote to him again on 9 December requesting him 'for your own interest's sake' to bring the Swiss treaty and the Mortara case before the Senate. He comments: 'The Democratic Party is too much identified with Jesuitism and Catholicism, a fact which estranges to her the liberal class of the northern population. The Israelites especially have lately been frightened away from the Democracy by the Swiss Treaty.' Again, there is no indication that Douglas sent a reply, though the warm tribute which Wise paid to Douglas when he died in 1861 shows that Wise had not lost his admiration for him. What the first letter reveals is that in November 1858, when the hopes for Zion College and a synod had collapsed, Wise was toying with the idea of entering daily

[201] *Reminiscences*, 327.
[202] Wise's letters to Douglas are preserved in the Stephen A. Douglas Collection, University of Chicago Library.

journalism in support of a political cause. The role of rabbi of a single congregation and editor of a Jewish weekly was too confined. In 1858 there was no immediate prospect of re-establishing these ventures, and the attractions of politics may have entered his mind again. In the election of that year one of the Cincinnati candidates was a minister, and Wise had made enough beginnings to be ready, if he could project himself sufficiently into the arena, to be the first rabbi to stand for Congress.

Politics did enter his preaching. The minutes of Congregation B'nai Jeshurun show that on 14 April 1860 the board resolved 'to notify the Rev. Dr. Wise that the Board disapprove of all political allusions in his sermon and to discontinue the same (the political allusions) in future'.[203] At the next meeting (12 May) the president reported that there had been a satisfactory interview between Wise and himself on the subject of the above resolution, which the board thereupon ordered to be expunged from the minutes. However, Wise must have asserted rights which his board was not prepared to concede, for the resolution of 12 May continued: 'the secy, in acquainting Dr. Wise with the above, notify him also that the Board will by no means yield their right of instructing the officers of the congregation as the case may be'. Not long afterwards Wise was declaring in the *Israelite* in an article entitled 'No Political Preaching': 'Not one single word have we, as yet, said in the pulpit on the politics of the day. Fifteen years we have preached in this country . . . we never said one word on politics.'[204]

12. THE CIVIL WAR

When the possible dissolution of the Union first entered men's minds, Wise was once again hoping to realize his plan of establishing a college, but the issues which led to secession must have forced themselves on his attention. Cincinnati stood on the border between free and slave states; its environs were the first stage on the 'Underground Railroad' by which slaves were taken to Canada for liberation; it was near the scene of attempts, sometimes the cause of riots, to arrest and return slaves under the Fugitive Slave Law.

Something of a panic followed the presidential election of

---

[203] Minutes, Congregation B'nai Jeshurun.
[204] *Israelite*, 7 (1 Feb. 1861), 244.

November 1860. Wise took a 'plague on both your houses—why all this fuss' attitude—the situation was 'artificial' panic, 'no more than the produce of the present state of politics and the cunning contrivance of bankers, stock jobbers, brokers, etc.', and he forecast peace: 'The republicans have turned lamkins, tender and innocent, immaculate and bashful ... They are as tame and obliging now as the peasant the first time in the city ... The same thing ... is the case in the extreme south with fire eaters, seceders and political circus riders.'[205]

The belief that the fires would cool was widespread, and Wise was by no means alone when he remarked that 'the two extreme factions will be cooled down before the year ends'.[206] However, there is some interest in the decided view of human nature on which Wise based his conclusion: 'people care very little for abstract ideas, extreme views or false conceptions of honor when their material interests are neglected or even ruined'.[207] And this worldly view he backed with the affirmation that, threats of secession notwithstanding, he was still prepared to take payment for the *Israelite* in bills payable in any state of the Union.[208]

The crisis did not abate. South Carolina's secession occasioned a lengthy editorial in the *Israelite*:[209] 'The fanatics in both sections of the country succeeded in destroying the most admirable fabric of government. Under the pretext of progress and liberty, state rights and personal freedom they have made the beginning of destroying the proud structure of liberty to which all good men looked with hope and satisfaction.' Here, as before, the 'plague on both your houses' note is sounded, but as the article proceeds the balance shifts somewhat against the Abolitionists.

Demagogues who sought office at any price, red Republicans and habitual revolutionists who feed on excitement and civil wars, German atheism and American puritanism who know no limits to their fanaticism, visionary philanthropists and wicked preachers who have that religion which is most suitable to their congregations, speculators in property, stockjobbers and usurers whose God is Mammon, thoughtless multitudes and hired criers in the South and North succeeded in breaking down the fortress of liberty, the great bulwark of our best hopes.[210]

---

[205] *Israelite*, 7 (30 Nov. 1860), 172.   [206] Ibid.   [207] Ibid.
[208] Ibid. The tone of Wise's approach is worth considering for its contrast with Einhorn's, which was based strictly on principle.
[209] Ibid. 7 (28 Dec. 1860), 205.   [210] Ibid.

Wise continues in the pessimistic note: 'either the Republican party must be killed off forever by constitutional guarantees to the South, to make an end forever to this vexing slavery question, or the Union must be dissolved'. For the desired course, the necessary majority of three-quarters of the states could not be obtained, 'because we have too many demagogues and fantasts, therefore we maintain this Union is as good as dissolved'.[211]

The dissolution of the Union is a theme to which Wise reverts when, in the following week's issue of the *Israelite*, he indulges in prophecy for the New Year.

The year 1861 must witness either the end of the Republican party or the dissolution of the Union. The Republicans know this very well and talk quite freely of the final and perpetual separation of the North and South. All their manœuvres are intended to that point. They want neither war nor coercion nor compromises. Separation is their final object. They maintain their object of Abolitionism can best be achieved by the separation of the South from the North.[212]

In December 1860, President Buchanan had called upon all denominations to observe 4 January 'as a day of fasting and prayer, that God might have mercy upon us and save this Union'. The *Israelite* published a sarcastic reference to Buchanan's action, describing him as one of the principal agents of the calamity and as being possessed of 'hatred and feeling of vengeance'.[213] On the same page, there was an announcement of a special service for the following Friday morning—the day appointed by the president—in the Lodge Street synagogue, at which the 'Rev. Doctors Wise and Lilienthal' would preach. Evidently some incident must have arisen which prevented Wise from using the pulpit of his own synagogue, for in the 'No Political Preaching' article Wise declared that it had been his fixed principle not to say a word in the pulpit on the politics of the day 'and for that very reason refused to preach the fourth of January last, in order not to violate our principle'.[214] No hint is given as to what was at issue.

---

[211] Ibid.   [212] Ibid. (4 Jan. 1861), 212.   [213] Ibid. (28 Dec. 1860), 206.
[214] *Israelite*, 7 (1 Feb. 1861), 244. The minutes of the Board of Trustees of Congregation B'nai Jeshurun make no reference to any incident in connection with this service.

In the course of a lengthy article, Wise, in giving his reasons for refusing to 'preach politics', makes some scathing comments on the nature of politics. Whether this sudden awareness of the seamy side of the political process was stimulated by a personal set-back in the political arena cannot be stated.

Politics in this country means money, material interest, and no more. The leaders of all parties are office-seekers or office-holders. They hold or seek offices, not in order to benefit the community, but to benefit themselves ...

Land speculators, who bought large tracts of land in Kansas, exercised every sort of influence to make her a free state, in order to increase the price of land. Other speculators ... exercised all their influence in order to make a slave state of Kansas, in order to direct the current of migration to such states or territories where they possessed land, so as to dispose of it at improved rates. Slave holders favor the extension of slavery because it increased their wealth, and land speculators oppose it, because they find their present account by it. Politics and money are synonymous, however holy, exalted or lofty these things may appear to the myriads of honest men who are dragged along by party leaders ...

Politics is a business, and in many instances a mean business, which requires more cheat and falsehood than a vulgar scoundrel would practice. Philosophize over it as you please ... it remains a vulgar business ... with which we are fairly disgusted on account of its dishonesty and violence.[215]

In the context in which they were written—the issues before the American people just before the Civil War broke out, and the particular incident of the day of national prayer—such words give the impression that for the most part they were not issues worth fighting for. Freedom or servitude for the Negro, Free Soil or the extension of slavery to the territories, the right of secession or the indissolubility of the Union, seem to have been placed by Wise on the same level as controversies over the spoils of office or the granting of land to a railway.

The fact that Wise treated opposition to the extension of slavery as a pretext indicates that he did not regard slavery as an issue;[216] his repeated verbal assaults on 'fanatics' suggests that he looked upon the Abolitionists as disturbers of the peace. Some controversy has arisen

---

[215] *Israelite*, 7 (1 Feb. 1861), 244.

[216] May, *Isaac Mayer Wise*, 243, states that Wise 'did not zealously advocate the abolition of slavery'. If May meant to imply that Wise advocated abolition, though not zealously, he does not support his contention with evidence.

as to whether Wise actually favoured slavery. The issue was faced squarely by other Jewish teachers—David Einhorn and Sabato Morais expressed themselves against slavery; Morris J. Raphall, supported by Isaac Leeser, took the view that it was an institution sanctioned by Judaism. Writing many years afterwards, Max J. Kohler (a grandson of David Einhorn) said that Wise, in the *Israelite*, expressed approbation of Raphall's stand.[217] This is not true. Alluding to press comments on Raphall's pro-slavery sermon, Wise wrote 'that among all nonsense imposed on the Bible the greatest is to suppose the Negroes are the descendants of Ham, and the curse of Noah is applicable to them'.[218] But, though he contested the view that Negro slavery was supported by scriptural texts, the issue of slavery was not one on which he felt strongly. True, he did say that he was against it, but in terms which, having regard to the issues, amounted to acquiescence in continuance. His position comes out more clearly than anywhere else in an article printed in *Die Deborah* in December 1859. 'We are no apologists for slavery. We have always declared our view candidly that by constitutional means it should be kept far from the territories of the great West. But we have no constitutional right to snatch from the South its slaves through revolution and abolitionist agitation.'[219] Union is the dominant idea. In Germany and Italy the striving after union went hand in hand with the striving after liberty; in America the achievement of union had meant the achievement of liberty. Destroy the American Union? Here his mind may have lingered on the miscellaneous assortment of stuffy German principalities that spotted the map of Europe and held back progress because the dignity of their rulers had to be maintained, or on divided

---

[217] *Publications of the American Jewish Historical Society*, 5 (1897), 140.

[218] *Israelite*, 7 (18 Jan. 1861), 230.

[219] *Die Deborah*, 5 (16 Dec. 1859), 94. May, *Isaac Mayer Wise*, 245, attacks Kohler's statement that Wise approved of Raphall's position, but does not make clear what Wise's position was. Korn, 'Isaac Mayer Wise on the Civil War', *Hebrew Union College Annual*, 20 (1947), 638, states that Wise was 'prepared to see slavery established as a permament American institution, to save the Union', but was not 'pro-slavery'. On p. 640 he observes: 'Long after the final draft of the Emancipation Proclamation was issued, Wise finally gave an expression of his views on slavery in the Bible. He showed no unwillingness to state his beliefs once slavery had ceased to be a political issue. They are, of course, the ideas of a man opposed to slavery.' Still, it would not prove that Wise was anti-slavery before the Emancipation Proclamation, even were he shown to be equivocally so afterwards. Korn adds, 'Wise was still unwilling to come to grips with the evils of southern slavery which so infuriated the north, or with the economic conditions which perpetuated those evils' (p. 641).

Italy, subject here to the ignominy of priestly rule and there to the humiliation of foreign domination. And if America were divided, would its liberties remain free from the encroachments of European empire builders? It was the Union, blemished slightly though it might be by Negro servitude, which had guaranteed freedom to Whites who had fled the shores of Europe, and that came first.

Wise's attitude also emerges in his fervent memorial tribute to Stephen A. Douglas, who died shortly after the conflict began. Douglas, to be sure, had supported war as a means of preventing secession, and that was further than Wise was prepared to go,[220] but it was Douglas who had proposed that the question of slavery be left to the people of the Territories to decide as they organized themselves into states.[221] This corresponded to the kind of sentiment that was fairly strong in Ohio. Its mainspring may have been prudential considerations natural enough in a border state, but there are grounds for believing that Wise's feeling as a Jew played a part. Wise 'was essentially a middle of the road man, not only in religion, but also in politics. The only exception was where politics touched Jewish emancipation and liberty. Then he was an implacable extremist and demanded immediate change.'[222] Rightly or wrongly, Wise appears to have suspected some of the Abolitionists of a disposition to tamper with the liberty and equality the guarantee of which he regarded as the crowning glory of the American state and Federal constitutions. Massachusetts was a centre of Abolitionism; Massachusetts was also anti-alien—specifically anti-Irish, but what immigrant was to know where the canker would spread? Therefore, Abolitionists were hypocrites. Such a picture may be over-simplified, but the lines are clear in Wise's view of the Abolitionists. He regarded them as ethically inconsistent for having adopted, in Massachusetts in 1859, a law requiring of aliens seven years' residence and naturalization as a qualification for holding public office.[223]

That Abolitionism was espoused by the Christian clergy in the North did not endear the cause to Wise. He denounced vehemently

---

[220] *Israelite*, 7 (7 June 1860), 386.

[221] *Encyclopædia of the Social Sciences* (1930–5), v. 227.

[222] Jacob R. Marcus, *The Americanization of Isaac Mayer Wise* (Cincinnati, 1931), 10. This has been drawn upon generally for its assessment of Wise's political ideas.

[223] *Israelite*, 7 (25 Jan. 1861), 238. Wise's view is cited not for its logical consistency but for its reflection of an intense dislike of enacting distinctions between different sections of the population.

the slightest interference with separation of church and state; he suspected the 'political parsons' of trying to inject Christianity into the Constitution.[224] He was grateful for the liberty and equality afforded by the open frontier, the open society, and the political system of the United States, and there, of all places, he seems to have felt, men should live and let live. He saw in the Abolitionists not men who wanted to grant liberty to slaves, but men who wanted to interfere with the liberty of the states. He lumped them together with those who would restrict the liquor traffic, enforce Sunday observance, and somehow make Christianity a legally established religion.

If Wise regarded all other considerations as subordinate to the maintenance of the Union, it follows naturally that he deplored secession—'this is the most terrible blow the cause of humanity is likely to suffer in the year 1861', Wise wrote while the crisis was yet building up. Even for the Union, however, coercion was not his line: 'Force will not hold together this Union; it was cemented by liberty and can stand only by the affections of the people . . . Force and liberty are antagonistic. Either must fall to the ground.'[225] So, though he deplored secession, Wise held that the right to secede was there. The foregoing was written in December 1860. By March 1861, an

---

[224] *Israelite*, 8 (18 Oct. 1861), 124, despite its self-denying ordinance of 19 Apr. 1861, contains an article in violent tone, headed 'The Wrong Influence of the Church': 'Who in the world could act worse, more extravagant and reckless in this crisis than the Protestant priests did? From the very start of the unfortunate difficulties, the consequences of which we now suffer so severely, the Protestant priests threw the firebrand of abolitionism into the very heart of this country. . . . Remember the violent abolition speeches and denunciations of all opponents from the Henry Beecher Ward and Theodore Parker factions and another host of eccentric minds. . . . Remember the petition to Congress by the Presbyterian synod of Pittsburgh, Pa., at the beginning of this war, praying to acknowledge God and Jesus, and abolish slavery.' A few months later he was writing: 'Years ago we knew nothing of prayer meetings, Sunday laws, Christian country, Christian legislations, and all that sort of new fangled theories, nay most of our eminent statesmen were not even baptized . . . Now we have plenty (and yet more every day) of prayer meetings, Sunday laws, temperance laws, Christian states and legislations, Christian chaplains in the Army, Navy, hospitals, legislative halls and elsewhere, with a masterly inactivity, a lack of energy and vigor, a want of strength and honesty of purpose, plenty of blunders, weakness, fraud and selfishness almost everywhere. . . . How sick is our moral nature, if we stand in need of such artificial means and priestly guardians, and submit to them! The better nature of moral freemen must revolt against the impertinence of men to be our guardians in religious matters, in matters between man and his God.' (Ibid. (24 Jan. 1862), 236.)

[225] *Israelite*, 7 (28 Dec. 1860), 205, 206.

antisemitic aside in an attack on Judah P. Benjamin by Senator Henry
Wilson of Massachusetts had provoked Wise to look on the act of
secession in a more favourable light.[226]

On 14 April 1861, Fort Sumter surrendered to the Confederate
forces. The fire of that bombardment fused into a single mass the
diverse elements that had existed on each side. Lincoln's call for
volunteers met with an overwhelming response. The *Jewish Messenger*,
of New York, reported from Cincinnati that 'the Jewish young men
of this city have entered into the war excitement with considerable
enthusiasm; over fifty of our finest Jewish young men have enlisted
into actual service, and many more are about following'.[227]

A little before, Wise had expressed himself in a manner which fell
short of enthusiasm. Under the heading 'Silence, our policy', he had
written:

We are the servant of peace, not of war. Hitherto we thought fit to say
something on public affairs, and it was our ardent hope to assist those who
wished to prevent civil war, but we wasted our words. What can we say now?
Shall we lament and weep like Jeremiah over a state of things too sad and
too threatening to be looked upon with indifference? We would only be
laughed at ... or probably abused for discouraging the sentiment. Or should
we choose sides with one of the parties? We cannot, not only because we
abhor the idea of war, but also we have dear friends and near relations,
beloved brethren and kinsmen in either section of the country, that our heart
bleeds on thinking of their distress ...

Therefore silence must henceforth be our policy, silence on all the questions
of the day, until a spirit of conciliation shall move the hearts of millions to a
better understanding of the blessings of peace, freedom and union.[228]

The outbreak of war must have embarrassed Wise personally,
because many of the subscribers to the *Israelite* lived in the South
and became cut off, and many of those in the North cancelled their
subscriptions. There is something quaint, however, in his lament,
published in June, that the postmaster-general had stopped mails to
the seceding states, and his suggestion that this action was unconstitutional.[229] The assumptions of total war were something which
society was still spared.

[226] *Israelite*, 7 (22 Mar. 1861), 386. In *Israelite*, 9 (27 Feb. 1863), Wise again
associates Abolitionism with attempts to Christianize the Constitution.
[227] *Jewish Messenger*, 9 (3 May 1861), 133.
[228] *Israelite*, 7 (19 Apr. 1861), 334.   [229] Ibid. (14 June 1861), 396.

1. Isaac Mayer Wise and family, 1850. *Right to left*: Theresa Bloch Wise, Leo Wise, Dr I. M. Wise, Julius Wise (partially obliterated). *Standing*: Emily Wise

2. Isaac Mayer Wise, *c.*1855

3. Cincinnati, Ohio, 1855. *Cincinnati, Covington, and Newport:* a coloured lithograph 16 in. x 11 in. showing the appearance of Queen City from across the Ohio River. The tallest steeple in the left background is St Peter's Cathedral, completed in 1844 and still standing. The round building on the hill at the extreme rear right of the view is the old observatory, erected in 1845 by Nicholas Longworth. Cincinnati received its present name in 1790, in honour of the society of Revolutionary War Officers of that name. In the foreground of the picture, in the angle made by the junction of the Licking and Ohio rivers, is the Newport Army Barracks as completed in 1855. Covington, Ky., is shown in the left foreground

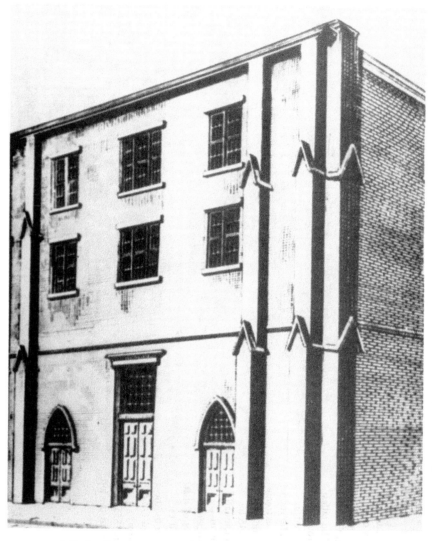

4. Lodge Street synagogue (B'nai Jeshurun), Cincinnati (1848–66).
(*Courtesy Isaac M. Wise Temple*)

K. K. BENE JESHURUN.

5. Isaac M. Wise Temple, 8th and Plum Streets, Cincinnati, Ohio (exterior).
(Photo taken in 1888)

6. Isaac M. Wise Temple,
Cincinnati, Ohio (interior)

7. First building of Hebrew Union College, 724 West 6th St., Cincinnati, Ohio

8. Hebrew Union College–Jewish Institute of Religion (aerial view taken in 1962)

The absence of any support for the Union cause from Wise did not pass unnoticed in Cincinnati. The Revd Moncure D. Conway accused him of unfair motives, to which Wise replied that he never preached on politics.[230]

The weeks rolled on with only the faintest suggestion of war penetrating the columns of the *Israelite*. The topic was avoided in the reflections Wise wrote for the New Year 5622,[231] and twelve months later the same policy was observed.[232]

Early in the Civil War, Wise attributed the want of officers in the Army and Navy of the United States to the neglect of learning, though in such terms as not to refer to the hostilities which by then had started.[233] In November 1861 he covered a whole page of the *Israelite* with a lament over 'the lessons of the age'.[234] The schools were yet too young and the colleges too superficial to make the Americans an enlightened people. As for the press—'any corruption that pays finds its advocates'. The two principal abuses of the wealth and freedom of America were materialism and neglect of science. 'Without money an honest man in our cities is an ass, looked upon as a cypher, treated as a superfluous thing, while we do homage in the most obedient manner to the rich scoundrel, the wealthy blockhead, and the opulent ignoramus.' Science, he said, was being choked by the all-absorbing ambition to make money as early and as fast as possible: 'any quack can be our physician, any well-spoken man our teacher, any humbug a professor, and any comedian a preacher'. Concluding, Wise refers to the lessons to be learned from 'the ordeal through which we are passing'. That is the nearest he gets to mentioning the war in a long article.

In the Fourth of July sermon which Wise delivered in 1863, he lamented the war and desolation that had overtaken the country, but

---

[230] Ibid. (31 May 1861), 380.   [231] Ibid. 8 (6 Sept. 1861), 76.

[232] On this occasion the Civil War was alluded to though without any opinion being expressed (*Israelite*, 9 (26 Sept. 1862), 92). A week earlier there had been a reference to the interruption in production caused by the proclamation of martial law in Cincinnati.

Occasionally notes were sounded which might be considered ambivalent, e.g. 'Should this war result in an entire restoration of this union to its former majesty and integrity' (ibid. 8 (Feb. 1862), 269); the reprinting 'as somewhat of a curiosity' of a form of prayer for the Confederacy introduced by the Revd Dr Bernard Illowy into some of the synagogues of the South (ibid. (14 Feb. 1862), 263); and an editorial headed 'To Preachers', commending the vacant pulpit at Charleston, SC (ibid. (7 Mar. 1862), 285).

[233] *Israelite*, 7 (19 July 1861), 20.   [234] Ibid. (8 Nov. 1861), 148.

in attributing them to the sinfulness of the people is careful in balancing the faults between one party and the other. The past years of the country, he said, were each a link of a long chain of prosperity without precedent in history. Wealth, however, had led them to 'an insane, corruptive and demoralising luxury'. They had danced madly round the golden calf and therefore stood disgraced before the civilized world.[235] No doubt the tenor of his observations during this period was affected by sorrow at the destructiveness of the war; probably there was more of a long-range feeling—doubt as to whether the Union which meant so much to him could survive the conflict.

Although Wise placed the main issues of the war outside his purview, his thunder pealed forth when the rights or the honour of Jews were touched; when antisemitic accusations were made; when Congress failed to give Jews the right to have army chaplains; or when General Grant issued his notorious General Order No. 11 expelling Jews from the areas under his command[236]—which Wise did not overlook years later when Grant was nominated for the presidency. More surprising, however, was another of his sudden incursions into politics, at a time of acute controversy and when the Union cause was greatly harassed by war-weariness and internal dissension.

Writing of the American people some years after the Civil War, James Bryce observed that 'they have what chemists call low specific heat; they grow warm suddenly and cold as suddenly; they are liable to swift and vehement outbursts of feeling which rush like wildfire across the country, gaining glow like the wheel of a railway car, by the accelerated motion'.[237] When the guns roared at Fort Sumter, a war fever spread through the North, a fever in which all parts of Ohio shared; when the war proved to be something less agreeable than a picnic, when the Union cause suffered in battle and recruits for the army had to be drafted, defeatism became open. At Ohio's state elections in 1861, the Union Party, a coalition of Republicans and War Democrats, carried the day, but the regular Democratic organization, which, while not clearly opposed to the war, favoured peace through

---

[235] *Israelite*, 10 (10 July 1863), 12.

[236] This whole episode is dealt with in detail in Korn, *American Jewry and the Civil War*, pp. 121 ff. See also Ellis Rivkin, 'A Decisive Pattern in American Jewish History', *Essays in American Jewish History* (Cincinnati: AJA, 1958), 37–8.

[237] *The American Commonwealth* (New York, 1888), ii. 253.

a constitutional convention, remained intact. This sentiment was fed by weariness with the fighting, dismay at maladministration, and resentment at the unaccustomed powers exercised by the Federal government. The outstanding leader of the Peace Democrats was Clement Vallandigham, who sat in the Congress as representative for the Dayton district of Ohio. His attacks on the Lincoln administration were merciless, and it appeared as if he desired the defeat of the Union forces in order to achieve peace. In the 1862 congressional election, the Democrats in opposition to Lincoln won fourteen districts out of nineteen in Ohio.

Sympathy with Vallandigham's movement expressed itself early in 1863 in the less constitutional forms of desertion from the army and armed resistance to conscription. Vallandigham, who continued to demand conciliation and to attack what he described as the unconstitutional measures of the Lincoln administration, was arrested in May, and a military court sentenced him to confinement. He was sent behind the Confederate lines but made his way to Canada and, establishing himself at Niagara Falls, continued his propaganda. The arrest of Vallandigham strengthened the hold of the Peace Democrats on the party organization, and almost unanimously he was nominated as candidate for the governorship.[238]

The election was bitterly fought, and it was under these conditions that Wise, who had previously been adamant in his refusal to talk politics, suddenly descended into the arena. Cincinnati's *Daily Enquirer* of 6 September 1863 reported the Democratic County Convention held at Carthage on the previous day. Wise had not been present because it was a Saturday, but in the ballot for nomination of two state senators he received 280 votes out of a possible 312. The newspaper, which was the leading supporter of the Vallandigham cause, commented: 'Dr. Wise is a gentleman of learning and accomplishments—is well known as an estimable Hebrew rabbi of this city. He would make an excellent Senator.'

The scrimmages in which their minister had been involved have left little record of reaction on the part of the flock. Perhaps his strength of personality intimidated them, perhaps the terms of his contract. But while his quarrels with Einhorn as to the correct attitude to the Talmud were remote from their concerns, politics, especially

---

[238] See generally E. H. Roseboom and F. P. Weisenberger, *A History of Ohio* (new edn., Columbus, 1953), 282.

in a time of war, was something on which they had opinions of their own. The news of the nomination must have agitated some part of the congregation, because two days after this report—that is, on 8 September—there was a special meeting of the board of trustees 'to take in consideration the nomination of Dr. I. M. Wise as State Senator'. 'After some discussion,' the minutes of the meeting tell us, 'a Committee of 3 ... were on motion appointed to draft suitable resolutions, expressing the sentiments of the Board in relation to this matter, who reported the following communication to Dr. Wise, which was unanimously adopted and the Secy. ordered to forward the same, after which the meeting adjourned.'

The letter appended to the minutes bears the date 7 September 1863—the day prior to the meeting—and under that date it was subsequently published. It is couched in respectful terms.

Rev. Sir—By unanimous desire of the Board of Trustees of K. K. Bene Jeshurun, I am instructed to communicate to you that the subject of your nomination as State Senator by a Convention held at Carthage, on the 5th inst., has been fully deliberated upon.

The Board feels greatly honoured by this demonstration of confidence bestowed upon you; they are also well aware of your sincere attachment to our common country; nevertheless, as it is an established law with us that our minister should be present in the synagogue whenever divine service is held, and also, your services otherwise being indispensably necessary in our congregation, as well as in the scholastic department, you are hereby politely, but most emphatically requested to decline the said nomination at once.

With due regard, I have the honor to be, Rev. Sir, your obedient servant,
                                                                    Fred. Eichberg

Sec'y of the K. K. Holy Congregation Bene Jeshurun

The suavity of the language does not conceal the 'emphatically' and 'at once' in its operative words.

Under the same date, the board of directors of the Talmud Yelodim Institute wrote to Wise, forwarding a resolution passed that day. This wears no velvet glove:

The Rev. Dr. Wise is engaged as school superintendent, with a fixed salary attached, and the duties of the superintendent are such as to require his attendance almost daily at the school.

Resolved, that we remonstrate to the acceptance, by the Rev. Dr. Wise of the above named nomination.

Resolved, that we desire the Rev. Dr. Wise to decline the nomination, and for particular reason, that the duties and obligations due to our Institute are paramount to any other engagements.[239]

The trustees of the congregation held their quarterly meeting less than two weeks later (19 September), and a general meeting took place on 20 September. The minutes of neither meeting make reference to this incident. In the meantime, however, Wise had replied to the communications addressed to him, stating in the course of his reply:

'I beg leave to state that the duties I owe to the congregation and the school are prior to those of any other office to which I might be elected hereafter; therefore, as long as I am not dispensed of the first, I cannot enter upon any other. As you maintain you cannot dispense with my humble services for the time I might be obliged to spend at the Capital of the State, and the law of the congregation especially ordains it so, I certainly feel obliged to decline a nomination so honourably tendered, notwithstanding my private opinion, that I might render some services to my country, not altogether unessential, especially as those who nominated me know well my sincere attachment to this country and government. God will save the Union and the Constitution; liberty and justice for all, without my active co-operation, being, after all, without any political aspirations—only an humble individual.[240]

[239] *Cincinnati Daily Times* (10 Sept. 1863), 3; Minute Book, Talmud Yelodim Institute.

[240] Minute Book, Talmud Yelodim Institute. This appears to have been the only occasion on which rabbi and congregation stood face to face. In connection with Wise's decision ten years later to leave for New York, the *History of the K.K. Bene Yeshurun of Cincinnati, Ohio* (Cincinnati, 1892), attributed to Wise and his grandson Max B. May, states that 'the unpleasantness was amicably adjusted', but it is not certain whether the 'unpleasantness' referred to was the cause or the result of Wise's proposed departure. If the former, no evidence of it appears in the minutes of the congregation. The minutes tend to be sparse in their references to Wise, but the following is a summary of some of the incidents in the record of disagreements. Even when telescoped together they do not amount to anything substantial, and none of the incidents immediately preceded 1873.

Soon after the consecration of the Plum Street temple—at the meeting of members on 14 Oct. 1866—changes in the times of services advocated by Dr Wise came up for discussion. One motion was made that the Friday evening service commence half an hour before sunset and an amendment was offered that the matter be left to Dr Wise. This apparently was unacceptable (though the minutes are not clear on the point) but by 43 to 34 the congregation agreed that it be left to Dr Wise in conjunction with the Committee on Religious Rules and Regulations. This, according to the report presented by the president to the annual meeting in the following year, 'created almost a split in the congregation'—presumably being a defeat for Wise. (At the meeting two years later (23 Sept. 1868) proposals he brought forward with the endorsement of the committee and the trustees were defeated by 36 votes to 27.) On 26 Oct. 1866 a meeting of the trustees took place, the principal object being to request 'the several officers who had tendered their resignations to withdraw the same'. That the resig-

The tone is distinctly more chastened than that of the fighting editor of the *Israelite*. And perhaps the denial of political ambitions and the expression of belief in the Union at the end only calls attention to that which it professes to disavow.

---

nations did arise out of a quarrel in which Wise was involved is evident from what the minutes of that meeting describe as the 'ascessions [*sic*] made by the Rev. Dr. Wise', in consideration of which the resignations were withdrawn. These were 'That he will cooperate with the Board of Trustees in any matter whatever; that he will at no time interfere with the established rules and regulations adopted by the Congregation and if any alterations should in his judgment be made hereafter, that all his actions would be guided by the wishes of the Board of Trustees.' The president, reporting to the next annual general meeting, said that 'only after a considerable exertion on my part in inducing the Rev. Dr. Wise to make considerable concessions to the Board they could be induced to remain in their positions'. Thereupon the matter appears to have been settled. At the meeting on 10 Nov. a member of the board of trustees requested the Committee on Religious Regulations 'to change the time of the Friday evening service to 5 o'clock and that the order of service as prescribed in the Prayer Book should be strictly followed'. To which there is added the word 'Carried!!', suggesting that perhaps the old difficulty had not been resolved. One's impression is that Wise was determined to go his own way, whatever the congregation thought. Next it was Wise who complained. At a special meeting of the trustees on 27 Jan. a communication was read from Wise complaining 'of the expressions made use of by the Vice Pres. as derogatory to his character in his position as minister of the Congregation'. The vice-president said he 'did not remember of having made use of any such language and in no wise intended to give offense'. Nothing further is recorded. At the ensuing annual meeting (5 Oct. 1867) the president, vice-president, secretary, and several of the trustees retired. The president in his report made several references to opposition and want of harmony—one instance has been quoted. Whether, and, if so, how far, one party was grouping round the minister cannot be stated.

On 25 Nov. 1869 the trustees held a special meeting to consider a request by Wise for the use of the Temple for three lectures. This was granted 'after a lengthy debate by five votes to three'. In the same year Wise got his way with regard to a change in time of Friday evening services, the general meeting on 26 Dec. agreeing to a service at 7 p.m.

What to all appearances was a rebuff was suffered by Wise at the annual meeting of his congregation held on 2 Oct. 1870. Mr A. Aub offered a resolution commending the work of those rabbis who had met earlier that year in Cleveland to revise *Minhag America* and concluding with a message of thanks to Wise 'for his successful labors in behalf of Israel's sanctuary, which he has so masterly and generously elevated'. The meeting rejected the resolution; we do not know why.

On 9 Feb. 1871 there came before the trustees a communication from Wise requesting what the minutes refer to as a 'Private Department [*Apartment?*] in the basement of the Temple for his special use'. The Board appointed a committee to go into the question. The Committee reported on 27 Apr. that the president of the Talmud Yelodim Institute thought that it needed all the rooms, but would bring the matter before his board. Probably there was in B'nai Jeshurun what one sometimes finds in a congregation with a strong spiritual leader—an underground opposition ready to come to the surface if opportunity arose.

Some hint of these proceedings appears to have been dropped in the ear of the press. On 10 September, the *Daily Times*, an evening paper, published the correspondence, and on the following morning the pro-Vallandigham *Daily Enquirer* came out with this announcement:

The Rev. Dr. Wise has been forced, by outside pressure, to decline the democratic nomination for State Senator. Had his name been on the other ticket, the Shoddy Contractors, who have been so busy in pulling the wires to produce this result, would have been contented to let it remain. The names of these Shoddy Contractors do not appear on the record, but they are known nevertheless.[241]

Wise's association with the Vallandigham Democrats is a development of the attitude he expressed earlier towards secession and peace. It is conceivable that a specifically Jewish interest may have drawn him to Vallandigham. The member for the Dayton district had earlier exerted himself to protect Jewish rights. On 12 July 1861, he had moved an amendment to a bill before Congress to remove the restriction to Christians of chaplaincy appointments. His amendment was rejected, and Wise protested in the *Israelite* against 'this unjust violation of our constitutional rights', adding: 'Keep this paper for future reference. Peace will be restored to this country, then we will square accounts.'[242] Vallandigham had also proved helpful to the Jewish cause in connection with the Swiss treaty and the Mortara case. These actions may have had something to do with Wise's support.

13. AT NORTH COLLEGE HILL

The outcome of the Civil War was far from certain in December 1861 when Wise took another of those steps which showed that he was ready to strike out on his own path: he bought a large farm between North College Hill and Mount Healthy, and made it his principal residence. The farm lay nine miles north of Cincinnati. It is unusual, even in these days of instantaneous communications, for a clergyman to live at such a distance from the scene of his activities; in 1861 it must

---

[241] *Cincinnati Daily Enquirer* (11 Sept. 1863), 2. Earlier that year this paper, when dealing with General Order No. 11, had criticized the Jews for being mostly Republicans, which would help to explain the step forced on Wise.

[242] *Israelite*, 8 (19 July 1861), 23.

have been unprecedented. Cincinnati was a city turbulent enough in times of peace, and the excitements of the Civil War must have added to the violence. It was still confined to the river basin and could be prostrated by a sweltering summer. Isaac and Theresa Wise had a family of ten children, and Wise may have calculated that, apart from other advantages, the produce of the farm would at least fill the mouths of his brood. More, there were educational institutions at North College Hill to which he could send them; and he hinted that he might use them as a stepping-stone to a college under his own control.[243]

His congregation did not demur at Wise's removing himself a distance of nine miles, and Wise, of whose endurance as a traveller there is ample evidence, presumably found driving to and from the city no strain. The picture retained by his family, presumably formed out of his later years, is one of him sitting in his study at the farm, writing without intermission for hours on end. He had an eye for the panorama of nature, and this probably gave him strength when he withdrew, as from 1861 he was able to do regularly, from the turbulence of the city. The vista which lay before him he painted in an article in the *Israelite*.

Arrived upon the top of the hill the grandest scenery imagination can depict bursts into sight. For ten miles in all directions except the north the landscape stretches away under our feet. There lay open to the eye all the hills and valleys over to Kentucky, including the western part of Cincinnati. On the other side Glendale, Carthage, Springrove, Clifton and the villas between present themselves to view, and the houses look like gems set upon the dark carpet of groves and parks. It is a birdseye perspective which one has no opportunity to see again for hundreds and probably for thousands of miles.

On the hill the atmosphere is entirely different from the city. The air is pure, light, much more transparent, therefore also the blue of the skies is different and resembles fully the Italian sky. The hill is studded with fine wells, pure water, rich gardens, fine residences and a healthy people.[244]

In the noisy, smoke-filled city, scenery and atmosphere were entirely different. Wise's comments when he had decided to move may be inspired by self-justification, but they are borne out by the comments of others. 'The traveler distinguishes nothing but a smoky heap, here

---

[243] In *Israelite*, 8 (15 Nov. 1861), 156, when he was contemplating his removal to North College Hill, Wise wrote candidly about the limitations of Cincinnati.
[244] Ibid.

and there relieved by a church spire ... Cincinnati, to the stranger, has the appearance of a beautiful woman, dingily apparelled.'[245]

We have no information as to the role played by Mrs Wise in the decision, peculiarly within the concerns of a wife and mother, to move the family home. Family recollections suggest that the decision was that of the husband, and that the wife acquiesced reluctantly.[246]

Altogether Theresa Wise appears as a shadowy figure in her husband's *Reminiscences*. She was concerned about his health and his absent-mindedness; she took a stand when he wanted to return to Europe in 1848 and when it was represented to her that Charleston, whither he proposed to move in 1850, was dangerous because of the yellow fever; she wept in times of trouble. Wise's frequent journeyings do not suggest that he felt chained to his home, and his *Reminiscences* do not point to his wife as the inspiration of his activities. 'My wife learned nothing of all this,' he wrote of his disappointment at the failure of his first plan to unite American Jewry. 'Even later I never drew my wife into my struggles and sufferings ... Selfishness had something to do with this, as I did not wish to be disturbed in my home life ... Serene peace ruled in my home ... No matter what took place outside, not a word was said about it at home.'[247]

Domestic tranquillity was not Wise's lot after his removal to North College Hill. Theresa Wise was overcome with illness; she lived until 1874, but the last decade of her life was almost uninterrupted sickness and suffering. There was reticence about the nature of her illness. In the preface to *The Cosmic God* (published in 1876) we have one of the few occasions on which Wise lifts the veil on his private life. 'My wife was prostrated with an incurable disease. For nearly two years she lived the life of a shadow, without affection or clear consciousness, no more herself than the ruin is the castle.' He describes the book as 'conceived in sorrow, composed in grief and constructed at the brink of despair'. He goes on to refer to 'Ruthless attacks upon my character, restless assailants from the camp of implacable foes', which is familiar enough. However, the presence of domestic misfortune beyond remedy is to be borne in mind when considering Wise's public contentiousness at this period.

---

[245] *Jewish Messenger*, 45 (7 Mar. 1879), 1.

[246] The *Reminiscences* were written as contributions to *Die Deborah* between July 1874 and Aug. 1875; Theresa Bloch Wise passed away on 10 Dec. 1874. A memoir of her life was written by their daughter, Theresa Wise Molony.

[247] *Reminiscences*, 93.

14. FIRST FRUITS IN CINCINNATI

Heavy as was its toll of life and property, the Civil War stimulated rather than retarded the development of the United States. The Union was now impregnable, and it was made stronger by economic development on a vaster scale than had yet been conceived. The Homestead Act of 1862 and the rapid development of the railways encouraged settlers to push the frontiers further and further west; the stream of immigrants flowed on without diminution; the value of agricultural produce and minerals bounded upward rapidly; industries which the war had enlarged found their capacity still required after peace was restored. In an economy so dynamic, many a pedlar became a storekeeper, many a storekeeper became the owner of an emporium, and many a small manufactory became a large one. There would be no purpose in describing the post-bellum era as one of high idealism (Wise himself suffered from no such illusion). Any generalization must be used with caution, but the age can be characterized by strident materialism and political corruption.[248] Nevertheless, the country was forging ahead. The Jewish communities were increasing in size and Jews as individuals were sharing in the prosperity of the North as a whole, and had become more attuned to American life. As the railway network became denser, communities became less isolated, and the waging of a successful war in defence of the Union strengthened the centripetal forces in subsidiary branches of the national life. For his 'bold plans' Wise now had a more solid foundation on which to build.

Still, first thought was for matters of immediate congregational interest and prestige. As early as 1860, Wise's own congregation had found the Lodge Street synagogue inadequate. The war postponed efforts to build a new house of worship, but in 1863 a site was bought at the corner of Plum and Eighth Streets, and building started two years later. On 24 August 1866 the Plum Street temple was dedicated. The new edifice, constructed in the Moorish style, was a large one, seating over two thousand worshippers, and it was consecrated with all the grandiloquent ceremonial that was customary in those days.

The dedication service began at the Lodge Street synagogue, and a procession, preceded by music and banners and including the Scrolls of the Law, wound its way to the new temple, where a second service

[248] *Cambridge Modern History* (1st edn.), vii. 654, 697, 698.

was read. The ritual included the five verses of a hymn written by
Wise for the occasion and set to music by Mozart. The first verse ran:

> 'Let there be light,' a second time
> The Lord of Hosts proclaimed;
> 'Let error yield to truth sublime,
> And justice reign supreme!'
> The sun then rose on Sinai's height,
> And poured on thee a flood of light.

There was another hymn, also written by Wise, of which the first
verse ran:

> Resound, ye domes, with holy hymns,
> Break forth in joyous lays,
> To Him whose glory suns bedims,
> Whose love outlasts all days;
> Ye gorgeous pillars sing
> The praise of Isr'el's King!

The choral parts of the service were sung by a choir of forty-five
vocalists, supported by the organ and an orchestra; the cantor of
Temple Emanu-El, New York, was brought to Cincinnati to officiate;
the most prominent citizens were found in the congregation. Altogether the move from the insignificance of Lodge Street to a prominent
site opposite the cathedral meant that Judaism had arrived.[249]

Wise used the occasion of his dedication sermon to expound 'the
leading points of American Judaism, the new school in Judaism'. This
too was elaborately staged; it was based on the Psalm 117 ('Praise the
Lord, all ye Nations'), and when, after a few introductory paragraphs,
Wise first set forth his text, the choir and congregation joined in
singing it. He concluded by invoking

the great Elohim, who is the Creator of the universe, to consecrate this temple
by His holy presence ... the All-wise Adonoi, who is the everlasting Governor
of the universe, to consecrate this temple with His divine wisdom ... the All-
good El-Shaddai the bountiful Preserver of the universe, who revealed himself
to our fathers Abraham, Isaac and Jacob, to consecrate this temple with His
divine goodness ...
... the Great I am who redeemed our fathers from bondage, to consecrate
this temple with His divine grace, ...
... the All-mighty Yah, who is 'my might and my music,' whose powerful
arm revealed itself to our fathers at the Red Sea, to consecrate this temple

[249] *Israelite*, 12 (31 Aug. 1866), 4.

with the fullness of His might, and the glory of His name ...

... the Lord Zebaoth who revealed His truth and light to Moses and the Prophets, to consecrate this temple with His everlasting light and truth.

... the Great and Ineffable One, the Most High and Most Holy, who alone is God, and none beside Him, the only and sole sovereign of all that was, and is, and will be, to consecrate this temple and this congregation with His everlasting majesty and refulgent splendor, now and for ever.[250]

Each of these invocations concluded with the doxology 'Now and forever, Amen, Hallelujah', and on each occasion the choir repeated the words 'Amen, Hallelujah'.

In his crude little place of worship in Albany, Wise had been wafted aloft by thoughts of synagogue music after the grand manner which Sulzer had introduced in Vienna. Now, twenty years after his arrival in America, he found himself the centre of a more elaborate pageant in a larger house of worship than anything known to the Jewish community of the imperial city of the Habsburgs.

Apart from his role in the ceremonies of the day, Wise was not forgotten by his congregation. Before the grand procession left the old synagogue, the president delivered an address in the course of which he reviewed the history of the congregation, then twenty-seven years old. He left no doubt that Wise's coming had transformed the congregation.

The real history of the progress of our congregation dates from the time when our esteemed Rabbi, Rev. Dr. Wise, was chosen as our spiritual guide, for to him we are indebted for the position which we now occupy in the community and among our sister congregations. It was he who commenced fearlessly, and in opposition to all existing obstacles and prejudices, to remove the superficial practices in our service, and he slowly but surely created order and system out of chaos.

His excellent teachings found a willing ear in his congregation. He not only managed to retain in our midst peace, harmony and concord, of which this congregation has always been characterized, but he extended the same wholesome influence over the majority of the congregations in the West, who are co-operating with us in the onward march of progress, enlightenment, and true religion.[251]

Few rabbis could be identified with the progress of their congregations as Wise was by his president.

---

[250] *Israelite*, 12 (31 Aug. 1866), 5. Concerning the dedication ceremonies generally, see Heller, *As Yesterday When It Is Passed*, 107 ff.
[251] *Israelite*, 12 (31 Aug. 1866), 4.

The glow of satisfaction which the ceremonials of August 1866 exuded must have persisted for a long time thereafter. Two years later Wise was to speak at the dedication of a yet larger temple, the new Temple Emanu-El in New York. Even in comparison with the Fifth Avenue sanctuary his own temple must have ranked as one of the show places of the American Jewish community, and merely to possess it must have lent support to the efforts which the rabbi made to put into operation plans for American Jewry as a whole.

The consecration of a new temple was one of the extraordinary occasions of a rabbi's career. How did Wise acquit himself under workaday conditions? What impression did he give? Little information has come down, as is only natural. His was an age when virtuosity in the pulpit could make a clergyman's career, and the position which Wise attained, and the fact that he was constantly in demand for special occasions, suggest that his accomplishments were at least above average. On the other hand, the tributes paid to him do not single him out as the great rabbinical orator of his day.

In March 1879 the New York *Jewish Messenger* published a description of a Sabbath morning service at the Plum Street temple, attended apparently by 'hundreds of people entering quietly and decorously, who took their seats just as noiselessly as they had entered'. The report concerning the rabbi's part is what engages our attention.

A tall man, whom we had not previously noticed, slowly arose from his seat on the platform, and with slow, almost unsteady gait, ascended the pulpit. A tall, lean man, with stooping shoulders, and walking as if he were suffering physical pain. His full black dresscoat sat loosely around him—it was not an impressive figure. A lofty forehead, a pair of brilliant blue eyes, were the only marks of beauty upon his otherwise uninteresting countenance. Nervously his hand grasped the pulpit, as if his body needed support in the mental exercise that was to follow. The text was given out in a low, undetermined voice. But as soon as the first words fell from the preacher's lips, his hand forsook its hold, his stooping shoulders raised, his eyes became still more brilliant, his form became erect, his nostrils elated, and a mighty man stood before my astonished eyes! His whole face lit up with the electricity of mental exercise, and as the words rushed from his mouth in a mighty current, I recognized Isaac M. Wise. It was a masterly effort, though not a new one. Perhaps in that moment, when he discoursed upon 'Prophecy,' the good doctor was not aware that years before he had laid down the same principles in the third chapter of his 'Origin of Christianity'. But his old principles, dressed in fresh thought, and presented in sturdy, solid English, fell delightfully from the lips of the man who had revolutionized Western Judaism during the last two decades. And there was not a soul amongst the vast audience who for three quarters of an hour did not follow the lecturer with the closest attention. It is no surprise to me now that Dr. Wise is the idol of thousands, who love him the better as they recognize the fact that he has his faults.

Such an array of solid facts, such rushing torrent of eloquence, such fervor and conviction in the existence of the Great Jehovah, are seldom perceived within the space of one discourse, and to listen to such a man for weeks and years, to perceive as he proceeds glimpses of genuine inspiration combined with solid learning, is a delightful improvement upon the hackneyed, second-hand sermons to which one is occasionally compelled to listen. When he stands before you, addressing his congregation with the earnestness of con-viction, you forget that his tearing down of old landmarks inflicts pain in the breasts of thousands, who are averse to his teachings, but you only recognize the fact that that man, with the fire of genuine enthusiasm in his eye, his noble aspirations towards elevating the nation he loves so well, would seal their happiness with his heart's blood. You forget that in past years the measures he used towards attaining his ends, were autocratic, and he only appears as a thorough physician, who invents radical cures to stem the tide of disease and infection. And when you see him in his pulpit, you also forget the journalist who for years has dealt partisan blows to his opponents right and left, and you see him in his real attire, that of a venerable, loving man, who has no quarrel with anybody, but who would be fain left to mind his own business, which is the propagation of the word of God as he understands it, unto those who are willing to listen to his ministrations.[252]

We may make light of the journalistic garnish which decorates this description, but there remains a solid tribute to Wise's powers as a preacher, and one which is the more telling because it appeared in a weekly which was generally opposed to his influence. From about the same period comes another characterization which is more clearly suffused with an animus against him. Henry Illowizi, rabbi and writer, who appears to have arrived in the United States shortly before, had been advised to seek out Wise for help in obtaining a pulpit. In *Through Morocco to Minnesota* he recalls his encounter and not only reflects on his preaching style but also on his style of living, describing in particular a Sabbath meal in a saloon in company with the lower orders.

Arrived at Cincinnati on a Friday, we embraced the first opportunity of introducing ourself to the great Jewish reformer, author, orator, philosopher, pamphleteer, publicist, politician, and theologian of the West. The oppor-

[252] *Jewish Messenger*, 46 (28 Mar. 1879), 1.

tunity was afforded in the vestry-room of his temple, where we found him next morning,—a somewhat bent, unsteadily walking figure, crowned with a capacious head, of a physiognomy that bespoke a restless mind, a mental vigor seldom found in a man who has passed three-score. 'I heard of you,' he said, 'and there is no reason why you should not get a good position in America. Where is the *Israelite*? Here are three positions advertised; write to all them; do so at once.' Upon our remarking that the Sabbath was not a fit time for a Jewish minister to apply in writing, the venerable gentleman unhesitatingly honored us with an emphatic *shote* [fool], and added that we were unfit for this country,—a revelation which aroused in us some serious doubts about Mohammed being the last prophet. With this the matter ended so far, and our curiosity was not small to hear this 'light in Israel' discourse. His lecture was most assuredly a curiosity of homiletics, the stomach being the sacred centre round which all his ideas clustered. With an amazing waste of erudition, copious quotations from various literatures, he succeeded in strengthening his position until it seemed positively impregnable. The effect on the audience was magical. It is true some became drowsy and began to snore; but then, others did not sleep at all; while only one gentleman before us glanced at his watch now and then. The edifice is one of the most magnificent we have ever seen. When all was over we felt sure of one thing: there was a 'stomach' in the matter.

... After service we accompanied Rabbi Wise, who led the way to an inn or saloon, where, to our great astonishment, he ordered luncheon served on a bare table, chicken, beer, etc.,—amid a crowd of lower humanity, he talking theology and philosophy all the while. We were not invited to eat, but to listen,—an enjoyment not quite as nutritious as the meal proper. It was easy to see that the reverend gentleman must be a pleasant boon companion when in congenial company,—ever ready to tell a good story, enjoy a joke, have a hearty laugh, drink a glass or two, and have a good time. He is 'a good fellow', as the phrase goes; those he likes he will uphold with might and main, by means allowed or forbidden; for opponents he has 'immortal vengeance and hateful ire,' and handfuls of mire besides. His influence is kept fresh by two weeklies,—the *Deborah*, in German, and the *Israelite*, in English,—both edited in a spirit characteristic of the American politician, not as veracious as George, who would not tell a lie.[253]

Whether as a result of this encounter, or the horrified Illowizi's description of it, some ill-feeling arose between the two men: Wise described Illowizi as 'an inveterate liar'[254] and Illowizi threatened Wise with a suit for libel.[255]

[253] Illowizi, *Through Morocco to Minnesota*, 88.
[254] Ibid.   [255] Ibid.

The compliments addressed to Wise in 1866 were the first of a series of tributes which now mark his career. They were renewed and intensified three years later at a festival of which he was the centre. Wise and his wife celebrated their silver wedding on 6 June 1869. 'Young and old, male and female, Jew and Gentile—all were there, without distinction of creed or nationality,—to celebrate the day,' wrote the *Israelite* of the reception which the couple gave at their country home.[256] The choir of the temple sang a hymn; Lilienthal spoke on the text 'God is with thee, thou brave warrior', and later read an address signed on behalf of Congregation Bene Israel. Naturally, the principal address came from Congregation B'nai Jeshurun, and it was accompanied by a gift of $5,000. The boys of the top class of Wise's school presented him with an easy chair. There is scarcely need to allude to, let alone recite, the compliments which the great day brought forth, for his support of the orphan asylum, for his instruction to the young, for his efforts to establish a college, for his defence of the Jew against prejudice and bigotry. The struggles were not yet over, but at this milestone of his life Wise could feel that he was beginning to reap the harvest.

15. WIDER AMBITIONS

Assurances of the esteem in which he was held came to Wise when he was girding himself for a fresh assault on the giant of indifference and jealousy that stood in the way of the 'bold plans', to further which he had made Cincinnati his base in 1854; and they mark the end of a period, extending longer than a decade, in which he had been, not becalmed, but never able to catch the trade wind which would send him to his goal.

Wise's public imperviousness to the cyclones blowing around him during the war becomes all the more evident as we note his uninterrupted harping on the more parochial interests which he had taken up when he came to Cincinnati. If the wind was not blowing in his direction, he could tack at every turn of the breeze in the hope of manœuvring the vessel in the direction he wanted. The Federal army's lack of officers (most had come from the South) flowed from the supremacy of Mammon over learning in the North—and hence, presumably, indicated the importance of colleges.[257] Under the stress

---

[256] *Israelite*, 15 (11 June 1869), 4. [257] Ibid. 6 (19 July 1861), 20.

of war, antisemitism was raising its head; one answer was 'educate your children ... withdraw your children as much as possible from commerce ... Let us have men in all branches of science and trade, let our innate talents be turned to the different occupations of the citizens, and prejudices will vanish as the mist before the rising sun.'[258] Thus the emphasis shifts, at times, from the training of American rabbis to education as an antidote to antisemitism.

The specialized function of the college in which he was most directly interested he did not forget, even during the dark years of the Civil War. The New World, he argued in an article entitled 'The Want of Ministers', would revolutionize the old in all departments of the mind; every sect but the Jews had its advocates and expounders; in the absence of such the Jews must remain strangers to the world. 'The remedy is a college of our own, in which young men are educated for all vocations of life and those who feel the desire be prepared for the ministry.'[259]

The fear that Jews might 'remain strangers to the world' sounds a note which appears with a different accompaniment also. He urges the Americanization of the Jew in the same breath as he says 'withdraw your children as much as possible from commerce'.

We must be naturalized not only in the political sense of the word, but also in its social signification. Be no Germans, no Polanders, no Englishmen, no Frenchmen, be Jews in the synagogue and Americans everywhere outside thereof ... Be Americanized in language, manners, habits, and appearances.[260]

With this viewpoint he inveighed against exclusively Jewish clubs, not acknowledging apparently that they were a phenomenon which non-Jewish attitudes had a large share in creating.[261] Far more persistent were his attacks on 'The attempt at Germanizing the American synagogue'. This he did on numerous occasions and various grounds (though the name Einhorn and the prayer book *Olath tamid* are written large every time).[262] It had an obvious relationship to his

[258] Ibid. 10 (2 Oct. 1863), 108.   [259] Ibid. 9 (2 Jan. 1863), 204.
[260] Ibid. 8 (4 Apr. 1862), 316.   [261] Ibid. 10 (2 Oct. 1863), 108.
[262] Ibid. 8 (12 July 1861), 12. See also ibid. 8 (11 Apr. 1862), 324. 'Every teacher and preacher can, should, must learn English.' (*Die Deborah*, 13 (30 Nov. 1866), 82), as cited by Rudolf Glanz, 'Source Materials on Jewish Immigration', *YIVO Annual of Jewish Social Science*, 6 (1951), 145.

thrust for the training of American rabbis and the establishment of a college for that purpose.

Seeking at every turn a hearing for his plans but never receiving the response which would suggest the opportunity of executing them, he gave expression to the sense of victimization exhibited time and again in his writings. In January 1862 we find him deep in depression. The *Israelite* and *Die Deborah* must have been in low waters owing to readers in the South being cut off and those in the North finding reasons to discontinue.[263] Wise appealed to his readers to find new subscribers or pay the subscriptions of those who could not afford to do so themselves. This appeal was preceded by nearly two columns of complaints concerning unnamed enemies: 'The opponents of the *Israelite* and *Deborah* . . . exert all their influence and ingenuity to break down this establishment . . . We have been and are persecuted by the mean and despicable envy of men who want honor without labor.'[264] By allusion he pointed to the Orthodox on the one hand who were grieved to see him diffuse light and truth, and 'the other camp of modern society' who were aggrieved that he did not 'write in favor of pork . . . against the rite of circumcision, the fasting on the day of atonement, the rest on the Sabbath-day . . . '.[265] 'We wanted a college', he wrote eighteen months later, 'there came insult and sickening opposition from eastern cities because the college was to be in the West . . . We proposed a synod . . . we proposed a union of the synagogues by the *Minhag America* . . . and were attacked like a criminal with passionate fury as if we had proposed the destruction of the world.'[266]

Wise's concern for the maintenance of the American Union reinforces his pursuit of the idea of the union of American Israel. Noting that the reformers wished openly, systematically, and self-consciously to reconcile Judaism with the spirit of the age, he de-

[263] At this time, *Israelite* was publishing the names of subscribers who had 'stopped without payment or notice'.

[264] *Israelite*, 8 (10 Jan. 1862), 220.

[265] Ibid. No indication is given of the acts of persecution. He may have been aggrieved at the refusal of wealthy friends to rescue his newspapers out of their difficulties: 'people think it a matter of charity to pay a few dollars for a journal that continually fights their battles and find ready excuses to discourage it as much as in their power'; ibid. 10 (24 July 1863), 27.

[266] Ibid. 10 (24 July 1863), 27: 'personal attacks and even violent tirades against the editor' were, he said, the reward of his efforts to create the institutions which the community needed.

precated the fact that every rabbi reformed as he thought proper and every congregation behaved as a distinct sect. 'They call that the free development of the religious idea, we call it anarchy . . . common sense says "united we stand" there is strength in union.'[267] He rounds off his arguments with a plea for a uniform liturgy, music, catechism, and qualifications for rabbis—and of course a college.[268]

This was in January 1863. That summer he visited Chicago, Cleveland, and St Louis and returned filled with enthusiasm for the progress of Reform in those parts but infected with a fresh dose of resentment against those, the Reform leaders of the East, who had killed his proposals for a college and a synod. He repeats his call for a union, but this time it is not a union of all American Israel but a 'union based on the progressive principles of "Reform" '.[269] Moreover, he is toying with the idea of leaving out the East.

Early in 1864 Wise had been ready to carry into effect the kind of scheme he had in mind before the Civil War intervened[270]—a private institution under his personal control. He had come into possession, he said, of a house equipped as a residential school near his residence on North College Hill and he proposed to open it as such to prepare pupils 'for any and every professional study, including the ministry, which they may choose'. The fees would be $400 per annum, and as soon as twenty-five students had registered and $10,000 been pledged, the scheme would proceed.[271] Nothing further was heard of the matter.

In the absence of any move on the part of the better-off Jews of America to send their sons to the college which he had proposed to set up as a private institution, Wise had been unable to proceed; but his mind had not yet ransacked all the possibilities of engaging support. What about the B'nai B'rith? The congregations were independent republics, jealous of their sovereign rights; but the B'nai B'rith Order was a federal system, lodges being integrated with the national body. Here, then, was an organization which could take up a project that was national in scope. Wise had been active intermittently in the affairs of the B'nai B'rith, and in July 1865 sought the agreement of District Grand Lodge No. 2 to a resolution the effect of which would have been to replace the 'Orphan Asylum Fund'

[267] Ibid. 9 (30 Jan. 1863), 236.   [268] Ibid.
[269] Ibid. 10 (14 Aug. 1863), 352.   [270] See ch. 3 sect. 7 above.
[271] *Israelite*, 10 (12 Feb. 1864), 261.

which the district was then collecting by a 'Teachers Seminary Fund'. The proposal was heavily defeated. A year later the Constitution Grand Lodge (i.e. the governing body of the order, embracing all the districts) met in Cincinnati. B. F. Peixotto, the grand master of the order, urged, it is said at Wise's instigation, the consideration of a plan for the foundation of a university, one of whose objects—its principal object, perhaps—would be the training of Jewish ministers. The opponents of the scheme sought to deprive the proposal of its momentum by deleting the part which related to the training of ministers, on the grounds that it was one of the order's principles to keep aloof from doctrinal and congregational matters, and then they allowed the indifference of the separate lodges and districts to put it to death.[272]

Despite this rebuff, Wise did not revert to the idea of a college as a private institution; he now preferred a public institution supported by the Jews of America. His optimism and his zeal made it all appear very simple: each congregation was to enact a law that each of its members was to pay with his dues a dollar a year to a college fund, and to set up a committee to collect a dollar a year from non-members for the same purpose. These means, Wise declared in March 1866, 'will secure to the Hebrew community ... one of the best endowed colleges in the United States'.[273] Support for proposals along these lines was voiced in St Louis[274] and Buffalo,[275] but again they came to nothing. Wise would have been in a stronger position to badger other congregations into adopting the dollar-a-year levy had he been able to get his own to take up the idea. B'nai Jeshurun had bitten off as much as it could chew with building the Plum Street temple. For whatever reason, no move was reported from Cincinnati.

In 1866 the opening of the Plum Street temple brought Wise again to refer to the need for a college. The dedication of so fine a structure drew some antisemitic comments from the local Presbyterian news-

---

[272] The statements in the text are abstracted from an article by Isidor Busch entitled 'The Jewish Orphan Asylum, Cleveland, O. Some Glimpses from its Early History', *Menorah*, 5 (July 1888), 24 ff. The article displays a clear animus against Wise, and subsequent issues of the magazine show that it drew protests from the *Israelite*. However, the record of the proposals was not challenged, and David Philipson's *History of Hebrew Union College* confirms that Wise tried to enlist the support of B'nai B'rith at the period mentioned but failed.

[273] *Israelite*, 12 (23 Mar. 1866), 300.   [274] Ibid.

[275] Ibid. (27 Apr. 1866), 341; (4 May 1866), 348.

paper. In the *Israelite* Wise gave the writer more than seventy-five column inches of reply in the implacable style which he adopted whenever faced with an attack on his people. But he had not done with the *Presbyterian Witness*. That paper had criticized his dedication sermon as infidelity, which prompted Wise to suggest that it was the duty of Jews to inform the millions of Gentiles who disbelieved in miracles how near they were to his view of Judaism; and for that purpose they needed 'a college and a seminary to educate preachers, teachers, writers, advocates and expounders of our cause'.[276]

Wise had not given up hope of support from B'nai B'rith. In January 1867 he wrote in terms which implied that the college scheme was either about to be submitted to this order or was already under its consideration. This time he emphasized its character as an institution of general education. Again the enthusiasm of Wise's advocacy found no response.

When Wise urged the college upon B'nai B'rith there was no point in associating with it the project for a union of congregations. In general, however, the advantages of a congregational union also continued to occupy his mind. On this theme his writings abound, and one more example will suffice. In 1867 the summer conferences of the other religious denominations had impressed Wise with their ability publicly to demonstrate their existence, and he contrasted the absence of a recognized voice for Judaism: 'only the Israelite is dumb, he shows no public signs of life and activity'. Union, he suggested, was impossible while the Jewish community was two-thirds foreign, retaining prejudices brought over from other countries.[277] This gave him cause to advance the claims of his *Minhag America* not merely as the ritual expression of the rational purified Judaism, but as the instrument of further union: 'whenever one hundred congregations shall be liturgically united under the *Minhag America*, . . . the basis to a lasting union of the American Israel is laid out, upon which all the superstructures of the synod, the college, the seminary, &c., will easily be reared'.[278]

The right asserted by every 'rabbi, preacher, cantor or teacher' to 'manufacture a new prayerbook . . . to write a catechism and a historical abstract of the Bible, to produce the most horrible confusion of ideas in Judaism' Wise asserted to be 'of European birth, and . . .

---

[276] Ibid. 16 (12 Oct. 1866), 71.   [277] Ibid. 13 (21 June 1867), 4.   [278] Ibid.

entirely averse to the spirit of our country, in which the idea of union, the harmonious cooperation of many to one purpose, is manifestly predominant'.[279] This was written in 1868, when the American Union had emerged strengthened from the crucible of the Civil War. Probably the fact that Einhorn was pushing *Olath Tamid*, and in its favour had displaced *Minhag America* from the synagogue in New York to which he had been appointed two years before, was irking Wise. When Wise is in this mood, congregational autonomy is an obstruction to be overcome, rather than the immoveable cornerstone of Jewish life.

He was not always in the same mood. A year before (1867) one of the spokesmen of Orthodoxy had made against reformers in general an accusation not far different from the one which Wise later levelled at those reformers who rejected his ideas. The New York *Jewish Messenger* declared that the Orthodox 'would hail quite cordially the convocation of an *authority* to consider, discuss, and, if deemed wise, to modify the ritual'; the reformers, on the other hand were content 'to follow implicitly and like sheep the dictation of their momentary spiritual leader'.[280] This wound up Wise for one of his periodical outbursts about the reception accorded by both Orthodox and radicals to the Cleveland Platform twelve years earlier:

Did not the orthodoxy howl at the Cleveland Conference as disgustingly as the radicals did? If that gentleman thinks that we sit still, stand by inactively, slovenly, sleepingly, and rot upon a rotten couch, till all those gentlemen please to move with unanimity, and let our sacred cause go to destruction, because those gentlemen love to sleep;—if he thinks, we say, because they do nothing, we must do nothing; because they sleep we must dream—that gentleman believes a mistake. We do. The calls, the most vehement calls, on the American Jews to rise and unite, invariably met deaf ears. This forced us to the conviction that we must act independently of those who sleep, those who are noisy on small things, those who do nothing. Authority or none, right or wrong, go on! Was the motive on the side of reform and progress, and, if they do not like it, let them unite and constitute an authority to do things better. But we must do, or else time will upset us, together with the cause which we neglected.

In April 1867 he pointed out that certain biblical laws were temporary

---

[279] *Israelite*, 28 (28 Aug. 1868), 4. Wise uses this occasion to take a swipe at Maimonides College—'The Polish *Cheder* is imported into Philadelphia and labeled a College.' As to his attitude to Maimonides College, see ch. 3 sect. 18 below.

[280] Quoted in *Israelite*, 13 (13 July 1866), 4.

in character and that the rabbis had not hesitated to change them. 'This was not always done', he said, 'by a Sanhedrin or a synod, it was frequently done by persons in high authority.'[281] It was extremely easy, therefore, to establish a firm basis for modern Judaism—after the fashion he had set forth in *The Essence of Judaism*. 'We only need establish the doctrines of the Bible, the law of the covenant as expressed or implied in the Decalogue, and the temporary laws which may be changed and have been frequently changed.'[282] The question arose, then, who was to declare the changes authoritatively. For the individual Jew, it was his own conscience. For the congregation, 'in order to maintain union and concord, an authoritative body, a synod, should decide, as was always the case in Israel'. Wise next considered the position should no synod be established.

It is the duty of every congregation to proceed in strict accordance with the doctrines of Judaism, the law of the covenant and the just demands of the age and especially of her members. The rabbi must conscientiously watch over Judaism and permit no misinterpretation of its doctrines and no violation of the laws of the covenant; in all other respects he is entitled to consult the interests of his cause, the demands of the age and the wishes of his congregation.[283]

He gives instances of what would be 'a violation of the laws of the covenant'. These would include a proposal to abolish the Sabbath or to adopt an 'anti-biblical doctrine', and if the rabbi could not prevent them it would be his duty to resign. However, there were reforms of another class, and in regard to these it would be the rabbi's duty to yield. Thus, if the congregation desired to introduce a choir, an organ, or the *Minhag America* prayer-book, or to abolish talmudical festivals (in fact do the kind of things Wise had done), then 'the rabbi must be guided by the wishes of the congregation'.

Wise completes this delineation of the system of authority by fitting to it his own actions during his ministry in America. He had worked for years, he said, to establish a synod, but after the Cleveland Conference in 1855 nothing came of the project. All that was left was the *Minhag America*, which 'was indorsed by the votes of thousands of Israelites'. As for the rest, the absence of a synod justified his independent actions.

---

[281] Ibid. 11 (5 Apr. 1867), 4. [282] Ibid. [283] Ibid.

Whenever the congregations will adopt the status quo, and pass laws in favor of a synod to conduct uniformly and lawfully the development of the American synagogue, we shall be the first to co-operate fully and conscientiously. As long as they act not, we must.[284]

Before either Wise or anyone else was able to renew the venture started in Cleveland in 1855, there passed away the man with whom he had collaborated in his first attempt to unite American Jewry and who had set his hand to that project even before Wise had arrived in the United States. Isaac Leeser died on 1 February 1868. Leeser's career runs parallel to that of Wise in many respects. Not only did he strive, both with and apart from Wise, for the union of American Israel, but he recognized that the mother tongue of American Israel would be English and, though brought up in Germany, he wrote and preached in the English language. He travelled tirelessly to the scattered congregations of the country; he started the *Occident* and a Jewish publication society; he translated the Scriptures into English; he produced an American edition of the prayer-book; he was an early advocate of a college for training rabbis and actually got the project under way.

Leeser received a better secular education than did Wise and was his superior in style. Wise had a better command of Hebrew and talmudic literature, but, far more important, there seemed to throb through his veins a red blood which gave him a forcefulness lacking in the over-modest Leeser. Wise was possessed by a belief in himself as the champion and saviour of American Jewry; Leeser was forever apologizing for his inadequacies. Wise, towering in energy and vision above his followers, but never so far ahead of them that they could not see him, based his system on the Ashkenazi *minhag*, familiar to the great majority, and added enough of current popular knowledge to give it the attraction of novelty that was so important in the New World. Leeser clung rigidly to the strict demands of Orthodoxy, and clothed it in the pure but unfamiliar colours of Sepharad. When Leeser died, Wise still had thirty-two years of active life ahead of him.

A melancholy tribute to Wise's influence had come from Leeser three months before his death. With little of his earnest life to run, he turned once more to the need for 'a due training of youth in

---

[284] *Israelite*, 11 (5 Apr. 1867), 4. Wise's meaning is not clear in every detail; the 'status quo' may refer to the former institutions of sanhedrin and synod.

religious knowledge', and in the course of comments on the general preference for money-making over education that run parallel to those which Wise made in the *Israelite*,[285] he observed: 'The learned stand at such an elevation above the people that, if they have influence, they can lead the congregation as they please. We have in our mind especially *one*, who resides in the West, we may as well name him, Dr I. M. Wise, who seems to have obtained almost unlimited control over entire districts.'—Wise must have read those words with great satisfaction, though what immediately followed must have reminded him that his authority was not unchallenged—'and he would be irresistible, were it not that an antagonistic influence, of a more radical kind yet, has been brought forward in the person of Dr Einhorn'.[286]

In the *Israelite* for 14 February 1868, Wise paid a tribute to his departed associate and antagonist with a sobriety which suggests that the news had affected him. It is difficult to accept the statement that 'we never became so far estranged to each other, that we were not on speaking terms, or could not meet each other cordially on any occasion, because we never offered each other personal insult, nor did we at any time disrespect each other'.[287] Leeser may have done so, but Wise did not conduct his relationship on that kind of basis. When he left the level of personalities Wise moved to surer ground.

He was the banner-bearer of American Jewish conservatism. All the rest of their leaders are of local importance only, while he, by his literary efforts, his travels, his numerous acquaintances, his unfeigned attachment to his cause, and his consistency, had a wide-spread influence. We know of no man in America who will replace Isaac Leeser in the orthodox camp. He had a cause to plead, and he did it without fears or favors. He did not yield an inch to any body. He unfurled his true colors on every occasion, and proved himself by far more consistent and by far more honest than many in that camp who are prudent enough to be every thing to everybody.[288]

And of his final epitaph there is no reason to doubt the sincerity:

We sincerely regret the loss of a man whom we esteemed highly, although we could but rarely agree with him. We have struggled; the victory is his, for he has arrived in yonder region where the enigmas are solved and the

[285] See *Israelite*, 7 (8 Nov. 1861), 148.   [286] *Occident*, 25 (Dec. 1867), 422.
[287] *Israelite*, 12 (14 Feb. 1868), 4.   [288] Ibid.

questions are answered. Peace be to his ashes, happiness to his soul, and blessing to his memory.[289]

Less than five months later Wise had occasion to note the death of another champion of Orthodoxy, Morris Jacob Raphall.[290] He was a talented and scholarly orator rather than a great leader.[291] Deafness and other disabilities had limited his effectiveness,[292] and apparently he died in such poverty that his library was raffled to pay his debts.[293] 'We know of no man in America who will replace Isaac Leeser in the Orthodox camp,' Wise had written.[294] Indeed, once Leeser could not hold it up, American Orthodoxy collapsed, until at the end of the century a second Jewish community revived it. In the mean time, was the leadership of American Jewry passing to Wise by survivorship?

Yet it was precisely in the few years following Isaac Leeser's death that the onlooker might have thought Wise condemned to the role of perpetual brawler, his pretensions to national leadership defeated. For as the ranks were thinned out on the right, those on the left were reinforced. The flow of immigrants never ceased, and among them were a number of rabbis, for the most part of a Reform outlook. Wise, who frequently recalled his own pioneer status as an American rabbi and the need for others to shoulder the burden, noted with satisfaction that in addition to the 'grand temples erected, erecting or projected' in the post-Civil War period, learned rabbis had been called from Europe—Mielziner and Huebsch to New York, Hirsch and Jastrow to Philadelphia, Kleeberg to Louisville, and Kronik to Chicago— 'gentlemen known not only as accomplished orators, but also as prominent scholars and writers of importance'.[295]

To the names which Wise mentioned we may add Samuel Adler, who had been in New York since 1857. In 1869 Kaufmann Kohler and Lippman Mayer came to America. The Hirsch mentioned in the *Israelite* was Rabbi Samuel Hirsch, whose *Religionsphilosophie* had influenced Wise so greatly a quarter of a century earlier and who now went to Congregation Keneseth Israel, Philadelphia, to replace David

---

[289] *Israelite*, 12 (14 Feb. 1868), 4.
[290] Ibid. 14 (26 June 1865), 6. Raphall died on 23 June 1868.
[291] *Dictionary of American Biography*, xv. 382.
[292] Hyman B. Grinstein, *The Rise of the Jewish Community of New York* (Philadelphia, 1945), 98.
[293] *Israelite*, 14 (3 July 1868), 4; ibid. 15 (2 Oct. 1868), 4.
[294] Ibid. 12 (14 Feb. 1868), 4.   [295] Ibid. 13 (7 Dec. 1866), 4.

Einhorn. The latter had moved to Congregation Adath Jeshurun, New York, insisting, as has been noted before, that his new congregation replace Wise's *Minhag America* with his own *Olath Tamid*.[296]

The newly arrived rabbis preached and wrote in German; they had the advantages of a German university education, which had been denied to Wise; and it would not be surprising, especially as they belonged to the first generation of rabbis so endowed, if they brought with them a sense of caste by which they marked themselves off from the lesser breeds and a consciousness of the superiority of the theologically more developed atmosphere of German religious life. Here probably is the basis of Wise's complaints at the Germanization of the American synagogue.

In the meantime, Wise had become the community's rabbinical spokesman in the English language. He did not conceal his dislike for New York, nor the dislike that existed for him in New York. 'There is great prejudice in New York against your humble writer,' he wrote in the *Israelite*; 'In the Emanuel Congregation many think I am too orthodox.'[297] A year later he had been chosen to preach at the dedication at the great new Temple Emanu-El in Fifth Avenue (and three years after that he was being excluded from its pulpit). The dedication was an outstanding occasion in the American Jewish calendar, and if Wise considered the invitation something of an accolade he would have had ample excuse.[298]

For this kind of honour Wise was greatly in demand, and, no doubt, was equally ready to project himself. In the same year as he spoke at Temple Emanu-El he spoke at the opening of the B'nai B'rith Orphan Asylum in Cleveland and at the dedication of the temple in Louisville. Two years earlier (1866) we find him at the dedication of the temple

---

[296] Ibid. 12 (22 June 1866), 405.   [297] Ibid. 14 (9 Aug. 1867), 4.

[298] The congregation was without an English preacher at the time. Earlier in 1868 Max Lilienthal had accepted an appointment but had withdrawn, and the Revd J. K. Gutheim, who later took up office, was unable to be present at the consecration. Wise was invited to participate at short notice and was rewarded with the gift of a $500 US bond. In Jan. 1870 Wise wrote to Temple Emanu-El asking for the use of the temple choir and organ for three evenings for the purpose of holding three lectures on Talmud and the Gospels. A special meeting of the trustees was called for 17 Jan., the minutes recording that 'Although it was the wish of every member of the Board, to oblige Dr. Wise, as we consider our congregation somewhat under obligation to him there could be no departure from the rule to refuse such requests'. Presumably these were the lectures which eventually were delivered in Steinway Hall.

at Evansville, Indiana,[299] and in 1867 he performed a similar office for the new Temple Beth El in Detroit. In that year also he travelled south to consecrate the new synagogue in Richmond, Virginia, involving himself in forty-four hours of steady travel.[300] Wise arrived at the Philadelphia Conference (1869) after it had started because he had been engaged on a visit to Nashville, Chattanooga, Atlanta, Augusta, and Charleston. In 1872 we find him heading in another direction—to Easton, Scranton and Titusville, Pennsylvania, and Hartford, Connecticut.[301] Once Leeser had become feeble there was no other rabbi who made the whole country his congregation in this way.

Wise must have been one of the first rabbis to turn to professional lecturing. In February 1871 he gave three lectures on the origins of Christianity at the Steinway Hall, New York—tickets of admission (50 cents each lecture) were sold at the door. This 'line' was probably a by-product of the practice which he introduced of giving lectures in series at the Friday evening services of his temple in Cincinnati. His course on the 'origin of Christianity' Wise repeated during 1876 at New Orleans, Memphis, Chicago, Milwaukee, and Detroit. The audiences were small, admittedly, but this was because 'the intelligent and liberal portion of the community is small almost everywhere'.

The fame of Wise's work as a preacher spread abroad. In August 1870 the *Israelitische Wochenschrift*[302] of Breslau published two articles from its New York correspondent, who divided the champions of Reform into two categories: 'the screaming and the discoursing, or also, if you choose, the itinerant and the stay-at-home. At the head of those who scream and travel stands the "Wise man of Cincinnati".' The writer expended much sarcasm on Wise's activities, but in far away Germany the editor felt impelled to append this note:

So as to give credit to the truth we annexed this sketch moreover to a well known person who has lived in America for a long time. He tells that Mr. Wise is certainly regarded as a good speaker and through his journies has contributed much to imparting a favourable view of Judaism to Americans, particularly in the West, where twenty years ago Jews were hardly known.[303]

Nevertheless, at this period the German element in American

[299] *Israelite*, 13 (10 Aug. 1866), 4.   [300] Ibid. (14 June 1867).
[301] May, *Isaac Mayer Wise*, 290.   [302] See *Israelite*, 17 (26 Aug. 1870), 9.
[303] *Israelitische Wochenschrift* (Breslau), 2 (10 Aug. 1870), 266.

Reform had received an accession of strength and energy, especially in the large Jewish communities of the eastern seaboard. The plutocracy of the East looked to Paris for its fashions, not to the prairies, and likewise the theology of Berlin was to them more attractive than that of Cincinnati. Just when it might have been thought that the tide of assimilation would be washing away inherited German characteristics, the additions to the rabbinate, the prestige conferred by the enhanced status of Temple Emanu-El, and David Einhorn's removal to New York served to reinforce the German influence.

In March 1869 Einhorn acquired an organ of the press. A new weekly journal, the *Jewish Times*, in German and English, began publication. The editor was Moritz Ellinger, a schoolmate and lifelong friend of Einhorn's, and it is clear from its contents that Einhorn was the paper's *spiritus rector*.[304] Kaufmann Kohler goes so far as to say that the launching of the *Jewish Times* 'paved the way for the enunciation of the Reform principles by the Rabbinical conference held at Philadelphia in November of the same year'.[305]

While the Eastern Reform group was gathering strength, the moment seemed to be approaching when, out of the seed which Wise had been scattering for years, a plant was about to spring forth. In February 1869, either because he had definite plans or because he was trying to raise the wind, he announced the convening of a synod to meet that summer in Cincinnati—'a conference . . . to be composed of all Hebrew ministers, teachers and Representatives of the Congregations, and Young Men's Associations'.[306] The announcement

[304] Kaufmann Kohler, *Studies, Addresses and Personal Papers* (New York, 1931), 527; id., *A Living Faith* (Cincinnati, 1948), 266–71. At the general meeting of Temple Emanu-El on 24 May 1868 a communication was read from Congregation Adath Jeshurun—Einhorn's—requesting co-operation in establishing an organ of Jewish reform, and in accordance with the authority granted to him the president appointed representatives to a joint committee for this purpose. (Minutes, Congregation Emanu-El, New York.) It is possible that this was the origin of the *Jewish Times*. The interest of the two congregations in establishing such an organ would be likely to have arisen from the fact that the *Jewish Messenger*, at that time New York's Jewish paper, was in Orthodox hands.
[305] Kohler, *A Living Faith*, 268.
[306] *Israelite*, 15 (26 Feb. 1869), 4. Evidently a serious attempt was made to convene a synod. The minutes of the meeting of the Adjunta of the Congregation Mikve Israel, Savannah, Georgia, for 8 Apr. 1869, record that the president stated that he 'had a circular from Dr Wise and others inviting the congregation to send a delegate to a convention to be held in Cincinnati on the 15 June next.' The congregation promised its co-operation, though not having a minister it felt it could not send a delegate. The 'others' presumably, are the committee mentioned on 21 May (see

is given in a brief paragraph, without accompanying rhetoric and exhortation.

Exhortation came in full measure a week later. In an article entitled 'Our American Israel', Wise called upon rabbis and presidents to 'Act Speedily and Together'.[307] The matters he specified as requiring concerted action were the need for Jews to express their view in the conflict over the use of State funds for sectarian education, the need to have American preachers and teachers (here he gives renewed expression to his laments over the Germanizing of the American synagogue), the need 'to bring system and uniformity into the religious school, in plan, system, subjects, and text books'. He wanted the conference to take the younger generation in hand 'to marshal this intelligent host to a body guard of our cause', and one task which he wanted to assign to them was the establishment of Jewish libraries. The programme, in so far as he goes into details, is concerned entirely with practicalities.

He does not use the word reform, though a passage quoted below might make it appear that reform of worship was one of his objects.[308] In denouncing the inactivity of the Jewish community with regard to the threat of sectarianism in public affairs he asks rhetorically, 'Will you cling to the spirit of darkness to save a piece of talmud and your Midrash quibbles?' but there was no attack on Orthodox doctrine or practice. *Minhag America*, which he loved to advocate and whose acceptance in any congregation he never failed to record, does not get a mention, but he does emphasize the need, not merely for union, but for uniformity.

The synagogue ... must be placed on a footing of uniformity and must be brought into harmony with the spirit of the age. It matters not to us,

---

p. 211, at n. 311). In his Introduction to *The Controversial Letters and the Casuistic Decisions of the Late Rabbi Bernard Illowy Ph.D.* (p. 6) Dr Henry Illoway, who was practising medicine in Cincinnati at the period in question, states that 'About the year 1866 Wise came to the conclusion that another Rabbinical Conference ... would be timely,' but that Lilienthal was not willing to unite with the unqualified ministers who had become accustomed to relying on Wise's leadership and whom he wanted to summon. When Lilienthal could hold the matter back no longer he acted as intermediary between Wise and the Eastern rabbis who were unwilling to act with Wise, and he suggests that as a result of his negotiations Wise was invited to the Philadelphia Conference of 1869.

[307] *Israelite*, 15 (5 Mar. 1869), 4.   [308] Ibid.

which particular system of public worship may prove most acceptable to the congregations, if it be only in harmony with liberal principles and American wants. Uniformity and firmness are things we need. We need uniformity, that the Israelite of any place find himself at home in any other place of worship which he may chance to visit; that books and music can be stereotyped and sold at such low figures, that they become accessible to all; that the divine worship can be taught in the schools. We need firmness in the form of worship to give it holiness, and commanding respect.[309]

On 30 April Wise was writing as if he was discouraged that his announcement of a conference had not brought the overwhelming response to which, in his view, the urgency of the subjects to be discussed entitled it. In *Die Deborah* he published a letter from Schlesinger of Albany urging him to write again about the necessity of a conference, and, commenting on it in that week's *Israelite*, he alluded to the 'personal abuse' he suffered at the hands of the opponents of the Cleveland Conference. There followed more about his being a scapegoat and the object of causeless hatred, leading up to the declaration that if twenty-five congregations made it clear that they wanted a conference, a conference would be called. After further strong exhortations for action came the last-minute information, received after the article had been set in type, that the congregations of Detroit and Memphis had resolved to join in the call for the conference.[310] On 21 May he was able to announce that altogether eleven congregations had agreed to participate, contributing to the total of twenty-five. By this time Wise had assembled a conference committee consisting of Rabbis Lilienthal (Cincinnati), Kleeberg (Louisville), and Mayer (Cleveland), and Messrs Henry Mack and Louis Freiberg (both of Cincinnati).[311] No word in any of the printed propaganda suggested that members were to be drawn from Western communities only, but the East had no share in the arrangements.

16. AMONG THE GENTILES (1867–1878)

Meanwhile, while Wise's plans for the American Jewish community were sometimes moving forward but equally often becoming becalmed or storm-bound, he was involved in a divergent association, albeit one less central to his concerns. Octavius Brooks Frothingham (1822–95) a leading radical among Unitarian ministers, had become president

---

[309] Ibid.   [310] Ibid. (30 Apr. 1869), 4.
[311] Ibid. (21 May 1869), 2.

of the Free Religious Association, founded in 1867. The leaders were a distinguished intellectual group from the National Conference of Unitarian Churches who could no longer accept the more traditional position of the national body. The Free Religious Association was avowedly of a non-Christian character—a standpoint that had become a matter of contention within the official Unitarian camp. The objects of the association were 'to promote the interests of pure religion, to encourage the scientific study of theology, and to increase fellowship in the spirit'. In practice the association reflected the humanistic theism espoused by Frothingham.

Support for the Free Religious Association came from the New England intellectual élite—the 'cod-fish aristocracy' whose conceits had aroused the unaffected man of the West not long before. Jewish–Gentile partnership in religious discussion was something of a novelty, and an invitation to join such a group was indeed flattering. In 1872 Wise became one of its vice-presidents. He spoke for the association and dedicated *The Origin of Christianity* (1868) to it. In the avidity with which Wise took up this relationship it is not difficult to suppose an element of one-upmanship *vis-à-vis* his opponents in the advanced Reform camp. Yet it may have responded to an earlier optimism that ran deeper. In 1799 David Friedlaender (1750–1834), a disciple of Moses Mendelssohn, taking the view that the eternal truths round which Jews and Christians should unite were synonymous, sent an open letter to Pastor Teller, a Berlin church official, stating that many Jews were willing to accept baptism provided that they were not required to confess the dogmas of orthodox Christianity. Was Wise, also a child of Mendelssohnian ideas, inspired by similar feelings, though moving from a converse position? Liberal Judaism, in his view, was the ideal of a liberal religion; it was a religion without mysteries or miracles; in free America the Gentile avant-garde were moving to that position, and the invitation to a rabbi to join their work confirmed it.

Such feelings persisted in Reform Jewish circles. Speaking in 1919 at a centenary tribute to Wise, Kaufmann Kohler could assert, 'Never before was the outside world so eager and willing to listen to the view of progressive Judaism and to accept its doctrines as it is today.'[312] Yet more pointed is Kohler's next statement that in his intimate circles Wise had expressed the view that within fifty years Judaism's

[312] *Central Conference of American Rabbis Year Book*, xxix (1919), 280.

teachings would have become the common property of the American people.

Wise's connection with the Free Religious Association did not last. In 1878 Felix Adler who, after being trained for the Reform rabbinate, had disavowed Judaism and founded the Ethical Culture movement, succeeded Frothingham as president of the Free Religious Association, and thereafter Wise withdrew. Was the apostle of religion conformable to reason simply moved by a 'gut reaction'? In his eyes Adler was a renegade, and while he was happy at the thought of defections from Christianity, he could stomach serving under an apostate from Judaism no more than Pastor Teller, the deist, could stomach baptizing Jews who disavowed belief in Jesus. On both sides the desire to build bridges was held out, but on both the unspoken assumption was that the other side would use the bridge to cross over. All the time Wise's main concerns were with his fellow Jews. Playing second to an authentic Gentile may have helped them, but not playing second to the young Felix Adler.

17. YEARS OF SORROW AND STRIFE (1869–1874)

When, after an interval of four years (1869–74), Wise's conference of congregations was to assemble, he was to be involved in strife as violent and extended as any he had known. Over the years he had impugned the bursting of the bubble floated at Cleveland as a matter of personal victimization, and the renewal of hostilities may be seen as a mere livening up of a conflict that had proceeded almost since he arrived in America. Instead of the frenzy abating as the years went by, it seemed to intensify. When he began to write his *Reminiscences* in July 1874, conflict with the forces of evil, the struggle against demons—'hollow eyed ghostly grinning dwarfs, lascivious, ragged, goblins and tiny poodles with large hollow puffed out hands'—came to the fore as he recorded the dream which he says came to him as his ship neared New York. In 1876 the same mood assumed a more contemporary application: in the preface to his lectures on *The Cosmic God*[313] he says, in a vein which again calls to mind the dream, that at this period

Ruthless attacks upon my character, of restless assailants, from the camp of implacable foes, embittered my joyless days. My energies failed. Insanity or

[313] 'The Cosmic God: A Fundamental Philosophy in Popular Lectures' (Cincinnati, 1876).

suicide appeared inevitably. In this state of mind, the Satan of Doubt persecuted me with all his furious demons. My convictions were uprooted, and my faith was shaken; I was myself no longer.[314]

'Insanity or suicide appeared inevitably.' Could Wise have invented this? Could so tough a fighter have taken the attacks of his enemies so much to heart? Was he projecting on to himself a fate which he saw endangering one near to him? It may be that his demeanour had its roots in an incurable domestic anguish. Theresa Bloch Wise died on 10 December 1874. A contemporary notice declared:

The last decade of her life was trying. She was continually sick or sickly, and the numerous physicians consulted differed widely as to the root of the evil, until at last, in February, 1873, she was prostrated by a disease of a delirious character, the cause of which was never fully agreed upon by her physicians. After three months, she recovered so far, that she could be removed to her country residence, without fully recovering, however, her mental powers of former days. In the fall of the year, she was quite well, but then she fell out of a window from the second story, and was prostrated for twenty weeks with a double fracture of the leg. Still in spring 1874, she was well enough to go back to the country, and there she kept herself up to the end of August, when she was seized by spasms, followed by a hectic fever, from which she never recovered. Early in September she was moved back to the city, and since the tenth of September she was never up again.[315]

This language suggests some kind of mental derangement. How far back in time this illness reached we do not know. The preface to *The Cosmic God*, quoted earlier, suggests that the illness had been serious for two years. One notes that at this period of suffering Wise found it possible freely and jokingly to publish his reminiscences; one asks whether an implacable public demeanour did not reflect helpless suffering in the personal sphere.

Wise's movement for a conference was gathering strength when the Eastern reformers decided to act, with the result that instead of seeing his aspirations for a united American Judaism under his leadership consummated, he found himself diverted again and engaged in the fierce conflicts reflected in his writings.

The focus of the strife was two sets of conferences called with differing objects by men who had developed strong personal antagonisms. Wise, in pursuit of long-standing aims, brought together a

---

[314] As quoted in Wilansky, *Sinai to Cincinnati* (New York, 1937), 287.
[315] *Israelite*, NS 1/25 (18 Dec. 1874), 4.

conference of rabbis in Cleveland in July 1870. This adjourned to New York in October and reassembled in Cincinnati in May 1871. It then declared itself to be a permanent body, but in fact never met again. In the meantime, a conference of Reform rabbis had met in Philadelphia in November 1869, and Wise was charged with arranging for the sessions to be resumed in Cincinnati in November 1870. However, he backed away, and this move petered out. In the course of these manœuvrings Wise was solemnly condemned by his colleagues, but out of the ashes of these endeavours emerged the Union of American Hebrew Congregations, brought together by the lay leaders of Wise's community.

On 1 June 1869 Samuel Adler, of Temple Emanu-El, New York, and David Einhorn issued a 'call' inviting *die theologisch-gebildeten Collegen, welche dem entschiedenen religiösen Fortschritte huldigen* ('colleagues educated in theology who favour decisive progress in religious matters') to a conference to be held after the ensuing High Holidays with the object of securing an understanding between rabbis who were striving for the same ends on the principles—not the form—of the modern ritual and the solutions of practical religious questions, particularly those relating to the law of marriage.[316] Contrasts between their approach and Wise's appear at every turn. The limitation of the invitation to 'theologically educated colleagues' looks as if it might have been framed in conscious disdain for the 'mixed multitude' whom Wise was proposing to call together. And where Wise wanted a conference for the purpose of uniting American Israel, they had in mind the strengthening of a particular theological tendency; and even among those who agreed with that tendency they did not desire to encourage practical measures as much as to establish the formulae of a denominational standpoint.[317]

This 'call' must have presented Wise with a problem, but for the time being he showed unusual restraint, saying that he did not consider the call 'for a meeting of rabbis of the progressive school' to be in opposition to the conference of all congregations and their ministers which he had advocated.[318]

[316] In *The New World of Reform* (Bridgeport, 1974), I have given a translation of the proceedings of this conference, together with an introduction setting forth the background.

[317] This is made abundantly clear in an article accompanying the 'call' which appeared in *Jewish Times*, 1 (4 June 1869), 8.

[318] *Israelite*, 15 (11 June 1869), 4. He later complained that Adler and Einhorn had wronged him by calling the conference. See ch. 3 sect. 19 above. The question whether

The conference opened on 3 November in the study of Dr Hirsch in Philadelphia. Eleven rabbis were present. Wise was not among the eleven; he had gone south and did not arrive till the third session. One man—Einhorn—clearly dominated the proceedings. He arrived with a set of proposals in printed form which were made the basis of discussion, and the resolutions which emerged diverged little from their original form.

The resolutions adopted by the conference followed the line of thinking which Einhorn had first articulated at the Frankfurt rabbinical conference twenty-four years earlier.[319] Thus, they did not hope for the restoration of the Jewish state under a descendant of David; the destruction of the second Jewish commonwealth was not a punishment, but part of a divine plan to disperse the Jews so that they might realize their mission of leading the nations to a true knowledge of God; the destruction of the Second Temple had consigned priesthood and sacrifices to the past once and for all; any distinction between the priestly *kohanim* and other Jews was meaningless; the mission of Israel was to be emphasized; belief in bodily resurrection had no religious foundation; and though the cultivation of Hebrew was desirable, as it was unintelligible to the vast majority of Jews it must give way to prayer in an intelligible language. There were also a number of resolutions dealing with marriage and divorce: the bride was to be an equal party in the marriage ceremony; the traditional marriage formula and benedictions were to be replaced; polygamy, the special marriage laws concerning priests, *halitzah*, and *get* were abolished; presumption of death was to be a matter for the law of the land.[320]

These were not the things for which Wise had been agitating. Wise had been crying for a union and a synod which would make for the consolidation of American Judaism; Einhorn and his followers set out to assert a doctrinal standpoint, and, though they doubtless hoped

---

he should attend the conference required consideration, since the limitation to the 'theologically educated' might have placed a weapon in the hands of the convenors to repel those who were not university graduates; and later there was a suggestion that Lilienthal acted as intermediary to ensure that he would not suffer a rebuff (*Jewish Times*, 3 (26 Aug. 1870), 408.

[319] Julius H. Greenstone, *The Messiah Idea in Jewish History* (Cincinnati, 1906), 260–5.
[320] Philipson, *Reform Movement in Judaism* (1st edn.), 488–90. The resolutions are set out in *Protokolle der Rabbiner-Conferenz abgehalten zu Philadelphia* (New York, 1870), 86–8; and *The New World of Reform*, 116–19.

that it would attract adherents and even win a majority, to get the majority under the roof of a single organization was not their first concern. The line of division is that apparent in the controversy that followed the 1855 Cleveland Conference.

Which way Wise would jump was often unpredictable. It was he who raised the question of removing the requirement of circumcision in the case of proselytes (*milat gerim*) and Einhorn who declared the proposal inopportune.

Wise had not forgotten his practical plans. He proposed that the conference meet at Cincinnati in the following year, and that an assembly of the congregations be called at the same time. The proposal to meet in Cincinnati was accepted unanimously, but the idea of an assembly of the congregations drew from Einhorn the reply that the congregations were still not ripe to rise to the loftiness of Judaism; they (the theologically educated rabbis) would never be able to move forward if in their debates on religious questions people with the right to vote took part who possessed no sort of theological knowledge; even in the two Reform congregations of New York a great part was still not ripe for their conclusions, and the Leipzig synod of that summer, which could not carry through the triennial cycle of Torah readings, furnished striking evidence of the deplorable results which a meeting of congregations would produce for them also. Einhorn feared that the more advanced congregations would step backwards so as to produce agreement with the more hesitant.[321]

Despite this rebuff, Wise continued his participation in the conference. In fact, he acted as president for the concluding discussion and, together with Lilienthal, was chosen to constitute the committee charged with making arrangements for the 1870 meeting.

The attempts by the *Jewish Times* to explain the real significance of the resolutions of the Philadelphia Conference bear out Einhorn's prophecy that the congregations were not yet ripe for the viewpoint which he succeeded in getting his colleagues to endorse. The res-

---

[321] *Protokolle*, 44; *The New World of Reform*, 10. Wise was among the four members nominated for election as chairman of the committee to consider motions bearing on the Sabbath. Three, including Wise, withdrew their names (*Protokolle*, 43; *The New World of Reform*, 75). Wise declared later (*Israelite*, 15 (13 May 1870), 8) that he refused to serve on any committees because of the refusal to call an assembly of congregations. However, this can hardly relate to his refusal to go forward for election to the chairmanship of the above-mentioned committee, since that election preceded the motion concerning the calling of an assembly. Wise, moreover, did accept responsibility for the arrangements for the next conference.

olutions did not point to the solution of any of the problems which confronted the layman, but attacked institutions which he was prepared to respect if for no better reason than that they did not interfere with him. It was a matter of indifference to most people that, had they examined the blessings used in the marriage service, they would have found that the ideas they expressed rang strange. But the broadcast abrogation of these time-honoured modes caused unease. Two years before the Philadelphia Conference, reflecting on 'Some Lessons' drawn from visits just made to other congregations,[322] Wise gave characteristic expression of his middle-of-the-road point of view. After asserting that 'the benumbed conservatism, the congealed and crystalized dogmatism and ritualism, commonly but falsely called orthodoxy, takes no longer; it has outlived itself', he then pushes the helm over to prevent the course veering too much to the left.

Our travels teach another lesson still. Our people are much too pious and conservative in matters of religion, to be hurled and precipitated into extreme, radical and impracticable measures. Nobody believes that one must smoke cigars on Sabbath and eat pork in vindication of principle, in order to be considered an honest friend of Israel's consecrated cause. Nobody believes that any reform is necessary or lawfully admissible, unless it elevates Judaism and endears it to the thousands of Israel. Innovations for the sake of innovation, and reforms for the sake of reform, find no favor with our people, who, thank God, care little for the whims of fashion, and are pervaded with the desire to remodel the external appearance of Judaism to correspond with the modern standard of taste and the acknowledged canon of criticism. Extreme and radical measures in matters of religion, are naturally as odious to our people as is the attempt to Germanize the synagogue, and make Judaism a stranger in this land of freedom.[323]

He reiterated his expression of opinion on Hebrew.

We are Jews, and will steadfastly remain in the path of our fathers; we are the bearers and preservers of the great and holy book which God entrusted to our care and safekeeping; therefore we will preserve the Hebrew language in our schools and in our temples; the main portion of divine service must be in Hebrew, the balance of prayers, hymns, instructions and admonitions must be in the vernacular of the country.[324]

The implicit distaste for the Einhorn programme was made explicit

[322] *Israelite*, 13 (14 June 1867), 4.   [323] Ibid.   [324] Ibid.

by renewed animadversions on 'extreme and radical measures' and attempts to Germanize the synagogue. Seeing things in a cold clear light, Einhorn could be aloof to popular sentiment, confident that the strength of his feeling and the rightness of his position would draw others to the same lofty heights. Unlike Einhorn, Wise was always contriving to gain widespread popular support. Wise was convinced that the middle way was popular; the calls to preach in distant towns for special occasions and the circulation of the *Israelite* and *Minhag America* convinced him of it, and not long after the Philadelphia Conference he was edging back to that path.[325]

Amid seeming harmony, the conference dispersed on 6 November; the first jarring notes were sounded before the month was out. On 19 November Wise wrote that he had proposed the abolition of *milat gerim* merely as a test question to sound out the radicalism of his colleagues;[326] the following week Einhorn's organ, the *Jewish Times*, asked for an explanation and accused him of prevarication.[327] Wise was seeking cover. Could it have been that he found himself under pressure at home as a result of his unexpected lurch into the radicalism which he so often denounced and grabbed at the first means of retrieving his position that came into his head?

He went further. He invited debate on the circumcision question, making it clear that the conference decisions were not final; he complained that every proposition other than Einhorn's 'was treated with a sort of contempt for which we cannot account'; and he returned to his old standpoint of union above party—'To us all parties in Israel appear necessary ... We will not shout Amen to the resolves of the one or the other side. But we will hear all of them, work with each as far as we can go without the sacrifice of principle, and remain among the might columns of the center.'[328] There was nothing here that he had not said before; he was making it clear, however, that adherence to the Philadelphia resolutions made no difference. The following week he gave his attitude a practical edge by indicating that his own plan for a union was still being pursued.[329]

Before 1869 was out Wise took the opportunity of reiterating his views. In the *Israelite* for 24 December he published a letter signed

---

[325] In the article referred to in the preceding notes he refers to the popularity of his views; in *Israelite*, 15 (21 May 1869), 4, he notes that its success has necessitated yet another increase in size.

[326] *Israelite*, 15 (19 Nov. 1869), 8.   [327] *Jewish Times*, 1 (26 Nov. 1869), 5.
[328] Israelite, 15 (19 Nov. 1869), 8.   [329] Ibid. (26 Nov. 1869), 8.

by 'J.E.' of Cincinnati—reminiscent of 'One for Many' of 1850 in the *Asmonean*[330]—expressing regret in terms flattering to Wise that he should have adhered to articles that were so inconsistent with his teachings, and stating that 'it is the fervent desire of your many warm friends, that you will not permit your name to be longer couched [*sic*] with such of the proceedings of said conference as are incompatible with the true interests of Judaism'. This letter Wise used as a peg on which to hang a fresh gloss on his participation in the Philadelphia Conference—no sects or factions in American Judaism. 'All shades of opinion appear justifiable and necessary for a healthy development and sound progress. Not a step out of the center, is our invariable and unchangeable stand-point.'[331] Reform and progress were always necessary, but Judaism, not reform, was the main thing. On circumcision, Wise repeated the explanation of his attitude which he had given earlier. His correspondent had raised the question of Hebrew, and this gave Wise occasion to hoist the flag of *Minhag America*. 'While we are ready to correct such passages, of which there are very few if any, as are not in perfect harmony with the enlightened and broad principles of Judaism, we will not have the *Minhag America* replaced.'[332]

A fusion of prayer-books was one of the subjects on which a commission set up in Philadelphia was to report to the next conference;[333] now Wise was proclaiming the immutability of *Minhag America*—the old dividing line between him and Einhorn—and putting it forward as the basis (the sole possible basis?) of a union of American Israel. In the following week, he said, he would discuss the question whether the proposed congregation conference should be called immediately, and in the meantime he invited public expression of opinion on the matter. Here too Wise was keeping his independent plans alive, although the formation of a union of congregations (like the question of a rabbinical seminary) was among the questions to be considered at the 1870 rabbinical conference.[334]

---

[330] See ch. 2 sect. 6 above.   [331] *Israelite*, 16 (24 Dec. 1869), 9.   [332] Ibid.
[333] *Protokolle*, 42, 80; *The New World of Reform*, 74, 111.
[334] *Israelite*, 16 (24 Dec. 1869), 8; ibid. (31 Dec. 1869), 8. On 7 Jan. Wise was still not ready to show his hand, merely writing: 'We are not ready yet to give our argument on the congregational conference to the public. We expect many more papers on the subject, and we desire to let others speak first. The matter deserves full attention and cool deliberation. No factual movements must be initiated, no half work done, no new fire brand thrown into our midst. We must have union first, and then we can do great

By February 1870, Wise was sufficiently confident to press 'the necessity of a general convention of all American Jewish congregations'. The title of the article in which he did this ('The Convention and the Liturgy') indicates the point which he emphasized: that there was only one way of providing the reform whose necessity would be acknowledged by all thinking Israelites while guarding against 'lawless, arbitrary and unprincipled innovation with its destructive tendencies', a convention of all the congregations and a rule that the liturgy might be changed by the convention only.[335] Naturally, he did not forget *Minhag America*. He advised all congregations to adopt it and abide by it until the convention should decide otherwise; he asserted that it offered the only opportunity to effect a synagogal union. Nevertheless, he was willing to yield to the majority of the convention, even on the question of *Minhag America*. The most remarkable thing about this article is what it omits. Wise makes not even an allusion to the Philadelphia Conference. One might have thought that no such conference had met, had come to no decisions, had not planned to meet again later in 1870 under arrangements of Wise's making.

Two weeks later Wise remembered Philadelphia. A congregational convention which would found a union was a necessity, and twenty congregations had given his committee authority to call it; but there was disagreement among the committee as to whether to call it at once, with some arguing that the congregational convention would probably declare itself against the radicalism expressed at Philadelphia, and others urging it as a means of letting the radicals know where they must stop.[336] It would be best not to call the convention immediately, but to give the second session of the rabbinic conference the opportunity of adopting the plan. One can be sure that Wise's hardihood in suddenly conceding to the rabbinical conference the right to discuss the convention was not lost upon his critics.

This appeared on 4 March. A week later a signal came from New

---

things. Whoever wishes to speak publicly on the subject is invited to do so, and we will stand back until all have spoken who desire to be heard'; ibid.

[335] Ibid. 16 (18 Feb. 1870), 8.

[336] Ibid. (4 Mar. 1870), 8. At this time we find Lilienthal contributing regularly to the *Jewish Times*, the organ of the Eastern reformers, and it is a guess not too far-fetched to suppose that he was trying to restrain his impetuous colleague—certainly that he saw no chance of bringing in the powerful congregations whose rabbis had been present at Philadelphia unless those rabbis could be conciliated.

York which led to yet another turn on the part of Wise in his endeavours to attain a commanding position on the national scene.

18. FLIRTING WITH THE ORTHODOX

Wise's agitation for a convention had not made him forget his special concern for the training of rabbis in America, but here too he now harnessed it with his concern for an all-embracing union of American Jews. On 25 February he wrote in the *Israelite* contesting the view that the question of Reform or Orthodoxy must be decided before a seminary was founded, because then the institution would have to be either exclusively Orthodox or exclusively Reform. If that were so, Wise argued, they would need 'some dozens of seminaries; for not only have we a dozen of different reforms, but also a dozen of different orthodoxies, i.e., we have as many reforms and as many orthodoxies as we have rabbis, preachers, Hazanim, Parnassim and knowing ones, each of whom has his own Shulchan Aruch, his own Minhag, and his own ambition'.[337] After pronouncing on the mutability of these various forms (he likens them to Jonah's gourd, growing in the night and perishing in the night) he continues in the strain which he favoured at this time: 'there is something infinitely higher and holier in Judaism than all forms, modern or ancient'.

To be 'understood well and expounded right', this something had to be 'learned from the original sources which the Jewish mind of all ages produced'. A Jewish preacher needed to be 'well acquainted with the Jewish literature and its spirit'. Therefore, he said, 'dogmas, forms or reforms' did not concern Jewish students of theology; the Jewish preacher needed, together with a good collegiate education, a 'correct and comprehensive knowledge of the Jewish sources'. Therefore they needed 'but one seminary for all parties' but 'no school of training of the conscience'; and if the congregations united in a convention, they could easily provide a seminary whatever forms one or the other might prefer.[338]

This was received with joy in an unexpected quarter. On 11 March the New York *Jewish Messenger*, an organ of Orthodox viewpoint closely connected with the Board of Delegates of American Israelites, printed lengthy extracts, prefaced with an introduction in which the

---

[337] *Israelite*, 16 (25 Feb. 1870), 8, as quoted in *Jewish Messenger*, 11 Mar. 1870.
[338] Ibid.

editor praised Wise for having risen 'superior to personal or party prejudices' and sought his support for Maimonides College, notwithstanding the unkind things he had said about it.

Whether by coincidence or otherwise, the same issue of the *Jewish Messenger* announced that the next meeting of the Board of Delegates would take place on 23 May, and to this commendation of Wise's views we can trace his brief flirtation with the board.

The pleasure felt by the *Jewish Messenger* at Wise's views on rabbinic education must have been confirmed when a week later (18 March) he referred to 'the necessity of our Schechitah and Bedikah laws'.[339] He gave his approval to these examples of talmudic legislation on rational grounds: 'our laws need some improvements but on the whole they are an excellent protection against numerous diseases'.

Mention has been made of Wise's refusal to support the Board of Delegates when it was established in 1859,[340] and as late as 1868, in the course of a fulmination directed against a particular activity of the board, to be mentioned below, Wise was still ready to assail its representative character.

The record of the Board of Delegates belies any suggestion that it was established with the idea of imposing a single religious outlook. The impulse to establish under the board's auspices a college for training rabbis came from Isaac Leeser and a group of Philadelphia laymen. Through Leeser's perseverance the board resolved in 1866 to support the establishment of a college 'for the rearing of Jewish divines', and it opened in November 1867, with Leeser as provost and a faculty (largely honorary) which included Marcus Jastrow and Aaron Bettelheim, two Philadelphia rabbis with a good scholastic background which had been adjudged 'more than adequate'.[341]

Wise, the tireless advocate of an American-trained rabbinate, took a high line with Maimonides College.

It is our solemn duty to caution the community against every imposition in the province of our sacred religion. We cannot and dare not be silent, wherever and whenever, from ignorance or a love for notoriety, the cause of Israel is made ridiculous, and subservient to private whim. Therefore, we must again

---

[339] *Israelite*, 16 (18 Mar. 1870), 9.   [340] See ch. 3 sect. 10 above.
[341] See B. W. Korn, 'The First American Jewish Theological Seminary: Maimonides College 1867–1873', in *Eventful Years and Experiences* (Cincinnati, 1954), 151 ff.

raise our view against the establishment which is called the Maimonides College of Philadelphia.[342]

The 'solemn duty to caution' was occasioned by the report of the secretary of the Board of Delegates on the working of the college. That the secretary couched his report in enthusiastic, and even high-flown, language is obvious at a glance, but such language was merely conventional, and if Wise had attacked every report that lapsed from judicial sobriety he would have needed little else to fill the editorial columns of the *Israelite*. In this case he chose to wield a sledge-hammer. For example, he indicated that a course taught by Jastrow, a distinguished talmudic scholar, 'degrades the whole institute to a downright humbug' and, lest there should be any doubt on the matter, he added 'young men are invited to come and be figuratively slaughtered like sheep, and really killed off for practical life'. He wound up by suggesting that students keep away.

To parents and to young men we have to say beware of that humbug; it is a Polish Cheder in a modernized garb. The first object of education is, and must be, practical knowledge, which is there the last and least, according to that report. The main object of education is to liberalize the mind, which is obscured there by the Shulchan Aruch. The principal aim of learning is the development of reason which is crippled by the imposition of dead matter.[343]

By 1870 Maimonides College was a helpless orphan. It was a child of Isaac Leeser's, and when he died there was no one to apply his energies to its extension, or even its preservation. For an institution under Orthodox leadership, the reformers of the East were not disposed to concern themselves. They had—nominally at least—their own organization, the Emanu-El Theological Seminary Association, established in 1865. When Einhorn settled in New York, he endeavoured to enlarge its scope, and in the *Israelite* for 25 March 1870—four weeks after the editorial that had attracted the favourable notice of the *Jewish Messenger*—we find reference to a circular issued to the officers of reform congregations asking them to support the Emanu-El project by organizing similar societies in their own congregations, the representatives of all the societies to choose the governing body

[342] *Israelite*, 15 (21 Aug. 1868), 4.

[343] Ibid. There was a special reason for Wise to attack Maimonides College in respect of Jastrow's part in it since the two were locked in violent conflict at the time. See *Allgemeine Zeitung des Judenthums*, 31 (15 Oct. 1867), 842.

of the seminary.[344] Was there here the prospect of a Reform seminary, and even an embryo union of congregations, led from New York by elements unfriendly to Wise? Did he suspect, when the rabbis met in Cincinnati in November, and Einhorn's motion with regard to a seminary came to be discussed, as they had agreed at Philadelphia, that he would be faced with a *fait accompli* or something near it?

The friendly gesture of the *Jewish Messenger* won a response. Its editor was secretary of the Board of Delegates; by the time it met Wise had discovered that the Board 'offered a neutral ground to work for practical ends',[345] and, as he put it in the same article, the 'Secretary had smuggled me in as delegate to the Board for Portland (Oregon)'. The adherence of the Cincinnati rabbi was important enough to be mentioned by the *Jewish Messenger* in foretelling (29 April) 'the largest assemblage attending any annual meeting of the Board'.

Before the Board of Delegates met, a fresh opportunity came for Wise to demonstrate his lukewarmness to what had gone on in Philadelphia in November. The *Protokolle*, or official record of the discussions and resolutions, appeared and, beginning on 22 April, Wise devoted four articles to the conference. He mixes criticism with commendation, new points with observations he had made earlier. He was more explicit in the complaint that it was too much a 'one-man show'. Though the notice convening the conference had stated nothing specific about the business to be discussed, except with regard to marriage laws, Einhorn had once again arrived with a printed set of resolutions and 'it had to be eminently Einhornian or nothing'. The entire question was, whether the Einhorn propositions should be adopted as read, or the phraseology be somewhat changed. The substance was settled: when Kohler had 'the unhappy idea' of proposing a resolution concerning the Scripture lessons, his proposal was 'as a matter of course' tabled. The fact that Wise's own amendment regarding circumcision was rejected was 'proof positive that none but Einhorn's propositions would be entertained'.[346]

Wise still felt badly about the refusal to call a congregational conference: it was not only 'a proof of the unpractical turn of mind of the majority, but also an entire misunderstanding of the spirit, moving the majority of the American congregations'. The majority of

---

[344] See generally B. W. Korn, 'Temple Emanu-el Theological Seminary of New York', in *Essays in American Jewish History* (Cincinnati, 1958), 359.
[345] *Die Deborah*, 15 (24 June 1870), 2.   [346] *Israelite*, 16 (22 Apr. 1870), 8.

the congregations, he repeated, 'are in favor of progress, although they are opposed to radicalism. Why not consult the opinions of the representatives?'[347] Fear that they were not ripe for his opinions was just the reason why Einhorn did not want a congregational conference.[348] The conclusion which Wise drew from this refusal was ominous: 'we must open other avenues, if we desire to do something tangible. This is the reason why we refused to serve on any committee'.[349]

The last of the articles on the *Protokolle*, and the one which contained the phrase about opening other avenues, appeared on 13 May. But he had given an indication of what the 'new avenues' might be expected to be on 22 April, when the series opened, for the *Israelite* of that date contained an announcement that its editor would be attending the forthcoming meeting of the Board of Delegates;[350] and on 6 May, when his Reform adversaries would have been speculating as to what Wise intended to do in the Orthodox circles, he threw in yet another of his disparaging references to 'German prayers, prayer books, sermons and publications'.[351]

Wise's brief connection with the Board of Delegates was directed to one end: the setting up of a rabbinical seminary. The business included a resolution—probably framed in a spirit of routine—commending the work of Maimonides College. Wise offered a series of substitute resolutions setting forth a plan of action for founding a rabbinical seminary. Recollection of his previous attitude to Maimonides College gave birth to suspicions of his motives. Marcus Jastrow (who a short time before had been in bitter controversy with Wise) observed that, if the intention was to kill Maimonides College, it should be avowed openly.

After long debate, the board passed the resolution commending Maimonides College and set up a committee of five, with Wise as one of its members, to consider his plans for a rabbinical seminary.[352] This was in May. In July Wise said that he was working on the seminary scheme in connection with the Board of Delegates, but the committee could not meet until the winter.[353] By the time winter came

---

[347] *Israelite*, 16 (14 May 1870), 8.
[348] *Protokolle*, 44; *The New World of Reform*, 76.
[349] *Israelite*, 16 (13 May 1870), 8.   [350] Ibid. 16 (22 Apr. 1870), 8.
[351] Ibid.   [352] *Jewish Times*, 27 May 1870; 24 June 1870.
[353] *Israelite*, 17 (15 June 1870), 8.

other opportunities had come his way, and nothing more was heard of the matter.

Strangely enough, in view of his fierce opposition to attempts to 'Christianize' the Constitution, Wise succeeded in getting the Board to reject a resolution requesting the executive 'to keep in view the necessity of active remonstrance against the proposed amendment of the Federal Constitution recognizing Christianity, and of co-operating with practical local efforts for counteracting Christian societies having in view the conversion of the Jews'.[354] This resolution, we are told, Wise 'strenuously opposed' as 'unnecessary and superfluous'. They should not fight windmills and he had too much confidence in the American people to believe that they would pass any amendment recognizing Christianity. The question might have been asked, then, to what end were Wise's editorial fulminations? Perhaps he simply wanted to assert himself in the debate.

For the time being Wise seemed pleased with what he had done in New York.

> I managed very well with Orthodoxy, with which later I ate very heartily, drank and launched toasts.
>
> ... I chose to interest the representatives of the Orthodox side in the establishment of a rabbinical seminary and a publication society, and to me it seemed a capital thing. The gentlemen of the Board of Delegates know me for well nigh a quarter of a century; they know that not only have I always belonged to Progress, but have called it forth, fostered it and sustained it in American Judaism; they know that I am true to principles, consequently they must know I conceive the establishment of a rabbinical seminary entirely from the aiming at the study of sources and scientific education, so as to accomplish the unity of American Judaism, without dictating to either the rabbis or the congregations. In the seminary Jewish learning should be taught. ... What I believe to have been realised through the Board of Delegates is a better understanding between the parties, and that is also something.[355]

His new associates were not displeased either. The *Jewish Messenger* observed that the 'Rev. Dr. Wise made a very favourable impression and spoke with rare power'.[356]

Wise had equal right to be pleased with an honour he had received in Washington on the same trip: on 21 May, two days before the meeting of the Board of Delegates, he had delivered the prayer at the

[354] *Jewish Messenger*, 16 (27 May 1870), 8.
[355] *Die Deborah*, 15 (24 June 1870), 2.
[356] *Jewish Messenger*, 16 (27 May 1870), 2.

opening of the session of the Senate. Ten years earlier, Morris J.
Raphall had performed a similar function before the House of Representatives, but Wise was the first rabbi to deliver the opening prayer
in the Senate. At this distance in time such honours may be looked
upon more casually, but in 1870 Wise's co-religionists, not always
able to take for granted their position in American society, doubtless
felt uplifted by the recognition they had received. A little more than
two weeks before he appeared in the Senate chamber, but presumably
with the invitation in his pocket, Wise published a 'Retrospect' in
which he had waxed enthusiastic over the position which Judaism
had attained in America: 'It is no longer a fossil, a mummy or a
specimen of curiosity in some museum. It is a living reality, known,
appreciated and respected. It lives and enlivens. It exercises a telling
influence on the development of the religious idea in this country.'[357]
The honour also gave the opportunity to grind some familiar axes. It
had not been brought about by the Orthodox, he argued. As for the
German preachers and writers, he was prepared to concede that they
had done part of the work. But 'They may preach and write German
one century longer among us, without giving us a position in society,
without gaining public acknowledgement for the spirit and doctrines
of Judaism, without doing our Messianic work.' Who had done it?

A few men, about ten of them, have done this part of the work for Jews and
Judaism. Strange to say, about ten men, certainly no more, have revolutionized the opinions of this country concerning our religion and our
coreligionists. Those few men who spent their days and nights in mastering
the English language and requiring a correct knowledge of the spirit and
institutions of this country and this people, have done the work. Those who
were always wide awake, when the Jew or Judaism was misrepresented or
attacked, and always ready and capable to defend both in public print or
speech; who in books and periodicals expounded Judaism in the proper light
and made it accessible to the uninitiated; who from the pulpits and in public
spoke intelligibly, and by means of the press spread their speeches and
sermons before the community at large; those few men have done the work,
it can not be denied, and they have done it under steady combat against
their so-called orthodox coreligionists and in perpetual conflict with their
Germanizing cousins, always attacked or ignored by those whose cause they
plead and whose battles they fought.[358]

The picture of the champion of his people, lonely, traduced, but

[357] *Israelite*, 16 (6 May 1870), 8.   [358] Ibid.

eventually saving those who depended on him, is not unfamiliar. This time there is a note of triumph, proceeding, one feels, from knowledge of the honour that was about to become public.

Five weeks later, sustained by recollections of a successful visit to the East, Wise was still in a cheerful mood. He was chairman of the committee of the Board of Delegates that was to work on plans for a seminary; the committee could not meet until the winter, but he hoped to publish his plans and to hear of others so that the matter could be discussed and understood before the meeting.[359] There is no difficulty in believing that, had the road continued as Wise then saw it, the scheme would have been in being before the committee met. The mood of elation was reflected in the financial terms he stated: $300,000 was 'indispensably necessary', and he already asked for the first $5,000.

What of reform, which but a few months ago he had been discussing with his colleagues in Philadelphia? 'With a very few and unimportant exceptions in the Atlantic cities, the American Hebrew community is decidedly progressive and in full sympathy with the best ideas of the age', the feuds being merely personal. Having made his obeisance to 'the best ideas of the age', Wise then turned to reprimand the reformers: 'The exclusiveness and aristocratic air of certain reformers who consider only themselves and their friends capable of being free, enlightened and liberal, is ridiculous and injurious.' To the general indictment he subjoined a bill of particulars, by way of emphasizing, as he had done time and time again, the need for English preachers, but though no names were mentioned, the individuals who had sat round the table at Dr Hirsch's Philadelphia study must have known that they were being attacked. For good measure, an adjoining article added a more obvious touch of personal abuse. The Eastern reformers had remained silent all this time, but in an allusion to the meeting of the Board of Delegates the *Jewish Times* had so far descended into the arena as to permit itself the observation that the high priest I. M. Wise had joined the ranks of the Orthodox.[360] The man who laid so heavily about him had not become less sensitive to criticism, and Wise replied with his usual bluster.[361]

---

[359] Ibid. (15 July 1870), 9.   [360] *Jewish Times*, 2 (1 July 1870), 281.
[361] *Die Deborah*, 16 (8 July 1870), 9.

19. REFORMERS IN CONFLICT: EAST VERSUS WEST (1869)

In the meantime the conference which these German dictionaries had brought into the world was due to meet again in Cincinnati, with Wise and Lilienthal acting as hosts. Wise had criticized it, but he had not broken with it. He had indicated that he considered himself free to call a conference of congregations, and without stating that he had forgone that right he associated with the Board of Delegates on the footing that it was theologically neutral; but just as little did he cease to count himself as the friend of progress, numbered among the Reform rabbis of America and ready to take a hand in shaping their programme. What they thought of his blowing hot and cold over Philadelphia and his new love for the Board of Delegates is not difficult to guess. In view of the temperament of the parties, and in view of the absence of any general inhibitions against forthright public attacks on each other, it looks as if each side was waiting for the other to offer the *casus belli*.

At Philadelphia Wise had sung small, and when he sat among his intellectual superiors at the resumed conference his solo trumpetings could be easily squashed. So the Eastern reformers may have argued. It is clear that in June 1870 they still regarded as in force the decision to meet in Cincinnati later in the year.[362] At an earlier date Einhorn had shown himself disinclined to enter into polemics with Wise,[363] and the same attitude may have prevailed in 1870.

The breach came when in the *Israelite* Wise suddenly announced that he was going forward with his own conference.

On and after Monday July 11, 1870, in the city of Cleveland, O., the rabbis favorable to the preservation and further promulgation of the MINHAG AMERICA, will meet for the purpose of revising and re-editing the said *Minhag-America* Books. All rabbis, ministers, or representatives of congregations favoring the union of synagogal worship, are respectfully invited to attend the said conference, and to send their names in advance to the Rev. Dr. Jacob Mayer, Cleveland, Ohio.[364]

For all the complaints that at Philadelphia Einhorn's programme was

---

[362] Letters preserved in the Einhorn Collection in the AJA written to Bernard Felsenthal (24 June 1870) and to Kaufmann Kohler (22 June 1870).

[363] See his letter to Felsenthal of 25 May 1870, AJA.

[364] *Israelite*, 16 (17 June 1870), 8; repeated 24 June, 1 July, and 8 July. Ostensibly the invitation was not issued by Wise—no name was subscribed to it—but Wise wrote personally to colleagues soliciting their attendance. See *Jewish Times*, 2 (26 Aug. 1870), 408.

the fulcrum, here *Minhag America*, Wise's beloved, occupies the stage (though when it met the conference extended its interests); and, it being assumed that they accepted his prayer-book, Wise showed himself ready to welcome a 'mixed multitude', not only the 'theologically educated colleagues of a decided reform tendency'. This move seems to have taken Einhorn by surprise.[365] He regarded it as a breach of faith for Wise to have summoned a conference 'for a purely party purpose' prior to the rabbinic conference. Together with Samuel Adler, Einhorn now came to the conclusion that the meeting in Cincinnati could not take place,[366] and imputed to Wise the motive of calling his own conference in order to be released from the obligation of calling one which he would not dominate.[367]

The *Israelite* did not report the Cleveland meeting in detail. Thirteen rabbis attended, two of whom in addition to Wise had been present in Philadelphia: Adolph Huebsch from New York and S. H. Sonnenschein from St Louis. The meeting resolved to retain Saturday as the Sabbath and the basic structure of the traditional Hebrew service, omitting references to the personal Messiah, the return to Palestine, the sacrificial system and priesthood, and bodily resurrection, and leaving margin for vernacular (English or German) prayers and hymns. It began to revise *Minhag America*, but the heat was oppressive and the work could not be completed. The conference therefore adjourned to 24 October, and decided to resume in New York.[368] Among the motives for this procedure was a desire to bring in the Easterners.[369]

Wise trumpeted forth the significance of what had been done in Cleveland in 1870 in very much the same spirit that he had done concerning the Cleveland Conference fifteen years before. 'The Union of American Israel is fast becoming a fact', he wrote, opening an article in the *Israelite*. 'The cornerstone is laid, the structure will be finished in New York in October next', he proclaimed towards the end. As for the resumed conference that had begun in Philadelphia the year before, to that too he assigned a place in his scheme: 'the Cincinnati conference in November will find no difficulty in ratifying unanimously that which the New York Conference will have done in

---

[365] See his letters referred to in n. 362 above.   [366] Ibid.
[367] *Jewish Times*, 2 (26 Aug. 1870), 408.   [368] *Israelite*, 17 (22 July 1870), 8.
[369] Ibid.

October, and this is sufficient to unite the two conferences into one'.[370]
The article is headed 'A Perfect Union'.

Wise's recently found associates of the Board of Delegates may
have digested these arrangements with surprise, because they assigned
no place for that body. The omission was repaired two weeks later,
when Wise returned to the theme. 'Let Us Be One' was the title of
the article, and the opening words introduced a thesis which he had
been advancing now for nearly a quarter of a century: 'Let every
devout Israelite bear in mind, that the union of the American Israel
must be the first and last object of our public enterprises'.[371] The
focal points of union he was able to state quite simply.

In order to be one, we must have a center of unity. We must have a central
organization around which we revolve. This central organization is the annual
conference of the ministers, to decide theological questions, and the Board
of Delegates to do all the business of the community, both to co-operate as
co-ordinate instruments of the same body.[372]

Just as 'it must be the point of honour and of duty to every minister
to appear in person at the annual conference', so 'it must be a point
of honor and duty in every congregation to be represented annually
in the Board of Delegates'. But in Wise's view a single prayer-book
was as important as a single representative assembly as a focal point
of a united American Jewry, so again he thumps the table on that
subject: the congregations wanted it, the Philadelphia Conference
refused to provide it, the Cleveland meeting had been called to fill
the gap by revising *Minhag America*—any opposition to *Minhag
America* would be fruitless.[373]

The Eastern reformers, as represented by the *Jewish Times*, now
broke their silence and launched at Wise a quiverful of accusations.
He had been admitted to the Philadelphia Conference 'for the sake
of peace' and treated with every mark of respect—'all believed that
Wise had given up his old tricks, had turned a new leaf and could be
trusted. Henceforth there was to be no warring and disputing, no
more jealousies and bickerings, all laboring in one cause and for one
object'.[374] But when, on getting home, he found opposition to the
resolutions of the conference, he shifted with the wind—'to him

---

[370] *Israelite*, 18 (29 July 1870), 8.   [371] Ibid. 17 (12 Aug. 1870), 8.
[372] Ibid.   [373] Ibid.
[374] *Jewish Times*, 8 (26 Aug. 1870), 408.

principle was nothing, honor nothing, consistency nothing, religion nothing, but his situation everything'.[375] The Philadelphia Conference made an end of the plans for the synod for which Wise had been agitating.

He could not make up his mind yet to relinquish his plan altogether, and though he had given at Philadelphia his word of honor not to agitate that synod any further, as it would only interfere with the unification of Reform, so auspiciously inaugurated, he agitated the question anew soon thereafter. What is a word of honor to Wise? A thing not worth mentioning.[376]

His editorials 'teemed with open and concealed attacks' on his colleagues of Philadelphia, 'and when the time drew near that he was to issue the call for the second rabbinical conference, he caused an invitation to be issued in his paper for the rabbis, whose congregations had introduced the *Minhag America*, to assemble at Cleveland, in order to revise that failure of a prayer-book'.[377] The reason given for convoking the Cleveland Conference—that the Philadelphia meeting would have nothing to do with prayer-book revision— the *Jewish Times* terms a 'wilful and conscious falsehood', and in support it refers to the resolution on a prayer-book then under consideration by a committee. The onslaught was a lengthy one, and the editor of the *Jewish Times* pulled out all his stops for an angry roulade, playing the themes of Wise's perfidy, ambition, and lack of scholarship.

Wise replied in characteristic style. He answered none of the charges; he did not even refer to them by name; he merely questioned the manners and the motives of any who attacked him.[378]

A more substantial answer to the *Jewish Times* (though the New York weekly was still not mentioned by name) Wise published not in the *Israelite* but in *Die Deborah*, where a long article entitled 'Die Situation und die Conferenz' appeared on 23 September. He complained that Adler and Einhorn had convened the Philadelphia Conference when he was known to be at work on his own plans of unification, and he averred that he had abided by its decisions with regard to marriage and divorce. 'But since nothing was done in

---

[375] Ibid.   [376] Ibid.   [377] Ibid.

[378] Ibid. 17 (9 Sept. 1870), 8, contains another reference to the attack of the *Jewish Times*. Possibly this piece of extremely heavy satire is intended to refer to Cincinnatians who had assented to the criticism.

Philadelphia with regard to a uniform ritual as well as the solution of practical questions, and each proposal referring to such was laid upon the table, we had to look around for other opportunities of executing this highly important work.'[379] The 'other opportunities' were first the Board of Delegates. This would answer the needs of the time, if, as had been expressly promised to him, it did not occupy itself with purely theological questions.

We could not understand to what purpose a new body should be established if an existing one answering the purpose could be completed, especially if thereby cooperation for unity could be achieved so much easier. In solving practical questions that concern Judaism as a whole we have nothing to do with the ritual outlook of the members of each body. At the Philadelphia Conference we did not bind ourselves to secede from Judaism; it follows that its members cannot feel aggrieved that we agree with still another Jewish body. Those who had not yet adhered to the standpoint of progress will later rise up to it.[380]

The second purpose for which he said that he had to look around for other opportunities was a uniform ritual, and the revision of *Minhag America* was the task modestly and discreetly performed at Cleveland. It was disgraceful, he said, that so sacred a matter should be set about with such vulgar weapons—'One would have thought that this peaceful united and serious endeavour in the strictest tendency of progress would win the applause of all friends of progress'. Wise turned defence into attack by asserting that the Philadelphia conference had given no notice of any intention to come round to the prayer-book question and that therefore its successor was not entitled to deal with the matter. There was much more by way of complaint of being 'dragged through the mire, calumniated and humiliated by incompetent quill-drivers'—this last, no doubt, a personal reference to the editor of the *Jewish Times*.

At this stage Wise indicates publicly that he is ready to go on with the conference which was to have met in Cincinnati—on such terms, however, as would entitle him to exclude Einhorn and his friends: '... we cannot meet with gentlemen who have wronged and insulted us disgracefully and in public'. Once more Wise—the same Wise who not a year before had given his assent to all the radical propositions of the Philadelphia Conference—takes the opportunity to minimize

[379] *Die Deborah*, 16 (23 Sept. 1870), 2.   [380] Ibid.

the Reform label as far as he himself is concerned: 'We belong to no party in Israel because, thank God, we are raised above the spirit of party'.[381]

This trial balloon met with no response. But that did not matter. If the line that led from Philadelphia to Cincinnati was blocked, he could travel along the route that led from Cleveland to New York. He would have at least one conference.

This article in *Die Deborah* did draw a response, in that nine of the eleven rabbis who had met in Philadelphia published in the *Jewish Times* a declaration bristling with accusations against Wise—'a very double dealing attitude' towards their conference, 'a campaign against many of its resolutions, for which he himself had voted', 'abuse and derision at several of the prominent members', 'always with the phrase of unity on his lips he brought about a schism, in that he set up a separate group to decide a question which was already on the agenda of the second conference'. It was a requirement of self-esteem on their part to disclaim co-operation with Dr Wise;[382] and they could not 'interest themselves in a conference of rabbis which may take place in Cincinnati'. (This presumably was the second session of the conference inaugurated in Philadelphia, but there is no record that anything had been done to call it into being.)

Within limited circles, such a declaration may have caused great excitement. This one brought the rabbinic schisms into the open, and the observer might have concluded that, having provoked the antagonism of the country's most prominent Reform rabbis, Wise's plans were doomed to failure. What stands out is the apparent inability of Einhorn and his friends to carry forward the movement they had initiated, whereas the man who infuriated them simply bounced back.

The wrath of the reverend gentlemen who signed this 'Declaration' probably filled Wise with glee. Later he admitted that he had put a road-block in the way of the Philadelphia Conference. In the *Israelite* in 1871 he reviewed the rabbinical conferences that had taken place in America and said that no one could tell why the synod resolved upon in 1855 and the conference resolved upon in 1869 were not convoked. 'Strange, however,' he added, 'it was the influence of Einhorn and Wise which was at the bottom. Their mutual and unaccountable opposition upset both the synod and the conference.

---

[381] Ibid.   [382] *Jewish Times*, 2 (14 Oct. 1870), 521.

As far as this goes, they are even now. They have served one another exactly alike.'[383] This comes near to admitting that in 1870 he was getting his own back for 1855.

Though the '*Minhag America* Conference' had adjourned from Cleveland to New York partly in the hope of bringing in the Eastern rabbis, war was in the air. The meeting started with nine persons present; the number rose to thirteen, and by the conclusion had dropped to five. Wise was not among the officers, and there was a feeling that his influence did not dominate. Not long before, Wise had taken a high line about meeting the rabbis who he said had attacked him; throughout he had clung ferociously to *Minhag America*. Now, at the insistence of the St Louis congregation, the conference adopted a resolution inviting all who desired to 'further the liturgical unity in American Israel by the arrangement of a common prayer-book based on the principles of Reform' to 'participate in the composition and the editing of such a prayer-book', on the footing that 'in the case of such participation, all the prayer-books ... in use in American congregations be made the basis of the new prayer-book to be agreed upon'. Einhorn and his friends were to be invited in, and the basis was to be not *Minhag America*, but all the prayer-books in use. A committee was appointed to endeavour to reconcile the Easterners. It called on four of the New York rabbis. Three (including Einhorn) were not available; the fourth, Gutheim, indicated that he was in favour of a reconciliation but could not act without his colleagues. Nevertheless the committee was charged with continuing its endeavours and was reinforced by Lilienthal, the president of the conference. Dealing with its work, Lilienthal had observed that 'the time of infallibility and personal rule are past'—an allusion to the dogma which had been promulgated shortly before by the Vatican Council, which was echoed as signifying the end of Wise's personal control.[384]

---

[383] *Israelite*, 16 (2 June 1871), 8.

[384] *Jewish Times*, 2 (4 Nov. 1870), 564. There is, of course, no doubt to whom the *Jewish Times* was referring. The article, entitled 'The Adjourned Cleveland Conference', stated that 'most of the members of this adjourned Conference did not come here for the purpose of making a prayerbook, and certainly not for revising the *Minhag America*. The latter has been repudiated openly by the members of the Conference over and over again. The main object of the prominent members of the Conference seems to have been to endeavor to bring about a reconciliation between the opposing factions, of correcting the mistake which had been made in attending an anti-Philadelphia Cleveland Conference.'

The main business was to revise *Minhag America*, and here too Wise sustained a defeat that led to a threat of withdrawal. Mayer of Cleveland proposed that the name of the prayer-book be changed 'and none of the names of the existing prayer-books be adopted for the one to be published'. The debate was a protracted one, and fierce also. In the end, Wise's viewpoint that *Minhag America* was to be the basis of any revision was defeated by five votes to three, the other members declining to vote; and he left the conference, having declared in writing his inability to participate further.[385] The atmosphere became less heated during the night, and in the morning Wise signed a declaration which appears to have been prepared for the purpose by Adolph Huebsch.

From a former resolution of the Conference it is evident that, as long as no conciliation of the various parties (not represented in the conference) is effected, the Minhag America remains the basis of the prayer book to be compiled. If no such conciliation be effected, when the book is complete, I will certainly not object to the revisions of the title page. If such conciliation can be effected, the committee must not be embarrassed by either book or title page.[386]

Evidently the parties were not in a mood to give credence to oral statements. Huebsch brought the signed declaration to the conference, whereupon Mayer's proposition was dropped and Wise returned to

---

[385] *Israelite*, 17 (11 Nov. 1870), 10, stated that the controversy over the title-page of the prayer-book was not put on the minutes but was sent to the *Israelite* 'by an officious person'. This suggests that had Wise been in charge of the *Israelite* that week the report of the controversy over the names of existing prayer-books would simply have been suppressed. Wise's reasons for withdrawing, as given in *Israelite*, 17 (4 Nov. 1870), 10, were as follows: '1. The meeting (of the rabbis) has been convened, on the demand of honored colleagues, to revise the "Minhag America," not for the purpose of editing a new prayer-book. Had the latter object been mentioned in the call [convening the meeting] I would not have attended it. 2. In the face of all congregations to whom I have recommended the Minhag America, I have no right to assist in the abolition of the same, and in the compilation of a new prayer-book, without being enabled to refer to important reasons for the change. I am not aware of the existence of such reasons. 3. The name of Minhag America has been identified with the principles of union and progress of the masses of our coreligionists. I have no right to desert this principle, or to negate my past career in connection therewith. 4. While it might justly be expected of the respective congregations to adopt the revised Minhag America in place of the present edition, the introduction of a new prayer book, however, would certainly meet with obstruction which I do not wish to impose on myself.'

[386] *Israelite*, 17 (11 Nov. 1870), 8.

the fold. No one wanted to lose Wise, but they intended to make terms.[387]

Wise described the conference as 'a perfect success'[388] and commented 'Not a harsh word was spoken. No ill-feeling was entertained, none expressed.'[389] Again he beat the drum which told American Jewry that it was to be united in matters of ritual. Though he asserted that the German language would not last another fifteen or twenty years in the synagogue, he conceded that for the time being, in view of the numerous Germans in the congregation, there must be a free choice of German and English, besides the original Hebrew.[390]

'The new prayer book will be the Minhag of America, so much is certain,' asserted Wise confidently. '*Minhag America* is dead and the plates are for sale,' wrote Lilienthal.[391] But the story was not at an end. The conference did not complete the task of revising the prayer-book, and on adjourning it decided to resume in Cincinnati on 5 June 1871. There was still hope of bringing in the Einhorn faction.

The Cleveland meeting had been called for the express purpose of revising *Minhag America*.[392] The New York meeting was a mere adjournment from Cleveland, and it is reported in *Die Deborah*[393] under the caption 'Die Zweite Revisionversammlung'. Nevertheless, we find it dealing with matters outside the scope of prayer-book revision, such as the divorce laws of Indiana, the foundation of an educational establishment for higher Jewish learning, the second day of Rosh Hashanah, and the Jews of Romania. Wise himself noted that the New York meeting 'gradually assumed the character of a regular conference'.[394] Many matters, besides various aspects of prayer-book revision, and including the founding of a college, were referred to committees to report to the Cincinnati meeting; that assembly was announced in the *Israelite* simply as 'the next Conference of rabbis, preachers and delegates of congregations'.[395] Now it appeared that Wise's plan was achieving reality.

In May 1871, three weeks before the Cincinnati meeting, the Board of Delegates held its annual session in New York. Wise was not present; the committee on a rabbinical seminary, of which he was

[387] *Israelite*, 17 (11 Nov. 1870), 8.
[388] Ibid. 18 (24 Aug. 1871), 8.
[389] Ibid. 17 (18 Nov. 1870), 8.
[390] Ibid.
[391] Ibid. (2 Dec. 1870), 10.
[392] See ch. 3 sect. 19 above.
[393] *Israelite*, 16 (25 Nov. 1870), 2.
[394] Ibid. 17 (2 June 1871), 8.
[395] Ibid. (5 May 1871), 8.

chairman, was discharged, having failed to report; the *Israelite* does not mention the meeting. As the evidence goes, the brief flirtation ended without tears, and there was neither a whimper nor a scream about breach of promise from either party.

Geography, sentiment, and vested interests meant that co-operation with the Orthodox of New York and Philadelphia in reorganizing Maimonides College could hardly result in a college under Wise's control, and the bait of financial support for his own institution deprived the match with the Board of Delegates of any attractions it may have had. That financial support Wise had been able to announce in the *Israelite* for 9 December. Henry Adler of Lawrenceburg, twenty-five miles west of Cincinnati, had deposited $10,000 in trust with Congregation B'nai Jeshurun, Cincinnati, to be applied to the support of a college. 'Mr. Adler', wrote Wise, 'has the immortal honor of having made the first substantial move in this direction. . . . God bless Henry Adler.'[396]

The impetuous Wise may have been allowing his understandable enthusiasm to get the better of him, or he may have 'jumped the gun' deliberately, believing that a public statement would help to make certain that an intention was converted into a fact. No money had been deposited at the time of this announcement, and more than two years elapsed before final action was taken.[397] But it suited Wise to brandish the gift. Money attracts money, and the announcement that the college had $10,000 to start with might rally further support.

Another factor encouraged Wise to take action without reference to the Board of Delegates — namely, the establishment of a university

[396] We first meet the name of Henry Adler in Dec. 1870 when Leo Wise, an attorney, and presumably the rabbi's son (and who later took over the *American Israelite*) brought forward to a meeting of the board of trustees of Congregation B'nai Jeshurun held on the twelfth of that month a proposal by Adler to lend the congregation $10,000 at 8 per cent. A committee went into the proposal, which evidently did not mature. Henry Adler was a brother of Liebman Adler, a rabbi in Chicago.

[397] Henry Adler's offer to set up the trust bears the same date as a meeting of the trustees of B'nai Jeshurun at which it was read, together with letters from other Cincinnati congregations expressing willingness to join in deliberating upon the establishment of the proposed college. The delay may have been concerted so that the three-year period within which action was to be taken should not begin to run until those interested in the college could see the possibility of immediate action. 9 Dec. was not the first occasion on which Wise mentioned this gift. In *Israelite*, 17 (16 Sept. 1870), 8, he commended an unnamed donor who 'deposits $10,000 for the purpose of establishing a rabbinical seminary'.

in Cincinnati. Thus, when Lilienthal opened the 1871 Conference, he stated 'As soon as the McMicken University will have been opened and fairly started in this city, we intend to open a rabbinical seminary in Cincinnati.'

The 'Easterners' were not represented at the Cincinnati Conference, the Committee on Conciliation having to report failure owing to 'some personal differences of opinion'. Nevertheless, the number present in Cincinnati was double that in New York—twenty-seven against thirteen—though by all accounts the net drew in fish of more than one kind.[398]

At Wise's instance the conference declared its permanency, membership being open to all officiating rabbis, preachers, teachers of religion, and readers. More, he secured the adoption of a scheme for the establishment of a 'Union of Israelite Congregations of America', whose objects were to include the establishment and maintenance of a seminary, the provision of Bibles and textbooks, and the support of weak congregations. The union was to be governed by a synod, which was to meet biennially and to consist of the representatives of affiliated congregations together with their rabbis, preachers, or teachers of religion. A committee of five, appointed by the conference, was to call the synod into being as soon as twenty congregations ('adhering to reformed principles (none others)') with not less than two thousand members should have resolved to enter the Union.[399]

The conference also considered in some detail the curriculum of the proposed rabbinical seminary. It resolved to meet annually, except in the synodal year, and the 1872 meeting was fixed for the second Monday after Shavuoth (17 June), in Chicago.

Here, then, was what Wise had been fighting for ever since he had arrived in the country twenty-five years earlier. We need not suppose for one moment that he shed a tear at the absence of Einhorn and his friends—for one thing it spared him the sadness of parting with the title of his beloved *Minhag America*. He had organized a permanent rabbinical conference, and it had decided to call into being a congregational union, a synod, and a theological college; it was concerting plans for the conduct of religion schools, for the supply of textbooks, and for the organization of circuit preaching; the conference had 'finally settled the liturgical questions'. Well might he say towards

---

[398] The reports make clear that the conference was not confined to rabbis.
[399] *Israelite*, 17 (9 June 1871), 8, 9; (16 June 1871), 8.

the end of three long columns of enthusiastic summary that 'the Conference was a brilliant success'.[400]

But the clear blue sky gave way to a storm as fierce as any in which Wise had been involved; and instead of the speedy accomplishment of the intentions of the conference we have another interlude of violent recrimination, which doubtless led the 'old hands' to recall the conferences of 1855 and 1869 and to prophesy similar results.

Prayer-book revision was still one of the tasks of the Cincinnati Conference, and Wise, the critic of radical reform, suddenly swung to the side of a thoroughgoing reconstruction of the Yom Kippur service. His proposals were referred to the Prayer-Book Committee,[401] but on the following day (7 June) Wise moved that they be acted upon immediately. This gave rise to a heated debate, the following report of which is taken from the *Jewish Times*.

Dr. Wise offered a resolution that his report on reform in divine service be acted upon.

This gave rise to a discussion; Dr. Wise advocating a thorough change, and Dr. Hubsch and others favoring the old rites and forms of prayer. In the course of the discussion Dr. Hubsch spoke in praise of the so-called Spanish school of Jewish poetry. Dr. Wise said, he was not ignorant of the merits of that school, but thought its features too mystical and antiquated for this progressive age.

It was urged that Dr. Wise as a member of the committee on prayer-books could best submit and defend his views there, but Dr. Wise intimated that since his protest against the conservative course of the committee, he could not, in respect for himself, continue as a member of said committee. The discussion then assumed such an acrimonious character that Dr. Wise withdrew, whereupon a recess of ten minutes was taken, during which the doctor put in an appearance again, and quietly listened to the attack of Dr. Hubsch, after which he defended himself and the reforms, proposed by him, in an able speech. The animus of the whole debate showed that a majority of the meeting were not up to Dr. Wise's advanced and reformatory views.

Dr. Wise said, that the Yom Kippur (day of Atonement) was founded upon an entirely erroneous conception. That the idea of reconciliation or redemption is utterly anti-Jewish. That it is a law that sin is to be punished, not forgiven. That there is not to be found a single passage in the Scripture to the effect that sins are to be forgiven. That the idea of real reconciliation

[400] Ibid. (23 June 1871), 8.
[401] Ibid. (9 June 1871), 8. The actual wording of the report (cols. 3 (bottom) and 4) is 'referred to by the Committee on Prayer Book'.

in the Talmud dates only from the Pauline period, and is antagonistic to the spirit and tendency of the Hebrew religion.

Dr. Hubsch dissented from Dr. Wise's opinion and held that, if there be any God, He must be a merciful and forgiving God. Dr. Mayer agreed with Dr. Wise and maintained, that the idea of mercy or relenting toward the sinner is wholly incompatible with the conception of the attribute of God. He was not in favor of established or canonical forms of prayer, because prayers were necessarily addressed to a personal God, and many persons (of whom the speaker avowed himself to be one) did not believe in the existence of a personal god.[402]

Wise's motion was finally lost.

Though the report does not say so, it appears that in the course of the excited debate Wise expressed agreement with Mayer's denial of a personal God—and this was immediately reported in the daily press. Wise must have sensed the effect that his words would produce, so on 8 June he endeavoured to explain himself.

Dr. Wise obtained the floor and said that a word spoken here yesterday, and reported in the newspapers, would be likely to create considerable discussion, and was likely to be misconstrued outside of the conference. He would therefore propose, as one of the topics to be spoken on at the next conference, the following:

The idea of a personal God, accepted in theology as a technical term, is not Jewish at all. The God of the Bible is the Jehovah, i.e., the Infinite and Absolute, the Substance and Essence of all that is, was and will be. This Cause of all Causes, this Understanding supreme, Love, Justice and Holiness universal, cannot be thought or even imagined as personal. Theology bases the idea of a personal God upon the doctrine of incarnation.[403]

The non-Jewish press took up the original declaration, and there was even a cartoon in a humorous weekly. 'A converted Jew', said the *New York Tribune*, 'is always an anomalous object; but an unconverted Jew who has put behind him Moses, the law, or the prophets, is a something so far utterly inexplicable. We wait until he explains himself.'[404] In some circles the statements of Wise and Mayer were regarded as atheistic; they caused a sensation, and evidently the incident was referred to widely in the Christian press and pulpit.[405]

For Einhorn and his friends, the opportunity was not to be missed.

---

[402] *Jewish Times*, 3 (16 June 1871), 244–7. *Israelite* does not deal with this point.
[403] Ibid.   [404] As quoted in ibid.   [405] Ibid. 3 (30 June 1871), 280.

Here the man who had castigated them for their radicalism and even insinuated that they were deists and atheists was dragging the American Jewish community over the yawning abyss of unbelief. The *Jewish Times* used its most scathing denunciations, but the real thunderbolt came two weeks later in the form of a commination signed by fourteen rabbis of varying shades of opinion, most of them living in the East. The opening paragraph made clear their opinion of the Cincinnati Conference.

In the beginning of the present month a meeting took place in Cincinnati, Ohio, of a number of individuals, who, although for the greater part devoid of theological education and capacity and, hence, utterly incompetent to represent Judaism, assumed the style and title of THE CONFERENCE OF AMERICAN RABBIS.[406]

Having prepared the ground in general terms, they turned to the principal against whom they framed the indictment.

Things, which nobody deemed credible or even possible, took place then and there.—The originator of that conference positively repudiated the personal God and emphatically denied, that the belief in a personal God was taught by biblical Judaism. He, furthermore, designated the God of the Bible as being implacable, meting out punishment, but showing no mercy and forgiving no sin, under the plea, that the idea of a personal and pardoning God had its origin in Christianity.

'We should remain silent,' they continued, 'to such flagrant blasphemies, such unheard of, impious desecration of our sanctuary on the part of those very men, who profess to be its guardians and conservators?' 'Judaism is falsified, its purity defiled by the admixture of heathen elements, shamefully reviled before the eyes of the world'— therefore they could not abstain from publishing their 'unqualified and solemn protest against those false and non-Jewish declarations'. All this was merely by way of preamble, preparing the reader for the operative part of the declaration.

1. That the God of the Bible is not 'the substance of nature,' not identical with nature, but 'A PERSONAL GOD,' the Creator and Governor of the universe, infinitely exalted above the same, 'looking down upon heaven and earth'— and that whoever teaches the existence of an impersonal God has ipso facto renounced Judaism;

[406] *Jewish Times*, 3 (30 June 1871), 280.

2. That the interpolation of the idea of an impersonal God into the Bible is an infamous falsification of the Divine Word;

3. That in its records of revelation, in its entire literature and history, Judaism teaches Divine Grace and Mercy and consequently, holds out pardon and forgiveness to the repentant sinner, and that a denial of this fact is a slander upon Judaism and a blasphemy;

4. That a Conference which grants seat and voice in a Committee for the preparation of a prayer-book, to a man, who, in accordance with his notions of God, stigmatizes prayer as an absurdity, condemns, by this very action, itself and its work.[407]

Scratch these reformers and one found the *yeshivah bocher*: there is much in the tone and language of the declaration to remind one of an *issur* (rabbinical prohibition) which Orthodox rabbis might have issued against the reformers; but what does stand out is the desire to get even with 'that man'. Samuel Hirsch was not among the signatories to this Declaration. Together with Marcus Jastrow, the Orthodox rabbi of Philadelphia, he signed a separate Declaration[408]—probably nothing other than an opportunity to attack Wise could have brought them together—and in the *Jewish Times* for 7 July we find seven additional names joined to the indictment against Wise.[409]

Wise was equal to all these protests. Not that he stood firm as a rock, disdainful of the waves that broke against him; they goaded him into a frenzy (though not so much that he forgot to advocate his pet idea of a seminary), and he struck out. The preface to *The Cosmic God* shows that five years later he was still living through the experience.[410] With his usual instinct he did not address his replies to the charge brought by those who signed the denunciation but attacked their motives and their competence. When the attack appeared he averred that he did not acknowledge the rabbis of the Philadelphia Conference as his peers or equals in the realm of 'speculative theology'[411]—a large claim which was meat to his opponents. On 21 July his fulminations against those who had signed the protests extended over more than four columns; but they were directd to the point that these gentlemen were

unfit for the American pulpit ... They started from falsehoods, progressed in wickedness, and landed in a hell of absurdity. We pity the innocent poor individuals who have been beguiled by Satan to set their names to that

[407] Ibid.   [408] Ibid.   [409] *Jewish Times*, vol. 3, p. 298.
[410] See ch. 3 sect. 17 above.   [411] *Israelite*, 18 (24 Aug. 1871), 328.

protest; but you will agree with us that such innocent creatures were not intended by their Maker to preach Judaism in America. For the sake of God and truth, in the name of Israel and his sacred cause, let us have a seminary.[412]

Wise gives no sign of having mellowed since 1855; in fact his reaction was more violent than to Einhorn's attack on the Cleveland Platform. As then, the incident rankled for a long time. The Rosh Hashanah article in *Die Deborah* included the following:

Last year we indeed experienced the outrage of a few of our rabbis wanting to plant on the free soil of America the Inquisition proceedings that are disappearing in Rome; but a decayed plant could strike no roots in free soil; the Jesuitical bulls of excommunication have sunk like solid lead in the deeply moving stream of time, and the outrage had redounded on the authors of the new Jesuitry, who stand before their congregations blushing with shame and branded to the stars with the marks of Cain of their lies and malicious calumny, and must acknowledge that they have committed a disgraceful wrong. No shame accrues to American Judaism that it has learned to know its idle, envious and weakheaded passengers.[413]

That was in September 1871. In August 1872 the baptism of a Jewish minister in Mobile provoked Wise to reflect how for twenty-five years

the writer of these lines was persecuted, insulted and reviled, hatefully, fanatically and dishonourably, how for years in succession he was slandered, publicly insulted and stigmatized by irresponsible men such as Ellinger, Einhorn, Hirsch, Felsenthal and other such idle lodgers with Judaism, would take his motive amiss if he turned his back on Judaism to save his honour and attached himself to Christianity.[414]

Neither did he neglect the theme during the intervening months.[415] Dishonesty of purpose, personal hatred, a desire to harm the members of the conference and upset its work were the motives which Wise laid at the door of the protesters. And, no doubt, he saw 1855 over again, victory sucked from his grasp by an easterly gale. But there occurs in the long article this reference to his opponents:

Most all of them having been village parsons and village schoolmasters in former days, they must be excused, you say. But we say, some of them have

---

[412] *Israelite*, 18 (21 July 1871), 8.   [413] *Die Deborah*, 17 (15 Sept. 1871), 2.
[414] Ibid. (2 Aug. 1872), 2.   [415] See e.g. *Die Deborah*, 17 (29 Dec. 1871), 9.

seen better society, and ought to know how gentlemen speak, but they have never done it in treating things or persons unpleasant to them. Just think for a moment, young American Israelites, those whose calling it is, to cultivate, to refine, to elevate, to ennoble the taste, the manners, the feelings, the conceptions, are in a perpetual rage and use words and phrases like enraged village schoolmasters thrashing some refractory boys.[416]

The *theologische gebildeten Collegen*, to revert to the phrase which two years before had circumscribed the limits of those eligible to participate in the Philadelphia Conference, were trying to thrash I. M. Wise like a refractory village schoolboy.

20. ESTABLISHING THE UNION (1871–1873)

Little as the temptation to thrust at his critics could be resisted, there was more to do. The Cincinnati Conference had called for the establishment of a union, and when the adherence of twenty congregations had been obtained it would come into being. It was on 25 June 1871—barely two weeks after the close of the conference—that the first decision to join was made, by Congregation Bene Israel of St Louis. In *Die Deborah* Wise printed their letter in the course of an enthusiastic article headed 'Gott erhalt die Bene El Gemeinde von St. Louis!!!' ('God Preserves Congregation Bene El of St Louis') and concluding *E Pluribus Unum*.[417]

If he was to get the union going, he needed the support of his own congregation. When the Board of Trustees met on 31 August 1871 they received from him a communication setting forth the plan adopted at the rabbinical conference and pleading for the support of B'nai Jeshurun.[418] The board accepted the plan and recommended it to the general meeting of the congregation; and the general meeting which took place on 23 September 1871 accepted the recommendation.

B'nai Jeshurun merely joined those congregations which signified their willingness to join the union once established; it had undertaken no commitment to establish the union. Somehow the project lagged. Perhaps the 'Personal God' controversy frightened people off from Wise's enterprises; perhaps recollections of the false start of 1869

---

[416] *Israelite*, 18 (21 July 1871), 8.   [417] Ibid. 17 (7 July 1871), 2.
[418] Minutes, Congregation B'nai Jeshurun.

made them sceptical as to its realization; perhaps the absence of the influential congregations of the East made them dubious as to its value. Indubitably the communities were in closer contact than they had been when union projects had been discussed in 1848 and 1855, but still there were problems immediate and local in impact and far higher in priority than setting up a national organization. We cannot establish the influence of Mrs O'Reilly's cow on American Jewish history, but the disastrous city-wide fire which it started in Chicago in October 1871 engendered an immediate wave of sympathy, and led to considerable exertions to bring help to the sufferers, in which effort the Jewish communities involved themselves immediately. This too may have pushed interest in the proposed union into the background, especially as a new meeting place would have had to be found.

A conflagration ten times greater than that which laid Chicago waste would not have deterred Wise from acting on the 1871 resolution. In fact he tried in vain to breathe life into the rabbinical conference. On 10 May 1872 the *Israelite* reprinted the resolution passed at the Cincinnati meeting in the previous June, in which the conference had declared its permanency, resolved to meet on the second Monday after Shavuoth (17 June), and appointed an executive committee (Lilienthal, Sonnenschein, Wechsler, Welsch, and Wise) to convoke the conference. This resolution was again reprinted on 17, 24, and 31 May, but the wind must have been blowing strongly against Wise: no one made a move. On 7 June Wise tried a different tack. He declared that

the Executive Committee having failed to perform its duty ... I consider it my duty ... to declare 1. That I am ready and desirous to perform all the duties, which to perform I promised in Conference ... 2. That in my judgment the annual meeting of the Conference is necessary, and can result only in blessing to Judaism, progress and reform. 3. It being now too late to meet in Chicago the first Monday after *Shabuoth*, I propose to all expounders of Judaism ... to meet in Chicago, the second Monday after *Succoth* ... and I beg all coinciding with me on this point, to give me authority to issue a call to this effect, in their names and mine.[419]

This appeared a second time on 14 June, but again no one moved. Probably the bitter exchanges which had followed the 1871 meeting killed the chances of its becoming permanent, and this is confirmed

[419] *Israelite*, 18 (7 June 1872), 8.

by the fact that the executive committee made no arrangements to discharge their mandate to call a meeting in 1872.

Any likelihood that Wise's personal appeal for authority to issue a call would have received support was destroyed by yet another controversy which broke out a very short time after the appeal had been issued, with the result that, though there was no rabbinic conference in 1872, the public was still not spared the bitter personal exchanges with which the rabbis had come to be associated. In June of that year Wise solemnized the marriage of a man and the widow of his deceased brother, even though children were living, an action contrary to a traditional Jewish practice that was upheld even by the radical reformers, and it occasioned strong protest from Einhorn and Samuel Hirsch. One who was incessant in his urging of the need for a union and a synod might have made some attempt to consult his colleagues before taking so drastic a step, but Wise did not do so. Once the matter had been raised, the legitimacy of Wise's action received the support of eminent colleagues,[420] but in the meantime, the exchanges rang shrill. According to Wise, Hirsch even called upon the president of Congregation B'nai Jeshurun to suggest his removal from office.[421]

Arising out of this controversy an exchange developed between Wise and Bernhard Felsenthal of Chicago. Wise referred to Felsenthal as being a *trefessesser*,[422] and Felsenthal replied that after the Philadelphia Conference Wise had partaken of a *trefah* meal together with Dr Chronik and himself. Wise's reply, characteristically avoiding the question of what *trefah* meant, was 'ich überhaupt weder Schinken noch Speck esse', which is to be translated 'I do not eat either ham or bacon at all.'[423]

Cumulatively, these controversies account for why the union project had made no headway by the time of the next meeting of

[420] Dr Elkan Cohn, then in San Francisco, supported Wise; see *Central Conference of American Rabbis Year Book*, xxv (1951), 367.

[421] May, *Isaac Mayer Wise*, 290; see *Israelite*, 19 (12 July 1872), 10.

[422] A corrupted form of a term meaning one who eats food that is not kosher; by extension, a sinner in the wider sense.

[423] The word *überhaupt* could conceivably be translated 'generally', which would make the denial less emphatic. This controversy was conducted in the Cincinnati German newspapers *Wochenblatt* and *Volksblatt*. The letters were reprinted in the *Jewish Times* for 23 Aug. and 6 Sept. 1872 (vol. 4, pp. 526, 558). Henry Illoway in his 'Introduction' to *The Controversial Letters and the Casuistic Decisions of the Late Rabbi Bernard Illowy Ph.D.*, 2, 3, gives a picture of Wise's habits which would support his denial.

B'nai Jeshurun after that which had endorsed the idea. At the later meeting—held on 10 October 1872—the congregation took it up in a more decided manner, and also, as far as one can judge, took it out of Wise's hands. The president of B'nai Jeshurun, Moritz Loth, alluded to the need for a 'Jewish theological faculty' to train rabbis and suggested that the congregation appoint a committee of twelve and request the other Cincinnati congregations to do likewise, these committees jointly to take into consideration the calling of a general conference of all the congregations of the West, South, and North-west with a view to forming a union of congregations. There is no reference at all to the decisions of the 1871 rabbinical conference, no suggestion, even that anyone had ever thought of the idea before. Moritz Loth's proposal indicates a regional limitation, but there was a theological limitation also which ran counter to the 1871 decision that the union was to be confined to Reform congregations. The objects of the proposed union, Loth said, should be first to establish a Jewish theological faculty and second to publish books for Sabbath schools. The third object, he went on, would be

to adopt a code of laws which are not to be invaded under the plausible phrase of reform; namely, that Milah shall never be abolished, that the Sabbath shall be observed on Saturday and never be changed to any other day, that the Shechitah and the dietary laws shall not be disregarded, but commended as preserving health and prolonging life, as it has been statistically proved in such cities as London, Prague, Presburg and Pesth.

And it shall be a fixed rule that any Rabbi who, by his preaching or acts, advises the abolishment of the Milah, or to observe our Sabbath on Sunday, etc., has forfeited his right to preach before a Jewish congregation, and any congregation employing such a Rabbi shall, for the time being, be deprived of the honor to be a member of the Union of Congregations.

I hope that you will act favorably on my recommendation, and that it will receive the support of our sister congregation, which would lead to a Union of Congregations at large, and the adoption by that body of some safeguard against the so-called reform, which, if not checked, may become disastrous to our cause.[424]

---

[424] *Israelite*, 19 (18 Oct. 1872), 9; Union of American Hebrew Congregations, *Proceedings*, i, Introduction. Illoway (*Controversial Letters*, p. 5) observes that 'Cincinnati Jewry was at that time'—probably the 1850s is meant—'still very conservative and many of the prominent members of both temples and their families were quite orthodox, especially so in their households. These had to be reckoned with and they could be moved but slowly.' Moritz Loth (1832–1913) probably typified this conservative element.

Here we have an influential layman taking up the cause for which Wise had been fighting with relentless energy (there is no previous record of such support), but Wise's response is cautious, to say the least. He was not convinced, Wise said, of the 'justice or prudence' of excluding the congregations of the East. Loth's 'primary points' (as Wise described them), the union and the seminary, expressed his own innermost wishes—but the third, which made certain fixed rules the basis of the union, was 'casuistical, and ought to be left to a conference of Rabbis, or at least to men learned in Law'.[425] Wise expressed the hope that the move would be successful and urged the other congregations to co-operate.

Why was Wise's attitude so restrained? The religious bounds which Loth proposed to set look like a precipitate of the disavowal of radical Reform which Wise had emphasized time and again; was he so concerned to have a wide-ranging organization that he shied away from specifics which might alienate any particular section? The Philadelphia Conference had to be disavowed because it alarmed the moderates: Loth's setting of bounds to Reform could not be given an outright welcome because it might frighten off the liberally minded whom he also wanted to draw in. Wise visualized a comprehensive organization; better have all elements under one roof and cast upon any dissidents the burden of seceding than warn off this wing or that. More, he wanted it under his own leadership, and here was another, and a layman at that, formulating the platform. Loth had a mind of his own, and may have been conscious of the need for an active lay initiative. Not long afterwards he referred pointedly to the fact that the Union of American Hebrew Congregations had been 'planned and brought into being by humble laymen, and not by a Rabbi or Rabbonim'.[426]

What kind of discussions preceded Loth's move and whose sentiments he was representing we do not know. That Wise had attempted to indoctrinate the laity of the town and not least the president of his own congregation with his ideas is obvious; equally so that they had discussed among themselves the violent collisions through which the rabbi's pursuit of his goal had been deflected. Had the feeling crystallized that, because it was the only way either to attain the goal or to secure peace, they must take up the reins themselves? Wise

---

[425] *Israelite*, 19 (18 Oct. 1872), 8.

[426] *Union of American Hebrew Congregations Proceedings*, i (13 July 1875), 122.

expressed his reservations, but he was practical enough not to combat his president's effort.

The restraint paid off, so that during the first half of the 1870s Wise's career exhibited some of its sharpest turns. Set for a triumph in 1871, he had outraged the most influential rabbis in the country, and they joined not to support him but to condemn him. By 1872 reasonable men might conclude that it was right to dismiss him as 'the great Cincinnati agitator' whose personal ambitions had once again confounded his 'bold plans', this time for ever. But by 1873 he was moving again, this time on the road to achievement.

Under lay auspices, the movement quickly took shape, and Wise enthusiastically recorded its progress. The Cincinnati leaders set up their committees: we do not find Wise's name among the members. A call went out for a general convention of representatives of all congregations of the West and South to meet in Cincinnati on 8 July 1873. Wise was not among those who signed the call. He does appear as a delegate to the convention, representing not his own congregation but Congregation Zion of Shreveport, Louisiana. The correspondence presented to the convention showed that various congregations which were interested in the scheme put themselves in touch with Wise, and he served on the committee set up to draft a constitution. On the other hand we do not find Wise's name (nor that of any other rabbi) among those elected to the first Executive Board. Wise may have been keeping himself in the wings deliberately; or the laity may have felt that, were he allowed a position of prominence, the life of the newly born child would be endangered by the bitter feuds which had long divided the family.

By contrast with the gatherings of the rabbis, the founding convention appears to have transacted its business without displays of temperament and to have left no current of acrimony in its wake. There was agreement to call a second meeting in Cleveland in 1874, and it was decided that the new organization should be called the Union of American Hebrew Congregations.

The objects of the union as defined in its constitution failed to give expression to Loth's desire to set bounds to Reform; it also implied the end of the idea of a synod. Wise had long urged a synod, and the last rabbinical conference had supported it. In a draft constitution for the congregational union, which Wise published in May, the term is also used to describe the 'representative and legislative body of the

Union'.[427] A Mr Hirschberg, who represented Madison, Indiana, wished the convention to resolve that the establishment of a union was 'in no wise to be construed into the formation of a synod for the fixing of religious principles or the government of the several congregations'. The resolution was indefinitely postponed after considerable debate, 'in which it was urged that no threat had been made of interference with the principles of government of the several congregations, and that therefore no such disavowal was necessary'. But in the framing of Article II of the constitution heed was taken of the feeling expressed. To a statement of the objects which the union was to discharge, there was added the proviso: 'without, however, interfering in any manner whatsoever with the affairs and management of any congregation'. 'It is the primary object of the Union of American Hebrew Congregations, the constitution stated, to establish a Hebrew Theological Institute ... to provide for and advance the standard of Sabbath-schools ... to aid and sustain young congregations'. There is no suggestion of promoting a special religious tendency, and no suggestion of religious oversight, even by way of voluntary arbitration. The word 'synod' does not occur, even as the name of an administrative body; it was replaced by the more innocuous word 'council' (Article V). Here was something rather less than what Wise had been urging. If he felt a tinge of disappointment, he kept it to himself. In the light of the eventual outcome, the observer finds little reason to believe that the mould in which the union was set should have disappointed him. At least there was a union, Cincinnati-based, and a college was to follow. The clay had not been baked into brick, and Wise was sufficiently practical and self-confident to rest content in the belief that he would still be able to influence its permanent form.

Wise's enemies did not see the matter in this light. The new movement was excoriated by the *Jewish Times* as being 'on a level with all the plans and schemes that were ever set on foot by Dr. Wise. They can not rise above the niveau of the commonplace, and this last product of his fertile mind will fare no better: it will also end in dust and smoke.'[428] It went over the story of the previous conference which Wise had sponsored, treated this one as the latest of his enterprises, and expressed certainty that without the Eastern congregations his plans could not be carried into effect.

[427] *Israelite*, 19 (30 May 1873), 4.   [428] *Jewish Times*, 5 (25 July 1873), 344.

21. CALL TO NEW YORK (1873)

Five weeks after the Union of American Hebrew Congregations had been established—a victory, one would have thought, for Wise's cause—the *Israelite* contained the following notice:

The editor of the Israelite having accepted a call of the Congregation Anshe Chesed, of New York, has tendered his resignation as rabbi of K. K. Benai Yeshurun, of Cincinnati, to take effect at the end of September next. The Anshe Chesed Congregation of New York has elected him for life with a salary of $8000 per annum if superannuated. It is the first time in the annals of Jewish history in America, that such an offer has been made to a rabbi. The Anshe Chesed Congregation built the temple on Lexington Avenue, corner Sixty-third Street, which will be dedicated September 5. This brings the Minhag America permanently to New York, and decides forever the value of all protests and newspaper quarrels, which were spread so profusely during the two past years.[429]

Why did Wise, just at the moment when his hopes were nearest realization, consider pulling up stakes? Was he serious in his intentions to go to New York, or was the announcement basically a device for improving his position in Cincinnati? If he really meant to go to New York, what were the reasons?

The announcement in the *Israelite* brings out three points: the salary of $8,000, which was twice what he was receiving in Cincinnati; the new temple which the New York congregation was about to dedicate, which was presumably in a fashionable part of the city, and would give the occupant of its pulpit the possibility of a commanding position; and the opportunity of securing a lodgement in the East for his prayer-book and (though they are not mentioned) his ideas as to a union and a college.

Congregation Anshe Chesed dated back to 1828. Originally Polish-Dutch, it had latterly become almost entirely German—'Bavarian upstarts' was the description used by the New York correspondent of the *Allgemeine Zeitung des Judenthums*,[430] a characterization not unacceptable, apparently, to a Jewish newspaper published in Saxony. At the time when Wise's appointment was announced the congregation had been in a turmoil for nearly a year over the appointment of a rabbi.[431] Moses Mielziner, who had held office since 1865, resigned

---

[429] *Israelite*, 20 (13 Aug. 1873), 4. [430] Loc. cit. 37 (9 Sept. 1872), 608.
[431] Ibid.

in October 1872. (At times his Reform ideas had brought him trouble from a section of the congregation.) Wise preached to the congregation before the month was out, and it was said that there was a move to elect him rabbi forthwith.[432]

In the light of negotiations now known to have been pending, we can contrast the tone of an article entitled 'The Spirit of New York Affairs', which Wise published in the *Israelite* for 8 November, with the attitude to New York which he showed on other occasions. The belief that 'all things not belonging to business interest none in particular' was held only by people from outside 'who have very little opportunities to notice the agencies of culture working beneath the surface. . . . The supposed indifferentism of New York Israelites to Judaism and Jewish affairs is a mistake, without foundation in fact.' The next assertion which this visit had disproved for him was that Reform had proved a failure in New York. It was a success 'in spite of all the blunders made and making by reformers'. To this general proposition he added details which read like a pointer in the direction of Einhorn. One blunder in particular, he said, was 'a spirit of malice and bitterness, of reproof and reproach . . . which has been fostered in the pulpit and press of one class of representative men'. After more in this vein, Wise looked to the possibility that someone might come who would work in a different spirit. 'Whoever will succeed in uniting the discordant still homogenous elements to great public enterprises, will do a great and important work for the American Israelites. It would be done in love, through kindness, by charitable words, energy, perseverance, and enthusiasm for God and Israel.'[433]

This article did nothing to quench the belief among the leaders of Congregation Anshe Chesed that Wise was their man; before the end of 1872 Wise had been offered the pulpit for life, at a salary of $6,000 together with additional benefits. When the trustees met on 20 January 1873 they received a letter from Wise 'declining for the present' to accept the position.

The choice of the congregation then went to Samuel Isaac Kaempf, the rabbi and orientalist of Prague, whom we last met when Wise was deriding him for having delivered an old-fashioned *derashah* (sermon) at the Prague Hevrah Kadishah (Burial Society). The *Allgemeine Zeitung des Judenthums* for 8 July 1873 contains a dispatch from its

[432] *Jewish Times*, 4 (25 Oct. 1872), 689.   [433] *Israelite*, 19 (8 Nov. 1872), 9.

New York correspondent expressing surprise that Dr Kaempf should accept an appointment from such a congregation. Whether or not as a result of this article, Kaempf withdrew.

Congregation Anshe Chesed was minded to woo Wise again, and Wise was minded to be wooed. When the trustees met on 5 August, Wise had arrived in New York. He met the board on the following day and expressed his willingness to accept a call—at a salary greater than that contained in the earlier offer. One of the conditions was that his salary should commence on 25 September, which suggests that he meant to allow himself no more than six weeks in which to pluck up his Cincinnati roots and plant himself in New York. A meeting of the congregation took place the next evening (7 August), when the call was given.[434]

---

[434] The details of the negotiations between Congregation Anshe Chesed and the several rabbis have been taken from the minutes of the congregation, housed in the AJA. The following dispatch from New York, dated 12 Aug., which appeared in the *Allgemeine Zeitung des Judenthums*, 37 (9 Sept. 1875), 608, gives an opinion, apparently non-partisan as between the rabbinic factions, on Wise's standing and achievements viewed from New York at the time of his appointment to Anshe Chesed: 'The choice of a preacher which for a year has put the Anshe Chesed Congregation in tumult has at last been settled. After Dr. Kaempf of Prague had declined finally, the Board again entered into negotiations, which had been pursued earlier, with Dr. Wise of Cincinnati (editor of the 'Israelite') and last week he was appointed for life with a stipend of $8,000 . . . and insurance of $15,000. This sum, which seems fabulous to the European reader (here also it is the highest salary received by a Jewish clergyman) may possibly be capable of making many poorly paid rabbis over there long for the fleshpots of America; still, I am willing to offer no advice on the hazards of emigrating. As was already remarked of this place in an earlier correspondence, the pecuniary endowment is to be attributed more to a passion for show than to a truly religious need. Mr. Wise, who is in a position to give German and English sermons, is really the man most suited to this congregation. Since the congregation has placed itself under a great burden through the building of a new Temple at an expenditure of $250,000, it must naturally devise ways and means of winning new members. For many the preacher is the attraction; thus it is altogether natural that he should receive his share.

Whatever the opponents of Mr. Wise, particularly Dr. Einhorn and Mr. Ellinger (editor of the *Jewish Times*), impute to him he has earned good deserts for his services to American Judaism. Though inferior to many others in Talmudic learning, as a 'self-made man' he deserves full recognition. If in his case American humbug plays a big part, he shows thereby that he understands America. He represents Judaism with success towards the outside world; and with the American public particularly he stands in esteem. Thus, in the most recent period he brought into being a union of Jewish congregations which occupies itself particularly with the task of establishing an educational institution for teachers and rabbis. This union which was founded in Cincinnati at the beginning of July, will shortly (?) it is to be hoped, include all congregations in the United States. Though the need for a Jewish educational

The salient points in Wise's announcement of his move have been noted. Can we get any closer to the causes? 'Wise was undoubtedly influenced by the thought that he was being neglected by his congregation', wrote his grandson.[435] In what could this neglect have consisted—inadequate salary, being taken for granted, differences in policy? We have no information. There is a strong temptation to assume that, apart from the bait of a higher salary, the circumstances in which the Union of American Hebrew Congregations had been brought into being—by others, and not under his leadership—had something to do with his 'feeling of being neglected'. It is also likely that the desire to conquer the East—which, after all, is the reason indicated by Wise himself—played a significant part in his decision. The occasion was propitious. Samuel Adler, of Temple Emanu-El, had ceased to be effective and was retired in the following year; Gutheim had returned to New Orleans; Einhorn does not appear to have played any role outside the pulpit, and in the pulpit he appealed to the German-speaking element only.

Though Wise had secured a following in the West, they had constantly rejected the *Minhag America*, for which he had an absolute devotion. To maintain the lodgement of this volume in New York

---

institution becomes ever more urgent, great obstacles still stand in the way. The root of the evil lies in the wretched dissension which prevails among the spiritual leaders. The question here is neither of Reform nor of Orthodoxy (the practical distinction between the two parties is in the highest degree insignificant) but only of cliques and coteries. Without these mean petty jealousies many a creation would already have been called into being which till now is still the object of pious wish. If we have produced a few exemplary welfare institutions, such as hospitals, orphanages etc., these exist in no way through the united activity of the clergy but in spite of a disharmony that has become proverbial. It is really grievous to note how the different rabbis stand face to face like armed enemies. Just as soon as the energetic rabbis of the West, much under Wise's stimulus, propose a plan for an institute, those of the East are ready to protest. Thereby their effectiveness well nigh limits itself outside their congregations. How they will be roused from their lethargy through the appearance of Mr. Wise in their midst!'

The statement in the foregoing dispatch that the welfare institutions had been created in spite of the disharmony of the rabbis prompts the enquiry whether it was not this internecine warfare among the rabbis which caused the leaders of these welfare institutions to place them outside the reach of religious influences.

[435] May, *Isaac Mayer Wise*, 175. Wise may have been in financial difficulties at this period, and the prospect of an enhanced salary may have been important. This is alluded to in the fiftieth anniversary *History of the K.K. Bene Yeshurun of Cincinnati, Ohio* (Cincinnati, 1892), prepared by Wise and Max B. May. The pages of this work are not numbered, but the point is referred to in the section entitled 'The Period of Public Activity 1866–1892'.

when Einhorn had made Congregation Adath Jeshurun dispense with it, he had, so it appears, promoted a congregation which used it, but it appears to have gone out of existence in 1873;[436] he had been snubbed by Congregation Emanu-El in 1872. All this would bait a man of Wise's spirit to rise to the opportunity of going to New York with the design of conquering.

That Wise seriously thought of leaving Cincinnati at this period is supported by the incident relative to Temple Emanu-El. When he visited New York in October 1872 and his availability for the pulpit of Congregation Anshe Chesed was being canvassed, moves were made to invite Wise to preach, but the board was adamant in its refusal. Could it be that Wise had seen the chance to install himself in the leading congregation in the country, but that the leaders of the congregation, their minds on the fierce controversies in which he had been engaged, were determined to keep him at arm's length?[437]

Whether or not Wise seriously intended to leave Cincinnati, his congregation put him under severe and flattering pressure to remain. An influential committee had several meetings with the rabbi, and the upshot was a lengthy resolution adopted by the annual general meeting in September refusing to accept his resignation and requesting Congregation Anshe Chesed to release him. Wise had been introduced to the meeting before this resolution was adopted. He was given an ovation, and his salary was increased to $6,000, with additional benefits.[438] 'Unassailable' is not too strong a term to describe the position he now occupied.

To the story of Wise's relations with Congregation Anshe Chesed one footnote may be added. Before the year 1873 expired, Anshe

---

[436] Wise's visit to New York to consecrate the B'nai Maimunim synagogue is reported in *Israelite*, 14 (9 Aug. 1867). *Jewish Times*, 6 (18 Dec. 1874), 679, reports the death of Dr Jacob Wasserman, 'preacher in the B'nai Maimunim Congregation until its dissolution', which makes it not unlikely that the congregation had gone out of existence when Wise decided to go to New York. In announcing his decision to accept the New York appointment Wise emphasizes bringing *Minhag America* to the city: *American Israelite*, 20 (18 Aug. 1873), 8.

[437] Minutes of Congregation Emanu-El. At this time (Oct. 1872) the congregation was in negotiation with Dr Gustave Gottheil of Manchester, England. In the course of a letter, preserved in the AJA, which David Einhorn addressed to Kaufmann Kohler on 29 Oct. 1872, he wrote: 'Today Wise preached once in the Norfolk Street *schul*; it is said that he reckons on Temple . . .': the next word is indistinct, but at that time Emanu-El was the only congregation which used the term 'temple'. 'Norfolk Street *schul*' was Anshe Chesed.

[438] *Israelite*, 21 (3 Oct. 1873), 14.

Chesed had opened negotiations with Einhorn's congregation—Adath Jeshurun—for a merger, and the union was effected early in 1874. The combined body, of which Einhorn was of course the rabbi, took the name Beth El.[439] In the course of a few years, therefore, Anshe Chesed had run through the spectrum of Jewish religious colouration. It had baited Mielziner because he was too much in favour of reform, had wooed Kaempf who, though he had sympathies with Zacharias Fraenkel, was to all intents and purposes Orthodox, had chosen Wise, a moderate reformer, and had finally found itself under the spiritual guidance of his arch-enemy, the radical Einhorn. Wise's lack of a firm religious position was not unique.

22. 'WE MUST HAVE "UNION IN ISRAEL" '

Once Wise's position in Cincinnati had been confirmed, he resumed his agitation for support for the Union of American Hebrew Congregations, and in particular for the educational institution which it was its task to bring forth. 'Unless summoned from our post by a decree of Providence before it can be accomplished,' he wrote immediately after the formation of the Union,

we will not lay down our pen until there shall stand firmly THE Union of THE American Hebrew Congregations; until we shall have the Hebrew classical and rabbinical college on American soil. If we exercise any influence on the American Hebrews, and wherever we do or will exercise any, it will be used fully and vigorously in favor of 'Union' and 'College'. If we have any friends in this country, we will unceasingly entreat them to come forward liberally and generously in aid of 'Union' and 'College'.[440]

He gave himself to this task with an enthusiasm and a single-mindedness which recalls the spirit with which he had carried the flag of Zion College twenty years before. Harnessed to a practical task, working in the midst of an organized body of men, the goal of his strivings in sight, he found little occasion for personal complaints of persecution and victimization. 'We do not expect', he allowed himself to grumble, 'that this cause, however sacred and universal, will [not] receive much encouragement from either our denominational press, or our aristocracy, both of which have stood aloof of

---

[439] *Jewish Encyclopedia*, ix. 277. Congregation Anshe Chesed is not to be confused with the present-day New York congregation of the same name. Beth El subsequently amalgamated with Congregation Emanu-El.

[440] *Israelite*, 21 (8 Aug. 1873), 4.

all reform movements', but he had faith in the people and was confident of being able to push forward without the 'big men' of the East.

Happily we muster over twenty thousand men enrolled in congregations outside of our largest cities. If we can unite half of them to erect institutions to the glory of God, the elevation of Judaism, and the honor of Israel, the rest will come gradually, a little later, but they will. It is to those twenty thousand in Israel to whom the Congregational Convention has spoken, and upon whose fidelity and religious zeal reliance has been placed. . . . The people will move, the masses will speak, and they need no particular assistance; nor is their onward march much retarded by any single-handed opposition.[441]

Naturally anyone who was indifferent to the cause of the Union and the College incurred his wrath. 'The frogs quack and the earth moves forever' was the conclusion of an article built round a tale of some frogs who were troubled because the movement of the earth disturbed their sleep.[442] The names of neither individuals nor institutions were mentioned, but it is not far-fetched to assume that he was aiming at those who wanted to do nothing. In the same issue of the *Israelite* Wise complained about the absence of interest on the part of the congregations in California and Oregon. There was no excuse—that hundreds of miles of largely uninhabited country isolated the Pacific coast from Cincinnati does not appear to have entered Wise's reckoning; the cause was too big for regard for such trifles: 'We beg, not for ourselves, but for a sacred cause, for Israel's holy heritage, to be rescued from under the ruins of destructive materialism and crushing indifferentism, we beg.'[443]

Wise now became concerned at the fact that a large percentage of the Jews in Cincinnati and elsewhere were not members of congregations. 'Are You a Member of a Congregation?' is the title of an article expounding 'the solemn duty of every Israelite who has reached the age of manhood to join a congregation'.[444] An adjoining column carried an article with the simple heading 'One Dollar', and it reveals the cause of Wise's sudden feeling over the question of non-

---

[441] Ibid.   [442] Ibid. (5 Sept. 1873), 4.

[443] Ibid. In July and Aug. 1877 Wise visited the West Coast. His report showed that the congregations there looked upon the union and the college as being far removed from their interests.

[444] Ibid. (19 Sept. 1873), 4.

affiliation; a dollar per head per annum was the quota which each congregation was obliged to pay to the union. That was on 19 September. A week later he was upbraiding those who merely desired to be buried as Jews, but who stood aloof from congregational responsibilities during their lifetime.[445] Later he returned to the theme. 'It must become a general maxim among the American Israelites, that every one must be a member of a congregation, and every congregation a member of the Union. The one must make and support the other.'[446] This was the starting point, from which he proceeded to complain against several classes of 'outsiders'—'overdone individuals among us who are *too enlightened* to belong to any congregation . . . those in large cities who take all they can and pay nothing for it'. His desire to gather strength through the congregation for the union led him to declare that 'no minister of any synagogue ought to be permitted to attend to any wedding unless the groom is a member of a congregation; and to no funeral, unless the family is truly Jewish—i.e., members of a congregation'.[447]

With his upbraiding of those who stood aloof from the congregations (and thereby from the union) Wise combined appeals to observe the Sabbath, and opposition to every attempt to abandon 'the Sabbath of the decalogue, and . . . every proposition of adopting, in any shape or form, the day of resurrection as a Jewish holiday'. He also took up the cause of the Sabbath schools, whose improvement was on the agenda of the union, and in the same article denounced both the *chevras* who had no schools ('uncivilized *Tsaddikim*, who make noise enough in their little places of worship, and let their children grow up like heathens') and those who had religious schools without Hebrew instruction: 'Your Bible is Hebrew. You have no authorized version. A large portion of your prayers is Hebrew. The preservation of the Hebrew, and the purity of the Hebrew doctrine are inseparable.'[448]

While these things were being written, the union was taking shape

---

[445] *Israelite,* 21 (26 Sept. 1873), 4.   [446] Ibid. (19 June 1874), 4.

[447] Ibid. Probably with B'nai B'rith in mind, he at the same time inveighed against 'Jewish secret societies' that boasted 'upon their work in the elevation of Judaism and redeeming the world in general' but set themselves in opposition to congregations (ibid.). See also *Israelite,* 20 (28 May 1874); 22 (6 Aug. 1875); 10 Sept. 1875).

[448] See e.g. *Israelite,* 22 (3 Apr. 1874), 8; 25 (13 Aug. 1875), 5; 25 (10 Sept. 1875), 4. Kaufmann Kohler, an avowed opponent of the union, had begun Sunday services in Chicago when Wise denounced any abandonment of the Sabbath.

and plans were being laid for the opening of Hebrew Union College. As the day approached, Wise seems to have risen into something of a frenzy, not this time of denunciation or self-pity, darkened by premonitions of insanity or suicide, but of elation at the prospects which lay ahead. 'To our friends we must say, never stop agitating, never forget that we must have "Union in Israel," in order to do our duty before God and man, to us and to our children, to our country and the human family.'[449] And to this he appended a six-point programme which, verbosely enough for a summary, was still only a summary of what he had been preaching during the preceding months.

1. Every Israelite must keep his Sabbath, and not the Sabbath of the Pope and dead emperors.
2. Every Hebrew child must be sent to a well conducted Sabbath-school, to learn Hebrew, to be enlightened in the religion and history of our fathers, and to be trained to genuine piety.
3. Every Israelite, male or female, young or old, rich or poor, must be a member of some Hebrew congregation . . .
4. Every congregation must be a member of the Union of American Hebrew Congregations . . .
5. We must educate our rabbis from among our sons, who know our wants, feel our woes, and are inspired with our hopes and wishes; enlightened, patriotic and high-minded sons of freedom, who bear our banner and not that of England, Poland or Germany; who shall go before us, work with us and for us, and not for admiration in some foreign countries; who are with us, and remain with us, and not with one leg here and the other in Europe; who shall understand principles of honor and manhood, and not abuse one another in the Irish-Polish village style; . . .
6. We must advance the standard of intelligence among our people. The 'Union' must provide for academical education, for our sons and daughters, and offer the opportunity to be well instructed in the grand and opulent literature and history of the Hebrews.[450]

These six paragraphs do not say a word about 'reform', but the opportunity for a slap at Sunday services and the 'quarrelsome, selfish and silly demigods' imported from Europe could not be avoided. It is true that in the same article Wise says that it was the 'reform agitation' which had 'set in motion the indifferent mass' and was therefore responsible for the progress of Jewish life, but there is no hint of Reform in his programme.

[449] *Israelite*, 25 (24 Sept. 1875), 4.   [450] Ibid.

If he steered clear of the ideologues of Reform, he did not contemplate any going back on the kind of reforms which he had put into operation. In 1875, when dissension within Congregation B'nai Jeshurun, New York, over the introduction of an organ, mixed choir, and family pews reached the courts, Wise swore an affidavit affirming that organs and family pews had become a common custom in both Europe and America; and in his newspaper he inveighed lustily against any who thought that an American congregation could be restrained from adopting what, through his initiative, had become the American *minhag*.

The Judaism of this country is reformatory and progressive; it appeals to the reason, common sense and the innate feelings and convictions of the Jew, and not to the Talmud of that African *Azzuth Panim* [insolence] who whines stupidly in the *Messenger*, or of the outlandish and half-civilized saints of the *Beth Hamidrash*.
   ... The *Beth Hamidrash* rule is past and gone in this country, those gentlemen from Africa or Poland, however long their beards, awkward their garments and gait, and sanctimonious their countenances, must take seats in the background. They are shelved for good. This is a new country with new conceptions and a new future; we cannot afford to be schoolmastered by anybody. We understand our own business.[451]

Responsibility had still not smoothed down Wise's roughness; however, although 'hyper-orthodoxy' is one of the objects of his derision, the appeal is, above everything else, to what is American as against what belongs to the Old World.

Wise would not have been himself had he confined his enthusiasms and his expostulations to the editorial chair. Only twenty-seven congregations, most of them small, had been represented at the meeting which set up the Union in 1873; more needed to be enrolled and funds needed to be raised if it was to be other than a skeleton organization. The officers of the union might be devoted committee workers, but Wise alone had the strength or the competence to rouse the country to its needs. He raised the union flag in Philadelphia in September 1873. At the end of October he went to Indianapolis, Cleveland, and Detroit. This time his travels had no connection with the college or the union. Word had come to him on a Friday evening of the sufferings of the people of Memphis caused by an outbreak of

---

[451] *Israelite*, 25 (14 Aug. 1875), 4.

yellow fever. By 10 p.m. he had visited every newspaper office in Cincinnati, with the result that the following morning's papers contained an appeal for the relief of Memphis. With the same object in view he embarked on his out-of-town visits, which would have continued had he not received from the mayor of Memphis a telegram to the effect that no more relief was required.[452]

In February 1874 we find Wise in Chicago. The Constitution Grand Lodge of B'nai B'rith was holding its annual session there, and, notwithstanding previous failures, Wise tried once more to harness B'nai B'rith to the proposed college. He set down a motion that 'We, as B'nai B'rith, deem it proper to give our aid to the Union of American Hebrew Congregations, and to the institution that body may establish intending the elevation and promulgation of Judaism and Hebrew lore.'[453] But the dice were loaded against him. The president of the convention did not appoint Wise to the committee which considered this resolution—the chairmanship went to Moritz Ellinger, editor of the *Jewish Times* and Wise's principal journalistic opponent. Wise's motion was reported on adversely, and the convention adopted a report stating that 'This committee deem it not within the sphere of the Order to interfere with congregational or doctrinal matter in any shape or form.'[454] 'I can think of no single public act of injustice', Wise remarked in the *Reminiscences*, 'of which I have been the victim that was not inspired by B'nai B'rith brethren and leaders.'[455]

Still, to capture B'nai B'rith was not the only object of Wise's visit to Chicago. He spoke to three of the congregations in that city and to two in Milwaukee. There were no immediate results. Kehillath Anshe Ma'arav, Chicago, was one of the original members of the union, but the others did not respond immediately to Wise's visit.

In the early summer of 1874 Wise visited Pittsburgh and persuaded Congregation Rodef Shalom to adhere to the union.[456] For the rest of 1874 we do not find much travelling; this was the period when his wife was lying incurably ill, and in December she succumbed. In April 1875 he visited the East. In 1874 the Union had abolished the original limitation to congregations of the West and South when

[452] Ibid. 21 (7 Nov. 1873), 4.   [453] *Jewish Times*, 5 (13 Feb. 1874), 805.
[454] Ibid.   [455] *Reminiscences*, 265.
[456] *American Israelite*, 23 (17 July 1874), 4.

the Council of the Union decided to invite every congregation of the United States and its territories to join,[457] and the way was open to Wise to see that the invitation was accepted. The annual meeting of the council was due to take place in July, and, though he might have felt it unpropitious to attempt a direct assault on Eastern centres such as Philadelphia and New York, to reduce such outer strongholds as Washington and Baltimore was doubtless worth venturing upon. Hence he spoke in April—apparently in discouraging circumstances—to the Washington Hebrew Congregation,[458] and to Dr Szold's congregation in Baltimore. He won partial success, for on 7 May he was able to publish a stop-press telegram—such was the excitement of the chase—announcing that the Washington congregation had joined the union.[459] On 17 May he set out by river steamer for Huntington, and after spending a few hours of the following morning there left by train for Charleston, West Virginia, where he lectured at the Methodist Church on the doctrines of Judaism. On the following day he made calls (by way of propaganda for the union and the college, one assumes, though he does not say so) and on 20 May he proceeded to Richmond. There he preached in the synagogue and addressed the Sabbath school: 'I made my set speech for "Union and College;" and when I had done, the *Parnass* [lay head of Congregation] said to me: "Count us in; if the congregation does not pay, I will pay for it." '[460] When the Council of the Union assembled in the following month, Richmond was represented. On the Monday he went to Petersburg, Virginia—'I spoke earnestly, I believe fervently, which had the effect that this congregation at once voted itself into the Union of American Hebrew Congregations'. He had meant to go on to Norfolk but felt reduced by the heat, and instead spend a day resting in Richmond before he returned to Cincinnati.[461] In the meantime Kaufmann Kohler had launched a prepared attack on him in Chicago, but neither the fatigue nor the attack seemed to affect Wise's good humour. His nature had not changed so much that he was able to spare Kohler altogether; in fact he devoted to Kohler's address one and a half of the long columns of the *Israelite*, but still he rode the attack more easily than he had done a short time before. Then he could never have laughed at his

---

[457] *Union of American Hebrew Congregations Proceedings*, i (16 July 1874), 95.
[458] *American Israelite*, 24 (23 Apr. 1875), 4.
[459] Ibid. (7 May 1875), 4.   [460] Ibid. (4 June 1875), 4.
[461] Ibid. (11 June 1875), 4.

own style of reply: 'but now we have been attacked personally, unjustly, maliciously, horribly, shamelessly, unmanly, wickedly, terrible, insultingly, etc. (the balance in Webster's Dictionary)'.[462] For the rest Wise contented himself for the most part with heavy irony.

Once the Union of American Hebrew Congregations came into being, several projects were taken in hand—the provision of a cheap translation of the Scriptures, the sending of preachers to small congregations, and the improvement of Sabbath schools. The main challenge, in Wise's eyes, was the establishment of a 'theological institute'.[463] The meeting at Cleveland in 1874 of the first council of the union decided, upon the recommendation of a committee of which Wise was a member, that the institute was to be called Hebrew Union College and was to be under the 'control, management and government' of a board of governors of twelve members who were to have their own officers. The scheme also provided that the college should have three departments—preparatory, Hebrew classical, and rabbinical—and should be open to students of all denominations gratuitously. The provisions regarding the first two departments made it clear that the college was not intended for students of the ministry only. Here we have a reflection of Wise's old plan for a Jewish university. Cincinnati was designated as the seat of the college, and the governors were ordered to open at least the Preparatory Department by October 1875. Before it dispersed, the council elected the first board of governors, of whom Wise was one.[464]

The decisions taken at Cleveland raised Wise's spirits to fresh heights: 'Is it reality that all those cherished dreams of the past have been incarnated? Union and united action in the American Israel, the College and the resurrection of Hebrew literature and philosophy—are they indeed realities?' The meeting was as important in its day as were those under Zerubbabel, Ezra, and Nehemiah; the sons and daughters of future generations would feel happy 'if they discover the names of their sires among the men in Israel enrolled in the people's Council to guard and forward the most sacred cause, bearing the impress of God's seal of truth'. By this time he had begun to write his *Reminiscences* in *Die Deborah*, and the motif of his dream finds a place also in his words of advice. 'Go on, leap or climb over the rocks rolled in your path; creep through the thorny hedges in your way;

[462] Ibid.   [463] Ibid. 21 (31 July 1874), 4.
[464] *Union of American Hebrew Congregations Proceedings*, i. 99, 106.

swim the streams, circumpass mountains; go on and on and never pause.'[465]

Wise's enthusiasm extended, as is hardly surprising, to the choice of Cincinnati as the locale of the college; geographically it was in a central position; it was 'healthy, clean and in all moral points of view well governed'; on top of existing educational institutions a new university was growing; the spirit prevailing was one of 'liberality and literary ambition'. Moreover, Cincinnati was ideal because Cincinnati Israelites as a class occupied a 'high and respected social position' and because they had 'those large and costly temples in which wealth and art combined to glorify the name of God, elevate the character of the worshippers, and do honor to Judaism and the name of Israel'. Thirdly, Cincinnati was

the successful hot-house for the tender plant of American Judaism. . . . the *Zion of the New World*, which sent forth that light and spirit of progressive, liberalized and Americanized Judaism, now prevailing over the length and breadth of this country. . . . with us Judaism is nothing outlandish; it is no exotic curiosity; it is neither German, French, nor Polish: it is American, and fully so, in language, spirit and form.[466]

American in language, spirit, and form! Wise was now writing, not in the *Israelite* but in the *American Israelite*. Six weeks before (3 July 1874) he had changed the name of the paper—impetuously, one surmises, since the appearance of the first issue in the new guise was delayed and it did not mark a regular break, such as the beginning of a new volume. Wise claimed that the *Israelite* had fought the battles of the Lord 'for truth, reform, progression, light and charity' and had won—'It has emancipated and naturalized Judaism on the American soil'—and again he emphasized: 'the Hebrew is Americanized, and his religion naturalized; they are no longer strangers: they are perfectly at home in this blessed country.'[467]

But the decisions still had to be brought to fruition. The constitution of the union provided that when $60,000 had been raised the income should be applied to the maintenance of the college, and that when this had been increased to $160,000 the balance of $100,000 might be applied to the erection or purchase of a college building.[468]

[465] *American Israelite*, 21 (31 July 1874), 4.
[466] Ibid. (14 Aug. 1874), 4.   [467] Ibid. 23 (3 July 1874), 4.
[468] *Union of American Hebrew Congregations Proceedings*, i. 25.

When the council met in 1875, Moritz Loth was optimistic about meeting immediate financial needs.[469] This could only be because the college was to be opened on a modest scale. On 28 May Wise was able to confirm that the Preparatory Department would open early in the autumn, and that the board of governors was completing arrangements to establish a code of laws and to appoint a faculty. The laws were comprehensive enough, but the faculty was limited to one teacher apart from the president. Clearly the plan was to build slowly from the ground. Wise, we may guess, might have started with a completed structure in being, but, though he was the driving force, he had to reckon with the prudence of his colleagues.

The laws provided that the superintendence of the college should be invested in a president, and it appears that, although no announcement was then made, it was assumed when the council met in Buffalo that the office would devolve upon Wise. The college needed not only funds and a home and teachers, but also pupils. There was little suggestion that, despite Wise's pleas for a native rabbinate and a Jewishly educated laity, parents were anxious to enrol their sons; thus, if there was to be a college, Wise had to search for pupils also. In March 1875 the father of David Philipson in Columbus, Ohio, was surprised to receive a letter from Rabbi Wise asking whether he would like to enrol his son as a pupil at the new institution.[470]

Here the picture of another side of Wise's personality begins to unfold. We have seen much of Wise the fighter, the violent antagonist. Wise had asked Joseph Philipson to bring his son to see him, which he did in August, and David Philipson recalled the trepidation with which he entered the presence of the great man:

After the first few moments of the dreaded interview, the fear that possessed the lad disappeared entirely. The geniality of the famous rabbi put the quaking boy entirely at his ease and he left the house enamoured of the prospect of becoming a pupil of this remarkable man. The compelling personality of Isaac M. Wise impressed all, old and young, who came into personal contact with him in the same manner. Even bitter opponents who knew him only at a distance were disarmed when they were brought within the circle of intimate personal converse. His was the simplicity of real greatness and the lovableness of true humanity.[471]

---

[469] Ibid. 121.
[470] David Philipson, *My Life as an American Jew* (Cincinnati, 1941), 1.
[471] *History of Hebrew Union College* (Cincinnati, 1925), 21.

The evidence of Wise's solicitude for the young can be multiplied. Thus, a little later we find him writing to the board of governors:

There is now here a Russian-German boy, Morris Sachs, 14 years old, poor and friendless. He studied in the *Gymnasium* of Liba in Kurland, to the fourth class thereof, is tolerably versed in Hebrew and German, has a fair start in Latin, Greek and mathematics, and appears to be quite intelligent and desirous to study. His father is a poor immigrant, now in Chicago. The boy appears to me very promising and worthy of your support. He came to me penniless and friendless. I will keep him in my house till you decide what shall be done with him. He could conveniently go along with Grade D, and has the qualifications of the law, because he was in the Gymnasium. I recommend this boy to your particular grace, and, if you resolve so, I will keep him in my house till July next for half price, at $3 a week. I will also care for his clothing.[472]

When Wise had visited Richmond he was the guest of Dr A. S. Bettelheim, the local rabbi. The rabbi's 11-year-old daughter, later Mrs Rebecca Kohut, recalled in her memoirs what the presence of Rabbi Wise meant to the Bettelheim children when he stayed in their home:

This great man, who so thoroughly imposed his personality upon American Judaism, was a delightful talker and full of fun. Dignity and command were his, but not austerity. He encouraged us to be intimate with him. And our ease in his presence was in delightful contrast with the solemn reverence we had been taught to show our elders. . . . Only a man of his striking personality could have so large a following as his. As almost mere babies, I recall, we responded to the magnetism of the man. We liked to hear him talk, and to look at his wide expanse of brow, and his head which was so huge for his body, and the eternal spectacles perched upon his forehead, and worn under his hat.[473]

Another of his first group of pupils describes him as a 'mild, kindly and lovable' personality.[474]

Even the *Jewish Times*—Einhorn's organ—came near to admitting that Wise had likeable qualities: 'however often they may have been deceived or disappointed by the conjurer', it lamented,[475] people 'try

---

[472] *Union of American Hebrew Congregations Proceedings*, i. 322.

[473] Rebecca Kohut, *My Portion* (New York, 1925), 43.

[474] Henry Berkowitz, in *Central Conference of American Rabbis Year Book*, xxix (1919), 187.

[475] 7 (11 June 1875), 232.

him again and again. They cannot withstand his magnetic influence. We confess there must be a charm about him, irresistible to those who come within its radius.' The *Jewish Times* did not abate its criticisms of Wise and his enterprises, but all the critics could offer was criticisms. Wise, now 56, was donning his harness, and, if he survived, the charm which made him irresistible to the young would be the quality first remembered.

23. PRESIDENT OF HEBREW UNION COLLEGE

We have still not followed Wise into the presidency of Hebrew Union College. He left the second Council of the Union (1875) with his rapturous enthusiasm undimmed.[476] He was showing congregational presidents and boards of trustees how by helping the union they would be helping themselves, as the union would 'exert its influence to get every Israelite to observe the Sabbath and to be a member of the congregation', and would supply the congregations with rabbis to whose oratory it would be a feast of reason to listen.[477] In the same issue of the *American Israelite* he was, in a second article, showing parents that if they wished to prevent their babes from becoming 'social deformities for life' they must 'instill into them the love of observing the Sabbath and of practicing liberality';[478] and he entitled a third 'Social Deformities', who had 'no feeling for anybody or anything . . . Nothing is a reality but money, and if they cannot make any money out of it, they have no use for it; it is a waste of time, and they turn a deaf ear to every appeal.'[479] What was exercising him is made clear by the expression of hope in the final paragraph that the committees soliciting funds for the college would not meet such 'social deformities'.

On 28 August the board of governors resolved formally to appoint Wise president of Hebrew Union College. He performed his services gratuitously, and his only assistant was Solomon Eppinger, who had been on the staff of the Talmud Yelodim Institute.

Though there was no ready-made grandeur surrounding the presidency, Wise responded in a tone which suggests that the official appointment affected him deeply. He published a manifesto in the *American Israelite* which, while it is not self-effacing, is quiet in its self-confidence and comprehensive in its sympathies.

[476] See *American Israelite*, 25 (30 Aug. 1875), 4.   [477] Ibid. (6 Aug. 1875), 4.
[478] Ibid. 5.   [479] Ibid.

We deem it our duty to speak a few words for the President elected, and may say, that he considers it the highest honor which could have been conferred on him. Neither a seat in the Senate of the United States, nor the office of the Chief Justice, appears to him as responsible and honorable a position, as the presidency of the Hebrew Union College, where the finest opportunity offers to contribute largely to the education of the young people of our country; to lay a solid foundation to the future greatness of American Judaism; and to promulgate Hebrew learning, to raise high the moral and intellectual standard of Judaism.

An arduous task has been imposed on him with this honor. It is no small enterprise, to organize and to build up a seat of learning for the education of the rising and the coming generations. This will take more work than is commonly supposed, and can be successfully accomplished only by the earnest and unanimous support of the Board of Governors, the Faculty, the Executive Board of the Union, the confidence and hearty support of our co-religionists in general, upon whom he relies, and to all of whom he sends fraternal greetings with the solemn promise, always to do his duty fully, to the best of his knowledge and abilities. It will be his object of life and happiness, to afford the opportunity to the young Israelites of our country, to acquire an academical and enlightened education, to take out the treasures of Israel's rich literature, and to go forth into their various avocations enlightened, competent and upright men, apostles of truth and practical humanity; provided, of course, he shall meet with that aid and support which so sacred a cause richly deserves.

Isaac M. Wise has many and fierce opponents. He has projected and worked too much not to have them. But he has many more ardent and faithful friends, whose confidence he fully possesses and who are always ready to support him heartily. His opponents who are also opponents of the Union of American Hebrew Congregations, will, of course, denounce his election. But then the friends of the cause will justly tell them, if you are opposed to it, send your delegates to the next Council, to take place in July next in Washington, and instruct them to vote against Isaac M. Wise as President of the Hebrew Union College; have a better candidate to propose, and get for him the majority of votes in that Council, and the matter is settled. For whatever the Council resolves concerning any transaction, enactment, appointment or election of any of its Boards, that is law, and if Isaac M. Wise is defeated there, he stands defeated, and will stand it without a murmur. It will not cool off his enthusiasm for the cause, it will not diminish his zeal; he will remain the same warm advocate as heretofore of 'Union and College,' education, progression, enlightenment and learning. The evil, if such it be, can be remedied in the very next Council in the city of Washington. He has neither sought nor solicited the office, asks no remuneration, and is ready at any time, to vote a better man than himself into that lofty position.

The opponents will advance, that man Wise is not learned enough for the position, and he will at once admit, that there a good many men in this world who know vastly more than he and his opponents. But his friends will say, if all our rabbis educated in the Hebrew Union College will be able to give that satisfaction to their respective congregations as Wise has given to his in Albany and Cincinnati, if each of them will stand up before the American people in two hundred and more public orations and lectures, as Wise did; if they will wield as fearless a pen in behalf of Israel and his sacred cause, for a quarter of a century, as that very man Wise has done; the rising and coming generations will probably be well satisfied with the learning and ability of their rabbis. None of his opponents has examined him, none has pointed out any blunders in the books he has written, or the pubic orations and lectures he has delivered, although the American press all over this country has largely commented on them. If the rabbis of future days will do the same thing, the country will perhaps be satisfied with them.

He, on his part sends to his opponents the words which will be the motto of the College: 'Fullness of peace to those who love thy law,' and solicits the support of all. In his official capacity he recognizes no opponents, no enemies; he will work for the benefit of all, and however humble an individual he may be, he will always be guided by the principle: 'The disciples of the sages augment peace in the world.' He will have no ISMS and no SCHISMS to impose, no sophistries to defend, no superstitions to advocate, no prejudices to foster; exactly in obedience to the outspoken will of the Council and the Union, he will earnestly and steadily endeavour with the aid of a competent and distinguished Faculty, to open the treasures of Israel's literature to Jew and Gentile, reformer and orthodox, in justice to all and in offence to none. He will be the friend and patron of all young people who shall seek knowledge and thirst for that truth which our sires have amassed and crystallized in deathless words. The indigent student will always find him ready to help. It will be his pride to be a parental friend to the intelligent youth of our country, whose confidence he flatters himself to possess, and claims but the one reward, viz., success. What he may know less, the faculty will know more. With the help of God, he hopes to do as much good as he is able to accomplish.

To the young people all over this country, he sends paternal salutations, and the invitation 'Whoever are thirsty, let them go to the water.' Whoever desires to rise above the common level by steady and earnest study, whatever avocation he may choose in after life, let him come to Cincinnati and take advantage of the opportunities offered by the Union of American Hebrew Congregations. Whoever loves Israel and his sacred treasures, whoever loves knowledge and enlightenment, let him come and gather the fruits from the tree of knowledge, 'Hear, that your souls may live.' Come and work to become good, useful and prosperous men, citizens and Israelites. Young men, direct your full attention to Cincinnati, where the standard of intelligence will be rapidly advanced, the foundation will be laid to the usefulness and greatness of many a prominent man of coming days, and Israel's treasures will be rendered enjoyable to the American student. Young men, Isaac M. Wise says, he has worked for you long and steadily; you are not invited to work for yourselves.

We must say one more word to parents and guardians. The Hebrew Union College is intended for the education of all who seek education, and not only for the education of rabbis. So the Council decided. The advantages it offers to those students who will not choose to be rabbis are manifold. It offers them a thorough course of Jewish learning besides all the other branches of education. It places them under the parental surveillance not only of an eminent faculty but also of a committee of highly Honorable gentlemen from the Board of Governors, who will fully care for the well-being and conduct of the students. If offers them an enlightened religious and moral training in temples grand and gorgeous as well as in the orthodox synagogue, to see Judaism in its glory and to hear it expounded intelligently. Turn your attention to Cincinnati, to place your growing up sons where the opportunities are highly promising to educate them to be men, citizens and Israelites in the noblest sense of these terms.

The Board of Governors resolved to solemnize publicly in the temple, on Sunday evening October 3d. the formal opening of the Hebrew Union College, and Messrs. Solomon Levi, B. Bettman and Isaac M. Wise have been appointed a committee of arrangements, to carry out the wishes of the Board. We have no doubt it will be made a grand celebration of a great event, full of incalculable importance to the cause of Israel in this great country, where under the genial sun of freedom, in the centennial year of liberty, a new chapter of Israel's wonderful history shall be opened to the glory of God, the fraternization and elevation of the human family.[480]

Wise showed no intention of launching Hebrew Union College under the banner of Reform.

'No thunder of cannon, no ringing of bells announced to the world, which cared little enough, the great event when, in October, 1875, the Hebrew Union College opened at Bene Israel Temple in Cincinnati, one story below the surface of the earth.'[481] Wise's memory was at fault. Whether or not the world realized that this was 'a great event full of incalculable importance to the cause of Israel', Hebrew Union College had to be drummed up, and the modesty of the circumstances in which it began its work was drowned by the grandiloquence of the 'grand celebration' of a great event. At 7.30 on the evening of Sunday,

---

[480] *American Israelite*, 22 (3 Sept. 1875), 4.
[481] *The World of My Books*, 35.

3 October 1875, the Plum Street temple was filled 'to its utmost capacity by ladies and gentlemen, both Jews and Gentiles, of the highest intelligence of Cincinnati', if the enthusiastic report in the *American Israelite* is to be believed. The organ pealed forth a prelude; an augmented choir, accompanied by a full orchestra, sang a hymn, which must have been florid indeed if it matched the lyrical description in the same report.

There were speeches—from Bernard Bettman, chairman of the board (an office he was to fill for thirty-five years), from Rabbi Solomon Sonnenschein (of St Louis), from Max Lilienthal, and finally (and with the greatest brevity) from Wise; a psalm and a hymn, an overture and a symphony filled out the proceedings. How that day marked a milestone in Wise's life was best evoked by the simple words of the chairman of the board:

Postponing to a later day the election of a full Faculty, the Board of Governors, simply ratifying the choice of the people, have elected as President of the College, the man to whom indisputably belongs the honor of having originated and amidst discouraging conditions, persistently advocated it, the Rev. Dr. Isaac M. Wise. The occasion and the hour are too solemn and great for personal praise. All we say to him, on surrendering to him the college, is: Let your own conscience and the appreciation of those who know you best be your reward at this moment. Here is the college of which you have fought, for which you have worked, so long: may it, under your administration, grow into a full realization of your brightest dreams.[482]

[482] *American Israelite*, 22 (8 Oct. 1875), 4.

APPENDIX

The Principal Changes Introduced in
Minhag America

A DETAILED study of the changes in the liturgy found in *Minhag America*
and the derivation of those changes would form a monograph by itself and
would be beyond the scope of this volume. Fortunately, the reader can be
referred to Eric L. Friedland's *Historical and Theological Development of the
Non-Orthodox Prayerbooks in the United States* (Ann Arbor, 1967), where the
subject is examined in detail. Another valuable study from the pen of the
same writer is '*Olath Tamid* by David Einhorn', *Hebrew Union College
Annual*, 45 (1974), 307. Though not dealing directly with Wise it helps to
clarify the differences between him and Einhorn. The following notes select
some of the more obvious changes from the Ashkenazi text made by *Minhag
America*.

In the preliminary blessings of the morning service the thanksgiving for
physical health (*Asher yatsar*) is altered to one for the creation of the soul
(p. 5). The thanksgiving for the election of Israel (*Asher bachar banu*) has
joined to it a passage indicating Israel's duty to fulfil this role as a holy people
(p. 6). The series of fifteen individual blessings is reduced to seven (p. 7). It
opens with a blessing to the Almighty 'who hast made me an Israelite', for
which phrasing there is talmudic authority. In Reform prayer-books this is
sometimes used to replace the three blessings of thanks to God 'who hast not
made me a heathen', 'a bondman', 'a woman'. Wise, however, retains the
second, perhaps in tribute to the institutions of free America.

Turning ahead to the core of the service—the *Shema* with its blessings,
preceded by the Call to Worship (*Barekhu*) and the series of eighteen blessings
known as *Amidah* or *Shemoneh esreh*—the following are some of the changes
made by *Minhag America*.

In the first of the two blessings preceding the *Shema*, the *Yotzer* blessing,
the 'glorification of God in the visible universe leads to a poetic description
of the mystic worship rendered to him by the angelic hosts' (Hertz, *Authorised
Daily Prayer-book*, p. 110). Somewhat surprisingly, Wise retains the passage
which tells of ministering angels blessing the name of God (*Titbarakh tsureinu*)
(p. 17). Wise's English translation suggests that he may have read this passage
in an earthly, non-mystical sense. The paragraph mentioning the *Ofanim*

and *Chayot* (classes of angels) is omitted. The concluding passage of the benediction *Or hadash* (Cause a new light to shine on Zion) is omitted (p. 18).

In the second benediction, the *Ahavah* blessing, the passage 'O bring us in peace from the four corners of the earth' (*Vehavienu leshalom*) is omitted (p. 19).

The benediction following the *Shema*, the *Geulah* blessing, is considerably shortened.

The *Amidah* (pp. 23–31) exhibits the same policy of maintaining the old outward structure while making verbal alterations to make it conform to new ideas. The first two benedictions of the *Amidah* express ideas—the revival of the dead and the coming of the Messiah—concerning which Wise had nailed his colours to the mast in Charleston. In the first benediction, the word *goel* (redeemer) is altered to become *geulah* (redemption) (p. 25). In the second, Wise retains the invocation *mechayeh hametim* (who reviveth the dead) translating it 'granteth ... perpetual life to the dead'.

Interpolated in the third benediction is the *kedushah* (Sanctification) built around Isaiah 6: 3. Here Wise omits the conjunctive sentence 'Those over against them say, Blessed', presumably because it is a too explicit reference to an angelic chorus, leaving the second congregational sentence without an introduction (p. 24). The theologically innocuous sentence 'And in thy Holy Words it is written, saying', which introduces Psalm 146: 10, is likewise omitted. However, in the *kedushah* for the Additional Service on Sabbath (*Mussaf*) the appropriate introductory passages are in place (p. 92).

The seventh benediction begins *Re'eh na belachats achenu uge'alem* (O behold the oppression of our brethren) instead of *Re'eh veonyeinu* (Behold our affliction) (p. 25)—the prayer being not for 'us' but for 'our persecuted brethren'.

The tenth benediction was *Teka beshofar gadol lecheirutenu* (Sound the great horn for our freedom). It becomes *Toka beshofar gadol lecherut amim* (Let resound the great trumpet for the liberty of all nations). The former conclusion, *mekabets nidchei amo yisrael* (who gathers the banished ones of thy people Israel), is replaced by *mekarei nidachim* (who summons those who are banished); it is a prayer for human freedom, not for the redemption of Israel.

In the eleventh benediction, the first vowel of the first word is altered to change the meaning of the first phrase from 'Restore our judges as at first' to 'May our judges be as at first'. There is also probably similar intent to that in the seventh; namely, the prayer to remove *yagon va'anaahah* (grief and suffering) becomes a prayer to remove *aval vechamas* (injustice and violence).

The twelfth, *birkat minim*, anathematizing sectarians, disappears.

The fourteenth benediction (for the rebuilding of Jerusalem) is retained, but on p. 26 the phrase beginning *ki mitsiyon tetse torah* is inserted in place of *vechise David meherah letochah tachin* ('for out of Zion shall go forth the Law' instead of 'and speedily set up the throne of David'.)

The fifteenth benediction (for the coming of the Messiah) disappears.

The seventeenth benediction, which in the traditional form petitions for the restoration of the Temple service, has the references to the sacrifices deleted, but it reads *veheshev shechinatcha lidvir betecha* (let the glory of thy majesty return to the hall of thy house) instead of *vehashev et ha'avodah* etc. (restore the sacrificial service), while the insertion *Ya'aleh veyavo* has Messianic and particularist references deleted. The penultimate benediction has the narrative part of the insertions for Hanukkah and Purim, but not the introductory prayer *Al hanissim*—Wise did not believe in miracles.

The final benediction concludes on the universalistic note 'God, source of peace', instead of 'who blessest thy people Israel with peace'—the blessing of peace is invoked upon all mankind.

Turning to the concluding part of the daily morning service, we find that the verse *Uva letsiyon go'el* (And a redeemer shall come unto Zion) (p. 35) is retained, though in the afternoon service the whole collection of verses with which this begins does not appear (p. 39). They do form part of the Sabbath afternoon service (p. 107). In the *Alenu* prayer, the *shelo asanu* section, 'who hast not made us like the other peoples of the earth', has been deleted.

In attempting to elucidate a rationale for the changes made in *Minhag America*, it would be wrong to leave out of consideration the fact that the compilers were undertaking a novel task and worked in great haste.

Arising out of the rabbinic conference which Wise convened at that period, a second edition appeared in 1872. Such reports as have come from that period suggest that the revision was accomplished in an atmosphere of haste, as well as of personal controversy. The general framework of the order of services remains, but Hebrew and English are now printed on facing pages, instead of in separate sections. At certain points a German as well as an English rendering is incorporated.

Friedland (op. cit., 72) makes the following points with regard to the changes found in the 1872 edition:

A mood of rationalism was gaining strength. The biblical idea of six days of creation is systematically cut out, as in *ve-shamru* (short of *ki sheshet yamim* . .), *vayekhullu* (having just *vayevarekh elohim* . .), *yismehu* (minus *zekher lema'aseh vereshit*), and *attah yatzarta 'olamekha* (now replaced by *yismehu*). The marvels and wonders which attend our everyday lives are senselessly excised from the peerless *modim* prayer. . . . The tenet of a Davidic Messiah having been abandoned some time ago, the Davidic authorship of the Psalms comes next (*uve-shirey david 'avdekha* in *ha-mehullal be-fi 'ammo*). The ritual *mitzvot* and their attendant blessings, such as the fringes, phylacteries and the *mezuzah*, are eliminated. Of the Shema and its attendant paragraphs, the passage pertaining to the fringes (Num. 15: 37 ff.) is struck out, except for the lines beginning *le-ma'an tizkeru.*

Other reforms in the same vein came in view in the 1872 edition. In spite of these changes, undertaken exclusively under the auspices of Reform and free of all fear of incurring the disapproval of the traditionalist section, the M[inhag] A[merica], second edition, is surprisingly conservative. . . . Although Tish'ah be-Av is no longer marked, the same *tahanum (rahum vehannun hatati,* Ps. 6, and *va-anahnu lo ned'a),* Ps. 20, and *u-va le-tzion* stay and the Musaf is kept structurally intact. The daily Psalm (*shir shel yom*) continues to be prescribed in Hebrew for those who wish it. . . .

The most significant indication of Wise's underlying (and ambivalent) conservatism is his unremitting insistence on Hebrew as the language of prayer. All of Wise's rubrics are given in unpunctuated Hebrew. . . . The 1872 M[inhag] A[merica] reproduces the 1857 edition's *dinim ha-shayyakhim lehilkhot tefillah,* which are sundry inspirational sentences— rather than ritual directions as the title would seem to imply—relating to prayer from the Talmud and *Shulhan 'arukh* solely in Hebrew.

Was this more than a gesture inspired by memories of the Old World? Wise wanted something which looked like the old-fashioned *siddur.* If, however, it was to be used like the old-fashioned *siddur,* the Hebrew text needed to be accompanied by education in Hebrew, which Wise's programme did not provide. Further, it needed to be used like the old-fashioned *siddur*—in the home, day by day. Notwithstanding appearances, the Judaism countenanced by Wise slid into the most drastic reform of all, whereby the focus of Judaism was removed from the home to the synagogue and the priesthood transferred from the head of the household to the rabbi.

4

Fulfilment: Years of Harvest

1. DUTIES OLD AND NEW

Dr. Wise writes to inform his friends that up to twelve o'clock daily, Saturdays and Sundays excepted, he is to be found at No. 126 Dayton Street; from one to four p.m. at his office No. 150 West Fourth Street; from four to six in the Hebrew Union College; Saturdays and on Sundays up to twelve p.m. and from five to six p.m. in the Benai Yeshurun Temple.

American Israelite, 25 (8 October 1875), 4

If not before, when the glow of this ceremony had faded, Wise may have realized that his was the task to trudge on, now with one more burden on his shoulders. He was 56; he had fought his way upwards (as made clear in the dream) despite all the opposition of inferior beings, but the plateau he had reached was still not the summit. Over and above his duties to his congregation and his two weekly newspapers, he had to make Hebrew Union College mean something, lest the predictions of his enemies be confirmed and the presidency which had been vested in him with all the external marks of confidence was to go down as an empty and ephemeral title, with no more significance in the life of American Jewry than that of the other institutions which he had vainly attempted to bring to life.

Apart from these tasks, during the remaining quarter-century of his life Wise continued to travel and lecture, now being more in demand on account of his new office, and he added several books to his list of publications. At the outset Wise remarried. His old causes he continued to advocate, and he showed no abatement of vigour in contesting opposing views or in replying to his critics (or, as he would put it, enemies); but there is less of the unbridled passion and exhibitionist self-pity which figure so prominently in his earlier diatribes. The outbursts of frenzy he indulged in usually had a relationship to Hebrew Union College. He drummed up its virtues and paraded its achievements; he struck out at the failure of individuals to join a congregation, and the failure of congregations to join the union, as treachery to Judaism. Perhaps this mellowing can be attributed to the new satisfaction in his domestic life as well as to the broader responsibilities arising from his new office.

2. REMARRIAGE (1876)

The *American Israelite* for 28 April 1876 must have startled its readers with the following announcement:

The editor of the *American Israelite* has entered upon a life of co-partnership with Miss Selma Bondi, of New York, the daughter of the late Rev. Jonas Bondi, editor of the *Jewish Leader*.

The articles of agreement were signed, sealed, and delivered, Monday, April 24th, in presence of Dr. Joseph Lewi and lady, of Albany, N. Y., and various other ladies and gentlemen interested in the new firm.

Rev. Dr. A. Huebsch, of New York, performed the ceremonies, and the Doctor's excellent lady said the necessary responses.

The capital invested in the said firm, to be known hereafter as Isaac M. Wise & lady, consists of all the editorial and directing abilities of the first party, and the executive and corrective abilities of the second party.

The firm to be dissolved by mutual consent three days after death.

It is understood that Dr. Wise will attend to editorial and outside business as heretofore, and Mrs. Selma Wise will direct the home affairs at 126 Dayton Street.

In regard to sermons, it has been agreed that Dr. Wise continues to preach the sermons and deliver the lectures in the temple, and Mrs. Selma retains the privilege of delivering occasional curtain lectures; profits or losses to be shared equally, and no papers to be accepted or indorsed, especially no love-letters, except by mutual knowledge and express consent.

Friends are politely invited to call and inspect the new establishment.[1]

The *Jewish Times* overflowed with an indignation reminiscent of the post-Philadelphia controversies. It printed the *American Israelite* announcement, prefaced with a series of denunciations: 'that man Wise disgraces his own household, his grown up children, his profession as Jewish minister, Jewish morality, by making sport of his own marriage, by making a buffoon of himself and bringing ridicule on everybody connected with him'.[2] The *Jewish Messenger*, on the other hand, had no difficulty in offering a little gentle ridicule, slyly hinting that the alliance of the man of the West to a worthy lady from

[1] *American Israelite*, 22 (28 Apr. 1876), 4.
[2] *Jewish Times*, 8 (12 May 1876), 169.

New York might help to curb Wise's temper and bring about a union between the two factions in American Jewry.[3]

When he remarried, Wise had eight surviving children. By his second marriage there were four. In 1876 his older children had reached the adult stage. Emily, who had been born in Radnitz in the year of Wise's departure, had married Benjamin May in 1865. Their only child, Max B. May, a Harvard graduate, became a lawyer in Cincinnati and was judge of the Court of Common Pleas of Hamilton County from 1916 to 1919. He served Congregation B'nai Yeshurun as honorary secretary for many years. Max May was, in his own words, 'very close' to his grandfather and in 1916 published a biography of him.

Leo Wise, the eldest son, was destined first to become a lawyer. However, a more adventurous world beckoned, and in 1871, when he was about 22, he made off for the newly discovered diamond fields at Kimberley, South Africa. Whether through lack of success or pangs of homesickness, he returned home in 1875 and became first manager and later proprietor of the *American Israelite*. He succeeded in placing the enterprise on a sounder business footing, and his presence must have relieved his father not only of managerial chores but of a financial drain.

Leo Wise carried on the *American Israelite* until 1929, when the infirmities of age compelled him to dispose of it. Perhaps his most effective act to perpetuate the family name was to introduce his sister Iphigene (Effie) to a journalist friend, Adolph Simon Ochs, proprietor of the *Chattanooga Times*. In the *American Israelite*[3] the reader may have noted that the editor had made 'A Southern Trip'—to Chattanooga and Memphis—at an unusual time of year.[4] As to Chattanooga, there is nothing about the college, the union, a synod, or *Minhag America* arising out of the rabbi's visit; simply that

the very polite proprietor of the *Chattanooga Daily Times*, in his capacity of the reception committee of one took possession of his man and landed him in good trim in the house of Rev. Mr. Ochs, where besides that venerable gentleman, his excellent wife, three sons and a few daughters, were all ready to welcome their guest.[5]

It was a family 'get-together' prior to the wedding of Iphigene Wise and Adolph Ochs, which took place in Cincinnati on 13 February.

[3] *Jewish Messenger*, 39 (5 May 1876), 4.
[4] *American Israelite*, 29 (1 Feb. 1883), 4.   [5] Ibid.

In 1896 Adolph Ochs bought the *New York Times* and began a new era not only in his own life and that of his family, but in American journalism. Ochs showed himself a devoted son-in-law, and this spirit he exhibited in his helpfulness to his wife's family after I. M. Wise's death. In 1925 he became chairman of an appeal to raise a $5-million endowment fund for Hebrew Union College, to which effort the ability of the college to come through the Depression relatively unscathed was largely due. Due to his munificence the assembly hall at Temple Emanu-El, New York, was named in honour of Isaac Mayer Wise, and in the late 1920s he was projecting a complete edition of his father-in-law's writings.[6]

Wise's second son also laboured in the field of journalism, albeit under conditions less happy. Born in Albany in 1851, Julius Wise qualified as a physician and from 1875 practised in Memphis. When that city was ravaged by yellow fever in 1875, he tended the sick with great heroism. Unfortunately the ravages of the disease left their mark, and he was forced to abandon his profession. He turned his talents to journalism, and his contributions, signed 'Nickerdown', appeared regularly in the *American Israelite* until his death in 1902.

Elsa, the oldest of the children by Wise's second marriage, died in 1899 at the age of 22. Mention may be made of the twins, Rabbi Jonah Wise and Mrs Albert May, who became well-known figures in the New York Jewish community.

3. SUSTAINING THE COLLEGE (1875–1883)

In the meantime a college had come into being, and Wise was its president. However, Hebrew Union College was a mere name, without teachers, pupils, premises, library, or funds. It did not lack critics, or, to repeat Wise's preferred expression, enemies. They did not believe that America provided the soil on which rabbinic studies could be pursued, but the hostility had as its main focus the personality of the president. They did not trust Wise's scholarship; they looked askance at his designs; they bristled at his style. In theory, foundations for the college had been provided for. It was a branch of the Union of American Hebrew Congregations; the constitution of the union vested responsibility for its management in a board of governors,

---

[6] The onset of the Depression was probably the cause of the non-fulfilment of this project.

and the printed *Proceedings* of the Union with their well-drawn-up minutes and reports might suggest a smoothly running institution, ever moving forward under an established code of laws. The reality was different, and Wise's bombast in the *American Israelite*, his puffing of the college whenever opportunity came to him to report any event in its life, must have amused his detractors as much as it sustained his supporters. In fact, the college met in the basement of the Mound Street temple. The student body, as Wise recalled in later years, consisted of fourteen noisy boys, four of whom came to study and ten to create a disturbance. Textbooks had to be improvised because those available were in German, which the pupils did not understand. The library was not too large to be locked in a tin box at nights, a precaution taken not against thieves but against mice. Faculty? The president had the assistance of one underpaid teacher, which is testimony to the resources at the college's disposal. Orators might declaim in public at Union meetings about the significance of Hebrew Union College, but a sense of collective responsibility was not there; we are a long way from the era in which organized fund-raising on a national basis had become a commonplace of American Jewish life.

Out of these inauspicious beginnings something permanent arose. The college ordained more than sixty rabbis in Wise's lifetime, and he left it with its own building, a faculty of nine, and an ever-growing library. There was no aspect of the development of Hebrew Union College which he did not make part of his life, and no possibility of advancing its cause to which he did not harness his energies. He canvassed for funds, for books, for students. There are stories of students being admitted against the wishes of the governors (the college had no funds to maintain them)—Wise assumed responsibility for them. He acted as father to his students, was assiduous in finding positions for them, and advised them on their problems. How far he paid heed to the view of others must remain an open question. Nominally the curriculum was the responsibility of a committee set up in 1874. The recollections of one of its members, Dr Solomon Wolfenstein, are to the point:

We met a consecutive number of Sundays at Cincinnati. . . . Our meetings were very animated as a rule. Lilienthal and myself agreeing and Wise opposing us. . . . It was on one of these occasions when Lilienthal, lighting a fresh cigar, broke out in a laugh, in which he liked to indulge so heartily, and turning to me exclaimed: 'Wolfenstein, you are a fool and I am another. We quarrel with Wise, and, nevertheless, he will do as he pleases.' He certainly was right. When I attended the College examination in May or June, 1878, Rabbis Morais and Zirndorf (then in Detroit, and later on the faculty) were my colleagues. I did not find much of the program we had prepared carried out. Wise had cut down the scientific and theoretic subjects, laying stress upon matters touching and pertaining to practical life. Most probably he was right.[7]

The accepted technique was to present a good face to the world, but to the extent that the curtain has been lifted on the early struggles, one has a picture not only of Wise's energy and devotion but of his invincible optimism. In April 1886 he was able to look back on ten years of struggle:

Never has such a permanent establishment been erected and grown in America in such a short time as has the rabbinical college in Cincinnati. When the idea occurred to found it, everyone laughed mockingly, and they did not really believe that American-born children, who then did not know Judaism and had no apparent desire to learn matters relating to Judaism and Hebrew literature, could understand Mishnah and Gamorrah, Midrash and Philosophy. All thought it to be an impossible matter. 'Where is the American who would want to be a rabbi?' was heard from all Jews. 'The Torah has been forgotten in Israel, it has fallen and shall not rise again', they were thinking. People with widely varying opinions determined our policy, and therefore the student body consists of both Orthodox and Reform students. Nonetheless, we began. Don't ask how or with what! With one teacher I toiled daily in a dark room under a synagogue. I taught like an elementary school teacher who starts with the alphabet. I knocked on the doors of the rich to ask for some copies of the Pentateuch and old prayerbooks in order to have a text for 'The Sayings of the Fathers' and 'Psalms'. Now, thank God, we have a treasury of books which amounts to some ten thousand volumes and a beautiful and splendid building which is the finest of all rabbinical seminaries in the world.[8]

The impression that the achievement was the result of one man's tenacity is reinforced by the failure of parallel activities. The college was one only of the plans brought before the Union of American Hebrew Congregations, but it was the only one in which any achievement was to be recorded. Six months after Hebrew Union College opened, the presidents of the principal New York congregations called a convention for the establishment of a college of Jewish learning—

[7] From recollections published in the Wise centenary issue of *American Israelite*, 71/2 (Seventieth Anniversary Supplement) (24 July 1924).
[8] *American Israelite*, 32 (9 Apr. 1886), 608.

apparently to be an extension of the preparatory school previously established by Temple Emanu-El; despite the presence of a large Jewish community, the support of eminent rabbis, and the material resources at the disposal of the sponsors, the effort came to nothing. More than once Wise offered to resign. These offers the board of governors steadfastly refused. It is difficult to believe that they were intended as anything more than a feint: Wise would not have readily parted from his nursling. More than once suggestions came from the East that he should resign, because the college needed a president of more solid learning and less ribald manner. If these suggestions never went far, can it not be that no rabbinic scholar was willing to assume the burden that rested on his shoulders and no laymen were willing to assume the financial responsibility of bringing a distinguished figure from Europe? And if by the time of his parting he was acknowledged as first among the rabbis of America, this was due not to exceptional intellectual or oratorical power but to twenty-five years given to the nurturing of the American rabbinate.

In a sense, Hebrew Union College, like *Minhag America*, was a vestige of a more comprehensive scheme. The all-embracing synod, which would legislate for American Judaism and authorize an official prayer book as well as an official seminary for training rabbis, had been laid on one side. From time to time Wise still tried to raise the wind in its favour, but he found no support. The union, as established in 1873, was a deliberately circumscribed body, both as to the scope of its powers and as to the area of its membership. Wise's presence was felt, but in the wings rather than the centre of the stage. Within the union as a whole Wise remained backstage—one is tempted to ask whether the Cincinnati laity believed that the presence of a rabbi (particularly *this* rabbi) would be a stumbling block—and he took charge of one part only of the union's field of potential activity. The college itself, limited to the preparatory department of a rabbinical school, was only a first instalment of the comprehensive institution Wise had planned. If, as his critics charged, Wise was bent on becoming a 'western pope', being given the presidency of Hebrew Union College was hardly a coronation.

It was not long before the geographical limitation on the union's membership was removed. Negotiations reached a critical stage in the summer of 1877 and were accompanied by a fresh outbreak of contention between the journalistic representatives of the two groups. When on 1 June the *American Israelite* announced that the union council would meet in Philadelphia on 11 July it also mentioned that Wise would pay a visit to California and was willing to speak at stops *en route*.[9] He left on 1 July, and the timing of the visit raises the question whether his laymen feared that his presence during open debate in Philadelphia would be an obstacle to peace. From the point of view of raising funds for the union, the journey was unsuccessful; but the record published in the *American Israelite* is one of the most interesting pieces Wise wrote.[10]

Whether by coincidence or by design, a friend from his Albany days persuaded him to visit Saratoga, then a fashionable resort, in the summer of 1878. There he encountered a group of leaders of Temple Emanu-El, New York, with whom previously he had been unable to establish contact. Out of the informal discussions at Saratoga, an agreement was reached by which the union absorbed the ailing Board of Delegates of American Israelites, the protective functions of the older body being assigned over to a 'Board of Delegates on Civil and Religious Rights'. The negotiations which led to this enlargement of the union included the appointment of a special commission on the curriculum of Hebrew Union College, foreshadowing the development of a full programme of rabbinic education, and of that commission David Einhorn was a member.

The lodgement of the union in the East was symbolized by its meeting in New York in 1879. In the same week David Einhorn preached his farewell sermon (he died later that year); Samuel Adler, co-sponsor of the Philadelphia Conference, had retired in 1874. The field was becoming Wise's by survival. More advantageous, if Hebrew Union College succeeded, the American rabbinate would in time be populated by his disciples. Whether Wise calculated that his labours for the college would lead to the realization of his larger aims we do not know; such expectations would not have been far-fetched.

There seems to have been some belief among the Easterners that what had been started in Cincinnati would remain a preparatory school and that the seat (and inevitably the control) of the rabbinical seminary proper was still open for decision. It happened otherwise. The faculty was reinforced by the addition of Moses Mielziner, the New York rabbi, who had taught at the Emanuel Preparatory School

---

[9] *American Israelite*, 28 (1 June 1877), 4.
[10] This series of articles has since been reprinted by the Western States Jewish Historical Society.

and enjoyed a reputation as a talmudist; but possession is nine points of the law, and control remained with Wise.

Wise's career reached a fresh plateau in June 1883 when Hebrew Union College, its faculty strengthened and possessed of its own home, was ready to send forth a quartet of rabbis. For the first time, rabbis had been trained and ordained on American soil. In itself this was a notable event, and it was solemnized at the Plum Street temple in the grand style so beloved by Wise and his contemporaries. Wise did not wear a bishop's mitre, but his role in the proceedings as the master who transmitted rabbinic authority signified a primacy among his colleagues. Surveying the wider scene he would have found things going his way. Growth was the hallmark of American life. The German immigrants had established themselves, and Judaism had become naturalized. Of the two hundred congregations in the United States, all but a dozen had moved along the path of Reform. Many used *Minhag America*, but the parochial differences of the European past were being left behind; surely the American Judaism for which he had striven was emerging.

The perfection of the scene was marred somewhat by the incident of the *trefah* banquet. Wise had entrusted to a Jewish caterer the feast which was to celebrate the ordination but the first course provided was shellfish—manifest flouting of the Jewish dietary laws. Some traditionalists, who had participated in the event despite Wise's Reform leanings and whose presence helped to validate Wise's premiss that his seminary would train rabbis for all sections of American Jewry, departed in anger. Wise was not one to confess a mistake, and his making light of the incident could not have soothed their injured feelings. On the contrary, his derisory attitude to their complaints may have convinced them that at bottom he regarded the traditions of Judaism with contempt.

4. REFORM MOVES ON: THE PITTSBURGH PLATFORM

Even had it been in Wise to say 'I am sorry' instead of guffawing about 'stomach Judaism', it is doubtful whether his grand aim would have been consummated. Movements on Wise's left, as well as opposition on his right, diminished the possibility that a single American Judaism would emerge. Wise had stood for infusion of the past with a moderate element of Reform. In his youth he had imbibed the Mendelssohnian notion that Judaism was a religion conformable to reason. Alien elements, subsumed under such terms as 'kabbalism' and 'mysticism', had attached themselves to it, and these excrescences the enlightened New World could only discard. Nevertheless, the Bible was divine, revelation on Sinai a fact, and the Pentateuch the work of Moses. As to the Talmud, Wise was inclined to blow hot and cold; he had lost the *yeshivah* student's belief in its divinity and infatuation with its hair-splitting distinctions, but he retained the love of its contents: it remained the repository of traditions which he remembered with affection and which in the service of worship he sought to preserve.

The process of reform had gone hand in hand with the process of naturalization. The Constitution and the Bill of Rights, which placed all religions on an equal footing, had been settled before he arrived, but Wise had asserted the equality of the Jew and his religion with a forthrightness which no other public figure had shown. The large and ornate temple in Cincinnati over which hé presided was a visible reminder of the new-born status of Judaism. It looked the Roman Catholic cathedral on the other side of Plum Street straight in the face; it was not relegated to the ghetto, as were the historic synagogues he had known in Prague; it did not lurk in the shadow of St Stephens in Vienna, its existence hidden as far as possible by design, allowed by the authorities only on the footing that the facade on the Seiten-stettengasse gave no clue to the existence of a non-Christian place of worship. Within his temple the organ pealed and the choir sang as impressively as in any cathedral. The congregation was composed of established citizens, uncertain immigrants no longer, and here at full-dress ceremonies he conferred on young Americans the title and status of rabbi.

During the first three-quarters of the nineteenth century, many streams had bubbled forth within the bounds of American Jewish life. Wise's grand aim had been to assure the confluence of these streams, so that they formed a single pool under his direction. His ambivalence on the question of Reform proceeded from that ambition. This brought mistrust from both camps, but we have not yet reached the period when the two separated. By 1879 it looked as if Wise was on the way to success. In the end he failed; the two groups moved apart, and Wise had to find his constituency within the camp of Reform. The causes run deeper than the incident of the '*trefah* banquet' of 1883, or even the tenor of the Pittsburgh Platform of 1885. Given the influences bearing on Wise's constituency—the

American preference for freedom over order, the absence from recent Jewish experience of any extra-congregational direction of Jewish religious life—it was inevitable that the Jews of America would regard anarchy as less objectionable than hierarchy. The pool became a watershed, from which streams flowed in many different directions.

Movements on Wise's left as well as opposition on his right eroded the basis for a united American Judaism. Wise had stood for the modification of the past with an infusion of Reform, a religion, conformable to reason, without mysteries or miracles. But Wise's Judaism hinged on a miracle—the miracle of Sinaitic revelation. What if the continuing march of reason in fields such as geology and biology challenged the biblical account of creation, and in the field of literary criticism challenged the authenticity of the biblical record itself? What if the latest teachings pushed Moses into the shadows and exalted the Prophets as the founders of Judaism? Could it any longer be said that the books attributed to Moses were in fact his handiwork? Was revelation on Mount Sinai a fact? If Judaism conformable to reason was destined to be the universal religion, why let its particularism stand in the way of a greater universalism, now that reason was eroding the theological basis of Judaism and Christianity alike?

The career of Felix Adler (1851–1933) who, trained in Germany for the rabbinate of Temple Emanu-El, found Reform Judaism too narrow, may have been singular in its ultimate pursuit of the universalistic ideal, but it brought into focus a wider uncertainty. In 1876 Adler founded the Society for Ethical Culture. It had a vogue among the German Jews of New York and offered a challenge to those who assumed that their reforms had solved the intellectual problems of nineteenth-century Judaism.[11]

Wise, on the other hand, did not cease to be a child of the eighteenth century. His Bible history might be ignored by Christian theologians to whom it was out of date and might pass over the heads of German Jews recently settled in the United States who, had they been able to read it, would have found that it did not respond to their problems. The synagogue now had to deal with the children of nineteenth-century America. Wise might deride Felix Adler's ethical culture movement; he might forbid the teaching of Higher Bible Criticism at Hebrew Union College; but the new doctrines were making heavy

[11] See Benny Kraut, *From Reform Judaism to Ethical Culture: The Religious Evolution of Felix Adler* (Cincinnati, 1979).

weather for the churches; the theological atmosphere was charged with the teachings of Darwin and Spencer and Wellhausen, and directly or indirectly they raised and influenced attitudes within all sections of the Jewish community.

Against this background we come to an event which, even more than the repercussions of the '*trefah* banquet', thrust Wise unequivocally into the camp of Reform—namely the Pittsburgh Platform of 1885.

In that year the conservatives of New York acquired a vigorous champion in the person of Alexander Kohut (1842–94), rabbi of Congregation Ahavath Hesed. Kohut threw down the gauntlet at Reform in a series of sermons which Kaufmann Kohler answered under the general title 'Backwards or Forwards'. Impelled by the controversy, Kohler issued an invitation to 'all such American Rabbis as advocate Reform and Progress' to meet in conference in Pittsburgh. Nineteen attended (eighteen sent letters or telegrams of regret). Wise was given the honour of presiding, but Kohler, Einhorn's son-in-law, was the moving spirit. He produced a 'Declaration of Principles' as Einhorn had done at Philadelphia, and, as had been the case with Einhorn's draft in 1869, this emerged in the name of the conference as a whole, without substantial alteration. The source of the inspiration was made clear when the declaration was expressed to be 'in continuation of the work begun in Philadelphia in 1869'. This statement Wise lauded as a 'Declaration of Independence', and he did not demur at its acceptance.

Among the eight clauses the following stand out:

Second—. . . the modern discoveries of scientific researches in the domains of nature and history are not antagonistic to the doctrines of Judaism, the Bible reflecting the primitive ideas of its own age and at times clothing its conception of divine providence and justice dealing with man in miraculous narratives.

Third—We recognize in the Mosaic legislation a system of training the Jewish people for its mission during its national life in Palestine, and today we accept as binding only the moral laws and maintain only such ceremonies as elevate and sanctify our lives, but reject all such as are not adapted to the views and habits of modern civilization.

Fourth—We hold that all such Mosaic and Rabbinical laws as regulate diet, priestly purity and dress originated in ages and under the influence of ideas altogether foreign to our present mental and spiritual state. They fail to impress the modern Jew with a spirit of priestly holiness; their observance in our day is apt rather to obstruct than to further modern spiritual elevation.

Fifth—We recognize in the modern era of universal culture of heart and intellect the approach of the realization of Israel's great Messianic hope for the establishment of the Kingdom of truth, justice and peace among all men. We consider ourselves no longer a nation but a religious community, and therefore expect neither a return to Palestine, nor a sacrificial worship under the administration of the sons of Aaron, nor the restoration of any of the laws concerning the Jewish state.

Sixth—We recognize in Judaism a progressive religion, ever striving to be in accord with the postulates of reason. We are convinced of the utmost necessity of preserving the historical identity with our great past.[12]

There were also resolutions declaring the legitimacy of Sunday services, an innovation which Wise had repeatedly attacked, and appointing a committee (including Wise) to report to the next conference on the need for circumcision of converts (*milat gerim*).

Over a half a century later, Ismar Elbogen described the Pittsburgh Platform as

a peculiar document which can only be understood on the basis of contemporary intellectual currents. Nothing was said of faith or piety; the advantages of Judaism over other religions were indeed mentioned, but not clarified. It was not a *Confessio Judaica* but a homage to the latest European school of thought in science, in history of religion and particularly of the religious evolution of Israel. The laymen did not get much out of this platform; they did not learn what to believe and what to do, but only what not to believe and not to do.[13]

This assessment suggests that, though the occasion was Kohut's challenge from the side of tradition, Kohler's major concern was to disarm those who found Reform too traditional. Darwin and Wellhausen had reshaped the philosophical framework; Felix Adler was the standard-bearer of those who put modernity first.

Immediately in point is Wise's readiness to be associated with a standpoint antithetical to the point of view he had advocated throughout his life. The universal note in the first paragraph was in harmony with what he had preached, though it did not foreshadow the triumph of Judaism as the religion of the future. The second and third

---

[12] The effect of the Pittsburgh platform on the development of American Judaism was such that it is referred to in most histories of the subject. The text and background are conveniently set out in W. Gunther Plaut, *The Growth of Reform Judaism* (New York, 1965), 31–8.

[13] *A Century of Jewish Life* (Philadelphia, 1945), 344.

paragraphs reflect the influence of the biblical criticism, whose teaching at Hebrew Union College Wise forbade. Thirty years had elapsed since the Cleveland Conference, with its declaration that the Bible was of 'immediate divine origin', but Wise had not abandoned that standpoint. In 1872 he had published a catechism stating that 'God's words are preserved intact in the twenty-four books of Sacred Scripture'.[14] Most striking, in the very year of the Pittsburgh Conference he had weighed modern 'scientific' analysis of the Bible against the traditional Jewish approach and found it contradictory to Jewish feeling.

Must we not finally come to the conviction that we, who were, so to say, born with the Hebrew language and grew up with the commentaries on our lips, understand the Bible better than those few Protestant clergymen who are the authors of that negative criticism? Maybe we are too proud, too self-conceited to yield the palm, to abandon the Kether Thorah, to admit that all our fathers and forefathers, and among them the most powerful and independent reasoners, were blind, and all of us purblind, till those few Protestant clergymen professors came to open our eyes. Maybe we are all that; still we are used to see with our eyes and no others, to judge with our reason, and not with that of Kuenen or Wellhausen.[15]

Now there is an emphasis on the primitive element in the Bible. 'Torah' becomes 'Mosaic legislation' and far from possessing a divine supremacy is to be adjudged according to 'the views and habits of modern civilization'. Wise had belaboured radicalism for being part of Reform; now it is in the saddle and Mosaic and rabbinical laws are consigned to the unwanted past; now the reason of Kuenen and Wellhausen have taken over. It was as if the attitudes Wise had formed in the *yeshivot* and those he had learned from Herz Homberg were wrestling for control. The course of his writings, in particular the publication of *Pronaos to Holy Writ* in 1891, suggests that the outlook he had imbibed in childhood endured.

Reference to Wise's own writings fails to establish a rationale for his acceptance of the Pittsburgh Platform. The fact that he identified himself with another point of view is important for his own name. History accords him pre-eminence among the builders of American Reform; the Pittsburgh Platform stamped its identity on American Reform as did no other statement; and Wise's college became the one

[14] *Judaism: Its Doctrines and Duties* (Cincinnati, 1872), 10.
[15] *American Israelite*, 31 (13 Mar. 1885), 4.

rabbinical seminary in the world where the Bible criticism associated with the names of Kuenen and Wellhausen was accepted to full effect.

How Wise came to take this contradictory position is a tantalizing question. Of his impetuosity there is no want of examples; and one must add that, though the record is sketchy, the proceedings at Pittsburgh seem to have been offhand. In a couple of days the rabbis assented to a rewriting of the doctrines of Judaism on the basis of a document they had never seen before. The pace of these proceedings may be compared with the intense and laboured discussions at the three German rabbinical conferences (1844–6) which examined details of Jewish practice and their modification. Individual tendencies would have been enhanced by the impetuosity in the atmosphere.

Probably the tide had turned between 1869 and 1885, and Wise sensed the force of the new currents in the communities and among his colleagues. He could not be left behind, and the ability to unite was as important as the basis of the union. Thus we have Cleveland over again, only with an inversion of forces.

'Nothing practical had been done at Pittsburgh' was Wise's way of shunting off criticisms of the platform. It was intended that there should be a further conference in 1886 to carry into practical effect the programme of the Reform rabbis, and possibly Wise was looking to that to bring into being the authoritative synod which he had long advocated and of which he naturally hoped to be the leader (a conference did not have the same authority). For reasons which have never become clear this conference failed to meet. The Pittsburgh Platform remained in its place, stamping its identity on American Reform, so that Wise, pre-eminent as the builder of American Reform, became identified with it.

'Censure is the tax a man pays to the public for being eminent,' as Jonathan Swift wrote. In 1869 Wise had to face criticism from his local supporters for accepting the radical outlook expressed at Philadelphia. Considerable criticism was evoked by the Pittsburgh Platform; most of it was expressed in the East, and it focused on Wise, who was now not just the rabbi of a single congregation but also president of a rabbinical seminary that claimed to serve American Jewry as a whole. There were demands that Wise resign the presidency of Hebrew Union College, and a few congregations even seceded from the union. Wise rode the storm. (By now this was something in which he had a good deal of practice.) His following in Cincinnati remained loyal; the critics showed no readiness to assume his burdens, and forcing his resignation would probably have meant the end of the college.

To extreme statements of criticism Wise replied that the Pittsburgh rabbis had not pressed the transfer of the Sabbath to Sunday or the abolition of ritual circumcision: the course of studies at Hebrew Union College was not the work of the president or faculty but was prescribed by the Council of the Union of American Hebrew Congregations; they had not denied the divinity of the Bible. He was readier with attack than analysis, claiming for men who had adopted the Pittsburgh Platform the title-deeds to American Judaism.

That 'Declaration of Principles' presents a particular feature which must not be overlooked. It declares that we, the much abused reformers, radicals, decried, defamed and debased by the men of the minority who usurped for themselves the titles of conservative and orthodox or rather the Jews *par excellence*—*We are* the orthodox Jews in America, and they *were* the orthodoxy of former days and other countries. We can see no good reason why we should ogle you, allow you to act as a brake to the wheel of progress and confirm you in your pretensions. You do not represent the ideas and sentiments of the American Jew, this phase upon which Judaism entered in this country. You are an anachronism, strangers in this country, and to your own brethren. You represent yourselves, together with a past age and a foreign land. We must proceed without you to perform our duties to our God, and our country, and our religion, for *We* are the orthodox Jews in America.

Therefore, that 'Declaration of Principles' may properly be called the declaration of independence. No more flattery, hypocrisy, conspiracy, mutual admiration or mutual deception; you have to come to us or remain isolated; for we represent the orthodoxy of the American Israelites and the overwhelming majority of all American Jewish citizens. So sounds the language of honest men.[16]

As far as the college was concerned, Wise won through. But in winning he lost. A group of Easterners emerged from among the Sephardim and the more traditionalist Central Europeans who felt that they could not allow the training of rabbis to be left in Wise's hands. They set to work and opened the Jewish Theological Seminary in New York in 1887.[17]

Inevitably, the diversion of conservative interest to the second institution gave Hebrew Union College a more pronounced Reform

[16] *American Israelite*, 32 (4 Dec. 1885), 4.
[17] For the course of developments from the perspective of the Conservative group, see Moshe Davis, *The Emergence of Conservative Judaism* (Philadelphia, 1965).

coloration; and although in later years some Reform leaders were at pains to deny that the Pittsburgh Platform had any official status in the movement, it appears to have been accepted as the recognized yardstick. The idea of a single theological framework for American Judaism disappeared.

5. A NEW AMERICAN JEWISH WORLD

The battles over the Pittsburgh Platform were being fought over a terrain which other factors were already transforming. Large-scale migration from Eastern Europe had begun. The number of Jews in the United States, estimated at 250,000 in 1880, reached the million mark in 1900, the year of Wise's death. The acculturated community, speaking English albeit with a German accent, largely middle class, reformed in religion, was outnumbered by one that spoke Yiddish, belonged to the proletariat, and was untouched by Reform Judaism. The processes which Wise saw at work when he arrived in 1846 had to begin over again; but although many of the factors were similar, the answers were not necessarily the same. Incidentally, the presence of a second and larger Jewish community enhanced the importance of New York in American Jewish life and diminished the significance of Cincinnati and other Midwest communities where Wise had held sway.

The settlement in the United States of this second Jewish community made obsolete the mould in which Wise had been working, and it irritated him. He had sought and achieved the naturalization of the Jew and Judaism to American conditions. The boy who had outgrown the primitive Orthodoxy of the Bohemian village, who had tasted of the broader outlook of Prague and Vienna, who had been imbued with the Enlightenment of Herz Homberg and had heard his tales of the backwardness and superstition of the East, who had watched the Jewish immigrants to America go through similar processes while raising themselves on the social and economic ladder, now found all the elements of which he hoped Western Jewry to be redeemed planted on his own doorstep in America. Had Sisyphus laboured only that the stone he had pushed to the top of the mountain should roll back to its old position?

Moreover, the presence of the newcomers created problems which confronted the existing community day by day. Theological points concerned a tiny minority; ritual questions excited a wider group but still a minority; the record of Wise's efforts to give effect to his 'bold plans' suggests that a difficulty as great as any was that of getting people interested at all. The East European immigrants were visible every day, and from the point of view of charity or religious life or relations with the Gentile world they put an end to what had seemed to be stability. Incidentally, Wise's observations on the East European immigrants probably reflect arguments that were going on around him, and for that reason have an interest beyond that of his theological and institutional controversies.

Embarrassments at the level of social relations are clear when he argues against the opinion of a London Jewish weekly that the influx would mean the revival of Orthodoxy in America, or, as he put it, 'a retrogression of Judaism to the medieval and demi-cabalistic standard of the "Shulhan Aruch"'.

There are quite a number of very intelligent gentlemen in our country who apprehend similar results for the religious and social standing of American Israelites by the influx of an element so entirely foreign and, in many cases, altogether outlandish. This apprehension makes of them opponents of the immigration, especially in New York, Chicago, St. Louis and other places where such immigrants settle down in large numbers. We can not help admitting that, momentarily, those newcomers are of disadvantage to the Jews as a class, although those immigrants are certainly no worse than the Italians, Hungarians, or Irishmen who honor us with their presence. It is expected that the Jew be a decent, clean, civilized man, who submits gracefully to sanitary laws and police regulations, uses soap, and dresses like other people, which we hear is not the case with all those new-comers, for a good long while. This may produce and intensify social prejudices against our co-religionists at least for the time being, and ought to be counteracted by charitable people everywhere. Persuade them not to establish new Ghettos for themselves, not to live together in one narrow quarter, to send their children to public schools, to use more soap and less 'Shulchan Aruch'.[18]

The point he emphasized most was that the newcomers would exert no influence on American Judaism: 'They will come to us, we can never come to them ... There is no danger that the Russian Jews settling down in this country will abide very long in their inherited orthodoxy, which quite a number of them had deserted before they came to this country.'[19]

---

[18] *American Israelite*, 30 (26 Sept. 1884), 4, as cited by Dena Wilansky in *Sinai to Cincinnati* (New York, 1937), 178.
[19] Ibid.

That was in 1884. The problem did not abate in Wise's lifetime; and in 1887 we have the Midwesterner's view as to where the real America is to be found:

As far as American Judaism is concerned, New York and Philadelphia are outlying stations. Only a portion of their populations are Americans indeed, the bulk is as yet English, Polish, Roumanian, Galician, Hungarian, German or French, old-style Europeans, with the same notions and superstitions which their great grandparents brought out of the Ghettos. They have never been in America, they have been in New York or Philadelphia, which they look upon as being all there is in America. North of the Harlem River and on the other side of Germantown begins America, what they call there the West; there begins another life, other views prevail, and another spirit of the age is dominant. If it were not for the reform congregations of New York and Philadelphia, there would be as much difference between the Hebrew populations of those cities and of this great country as between us and the inhabitants of North Africa. It is next to an impossibility to associate or identify ourselves with that half-civilized orthodoxy which constitutes the bulk of population in those cities. We are Americans, and they are not. We are liberal, humane, cosmopolitan and broad in principles, and they are not. We are emancipated men and women, free, firm, and fraternizing, and they are not. We unite and they break up. We enlighten and they obscure. We appeal to reason and they appeal to their grandparent's habits. We are Israelites of the nineteenth century and a free country, and they gnaw the dead bones of past centuries. Besides the name we have very little in common with them. For the honor of American Judaism and our defense opposite the enlightened world, we do not want to have even that in common; we let them be Jews and we are the American Israelites. Write that to the 'Jeshurun'.[20]

It is a curious reversal of the opinion, attributed half seriously to the New Yorker, that there is no life west of the Hudson.

In a literal sense such statements were ill-considered, but this characteristic not only gives them their significance but also limits. Wise wrote 'off the cuff' and his concerns reflect fears that were felt throughout his constituency, arguments that were going on around him about the problems created by the East European Jews. Whether they necessarily represent a sustained or consistent attitude is another question.

The man who could write in these terms was resentful that anyone could suggest that he was hostile to the East European Jew. He was

[20] *American Israelite*, 32 (28 Jan. 1887), 4; Wilansky, *Sinai to Cincinnati*, 180. *Jeschurun* was the strictly orthodox periodical founded by Samson Raphael Hirsch in Frankfurt-am-Main.

vigorous in his denunciation of the tsarist persecution which drove them from Russia; he pointed with pride to the number of Russian Jews studying at Hebrew Union College: 'we welcome them as friends and brothers', he wrote, 'and are willing to assist them wherever we can'.[21] Russian persecution aroused his ire, and the relief of its victims engaged his solicitude. He was president of the first Immigrant Aid Society in Cincinnati; and it is reported that when in the pulpit one Saturday morning he was informed of the plight of a party of Russian immigrants who had been dumped in the city during the night, he immediately took a collection for their relief. The writings of Russian Jews caught his eye. Of a book by Nahum Sokolow, the 22-year-old editor of the Warsaw Hebrew periodical *Hazefirah*, he observed 'The work is well written, its author evidently has historical talent and is a good Hebraist.'[22]

6. SEVENTIETH BIRTHDAY: CENTRAL CONFERENCE OF AMERICAN RABBIS

Wise's combativeness did not abate once the storms generated by the Pittsburgh Platform had blown themselves out. The quarrels within the camp of what he called American Judaism simmered down, and time, the ever-active healer, transformed the 'great Cincinnati agitator' into the grand old man of American Judaism. He was still equal to the labours he had undertaken, but was now entering the time of harvest. Year by year the Hebrew Union College brought Wise to the centre of the stage at a grand ceremony. Six years after the first such ceremony, the Plum Street temple resounded with one with which he was yet more intimately connected, and which marks his entry into a golden age—the celebration of his 70th birthday, on 5 April 1889.

Admission was by ticket, so great was the number desiring to attend. Two thousand were present, the temple being filled from the moment the doors were opened. The official proceedings were lengthy, lasting from two until seven. The celebration opened with an orchestra playing Meyebeer's 'Coronation March' and ended with Weber's 'Jubel Overture'. Interspersed with musical items were addresses of one kind or another on behalf of the B'nai Jeshurun and Bene Israel congregations, the children of the Talmud Yelodim Institution, the

---

[21] Wilansky, *Sinai to Cincinnati*, 179.   [22] Ibid. 174.

Union of American Hebrew Congregations, the Board of Governors of Hebrew Union College, the University of Cincinnati, the Alumni of Hebrew Union College, and the students of Hebrew Union College. The music included a cantata, the text of which was written especially for the occasion by Moses Mielziner. Four rabbis participated, all of them Wise's students. When the exercises ended, Wise held an impromptu levee on the pulpit where he received the congratulations of no fewer than two thousand ladies and gentlemen, and then a smaller party sàt down to a supper which lasted till nearly midnight. The birthday was marked by a gift on behalf of the Union of American Hebrew Congregations of a town house, 55 Mound Street, purchased at a cost of $14,500.

If on such an occasion a man could look back with pride and look forward with hope, he might be excused feeling the burden of his years. Wise had begun to draw in his horns. He was devoted to his children and his pupils, yet a few months before he had felt compelled to decline the opportunity of being present when his son Harry married in Texas and his pupil Max Heller married in New Orleans: 'for the last two years,' he wrote to Heller, 'I always come home sick from every journey. I cannot without danger travel a great distance.'[23] In so indefatigable a traveller this was indeed a sign of weakening physical powers. There are indications that by this time the board of Congregation B'nai Jeshurun would have liked to coax him into retirement, but he would have none of it: he would die in harness. Presumably because it recognized a weakening of his powers, his congregation gave him an assistant—Rabbi Charles Levi—who was installed on 30 August 1889.

As if to point in the opposite direction, the same year brought Wise an additional office which consolidated his position on the national scene. A rabbinical union in one form or another he had never ceased to advocate, and there must have been a tired response to his urging to this effect in 1889. This time, however, it fell into place. On 9 July the rabbis, more than thirty in number, who were attending the Council of the Union of American Hebrew Congregations met and resolved to form the Central Conference of American Rabbis. On the next day the group approved a plan of organization: the basis of its work was to be the proceedings of all the modern rabbinical conferences from that held in Brunswick in 1844 and including all like

---

[23] Letter in Max Heller Papers, AJA.

assemblages since, thus indicating a Reform coloration. 'In spite of his strenuous protests', the report states, 'the unanimous sentiment' was in favour of Wise as president. To that office he was re-elected annually during his lifetime. The whole thing appears to have been unbelievably easy. As for Wise, he seems to have stepped out of the clouds of bitterness and contention into the clear sunlight. The report of the first annual convention of the new organization begins by referring to him as 'The venerable President'. This convention met in Cleveland, and Dr Aaron Hahn, the local rabbi, who delivered the address of welcome, said: 'At the head of our society there stands an old general, a veteran in the army of Judaism, Dr. I. M. Wise, great in age, but young and fresh in heart, in mind, in spirit.'[24] Wise was becoming the patriarch of the American rabbinate.

Here was the occasion for the first of Wise's presidential addresses, and he emphasized 'the right and duty to produce a uniform form of worship for all our houses or worship'.[25] The Central Conference set to work, with the result that the first part of the *Union Prayer Book* appeared in 1894, and on its acceptance Wise withdrew *Minhag America*. Again the design fell into place. The strife which for a whole generation had accompanied the production of prayer-books was totally absent. Wise concurred, although the new volume resembled in style Einhorn's *Olath tamid*. The only sign of contentiousness came from outside the Central Conference: Emil G. Hirsch of Chicago, Einhorn's son-in-law, found in the publication of the *Union Prayer Book* an occasion to issue a new English edition of *Olath tamid*.

The *Union Prayer Book* was not an 'authorized daily prayer-book' in the sense of the volume produced almost contemporaneously for the Jews of England, though in his advocacy of a synod which would give its seal of approval to *Minhag America* Wise appears to have been working towards such a situation. American Jewry was no monarchy, not even a federal republic. Congregations and rabbis retained their sovereign independence. There was no ecclesiastical hierarchy; the president of the Central Conference of American Rabbis did not acquire the jurisdiction of a chief rabbi, but he was naturally looked upon as spokesman for his group. Acceptance of Wise's role in this regard was enhanced by the fact that he held office for more than a decade, while a growing proportion of the members were his pupils.

[24] *Central Conference of American Rabbis Year Book*, i (1890), 7.   [25] Ibid. 10.

Thus it was natural that Wise should be invited to give the papers on
Judaism before the World's Parliament of Religions at the Columbian
exposition held in Chicago in 1893. Wise may have entertained the
expectation that the conference would publish his papers as an official
statement of Jewish doctrine, but it did not move in that direction.

As president, Wise had the opportunity to deliver an annual
message to the members, and these messages may be assumed to have
been more carefully prepared and edited than his newspaper articles.
In 1896 he was still affirming the ascendancy of Reform Judaism in
America. This was reminiscent of what he had written eleven years
earlier in the wake of the controversies over the Pittsburgh platform,
notwithstanding the continuous growth of the East European element.

American Judaism is identical with reformatory Judaism; the conservative,
orthodox or anachronistic parties are the minority sects whom we ought to
respect and treat with fraternal kindness and consideration, but no longer as
a vox populi or an influential factor in the historical process of the American
Judaism. An organised majority represents itself and the disorganised minority; the latter disappears under the former in the just estimate of the
world.[26]

It was Wise's address in the following year which was engulfed by
a changed tide in Jewish concerns and has been remembered most
assiduously. The Central Conference met on the eve of the first
Zionist congress. Wise was able to commend some aspects of the
Hovevei Zion movement, but Herzlian Zionism and its advocacy of
a Jewish state had no place in his scheme of things.

We are perfectly satisfied with our political and social position . . . We want
freedom, equality, justice and equity to reign and govern the community in
which we live. This we possess in such a fullness, that no State whatever
could improve upon it. That new Messianic movement over the ocean does
not concern us at all. But the same expatriated, persecuted and outrageously
wronged people came in large numbers also to us, still imbued with their
home ideas, ideals and beliefs . . . and compromised in the eyes of the public
the whole of American Judaism as the phantastic dupes of a thoughtless
Utopia which is to us a fata morgana, a momentary inebriation of morbid
minds, a prostitution of Israel's holy cause to a madman's dance of unsound
politicians.[27]

The language was strong, but the sentiment reflected the feelings of

[26] *Central Conference of American Rabbis Year Book*, vi (1896), 12.
[27] Ibid. vii (1897), 11.

the bulk of American Jewry. Herzlian Zionism did not represent the ideal which had drawn them to America.

One further extract from these addresses is given because it illustrates once more the part which feeling took in Wise's reactions. Though in *Minhag America* Wise was at pains to preserve the traditional contours of the Jewish liturgy, he accepted without demur the *Union Prayer Book*, in which the Jewish service of worship had been recast in a Protestant mould. The *Union Hymnal* was also Protestant in style, but no more so than the prayer-book. Here Wise disagreed.

The committee submits for our acceptance a Hymn Book containing upward of 400 hymns. We do not want them. We have the 150 Psalms which are our inheritance, the inheritance of Israel. In taking foreign hymns we make Judaism nugatory. I am opposed to any thing in the synagogue that is foreign to it ... When we reform, it is not towards Christianity, but towards the age before us, and not towards the age behind us.[28]

7. SUNSET

The sunset of the nineteenth century is brilliant in the world's industry, commerce, material wealth, comfort, intercommunication of nations, and the mechanical appliances, requisites and apparatuses in the service of these masters. There never were as many millionaires and multimillionaires in the world, or so few absolutely poor people in proportion to the rich, as there are now in the lands of culture; nor did the laboring class ever live as well and enjoy comfort and respect as they do now. In all material respects the progress of the race in this nineteenth century is undeniable and manifest everywhere where the progress of civilization was not retarded or shut out entirely. Materially the world is now in a much better condition than it ever was.[29]

Wise lived until 26 March 1900, and thus he saw the golden sunset of a golden century. The change in the calendar that January must have been arresting, and he marked it by a series of four articles entitled 'The Sunset of the Nineteenth Century'. 'Nineteenth-century optimism' is a phrase which the sadder twentieth century has often attached to the one which went before. As his own life drew to a close, Wise exhaled that feeling. The mood of satisfaction had a

[28] Ibid. viii (1898), 46.   [29] *American Israelite*, 46 (4 Jan. 1900), 4.

personal element. 'Early in life there wakened within me an unut-
terable instinct to achieve something in the world, preferably in
Judaism, and that not words but works ... In my dreams aboard ship
I had decided to conquer America.' This he had written in 1896, and
he was telling his readers that he had succeeded. There were good
reasons: he had risen from obscurity to prominence; Judaism had
experienced a new birth in the New World; America, where the
principles first enunciated by Moses were being realized, had become
a mighty power.

Wise did not put forward the brilliance of the sunset as self-evident;
he argued his case. And he did not confine it to the material sphere.
'We are entitled to the conclusion that the sunset of the nineteenth
century finds us far advanced in ethics, upon a height never reached
before. The nations are approaching the ethical ideal, individuals only
are immoral.' His optimism extended to the Jewish condition, and he
rounded off the series with a reaffirmation of a belief he had expressed
ever since he landed in the United States: 'We see in the 19th century
a glorious triumph of religiousness, and a long step towards the
fulfilment of the prophecies—Back to Mosaism.'

Thus it appears that the closing years of Wise's life were spent in
a mood of satisfaction. The structure for American Jewry which he
had laboured to build had not been completed to his specifications,
but the triad with which he was intimately connected—the Union of
American Hebrew Congregations, Hebrew Union College, and the
Central Conference of American Rabbis—had come near enough to
achieving his object. As a national figure on the American Jewish
scene he stood alone. (The rival seminary in New York was teetering
on the brink of dissolution.) He had the satisfaction of seeing synagogues throughout the country led by his disciples, but if anything
clouded the sunset, it was the future of the college. He had carried it
on his own shoulders for wellnigh twenty-five years. It was short of
funds, and he failed to see among the leaders of the Union the will
to ensure that Hebrew Union College was adequately supported.

In the spirit of the pioneer Wise had established himself in his
numerous roles, and in that spirit he laboured on. The summit having
been reached, the last decade of his life was not particularly eventful.
What today is chiefly remembered is his denunciation of the Zionist
movement when Herzl called it into being in 1897.

He expounded the theology of Judaism to the World's Parliament
of Religions, which met in Chicago in 1894. His opposition to the

current school of biblical criticism assumed book form in *Pronaos to Holy Writ* (1891). There were more anniversaries to commemorate— the fiftieth anniversary of his inaugural sermon at Radnitz (1893), the fortieth anniversary of his inaugural sermon at Cincinnati (1894), his 79th birthday (1899). His 80th birthday was marked by a special convocation of the Central Conference of American Rabbis (1899), with a celebration which virtually repeated that of his 70th birthday ten years before. The procession of cheering events was marred by a domestic tragedy: in 1899 his daughter Elsa was struck down by paralysis and died at the age of 22. Wise continued his regular writing, and the readiness of his comments did not desert him in old age. In 1898 he gave his name to Michael Rodkinson's quack translation of the Talmud, which drew a scathing riposte from Kaufmann Kohler.

Wise worked right till the end. On Saturday, 24 March he preached at the morning service, dined with his family, and then taught his class as usual at the college. On rising at the end of the lesson he suffered the stroke from which he died two days later. He lay in state at the Plum Street temple, and amid manifestations of grief throughout the land he was buried on 29 March 1900.

That Wise in his thinking remained a child of the eighteenth-century Enlightenment need not be repeated. But it is equally import-ant to note that he was a man of nineteenth-century America, the land of the pioneer, where it was the builder rather than the seer who was important. If the basis of government depended on the ideas of Thomas Jefferson, the readiness to act found its impulse in the spirit of Andrew Jackson. 'Tailors, cobblers, farmers, or clerks in stores are turned into physicians in thirty-two weeks,' wrote one traveller, 'policemen, watchmen and constables suddenly become lawyers; every man feels that he had the ability to be a preacher, teacher, politician, statesman and diplomat and soon finds his public and sphere of influence.' Those bred in the traditions of Europe might sniff, express outrage, or poke fun, but if the land was to be conquered by settlers, instead of the officers of a colonial power, there was no other way. Wise was one of the conquerors. His dream as the *Marie* approached New York was a dream of conquest, and he accomplished it.

8. THE LEGACY

What was Wise's legacy to the Jews of America? Voluminous as were his writings, they proved of little consequence, even in his own lifetime. An exception may be made for his prayer-book, but that did not so impress his colleagues and pupils that they refrained from superseding it. Wise's theology was soon outpaced by the very movement he laboured to foster, and he lacked the aptitudes of a critical scholar which would have enabled him to make a contribution to *Jüdische Wissenschaft*. But Wise did have vision, and this, coupled with his energy and persistence in building institutions, enabled him to bring about the naturalization of the Jews and Judaism in the United States. Jewish communities living under emancipation have usually been torn between the desire for integration and the desire for survival, and the experience of the twentieth century obviously causes us to question the need for integration in view of the need for survival. It is questionable whether Judaism would have survived in America in the nineteenth century had not Wise insisted that it could not exist as an offshoot of European Judaism but must adapt itself to American needs and American forms.

Inevitably the various elements in Wise's conglomerate fell apart after his death, not in the sense that they became alienated but because there was no longer any single directing spirit. The Union of American Hebrew Congregations and the Central Conference of American Rabbis played no role commensurate with the expansion of the American Jewish community. Wise himself had lamented that after the retirement of Moritz Loth, the Union had produced no leader of vision. The Central Conference provided a useful annual meeting for a widely scattered rabbinate, but without professional staff it could do little to offer continuing service. Hebrew Union College, on the other hand, was still in operation, and the community's need for rabbis and the college's need for maintenance made for a continuing relationship.

After a brief interregnum, the presidency of Hebrew Union College was vested in one of Wise's New York critics, Kaufmann Kohler. He was succeeded by Julian Morgenstern, a member of the college faculty and himself a graduate of the college. Trained in the methods of modern scholarship, they succeeded in giving the college an academic standing which it lacked in Wise's day, and under their leadership it could boast of a faculty that could stand comparison with the European institutions, which were the lodestars of that era, and buildings and a library which bore witness to America's zest for modernity and technical perfection.

At the same time, the Hebrew Union College felt the pangs of isolation. Cincinnati was part of the isolationist Middle West. Spiritually the college was anchored to the Pittsburgh Platform, of which Kohler was the author, and its support came from the established middle class, who had never felt the *Sturm und Drang* of the founders of Reform Judaism and to whom the Pittsburgh platform, more especially the things it rejected, was the guarantor of their religious contentment and social emancipation. They endowed Hebrew Union College with resources unequalled in any other institution of Jewish learning, but it was a college which spiritually had moved away from the comprehensiveness which Wise had sought.

Despite these limitations, it was still the most effective instrument in the hands of the Reform movement. Geographical and spiritual distance resulted in an inability directly and immediately to influence the crowded Jewish communities of the great cities, whose aspirations and ideologies remained alien, but who now greatly outnumbered the constituency on whom Wise had built. 'They will come to us, we can never come to them', Wise had predicted in 1884, and in many ways[30] he turned out to be right. This second community did come to the college, in the sense that from its sons came the recruits to the Reform rabbinate who in time were to transform both the college and the movement, pushing aside the ideological basis which it had developed. Moreover, the institutional pattern of the Reform group, which combined association with independence and put organization ahead of ideology, proved congenial to the climate of American Jewish life and set the pattern for the structure of other religious groups.

In time, America's powerful industrial society homogenized the American Jewish community, at the same time allowing for unforeseen divisions. The rejection of practices brought over from Europe, which characterized much of nineteenth-century Reform, abated as the immigrant generation disappeared, and nostalgia for the past helped to influence their descendants. As the twentieth century staggered to its mid-point, the scene was transformed in a more fundamental sense. In 1919, when the centenary of Wise's birth came round, Europe had

[30] *American Israelite*, 30 (26 Oct. 1884), 4, cited by Wilansky, *Sinai to Cincinnati*, 178.

306 Fulfilment: Years of Harvest

lost its hegemony in world affairs, and dominance could have been America's had not America preferred isolation; in 1946, at the centenary of Wise's arrival in New York, Europe lay in ruins, and world leadership had been thrust into America's hands. The old heartland of Jewish life did not just lie in ruins; it had been utterly destroyed. It was for the Jews of America to take up the torch, and to this task they applied themselves with energy and generosity. Unencumbered by ideological restraints, the institutions which Wise had fostered, amid doubts as to whether American soil could sustain them, showed themselves resilient enough to rise to the challenge.

Bibliographical Note

WISE'S activities were conducted within several fields of history. His experiences in Europe clearly set his outlook, but there is no record of his activities there; his active life was conducted in the United States, for whose political system he evinced the highest admiration. His concerns lay within the ambit of Judaism, and there is little sign that American religious thought influenced his outlook. Most of the works useful for further study were published in the United States, but it is anticipated that they will be accessible throughout the English-speaking world.

A major history of the United States is *A History of the American People*, by Samuel Eliot Morison (Oxford, 1965); smaller in compass are the two Penguin volumes by R. B. Nye and J. Morpurgo, *The Growth of the United States* (Harmondsworth, 1955). *A Religious History of the American People*, by S. E. A. Ahlstrom (Yale, 1972), is the standard work in its field. A series of four volumes, *Religion in American Life*, edited by James Ward and A. Leland Jamison (Princeton, 1961), may usefully be consulted.

Turning to the specifically Jewish field, there are several single-volume general histories of the Jewish people available: by Max L. Margolis and Alexander Marx (Philadelphia, Jewish Publication Society, 1927); by Abram L. Sachar (New York, Knopf, 1958); by Cecil Roth (New York, 1970); and by H. H. Ben Sasson and others (Harvard, 1976). For studies from a cultural viewpoint *Great Ideas and Ages of the Jewish People*, edited by Leo W. Schwarz (New York, Modern Library, 1956), may be recommended.

Especially pertinent is the last essay in *Great Ideas and Ages*, 'The Dynamics of Emancipation', by Salo W. Baron. For a detailed study of the period from the middle of the eighteenth century, see *The Course of Modern Jewish History*, by Howard M. Sachar (New York, Delta, 1958). The various aspects of the subject are dealt with extensively in *Encyclopædia Judaica*: see especially 'History (Modern Times)' viii. 703.

Jewish life in the United States is reviewed extensively in *Encyclopædia Judaica*, xv. 1585. There are numerous special articles dealing with an individual or a phase of the subject. Such articles are also a feature of the *American Jewish Year Book*. Mention may be made of three articles commemorating the tercentenary of the settlement of the Jews in North America appearing in vol. 55 (1954); and of 'A Century of Reform Judaism in America', by Sefton D. Temkin, in vol. 74 (1973). As a serviceable one-volume history, *Jews in America*, by Rufus Learsi (New York, Ktav, 1972), is recommended. *American Judaism*, by Nathan Glazer (Chicago, 1959), examines religious developments, as do two works by Joseph L. Blau, *Modern Varieties of Judaism* (New York, Columbia, 1966) and *Judaism in America* (Chicago, 1976). From a broader viewpoint, *Encounter with Emancipation: The German Jews in the United States, 1830–1914*, by Naomi W. Cohen (Philadelphia, Jewish Publication Society, 1984), describes the community in which Wise worked.

Monographs in the various fields of American Jewish life are without number. Some indication is given in the pages of *American Jewish History* (formerly *American Jewish Historical Quarterly* and *Publication of the American Jewish Historical Society*) and *American Jewish Archives*.

The number of works on Judaism makes it necessary to be selective. In *Encyclopædia Judaica*, x. 383, L[ouis] J[acobs] contributes the article 'Judaism', and in xiv. 23, J[acob] J. Petuchowski the article on 'Reform Judaism'. The first essay in *The Concise Encyclopedia of Living Faiths*, ed. R. C. Zaehner (London, 1959), is 'Judaism, or the Religion of Israel', by R. J. Zvi Werblowsky. *Judaism*, by Nicholas de Lange (Oxford, 1986), is a useful summary, as is *Judaism*, by Isidore Epstein (Harmondsworth, 1959) which is fuller but confines itself to the orthodox viewpoint. There is now a history of the Reform movement in Judaism which is both comprehensive and authoritative: *Response to Modernity*, by Michael A. Meyer (New York/Oxford, 1988). This supersedes *The Reform Movement in Judaism*, by David Philipson (New York, 1931), which contains useful material but is dated. The Reform viewpoint is also indicated in two volumes edited by W. Gunther Plaut: *The Rise of Reform Judaism* (New York, 1963) and *The Growth of Reform Judaism* (New York, 1968). The standpoint of the reformers can also be gleaned from *The Emergence of Conservative Judaism*, by Moshe Davis (Jewish Publication Society, 1963). *The Jewish People: Their History and Their Religion*, by David Goldberg and John D. Rayner (London, Penguin, 1987) treats the subject from the standpoint of Liberal Judaism.

Wise wrote voluminously; the most extensive collection is to be found in the American Jewish Archives, on the Cincinnati campus of Hebrew Union College. Bell & Howell have produced a microfilm edition of Wise's writings, with supplementary material.

Glossary

Note: words are sometimes given in a number of different forms, since the different forms of transliteration current in Wise's time have deliberately been retained.

bachur/bocher (*pl. bachurim*)	Young man; student at Talmudic academy (*yeshivah*).
beth din	Rabbinical court.
beth hamidrash	'House of study'; often applied to a chapel-like annexe attached to a synagogue and used for the study of rabbinical literature and for weekday services.
chalitzah	*See halitzah.*
chazan	*See hazan.*
chevras (*hebrot*)	pl. of *chevra(h)* or *hebra*, 'brotherhood' or 'society', sometimes used of small informal congregations, sometimes of special groups within a larger congregation.
get	Bill of divorce.
halitzah	Ceremony replacing observance of biblical injunction (Deut. 25: 5–10) on a man to marry the widow of his brother who has died childless.
hazan	Synagogue cantor.
kabbala(h)	Writings in the Jewish mystical tradition (lit. 'that which has been received').
kehillah	'Community' or 'congregation', sometimes designating the whole group of Jews living in a particular place, sometimes a single congregation within the group.
kehillah kedoshah	'Holy Congregation'; usually followed by name of congregation. Customarily abbreviated to 'KK'.
KK	See *kehillah kedoshah.*
mikvah	Bath for ritual immersion.
milat gerim	Circumcision of proselytes.

minhag	'Custom', more especially one concerning liturgical usage. This was apt to vary from place to place, and Wise gave the title *Minhag America* to the prayer book he compiled to indicate that America also was entitled to its liturgical usage.
mitsvah, pl. *mitsvot(h)*	'Commandment', in particular an act enjoined by the Bible or Talmud, but more generally any good deed. Also the various ceremonial honours that are part and parcel of the synagogue service.
Olath Tamid	'An everlasting sacrifice': phrase from the Pentateuch adopted as title for his prayer book by David Einhorn.
parnass (pl. *parnassim*)	Lay head of congregation.
piyyut (pl. *piyyutim*)	Liturgical poem(s) inserted within the regular prayers.
schochet	See *shochet*.
sefer torah	'Scroll of the Law': parchment manuscript of Pentateuch used for public reading in synagogue.
Sepharad	A location mentioned in Obad. 9: 20 and identified by the rabbis as Spain.
Sepharadi (pl. *Sepharadim*)	Term used to designate Jews and Jewish religious usages of Spanish origin.
shochet	Person qualified to slaughter animals according to Talmudic law.
shul (Yiddish)	Sometimes *shool* or *shuhl*, term for synagogue.
Shulhan aruch	Code of Talmudic law compiled by Joseph Karo in 1565 and in time accepted as authoritative by Orthodox Jews (lit. 'Prepared Table').
siddur	Prayer book.
sifrei torah	pl. of *sefer torah*, q.v.
taleisim	pl. of *talis* or *tal(l)it(h)*, shawl with fringes at four corners prescribed in Num. 15: 38, worn by adult males during morning services.
tallit(h)	See *taleisim*.
tefillin	Phylacteries, prescribed by Exod. 13: 1–10, 11–16, and Deut. 6: 4–9 and 11: 13–21; worn by adult males during weekday morning services.
trefah	Food that is not kosher.

tsaddikim　　　　　　　pl. of *tsaddik*, lit. 'righteous man'. Applied
　　　　　　　　　　　particularly to rabbis of the Hasidic movement,
　　　　　　　　　　　and often used ironically.

yeshiba/yeshiva(h)　　　Talmudic academy.
pl. *yeshib(v)ot(h)*

yeshiva(h) bocher　　　Student at Talmudic academy; often used to
　　　　　　　　　　　describe inexperienced youth.

Index

Printed and bound by CPI Group (UK) Ltd, Croydon, CR0 4YY

09/06/2025

14685817-0001